Spartan Reflections

Spartan Reflections

Paul Cartledge

University of California Press

Berkeley   Los Angeles

University of California Press
Berkeley and Los Angeles, California

Published by arrangement with Gerald Duckworth & Co. Ltd.

First California paperback printing 2003
© 2001 by Paul Cartledge

ISBN 0-520-23124-4 (pbk: alk paper)

Cataloging-in-Publication data is on file with
the Library of Congress

Printed in the United States of America

11 10 09 08 07 06 05 04 03
10 9 8 7 6 5 4 3 2 1

The paper used in this publication is both acid-free
and totally chlorine-free (TCF). It meets the minimum requirements of
ANSI/NISO Z39.48-1992 (R 1997) (*Permanence of Paper*). ∞

Contents

To the memory of my parents, Marcus (d. 1990)
and Peggy (d. 2000), and of my brothers,
Brian (d. 1949) and Tim (d. 1993)

SVTL

List of Plates

Preface

Twenty years ago my friends Brent Shaw and Richard Saller brought out a marvellously useful edition of a selection of the late (d. 1986) Sir Moses Finley's essays on *Economy and Society in Ancient Greece* (= Finley 1981a in the consolidated Bibliography below, p. 240). In a 'bibliographical addendum' (254-5) to Finley's still serviceable essay on 'Sparta and Spartan society' (Finley 1968) they commented, a touch acerbically perhaps, that 'not much of the social scientific approach' to the history of ancient Sparta that I had advocated elsewhere was 'readily available or obvious to the reader' in my 'general monograph' *Sparta and Lakonia. A Regional History 1300-362 BC* (Cartledge 1979, the book of my 1975 Oxford D.Phil. thesis).

I hope they will take the present selection of my own essays, on Spartan themes but always I hope with a wider Hellenic or just wider outreach, as part of my ongoing response or rejoinder to that criticism. Since 1976 I have I think established myself as one of the half-dozen international authorities on pretty well all matters ancient Spartan. I have authored or co-authored three books on the subject (Cartledge 1979, Cartledge 1987, Cartledge & Spawforth 1989, all shortly to be reprinted or reissued in revised and updated editions), and have published a score of articles and written a great many, perhaps too many, reviews. The late Russell Meiggs once remarked that one book on Sparta every two years was to be expected, but that two in one year might seem excessive. I am currently struggling with Meier 1998 and Richer 1999, and that is not to mention the volume of Spartan essays to which I myself was a contributor that was also published in that same year (Hodkinson & Powell eds 1999; see Cartledge 1999b).

Ancient Sparta, in other words, lives on and continues to exercise its fascination. Our everyday words 'laconic' and 'spartan' bear suitably laconic witness to that. I drink my coffee out of a mug bearing the logo of Rotterdam's Sparta football team – a gift from the talented graduate students in History at the University of Leiden who in 1999 generously participated in my Crayenborgh series seminar on ancient revolutions. Vince Lombardi, the great American football coach, earlier in the twentieth century sought to instil what he took to be 'spartan' values into his famously successful teams. The powerful anti-racist movie of 1967, *In the Heat of the Night*, starring Rod Steiger and Sidney Poitier, was set in

Sparta, Tennessee, one of many hundreds of such American Spartas (cf. Sparta, Wisconsin, as featured in Taplin 1989). Very recently, to move from the relatively sublime to the almost ridiculous, the American Hyatt Regency hotel chain thought they could increase their custom by reminding potential customers that the Spartans had lost the battle of Leuktra in 371 BC – so they should not expect to suffer 'spartan' accommodation in the chain's hotels! A final, up-to-the-minute illustration: Steven Pressfield's Thermopylae novel, *Gates of Fire*, is set to be made into a Hollywood epic starring George Clooney. Greater fame than that in this life is not readily to be expected.

The title chosen for the present collection, *Spartan Reflections*, is intended to capture the central and unavoidable influence of the Spartan 'mirage' (Ollier 1933-43), 'tradition' (Rawson 1969), or 'legend' (Tigerstedt 1965-78), and to indicate that these essays are meant to be both reflective and thought-provoking. Selection of essays has, however, been difficult, and I have been guided partly by the (relatively) objective evidence of citation-indexes (provided for me by my doctoral student Polly Low, who became an expert in BIDS, as the system was then called, without going near either an auction house or a bridge table), and partly by subjective local knowledge. The ordering (into Parts) and the order (both of the Parts and of the essays within each Part) are inevitably somewhat arbitrary and are not of course watertight. The reprinted essays are in all cases revised, rewritten and updated, and they are accompanied by essays that have either not been published at all before or not previously published in this form. The whole, it is hoped, will be greater than the sum of its Parts. Permission to reprint was generously granted by all copyright holders. I am especially grateful to the Princeton University Press for waiving its normal reproduction fee (Chapter 6) and to Giulio Einaudi Editore for permitting me to publish a version of the English original of Cartledge 1996a. I am also deeply grateful to my prospective doctoral student Ashley Clements for so cheerfully accomplishing the Herculean labour of retyping the printed originals onto disk.

Rather than reprinting or printing the essays 'cold', I have provided them all with brief new introductions, influenced to some extent by the practice of Sally Humphreys (1978 – her 'Additional Notes' range from a bare listing of subsequent related publications to fullscale re-evaluations) and Geoffrey Lloyd (1991) (where each reprinted article comes with a full 'Introduction' that summarizes its original purpose and subsequent 'reception'). I have also provided a new overall introduction to the volume as a whole, though here my task has been greatly eased by earlier reviews of similar purpose (Christ ed. 1986; Hodkinson 1999b; cf. Cartledge 1975 and my introduction to Powell ed. 1989) and by the bibliographical surveys of Vayiakakos & Taïphakos 1975; Clauss 1983 (with my review in *CR* 34 [1984] 344); and Ducat 1983. See also Chapter 1 below and, for a survey of British Lakonian studies, the New Introduction to Chapter 2.

Acknowledgments

Over the nearly thirty-five years since I began studying Sparta I have contracted many debts – to my teachers, pupils, colleagues, and publishers, many of them also friends.

In the first place, to the supervisor of my doctoral dissertation, 'Early Sparta c. 950-650 BC: an archaeological and historical study' (Oxford, 1975), Professor Sir John (then plain 'Mr') Boardman – see Cartledge 2000 for a small *antidôron*.

Next, to my many undergraduate and graduate pupils, especially Danielle Allen, Lene Rubinstein, and Polly Low (without whom this volume would not have happened), though I am bound to add that for some reason only one of my graduate students has ever chosen to work with me on a specifically Spartan topic. (Steve Hodkinson is a special case: I had the honour to assume the role of being his Cambridge Ph.D supervisor, but only in the sad event of the death of his original supervisor, Moses Finley.)

Penultimately, to my colleagues and former colleagues – to mention them by name is invidious, but I must cite at least Nota Kourou, Dimitris Kyrtatas, Anna Missiou, and Giorgos Steinhauer; Geoffrey Lloyd, and Paul Millett; Hector Catling (honoured, together with the British School at Athens, by the Municipality of Sparta in a special ceremony in September 1999), Bill Cavanagh, Nick Fisher, Lin Foxhall, David Harvey, Anton Powell, Graham Shipley, my co-author Tony Spawforth, Robin Waterfield (another collaborator), and Susan Walker; Joost Crouwel and Harry Pleket; Louise Bruit, Jean Ducat, François Hartog, Claude Mossé, Pauline Schmitt, Annie and Alain Schnapp, and Pierre Vidal-Naquet; Karl Hölkeskamp, Elke Stein-Hölkeskamp, and Wilfried Nippel; Mogens Hansen and Vincent Gabrielsen; Mariko Sakurai; Keith Bradley and Mark Golden; Bob Connor, Ed Cohen, Erich Gruen, Victor Hanson, Jody Maxmin, Ellen Millender, Josh Ober, and Barry Strauss.

Finally, to my publishers – Routledge (now Taylor & Francis) in the first and second instances and then, inimitably, Duckworth in its various metamorphoses and incarnations. The late Colin Haycraft commissioned and published my *Agesilaos* and will always occupy a special place in my

xi

Acknowledgments

– and by no means only my – affections. Deborah Blake has been the most sympathetic and efficient editor of this book that I could possibly have hoped for.

Trumpington, Cambridge
July 2000

P.A.C.

Part I

Sparta-Watching

1

'Sparta-Watching':
General Introduction

The fascinatingly complex Spartan 'tradition'[1] has been central to western political thought since antiquity, and images or myths of ancient Sparta – 'the Spartan mirage' (see Chapter 12, below) – are still unusually influential today. Sparta thus serves as a constant source of cultural reference and inspiration. Happily, this has now lost most of its peculiar association with authoritarian regimes, but alas the British National Party and the French Front Nationale still draw inspiration for their racist attitudes from their idea of Sparta.

When I began my doctoral research on the archaeology and history of early Sparta (1969-75), there was a cant Pentagon-inspired phrase, 'China-watchers', for American political analysts who specialised in Chinese affairs. China then, just about to be 'opened up' to the West through President Nixon, seemed to most of us a remote, alien and terrifying country. Winston Churchill's famous earlier description of Soviet Russia as 'a riddle wrapped in a mystery inside an enigma' could equally well have been applied to China. And, so it seemed to me, pretty much the same would have been said of ancient Sparta, by most non-Spartan Greek contemporaries. Though clearly Greek, Sparta yet seemed to many non-Spartan Greeks a place apart, in more than just a geographical sense.

I once had the notion that by using authentic, contemporary archaeological and epigraphical evidence I might somehow penetrate the smokescreen of the mirage to get to the 'real' Sparta concealed behind it. That notion now seems to me utopian (in the commonplace meaning of that abused word). Yet for all that, Sparta remains one of the only two ancient Greek cities (the other is of course Athens) for which there is anything like the right kind and amount of evidence for the historian even to contemplate attempting a convincing social portrait in the round. Modern scholarship on Sparta, as opposed to propagandistic exploitation of its image, began with the volumes of J.C.F. Manso (1800-1805), and continues with unabated vigour to this day (Baltrusch 1998; Meier 1998; Richer 1999; Hodkinson & Powell eds 1999).

I have already given several indications of how my general approach interacts with those of other scholars.[2] After some thirty years of practical

3

experience, on and off, I would now still recommend, as I did in 1980, just four main approaches as being both practicable and fruitful, singly or, ideally, in combination. The first is to confront the idea or legend or myth of Sparta directly, acknowledging that Spartan history must always be in a sense and up to a point the history of the idea, and then tracing in greater or less detail, more or less comprehensively, the genesis and evolution of the Spartan mirage.

Second, although archaeology may not permit access to unmediated actuality of a usefully reconstructible kind, there is still room for a full-scale monograph on Spartan or Lakonian artefacts (the regional nomenclature keeps open the question of the identity of the craftsmen – Perioikoi, Helots, or even déclassé Spartans: see Cartledge 1976a), from the Iron or Dark Age to the Hellenistic period, interpreted sociologically and not just art-historically or iconographically. More centrally, archaeology, especially in the form of intensive field-survey (see the next Chapter), must provide the basis of the regional approach to which the history of Sparta lends itself (cf. Cartledge 1979).

A third possible line is to apply the comparative method comprehensively. Succession to high office and royal patronage (Chapter 5), the age-graded educational cycle (Chapter 7), the Krypteia or 'secret service' (Chapters 7 and 10), institutionalized pederasty (Chapter 8) and the elaborate military organization (Chapter 11) are some of the topics that I have myself tackled from this point of view. Perhaps the key methodological points to keep in mind, however, are that comparison often most fruitfully serves to highlight difference, and that evidence from other *ex hypothesi* comparable cultures or societies may never be used as a substitute for the evidence we lack and shall always lack for ancient Sparta.

Finally, a quasi-biographical approach may recommend itself in one or two cases. My *Agesilaos* was written on the premise that, although we do not have the right sort of evidence to write a modern-style, inner-life biography of Agesilaos or any other Spartan – indeed, any other ancient, apart perhaps from Cicero, Julian and Augustine – the life of a powerful, central and relatively well documented figure like Agesilaos may act as a prism to refract the light intermittently reflected from the various facets of Spartan society, politics and culture.

I conclude with some remarks about historiography in general rather than the historiography of ancient Sparta in particular. Since I began studying and writing about Sparta, the most important single intellectual development within my general field of History (I call myself a historian who happens to study the ancient world rather than an 'ancient' historian) has been the 'linguistic turn' taken in so many of the social sciences and literary disciplines to which history in some form or forms is closely allied. Not so much what you say, but how you say it, and the status of the truth-claims behind what you write, have become of compelling, frontline concern. To such an extent indeed that a Cambridge colleague of mine has

4

felt the need to come out fighting 'in defence of history' (Evans 1998), that is, of his sort of non-postmodernist historiography.

I share that concern entirely. I applaud the debate that 'postmodernism' (an inexact but evocative term) has provoked, even within ancient history (see Morley 1999). I have myself written from within this po-mo perspective on Gibbon's *Vindication* of 1779, a brilliant treatise on the historian's calling as Gibbon presented it (Cartledge 1995a). But there too often remains a gap, as I am uncomfortably aware in my own case, between professions of historiographical faith and actual practice. I cannot prove that any of the events and processes I write about below actually happened, let alone as and why I think they did; and from some points of view that they they did or did not happen that way and for that reason is less important than the critical thought involved in reflecting upon them. Benedetto Croce's dictum that all history is contemporary history seems to me to have a particular resonance within this conceptual framework. Nevertheless, I do still have an ineradicable if sneaking desire to believe that they did, and the unquenchable hope that I will persuade others to share my point of view. It is in that spirit that the following essays are presented to and for their readers' reflection.

Part II

Polity, Politics and Political Thought

2

City and *Chora* in Sparta:
Archaic to Hellenistic

Introduction

This essay appeared originally as part of the published proceedings of the 19th British Museum Classical Colloquium (Cavanagh & Walker eds 1998: 39-47). It concluded with a résumé of 'British Lakonian Studies: Past, Present and Future', which I reproduce with slight modifications immediately below.

The first authentic British visitor to Lakonia to have left significant literary trace is the late seventeenth-century merchant Bernard Randolph. Randolph had of course been anticipated by scholarly travellers from the mid-fifteenth century, and it was to be almost a century and a half after Randolph before Britain seriously staked a claim in the burgeoning field of Laconian, or more accurately Morean, studies – thanks to Sir William Gell (1823) and (Colonel) W.M. Leake (1830). Even so, the early honours for the 'scientific' exploration of the Morea including Lakonia in the nineteenth century went chiefly not to Britain but to France (Puillon Boblaye, Bory de Saint-Vincent) and Germany (Ross, Stein, Philippson). It was presumably a mercy, though, that Heinrich Schliemann in 1888 could find 'not even a rubbish-dump' on the Spartan Akropolis and 'no trace of antiquity' in the hills bearing the main Mycenaean settlement and the historical Menelaion sanctuary (see further Hooker 1980: 20-4).

The twentieth century, however, does belong to Britain, or at any rate more so than to any other national group. Desperate for a historical site that would rival the German Institute's Olympia and the French School's Delphi, not to mention the Greeks' own Athenian Akropolis and environs, and one that would complement their own prehistoric Knossos and Phylakopi; and alarmed perhaps by the incursions into Lakonia of Christos Tsountas (prehistoric sites, esp. Vapheio) and A. Furtwängler (the Amyklaion, mainly of the historic periods), the British School at Athens settled decisively in the first decade of our century on Sparta – or rather, what is crucial for our purposes below, on Sparta as the centrepiece of Lakonia, the jewel in the crown. For before excavations began in Sparta itself, especially but not only at the sanctuary of Orth(e)ia, members of the School had first conducted extensive surface explorations in S.W. Lakonia and had sunk their spades, picks and trowels into Geraki (ancient Geronthrai) and Angelona (a heroön site). In the year that work at Ortheia itself began, 1906, M.N. Tod and A.J.B. Wace published their *Catalogue of the Sparta Museum* (still not entirely superseded over ninety years later).

So the pattern was set for the first quinquennium of campaigns (1906-1910) under R.C. Bosanquet and then R.M. Dawkins. The list of those participating both inside and outside Sparta reads like a roll of honour of British archaeological and ancient historical scholarship in the first half of the century – including as it does, besides those already named, G. Dickins, R.J.H. Jenkins (later an eminent Byzantinist), and A.M. Woodward. The ultimate fruit of this first period of work at the major site of concentration, publication of which was delayed by the First World War among other factors, was R.M. Dawkins ed. *Artemis Orthia* (1929, a supplementary volume of *JHS*). By then, however, the School had also completed, under Woodward, a second quinquennium (1924-28) of archaeological-cum-historical research in and around Sparta, the most significant results of which were the excavations on the Akropolis and in the theatre below it, and further extensive topographical surveys, all promptly published in the School's *Annual* (vols 26-30). An amusing sidelight on this campaign has recently been thrown by the publication of some brilliant caricatures by the draughtsman Piet de Jong: Rachel Hood, *Faces of Archaeology in Greece: Caricatures by Piet de Jong* (Leopard's Head Press, Oxford, 1998).

It is no exaggeration to say that the School's labours in the first and third decades of our century transformed not only Lakonian studies as a whole but also general perceptions of the nature and significance of early Sparta and especially Spartan culture. Guy Dickins (killed in World War I) was even able to persuade the editor of the connoisseur's *Burlington Magazine* (1908) to publish an article on Spartan art (*sic*), while Woodward's general summation of the implications of the new archaeological picture for the history of early Sparta, published in the most widely read British historical journal (*History* 1923), set the agenda and tone for the spate of reappraisals that has barely ceased to flow from the 1930s (Alan Blakeway, A. Andrewes) and 1940s (H.T.Wade-Gery) to this day.

Selection of representative examples from those fertile six-plus decades is of course invidious, but two interlinked chains of research and researchers seem unusually significant. First, there is a prehistoric chain started before World War II, at the prompting of Alan Wace, by Helen Waterhouse (née Thomas). Her research, expanded by the indefatigable legwork of Dick Hope Simpson, issued in a two-part publication in *BSA* 1960 and 1961 that was the immediate source of all postwar prehistoric extensive survey in Greece. It was largely due to their inspiration that Hector Catling chose to devote the principal energies of his Directorship of the School to Lakonia, a wise choice which justly earned him the sobriquet *philolakôn* used as the title of his 1992 *Festschrift* by grateful colleagues, pupils and friends (for my contribution, see Cartledge 1992b).

The second chain is a historical one. It begins with John Boardman's seminal re-examination of the (for its day) pioneering stratigraphy of Ortheia (Boardman 1963). From him, the torch was passed to his graduate pupil Cartledge, who in turn was fortunate to be able to collaborate with one of the leading experts in the epigraphy of Roman Greece, A.J.S. Spawforth (Cartledge & Spawforth 1989). Developing and (more often) revising Cartledge on Archaic and Classical Sparta has been Stephen Hodkinson, originally a pupil of Moses Finley, latterly of Cartledge. Hodkinson's *Property and Wealth in Classical Sparta* is forthcoming later in 2000 as I write.

Hodkinson will now, as will we all, have to take into account the heaps of new data and ideas being piled up by the interdisciplinary intensive Lakonia survey (Cavanagh et al. 1996-1997). Cyprian Broodbank, meanwhile, on the offshore island of Kythera is following partially in the footsteps of Coldstream & Huxley eds 1972. Also resuming and developing much earlier excavations, but in this case back in the central place, are Geoffrey Waywell and John Wilkes: much is hoped for from their work both on top of and alongside the Spartan Akropolis. But I conclude this too rapid résumé with a mention, *honoris causa*, of another work in progress. It is Dutch not British, but its director Joost Crouwel of the University of Amsterdam is almost a 'British' scholar by adoption, and, following on from his labours on the joint British School/University of Amsterdam survey, he has gone back to where the British left off at Geraki over ninety years ago.

For convenience I append in alphabetical order a select list of published British research, including all that mentioned above:

Andrewes 1954; Badian ed. 1966; Boardman 1963; Cartledge 1979, 1987, 1992b; Cartledge & Spawforth 1989; Cavanagh et al. 1996-1997; Chrimes 1949; Dawkins ed. 1929; Finley 1968; Forrest 1968; Hammond 1973; Hodkinson 1983, 2000; Holladay 1977; Hooker 1980; Huxley 1962; Jeffery 1961; Jones 1967; Lazenby 1985; Lewis 1977; Powell ed. 1989; Powell & Hodkinson eds 1994; Rawson 1969; Ste. Croix 1972; Sanders ed. 1992; Toynbee 1969 (but note that his work on Sparta had begun with topographical autopsy in 1911); Wade-Gery 1958; Walbank 1985; Waterhouse & Hope Simpson 1960-61.

*

The vexed problems of the rise, evolution and devolution of the state are ones to which ancient Greek historians and classical archaeologists may reasonably claim to have a special contribution to make. Thanks to the *polis* (however precisely it be defined) and to Aristotle, we are in there at the very beginning of the debate, so to speak.[1] Forty years ago Ernst Kirsten set the whole issue in its proper geographical framework, mapping the political ecology of the *polis* as a Mediterranean phenomenon.[2] Yet – such are the vagaries of scholarship – it remained stubbornly the case that 'A generation ago it was rare for British scholars writing about ancient history to bring the landscape into play alongside political accounts of antiquity'.[3]

Since then, however, the situation has happily changed. Human landscapes have become a central preoccupation of British ancient historians and classical archaeologists, particular attention being paid to the issue of core-periphery or town-country relationships.[4] So far as the history of ancient Greece is concerned, great enlightenment has been forthcoming in recent years both from François de Polignac's seminal volume on 'the birth of the Greek city'[5] and from the proper publication, at last, of some of the intensive field-survey work of the 1970s and 1980s, not least the British School/University of Amsterdam Lakonia Survey[6] and the Southern Argolid Survey.[7] In what follows I shall attempt to bring to bear the fruits of these complementary historical and archaeological approaches on the relationships between city and countryside (*chôra*) at Sparta during the last millennium BC. Specifically, I shall be asking how the Spartans of the centre or core settlements represented and conducted themselves in opposition to or distinction from the periphery of Perioikic and Helot inhabitants of Lakonia (and Messenia).

In my earlier work on Greek self-definition,[8] I preferred to emphasize cultural, symbolic and intellectual, rather than material, economic or social aspects. Here, I shall attempt to bring the material dimension closer to parity with the cultural, though the two are of course mutually implicated and conditioned. Topography, as Artemis Leontis has recently reminded us, is in the mind as well as on the ground.[9] Moreover, in the shape of the religious sanctuary, on which there has been a quite exceptional concentration of high-quality research published during the past decade,[10] the material and the cultural become almost one and the same – within the overarching framework of the political, to which I turn first of all.

Whether or not the ancient Greeks invented 'the political' or 'politics',[11] they certainly used them as a basic framework of theory and practice within which to define themselves. For them, it was of the essence of their self-definition as Greek citizens that their primary political loyalty and political identification, their 'nationalism' so to speak, were focused almost exclusively, not on the nation, let alone the nation-state, but on their own separate and radically self-differentiated political communities – as separate and different from each other as, say, Slovenia and Serbia, or France and England, are today.[12] I say 'political communities' advisedly. Comparative study suggests how difficult, if not impossible, it is to define 'state' or even 'city' with sufficient generality and precision. Nor does sticking to the

Greek word *polis* altogether help. In our terms, that word was used to denote both what some of us would call a 'city' and what some of us would call a 'state';[13] it served also to distinguish 'town' from countryside and to signify the Greeks' distinctive melding in one political entity of both town and country.[14] The *polis* of Sparta, as we shall see, affords unusual interest and typically complex variations on a common Greek theme from this point of view.

On the other hand, attention to the Greeks' own theoretical and practical usage, most notably in Aristotle's *Politics* (a title that means very specifically 'matters relating to the *polis*'), does reveal their overridingly concrete understanding. The *polis* was for them a question not only or primarily of some abstract entity but rather of men, specifically citizen men (*politai*). Put differently, the *polis* was a citizen-state,[15] in which citizens were those who enjoyed the public rights and duties of judgment and office. There was usually little or no State, capital S, in our modern sense of a governmental, judicial and military-police apparatus set apart from and above the common run of citizens (or subjects). Sparta represented the limit case in this regard. Nor – to introduce a specifically archaeological or artefactual dimension – was the *polis* necessarily and sufficiently defined by, though it might be optionally or optimally equipped with, certain material attributes. Several ideologically freighted texts (e.g. Thuc. 7.77.7) explicitly distinguish between the *polis* in the sense of its living citizenry and the walls of a *polis* (in the material sense of 'city'). The special relevance of this distinction will transpire as we bring out the peculiarities of Sparta by comparison or rather in contrast with Athens.

There were, in the Archaic to Hellenistic periods with which I am specifically interested, perhaps up to 1500 Greek *poleis* scattered almost all round the Mediterranean and Black Seas from the Pillars of Herakles (Gibraltar) in the West to Phasis (in ex-Soviet Georgia) in the far North-East. But there are only two, Sparta and Athens, about which we have anything like the requisite sort of detailed evidence to conduct a fruitful analysis within our appointed framework of city-*chôra* relationships. It is indeed precisely in terms of the politics of urbanization that Thucydides introduces the polar opposition between Sparta and Athens that underlies his entire History. Suppose, he wrote in the so-called Archaeology (1.10), that the central places, or civic centres, of Athens and Sparta were at some time in the future to be utterly destroyed apart from the foundations of some public and private buildings, observers would then be quite unable to gauge accurately the former power of the Peloponnesian War's protagonists: they would respectively overestimate that of Athens and underestimate that of Sparta.

Thucydides' prediction is in one sense quite accurate. There is no comparison today between the physical remains of the central places of the two antagonists. But in another sense it is self-refuting, since the survival of the literary work in which that prediction is contained is by itself

13

sufficient to establish an *a priori* case that there had once been some sort of parity of power between the two. However, what interests me principally here are the grounds for Thucydides' prediction regarding Sparta: 'the *polis* is not regularly planned and contains no shrines or other buildings of great cost or magnificence, but is simply a collection of villages (*kômai*) after the ancient Hellenic manner'.[16] Modern scholars have sometimes suspected that Thucydides was here indulging in some artistic licence, for the sake of his Athens-Sparta polarity. Certainly, as a self-declared Athenian (1.1), he was guilty of some chauvinist or ethnocentric special pleading. His definition of civilization in terms of citification, placing 'archaic' Sparta at the opposite pole from 'modern' Athens, does reflect a thoroughly Athenian viewpoint, and one with which Aristotle, for example, the Athenian metic originally from relatively tiny Stageira in Chalkidike who commended the Thessalians' practice of keeping their political agora distinct from their commercial one, would surely have taken strong issue. On the other hand, archaeology apparently bears Thucydides out. There would seem to have been a real difference between the urban development of central Athens[17] and that of Sparta.[18] What concerns me now are the origins and implications of this distinction and opposition, which, if my earlier argument is right, ought to have been located primarily in the political rather than the cultural or economic sphere. There is no better place to start from than the cities' very different constructions of citizenship.

To become a Spartiate (to use the term that distinguishes Spartan citizens from Perioikoi, who could both in appropriate circumstances be called 'Lakedaimonioi'), one had to pass successfully through the educational cycle known as the *agôgê*[19] and be elected to a dining society or 'common mess' (Singor 1999); and, in order to retain one's citizen status thereafter, one had to be able to contribute a certain minimum of natural produce to one's mess as a form of 'dues' payment. In these three ways, the Spartan citizens' qualifications and way of life contrasted with those of the Athenians, for whom it was sufficient to be of legitimate Athenian birth and registered as an Athenian at the age of majority. A further differentiating requirement imposed on Spartiates was daily attendance at the evening meal eaten communally in the messes. This, like the *agôgê*, was designed primarily to inculcate group solidarity, to the detriment of familial or any other kind of individualizing ties and values.

This universal dining requirement (coupled with an over-night communal-barracks sleeping obligation for the under-thirties) had a cardinal socio-political correlative. Not only did all adult male Spartan citizens act together politically in the central place but most of them also resided there more or less permanently. How come? Speculation as to the ultimate origins of messing as a social practice (one not unique to Sparta) aside, the answer briefly is that Sparta was in origins and essence a 'conquest' state.[20] Its territory, some 8000 km^2 in all, was easily the largest in the entire Greek world, and Sparta town was mapped ideologically in the image of an armed camp on constant military alert (*taga* may have been the technical term for this). This state of alert was directed not primarily against any external enemies, from whom they were cushioned and buffered by the so-called Perioikoi, who 'dwelt round about' them within the borders of the Spartan state, in personal freedom but political subservience.[21] The alert was directed rather against the enemy within, their many times more numerous labour force of serf-like Helots, though this siege mentality was not without a certain paradoxical quality. For it was the labour of the Helots that freed Spartan citizens from the necessity of productive labour, and enabled them to reside permanently in Sparta, often at a considerable distance from their Helot-worked estates. Yet, equally, it was because of the diehard hostility of at any rate the Helots of Messenia that the Spartans felt constrained to live or endure a military-style barracks existence in the central place.[22]

Sparta town, in other words, functioned politically to keep the non-citizens out – and down; to mark off the centre sharply from its immediate civic periphery. Why, then, did it not acquire what Thucydides clearly believed to be the normal accoutrements of urbanization, and in particular why did the Spartans not surround their central place, or part of it, with what by Thucydides' day had become one of the most normal of those accoutrements, an enceinte wall? Several reasons suggest themselves. First, weight of tradition. The Spartans notoriously over-valued the past (Thommen 2000), and, in part precisely because they too were no more immune from change than any other human community, they were keen to represent their way of life as having been frozen like a fly in amber from the earliest mists of their city's history. A key component of this Spartan ideological myth-history was their allegedly principled disdain of a city-wall, as a stigma of effeminacy, and privileging of the citizens' strong right arms. But actually not every Greek *polis* had had an enceinte wall to begin with, and by the time city-walls had become a normal feature of the Greek landscape the Spartans had evolved complicated alternative methods of central self-protection, partly material and partly symbolic.

The Perioikoi have been introduced above. Their strategic presence meant that an enemy from outside Lakonia or Messenia would have to fight through this substantial first line of resistance before reaching Sparta itself, as no enemy in fact did before 370/69, when crucially some of the Perioikoi of northern Lakonia had defected. A less obvious but none the less efficacious wall-substitute was provided by a cluster of religious sanctuaries around or in the close vicinity of Sparta town. A Greek sanctuary's basic function, as a place of human-superhuman intercommunication, was effected most conspicuously through a variety of sacrificial rituals, and most lastingly through the dedication of a multiplicity of votive offerings.[23] But although human-superhuman communication was a necessary feature of each and every sanctuary, this did not constitute a sufficient definition of all Greek sanctuaries' many and varied functions. For they were not merely places of worship and pilgrimage. Indeed, they were not always primarily, let alone exclusively, religious (as we would put it) in their functional significance. They might function also – or rather – as political entities in something like a secular sense.

Most relevant to us is the category of the limitary sanctuary. This comprised sanctuaries that were borderline in a literal as well as metaphorical sense, being located on natural or artificial boundaries within or between communities (including territories overseas).[24] As such, they might serve a variety of purposes: to articulate the necessary organic relationship between the countryside (the economic basis) and urban centre (the political superstructure), or to mark ritually the symbolic passage of citizens from 'wild' adolescence to 'tame' civic maturity (as in several Artemis sanctuaries), or to establish, consolidate or promulgate a state's claim to border-territory against a neighbour – which was always the prime cause and context of ancient Greek interstate warfare.[25]

The limitary sanctuaries that concern us here are of two main sorts: first, those which formed a kind of *pomerium* (to borrow the Roman term) or sacred boundary around Sparta itself and, second, those which served to define Spartan citizen territory, the *politikê gê*, against the territory of the Perioikoi.

So far as Sparta's '*pomerium*' is concerned, special attention should be drawn to the two sanctuaries of Artemis – surnamed respectively Ortheia and Issoria – on the east and west. Artemis herself was among other things a goddess of boundaries, separating the wild from the tame or cultivated. Regarding the area in the immediate vicinity of Sparta town, attention may be directed first to the Menelaion sanctuary (devoted to Menelaos and Helen, together with Helen's brothers, the Dioskouroi) in the north-east[26] and to the Eleusinion (sacred to Demeter and Kore) rather further to the south.[27] Both of those sanctuaries have long been known and, in the former's case at any rate, very well excavated. Much more recently, however, a most interesting sanctuary of demonstrable social and political significance, plausibly identified as a sanctuary of Zeus Messapeus, was discovered by the Lakonia survey at Tsakona some 4 km to the north of Sparta towards the perioikic town of Sellasia.[28]

Finds here include an unusual and distinctive plethora of ithyphallic terracotta votives that might well be accorded a monitory, territory-marking interpretation. Sir Kenneth Dover has characteristically cited in a comparable connection not only the statues of Priapus that dotted Roman orchards and fields but the threatening, boundary-marking ithyphallicism of 'watchful males' in 'some primate species'.[29] Given Tsakona's location so close to the centre of Sparta and to Sellasia, the nearest perioikic town across the border from Sparta's 'civic land', this sanctuary was surely a Spartan rather than a perioikic shrine, and it would not be implausible to see it as primarily serving a limitary political function.

16

However, by far the most important of these limitary sanctuaries in the immediate environs of Sparta was that of Apollo and Hyakinthos located at Amyklai a few kilometres south-east of Sparta town.[30] Significantly, it was here, at the Amyklaion, and not in Sparta town that the Spartans' principal 'national' religious festival was celebrated. To this we shall return. More immediately to the point, this physical separation of Amyklai, a constituent *kômê* or 'village' of Sparta on a par with the four contiguous villages of the central place,[31] was of course another reason why the Spartans did not at first build a city-wall round their central settlement. For by the time that Sparta did finally decide to do so, in the early second century BC, its geopolitical situation had altered, drastically, for the worse. All the Perioikoi and most of the Helots had acquired their independence, and Sparta's *polis* territory had been reduced to 'normal' Greek proportions, comprising the terrain immediately surrounding the central place in the Spartan plain.[32] A wall was therefore no longer a mere luxury or frippery that might be pragmatically dispensed with, and whose absence could be ideologically glossed. It had become an imperious necessity – regardless of the politico-military and symbolic cost of Amyklai's inevitable exclusion from its protection.

An Athenian comparison

In order to bring out further the peculiarities of Sparta's treatment of its *chôra*, we may briefly return to our comparison and contrast of the politics of urbanization at Athens, where they managed these things very differently, especially in the democratic period (fifth-fourth centuries). For a start, most of the 30,000 or so (on average) Athenian citizens did not reside permanently within the City (Astu) and Peiraieus area, enclosed as this usually was by walls of various kinds and periods. They lived instead in the surrounding *chôra* of Attica, in which were situated the vast majority of the 140 constituent *demes* or villages.[33] Thus whereas Spartan citizens compulsorily ate together every day in the central place as members of a citizen corporation, Athenians did so voluntarily and only on high days and holidays. And whereas presumably all fit Spartans always attended the Spartan assembly, at its relatively infrequent sessions, never did more than a maximum of half the citizenry attend the Athenian assembly, even though that was a truly decisive organ of government.[34] The Athenian assembly, in other words, was not located centrally in the City (on Pnyx hill) in order to differentiate and emphasize the hierarchy of centre and periphery. Most Athenian citizens were independent rural small farmers, and such town-country antagonism as did exist was as much a matter of elite snobbery as a structural factor integral to the functioning of Athenian political institutions – with the admitted exception of the strains imposed by Periklean policy during the Peloponnesian War period.

The reasons for the Athenian Assembly's central location were partly historical and symbolic – the Pnyx, like the Agora, was not far from the Athenian Akropolis, which had served as a central refuge and rallying-point as well as the heart of Athenian religious life since at least the foundation of the historical polis; and partly practical – Athens was by Greek standards a remarkably large and heterogeneous *polis* and absolutely required centralized governmental institutions. Hence Athens City was truly the seat of a 'national' assembly. Yet even that would not by itself have accounted for the remarkable urbanization of Athens attested by Thucydides. For this, two further factors, neither of which applied to Sparta, were chiefly responsible: the self-aggrandising Peisistratid tyranny of the sixth century; and the Athenian empire of the fifth. As a result, huge quantities of public and private resources were devoted to a largely religious building-programme rivalled in cost only by the secular reconstruction of the city-walls and walls linking Athens to Peiraieus at the beginning of the fourth century.

On the other hand, the Athenians' urbanism lacked one of the principal motivations behind Sparta's centripetal concentration. Despite the undoubtedly large numbers of slaves they possessed both individually and collectively, they had no serious cause to fear a servile enemy within (cf. Chapter 10, below). A continuing and probably unresolvable debate rages over the precise nature and extent of the connection, if any, between slavery and democracy at Athens. What is generally agreed, however, is that the Athenian slave body, being a heterogeneous polygot mass, did not pose the constant threat to the stability, let alone the continued existence, of the Athenian *polis* that the Helots did to the *polis* of the Spartans.

The festive dimension

From urbanism, with its vital religious components, I move finally and specifically to the politics of religion, with reference to civic festivals. Religion in ancient Greece was essentially, not just accidentally, civic in nature, the Greek *polis* being constituted as a city of gods as well as of men.[35] Indeed, according to a famous but controversial thesis of de Polignac,[36] the very origin of the Greek *polis* was owed to a primarily religious development, the integration of the central place with a major peri- or extra-urban shrine or cult place. Whether that thesis holds universally or not – and de Polignac himself [37] has significantly modified his own original position – religious festivals were indeed the beating heart of ancient Greek religion, and festivals somehow linking centre and periphery could thus perform a vital civic political function.[38] I have chosen therefore to compare and contrast one Athenian and one Spartan civic religious festival in order to illustrate the very different meanings and functions they could have for centre-periphery interaction.

The Panathenaia or 'All-Attican/Athenian' festival annually celebrated the birthday of the *polis*'s patron deity Athena Polias.[39] By its very name

18

the festival was overtly designed both to celebrate and to reinforce the political homogeneity and integrity of the entire *polis* territory, which was both unusually large by Greek standards, and by no means unitary in its origins. When the festival was founded in its 'classical form', traditionally in the 560s, homogeneity and integrity were probably a pious hope rather than an unmistakable actuality. Genuine politico-territorial unity was not to be achieved until the Kleisthenic reforms over half a century later, and even thereafter unity might still be seriously (con)tested at the margins. Those reforms placed the foundations of Athenian citizenship on the twin bases of birth and locality, and it was as members of their local demes that Athenians participated in the Panathenaia. Every four years the celebrations were conducted with especial magnificence, partly for the benefit of the non-citizens entitled or even required to participate. Yet the festival remained a triumphantly Athenian occasion, employed to present the desired face of Athens both to itself and to others. At the centre of that image lay the Akropolis, the hub of the Attic wheel. But just as a hub is useless without the wheel, so the Acropolis derived its significance from its location at the spiritual centre of the *polis* territory, and indeed of the wider Greek world within which Athenian citizens might be temporarily or permanently domiciled.[40]

Sparta had no precise equivalent of the Panathenaia, with its international as well as national connotations and reverberations. Its nearest counterpart was the Hyakinthia, in that that was the principal annual festival of Spartan 'national' or rather civic identity. But in almost all other respects it offers a clattering contrast. Sparta's patron deity, like that of Athens, was an Athena of the Polis,[41] but although Spartan Athena enjoyed at least one important festival, the Promakheia, the Hyakinthia was dedicated instead to Apollo, as were all Sparta's major festivals.[42] The Hyakinthia likewise took place in the political centre of the Spartan state, but significantly it was not a centripetal or monocentric occasion. Sparta town was, as we have seen, a dispersed scatter of five villages, only four of which were directly contiguous. The fifth was Amyklai, and it was here, eccentrically, just out of town, that the Hyakinthia was held.

Moreover, it seems to have remained a significantly Amyklaian as well as a 'pan-Spartan' festival. Thus only serving Spartan soldiers from Amyklai, and not also those from the other four villages, were automatically released from campaign to return home to celebrate it – in what was after all the height of the campaigning season. The non-Amyklaian Spartans processed solemnly from Sparta town down the Hyakinthian Way, symbolically marking thereby the political unity but at the same time also the separate identity of Sparta and Amyklai. Sparta, in other words, did not strictly have a festival which like the Athenians' Panathenaia consciously united in a single shared cult the entire civic territory of the Spartan *polis*. Indeed, the Hyakinthia, though national – yet retained a strongly separa-

tist and local flavour – harking back perhaps to the contested origins of th₁
Spartan *polis* in the eighth century.

One final contrast with the Panathenaic festival concerns the eligibility
for participation at the Hyakinthia. The procession and associated games
of the former were open not only to Athenian citizens but also to resident
aliens and foreigners; indeed, the participation of the latter two groups
was in certain aspects required. The Hyakinthia's military-style procession and musical and athletic contests, however, were open only to Spartan
citizens. Indeed, the only non-Spartans present at the Hyakinthia – in
contrast especially to the Gymnopaidiai festival, at which distinguished
foreign guests were made welcome, or the Promakheia, at which Perioikoi
were given a significant role – were Helots. It was not merely for geographical convenience, therefore, that the common messes in Sparta town,
those quintessentially Spartan civic structures, were situated along the
Hyakinthian Way.

The Hyakinthia, in short, like the Spartan system of urbanization as a
whole, was consciously designed to emphasize and reinforce the centre's
separation from and hierarchical domination over the periphery. Whereas
the normal and normative Greek *polis* united town and country in a
harmonious political symbiosis, Sparta was in this respect, as in so many
others, atypical, if not unique. The presence or (until the mid-Hellenistic
era) absence of a city wall was a clear ideological and spatial marker of
Sparta's difference.[43]

3

The Peculiar Position of Sparta
in the Development of the
Greek City-State

Introduction

The first published version of this essay originated in a paper delivered at
the Royal Irish Academy in Dublin, when I was a Lecturer in the School of
Classics at Trinity College Dublin, and was published in the Academy's
Proceedings. Since it was first published, in 1980, there has been a spate
of work on the political structure and history of the early, that is Archaic,
Spartan *polis*, most recently in the published doctoral theses of Meier
(1998) and Richer (1999). But no less interesting and important has been
the work done on the *polis* as such. My former graduate pupil Moshe
Berent, in his unpublished Cambridge doctoral thesis (1994), has in my
view seriously undermined the usual understanding of the *polis* as a State
(capital S) and rightly prefers to classify it comparatively as a 'stateless
political community'. Sparta, however, remains in his view relatively more
State-like than any other known ancient Greek *polis*, and I have therefore
not sought to confuse matters further by altering the title of my essay. The
other major research project on the Greek *polis* is collaborative: the one
currently being conducted by the Copenhagen Polis Centre directed by
Mogens Herman Hansen. For my views on that project, and a review of
four of its publications, including Hansen 1998, see *CR* n.s. 49 (1999)
265-9. For my views on politics and 'the political' in ancient Greece, see
Cartledge 1996b.

*

I

I begin with a quotation from the late Victor Ehrenberg's once standard
discussion of Greek political institutions in (roughly) the last eight centuries before our era. 'Sparta, so peculiar in many respects, represents a
difficulty; but following the practice of antiquity, which surely recognized

21

what was essential, Sparta too is dealt with inside the framework of the Polis.'[1] The word 'peculiar' denotes primarily a thing or quality that is the unique property or attribute of some entity or person. Secondarily, it means strange, odd, curious. As the Ehrenberg quotation implies, Sparta's political peculiarity is so striking that it can even be a matter for debate whether Sparta was indeed a *polis*.

In this paper Spartan 'peculiarity' in both senses of the word will be considered, with special emphasis on the political development of Sparta in the seventh and sixth centuries BC. This period of Greek history is often known as 'Archaic', a term devised by art-historians to characterize a period in the development of art-forms preceding a 'Classical' period, the latter representing the full flowering of tendencies merely budding in the 'Archaic' phase.[2] However, in the political sense Sparta's 'Archaic' period was also its 'Classical' epoch, a fact that has been used – rightly, as we shall see – to explain some aspects of Spartan peculiarity (in both senses).

II

A third preliminary question of terminology could hardly be more fundamental. Was Sparta in fact a *polis*? According to the 'practice of antiquity', it was indeed held to be one. Yet ancient practice is not as helpful as we could have wished. To quote Ehrenberg once more: 'To the Greeks themselves the word Polis was almost as general and vague as the word state is to us. Greek political thought and public law, in fact, knew of very few, if any, unambiguous concepts.'[3] Still, a brief and abstract description of the *polis* as an ideal type, at least as it was theorized by Aristotle, will enable us to pinpoint the areas in which Spartan 'peculiarity' is to be explored in our substantive discussion.

Aristotle was the greatest political scientist of antiquity. His *Politics* (meaning literally 'matters concerning the *polis*') was premised on the belief that man is a *zôon politikon*, a creature designed teleologically by nature to live in the *polis*, where alone the truly 'good' life can be lived. For Aristotle, the primary condition of a state's being ranked as a *polis* was that it should embody community of place, above all the unity of space and the identity of the territory of the state with the land held (on an *oikos* or individual household basis) by the citizens (*politai*, literally '*polis*-people').[4] Criteria for citizenship might of course be defined differently from *polis* to *polis*, but criteria there had to be, since, as Thucydides' Nikias remarked (7.77.7), 'men are the *polis*.' (This claim had of course a special point in the circumstances in which he and his men found themselves in Sicily in 413, but nevertheless it has also a generally valid application too.) Hence the fact that, instead of referring to the state of, for example, 'Athens', the Greeks spoke of 'the Athenians'. Now Sparta, strictly, fails to satisfy this first condition of *polis*-hood, because the name of the state, 'the Lakedaimonians', did not only denote the citizens of Sparta, who are usually called today, as they sometimes were in antiquity, 'Spartiates'.[5] Also included in the rubric 'Lakedaimonians', though primarily for military purposes, were the free but unenfranchised people known as 'Perioikoi' ('dwellers around'), who lived within the borders of the Spartan *polis* but in their own semi-autonomous towns.[6] Indeed, these towns could themselves loosely be called *poleis*, though they lacked *autonomia*. This was a foreshadowing of the general situation in the Hellenistic period, to the crucial significance of which we shall return (Section VI).

It will be enough to say here that in the Hellenistic period the *polis* had typically lost its second defining characteristic, the enjoyment of *eleutheria* (freedom) and *autonomia* (independence). By the fifth century BC these words, like so many others, had already entered the vocabulary of political propaganda and been emptied of much of their original content in the process. But it is clear that *autonomia* was normally conceived of as external freedom, freedom from external control or even interference; while *eleutheria* was the freedom of a *polis* to organize its political life as it chose.[7]

However, for political life to be regarded as truly that of a *polis* there was a third, 'constitutional', condition to be fulfilled. There had to be a relatively representative (in the non-technical sense) council the members of which (together with other officials) were elected, if only by a part of the citizenry, or otherwise selected; and there had to be meetings, ideally stated or regular ones, of a general assembly of the whole citizen body. Sparta, despite its lack of written laws, clearly counts as a *polis* on our second and third criteria: indeed, as we shall see at the very end of this paper, the Spartan *polis* in the fullest sense outlived most of its partners and rivals.

Similarly, Sparta embodied the polis to the fullest degree as regards the fourth ideal condition of *polis*-hood, *autarkeia* (self-sufficiency). The Greeks did not draw a rigid distinction between 'politics' and 'economics', an error often committed by modern scholars from which they were saved partly by their vocabulary, in part by the conditions of their economic existence.[8] They appreciated that the 'good' life in the *polis* depended on the citizens' securing not merely the necessities of life – these could be procured in the *ethnos* type of state too – but also what we might call the 'good things' of life. So the development of the *polis* was inseparably bound up with the development of economic exploitation through various forms of dependent or forced labour, above all (and eventually typically) chattel slavery. The connection between greater privileges and entitlements for individual citizens (though not necessarily their womenfolk) in the *polis* and increasing deprivation of rights for slaves has been rightly noted.[9]

However, this was not what was meant by the maverick Athenian oligarch Kritias, fervent admirer of Sparta, when he said (88 B37 D-K) that in Sparta the free were the most truly free, the slaves the most fully enslaved in Greece. For, as is notorious, the concept of individual rights as opposed to state prerogatives did not make much headway in this polity; and the Spartans' 'slaves' (*douloi*) were not chattel slaves but belonged to a category rather unhelpfully called 'between free and slave' in a second century AD lexicon (Pollux 3.83).[10] The essential point is that these Helots, as they were known, were not the heterogeneous, polyglot 'barbarians' (non-Greeks) bought and sold on the open market, who formed the bulk of the slave populations of most Greek states. The Helots were in fact themselves Greeks, compelled under pain of instant death to work the lands once owned by their ancestors whom the Spartans had conquered and enslaved. To use an anachronistic but not inappropriate terminology, they were a kind of state-serf, bound to the soil and owned collectively by the Spartan *polis* rather than by individual Spartan masters (or mistresses).[11] Thus, when Kritias called the Spartans 'the most free', he meant that they least of all lived for the sake of or under the constraint of others: on the contrary, they carried the exploitation of forced labour to its logical extreme and, thanks to the Helots, ultimately did *no* productive work whatsoever. Their sole skill and their major preoccupation was warfare,[12] precisely because, as we shall see, the Helots did not view their position in quite the same favourable light as their masters.

As far as the criterion of self-sufficiency is concerned, then, the Spartan *polis* was the same as most others, only more so and in a different way. On the other hand, strictly speaking it fails entirely to fulfil the fifth and final criterion, the possession of a truly urban centre. The root meaning of *polis*, indeed, seems to be 'akro-*polis*' or citadel, and the word may go back to a Mycenaean form *ptolis*.[13] However, since the discovery in this century of man's Neolithic ancestry, hardly two scholars can agree entirely on a definition of 'city' or 'urban'.[14] It is fortunate, therefore, that the Greeks were less exacting. A well-known passage from the Baedeker of antiquity, the second-century AD Pausanias (10.4.1), admirably conveys their general notion:

> From Chaironeia two and a half miles (twenty stades) bring you to the city (*polis*) of Panopeus in Phokis: if you can call it a 'city' when it has no state buildings, no training-ground, no theatre, and no market-square, when it has no running water at a water-head and they live on the edge of a torrent in hovels like mountain huts. Still, their territory has boundary stones with its neighbours, and they send delegates to the Phokian assembly (trans. P. Levi, slightly modified).

Had Pausanias been a historian or political scientist, he might have added a city-wall to his list of defining 'urban' features (those of Panopeus can still be seen); but his final comments on Panopeus' community of place and level of political organization clearly indicate that in his view the purely physical criteria of urbanization are less important than they.[15]

Likewise, some five and a half centuries before Pausanias, a critical visitor, Thucydides, had found it remarkable that the inhabitants of

3. The Peculiar Position of Sparta

Sparta still conserved an earlier pattern of settlement and lived 'in villages' (Thuc. 1.10.2). That is to say, the 'city' of Sparta had not been completely 'synoecised', and each of its five constituent villages still retained something of an independent identity.[16] In the same passage Thucydides had noted that from the ruins of Sparta's public shrines and private houses no future visitor would infer Sparta's past military might and political predominance. This was a brilliant prediction that has been fulfilled with lamentable completeness, although this does not of course mean that Sparta had once stood on the same level of 'urbanization' as tiny Panopeus. Thucydides too might have said something about Sparta's city-wall – or rather lack of one: the first such construction, completed more than two centuries after Thucydides' death, was an unmistakable sign of Sparta's political and military eclipse.[17] Anyway, all these factors amply justify Ehrenberg's description of Sparta as 'semi-urban'. But we cannot leave it at that: as a final oddity, one of the constituent villages, Amyklai, lay some five kilometres south of the main cluster, and its separate identity, fostered by geographical distance and historical tradition, was even less reduced than that of the other four villages.[18]

III

On balance, then, and with some important reservations, we may fairly characterize the Spartan state as a *polis*.[19] In the remainder of this chapter I shall attempt to answer the questions why, when and how it became one, and what contribution Sparta made in the seventh and sixth centuries to the development of the Greek *polis*, considering Sparta first as a discrete entity and then as one unit in an association of such entities. However, before we can tackle any of these questions, we must establish the limits imposed on us by the available written (literary or epigraphical) and material evidence.

As far as the Archaic period in general is concerned, it will be enough to convey the essential situation if I quote A.R. Burn's rather wistful comments on a fragmentary papyrus of a poem by Alkaios of Lesbos: 'In its suggestions of intriguing possibilities, while never once telling us all that we want to know, it is all too typical of the evidence for early Greek history'.[20] Moreover, the writing of history (in the modern sense of a critical and disinterested interpretation of the past) was not an invention of the Archaic period: that distinction is generally accorded to Herodótus, active chiefly in the third quarter of the fifth century, who rightly chose the middle of the sixth century as the starting-point for his history of Graeco-'barbarian' relations down to the Persian Wars of 480-79.[21] Regrettably, there simply is not enough written material surviving from the two centuries or so between the Greeks' rediscovery of literacy and invention of a fully phonetic alphabetic script around 775 BC[22] and the beginning of Herodotus' narrative in c. 550 BC for us to reconstruct an adequate political history of the period, and Herodotus' own utility increases noticeably the nearer he approaches to the Persian Wars. In fairness, though, I should add that we have learnt to squeeze the maximum from such scraps of poetry as that of Alkaios just mentioned and from Archaic inscriptions of various kinds.[23] So too we have come to see that archaeological (including art-historical) evidence is part of the historian's stock-in-trade, although experience and reflection have demonstrated that artefacts, even if they are authentic testimony to the times they represent, are not self-explanatory and cannot serve as a substitute for the written evidence we lack.[24]

The picture already looks bleak, but the evidence for the political structure and development of Archaic Sparta is, if anything, more than ordinarily poor.[25] In part, this is due simply to the absolute dearth of contemporary written evidence. Tyrtaios and Alkman were front-rank Archaic Spartan poets, but even Tyrtaios, by far the more explicitly 'political' of the two, was after all a poet (if a propagandistic one), not a political commentator.[26] Spartan epigraphy yields yet fewer inscriptions of political significance than can be counted on the fingers of one hand, and the one Archaic political document preserved by a literary source is, as we shall see, at once priceless and of uncertain value. Herodotus is invaluable for the Sparta of his own and, to a smaller extent, earlier times; but his brilliant successor, Thucydides, the contemporary historian *par excellence*, contents himself with enunciating one highly general (and not entirely self-explanatory) statement about early Spartan history (1.18).

It is with Thucydides' coevals, however, that the real trouble begins. For, starting in the late fifth century with the two works on Sparta by Kritias, the Spartan political and social system was exalted by its non-Spartan devotees into an ideal, at first from political, later from a mixture of political and philosophical motives. Hence F. Ollier's coinage of the evocative phrase 'le mirage spartiate' to describe these distorted idealizations;[27] hence also the fact that in a modern study of ancient utopias two chapters could be devoted to Sparta (the only actually existing *state* to be so singled out).[28] Our evidentiary problems are compounded by the fact that the only surviving extended accounts of Spartan society, Xenophon's misnamed *Constitution of the Lakedaimonians*[29] and Plutarch's hagiography of the legendary lawgiver Lykourgos,[30] both belong to the 'utopian' tradition. Sadly, the presumably more neutral *Constitution of the Lakedaimonians* by Aristotle (or his School) survives only in isolated quotations (frr. 532-45 Rose), which either add nothing to what he says about Sparta in the *Politics* or complicate and confuse the picture further.[31] Our loss is all the more keenly felt because we know Plutarch drew on the Aristotelian *Constitution* for his *Life* of Lykourgos.[32]

IV

What I have been trying to do is load the dice heavily on the side where I
think they ought to be loaded, that of uncertainty and caution. I do not
believe it to be fruitless to try to reconstruct Spartan politics in the Archaic
period. On the contrary, the attempt must be made, because it was in this
period that Sparta not merely brought its political institutions to full
maturity but also became the most powerful state in the Greek world,
powerful enough to play the ultimately decisive political and military role
in the repulse of the Persians in 480-79. And, as Thucydides (1.18) acutely
noted, it was Sparta's achievement of internal political stability at an early
date that enabled her to intervene in the affairs of other Greek states – at
first, we might add, for the benefit, later to the detriment of the admittedly
nebulous concept of 'Hellas'.

But just how early did Sparta achieve this stability, and was this
tantamount to its becoming a *polis* in the fullest sense?[33] In the thirteenth
century BC most of the area later occupied by the Spartan *polis* at its
greatest extent (between *c.* 545 and 370) was apparently divided between
two kingdoms situated on either side of the Taygetos mountain massif
(2407m). These kingdoms, like their counterparts centred on Mycenae,
Thebes and so on, represent as it were a political false start. For between
the world of the Mycenaean palace and that of the Hellenic *polis* there is
a gulf fixed, not only in time but in conception and organization; and that
gulf cannot be directly bridged. Politically speaking, the eleventh to ninth
centuries BC, sometimes labelled the Dark Age, mark an entirely fresh
start.

Into the void following the downfall of Mycenaean civilization – more
gaping in the Peloponnese, the Mycenaean heartland, than elsewhere –
there somehow stepped new arrivals.[34] These are known to Greek myth-
history as 'the descendants of Herakles', to modern dialectologists as West
Greek speakers, to historians ancient and modern more vaguely as Dorians.[35] The break which their arrival marked is nowhere more clearly
visible than in the very site of Dorian Sparta.[36] For this was a settlement
ex nihilo, on the other (western) side of the River Eurotas from what
British excavations have shown to be the chief Mycenaean centre of the
region.[37] The date of the settlement – or rather of the completion of a
perhaps drawn-out process of settlement – may possibly be fixed by
archaeological evidence to the second half of the tenth century. At all
events, no amount of juggling with pottery-chronology will sustain the
credit of the Spartans' own myth-historical traditions, which held that
Sparta was settled within the twelfth century (in our terms).[38]

Here we must pause briefly to look at these traditions a little more
closely, since they are intimately tied to one of our later preoccupations,
the survival into the Archaic – indeed, into the Hellenistic – period of a by
no means titular kingship (cf. Chapter 5, below). When the Spartans

27

sought to justify their land-grabbing operations of the eighth and seventh centuries, they naturally presented themselves as the legitimate successors of the last great powers thought to have occupied roughly the same area, the Homeric kings Menelaos and Nestor. The simplest and most convincing form of relationship, especially in a world dominated by aristocratic ideology, was that of blood. So the Spartans claimed that their rulers were lineally descended from the great-great-grandsons of Herakles who had together wrested the Peloponnese from Teisamenos, son of Orestes and grandson of Agamemnon.

The Spartans, however, had a difficulty not shared by their arch-rivals, the Argives. For they were ruled by two kings, from two distinct royal houses, the Agiads and Eurypontids. Their solution was blindingly simple: it was not one descendant of Herakles who had obtained Sparta and Lakonia (south-east Peloponnese), they argued, but two, who – naturally – were twins. But then how was it, a malicious enquirer might have asked, that the two royal houses were named, not after these twins, but after descendants of theirs? Since the Spartans had no satisfactory answer to this one, we may reply for them: because the kings before the eponymous ancestors were fictitious. If, however, we accept as genuine all the preserved names from the eponyms down to the Agiad Kleomenes I and the Eurypontid Damaratos, who were indisputably reigning jointly in 500 BC, and if we then assign a notional average reign of twenty-five years to each, we arrive at a date somewhere around 900 for the eponyms – an apparently brilliant concord of pedigrees and potsherds.

Unfortunately, the Spartan king-lists, central though they became to the ancient Greeks' reconstructions of their early history in terms of absolute dates, are houses of cards built on sand.[39] It may be that the first joint kings were really those for whom joint action (not simply coincidence of reign) is recorded, namely Archelaos and Charillos, who on one possible modern 'rationalization' of the ancient dates could have ruled together between *c.* 775 and 760.[40] Not long after this, probably, the Spartans incorporated Amyklai as the fifth constituent village of Sparta.[41] Does this imply that Sparta – i.e., the original Sparta, whose territory was confined to the east of Mt. Taygetos – had become a *polis* by *c.* 750?

However rudimentary may have been the interrelationship between Spartiates, Perioikoi and Helots at this stage; however slight the progress away from tribal monarchy; and notwithstanding the non-urban character of Sparta town, the answer, I believe, is that it had, though that answer is not so much based on positive contemporary evidence but rather an inference from two later episodes. First, in *c.* 735 Sparta embarked upon an aggressively imperialistic policy designed to annex at least the central alluvial plain of neighbouring Messenia and reduce its former occupiers to the status of Helots. Such an enterprise arguably presupposes some form, no matter how rudimentary, of *polis*-machinery. Second, shortly after the end of this (First) Messenian War, which lasted until *c.* 715, there occurred

28

the puzzling Partheniai affair. This abortive coup implies (see further Section V, below) that criteria of citizenship had by then been established.

Other scholars, however, are prepared to go much further, in order to save the credit of the much later literary sources. One, for example, has categorically stated that the Spartans 'were the first to give their state the shape of a *polis*'.[42] Justification of this bold assertion is sought by dating to before 750 BC the one Archaic Spartan political document that is preserved by a literary source, the 'Great Rhetra' (so called to distinguish it from several lesser *rhêtrai*).[43] It will give a fair idea of the problems this document presents if I say that, even though its authenticity is now generally accepted, the precise meaning of virtually every one of its fifty or so words (the unfortunately corrupt text is preserved in Plutarch's *Life* of Lykourgos, Ch. 6) is still hotly disputed.

V

Having established a cult of Syllanian Zeus and Athena, having done the 'tribing and obing', and having established a *gerousia* of 30 members including the kings, (1) season in, season out they are to hold Apellai between Babyka and Knakion; (2) the *gerousia* is both (a) to introduce proposals and (b) to stand aloof; (3) the *damos* is to have power to [in Plutarch's gloss on a badly garbled Doric phrase] 'give a decisive verdict'; (4) but if the *damos* speaks crookedly, the *gerousia* and kings are to be removers.

First then, its form. As Dr Jeffery's careful translation clearly conveys, the text falls into two parts, the verbs of action in the first being in the aorist tense, those in the second in the infinitive. We do not know whether this arrangement is meant to represent a temporal succession – *first* the establishment of the cult, etc., *then* the carrying out of provisions (1) to (4).[44] But it does seem probable that it was the four provisions in the infinitive which were the immediately crucial innovations.

Plutarch, however, or his source, considered that the fourth provision (usually known as the 'Rider'), was a later addition, tacked on to the other three at the instigation of the joint kings Theopompos and Polydoros, precisely because the *damos* (the people as a whole) *had* 'spoken crookedly'. In this Plutarch has been followed by Sakellariou, who then uses it as a supporting argument for his pre-750 dating of the rest of the text, since Theopompos and Polydoros could not have reigned together before (again, on a plausible modern chronology) *c.* 700 BC.[45] However, what Sakellariou omits to mention is that Plutarch may have been simply following Aristotle here (as elsewhere), and that Aristotle *had* to separate Rhetra and Rider, because for him Lykourgos (to whom Plutarch at least attributed the Rhetra), as co-founder of the Olympic Games (in what we call 776), belonged to an earlier generation than Theopompos and Polydoros.[46] It is, therefore, open to us to treat the Rhetra *plus* Rider as a unity and to interpret the Rider as specifying the meaning of what was presumably a general statement in provision (3). This view is supported by the fact that Tyrtaios (fr. 4 West), who is by far the earliest source to show any knowledge of the Rhetra, almost certainly attributed the complete text to Theopompos and Polydoros.[47] By itself this does not give us a firm date for the Rhetra, but it is, I think, enough to rule out the view of Sakellariou.

Granted, then, that the text was in some sense a single unit, what kind of document was it? The word '*rhêtra*' does not by itself decide the issue, since it just means something pronounced or spoken, hence anything from treaty or bargain to proposal to enactment.[48] Plutarch, however, our only ancient guide to interpretation, believed that the Rhetra was an oracle pronounced by the Pythia, Apollo's mouthpiece at Delphi: as he remarks elsewhere (*Mor.* 403e), Delphic oracles in prose were far from being rarities (and as a priest at Delphi he ought to have known what he was talking about).[49] Whether or not Plutarch was formally correct, it is more than possible that the Spartans would have sought Apollo's blessing for any major political innovation, as they later sought his blessing for a wide range of policy decisions. Under provision (1) they are instructed to 'hold Apellai' (the monthly Apolline festival) 'season in, season out'. Since this last phrase has distinctly poetic overtones (as does the word used in each case for 'kings'), I am inclined to follow those who see behind our text – and also behind Tyrtaios' elegiac couplets – an original hexameter oracle of the kind we know were recorded in Sparta in a later period.[50]

Precisely what the Rhetra was cannot, then, be established, but its unique preservation, in prose form, suggests that both at the time of its composition and in subsequent times it was considered to be of cardinal political significance. Can we ascertain more precisely what that significance originally was? Speaking generally, was the Rhetra designed to govern only a limited area of political activity, or was it, as it were, the cornerstone or blueprint of the entire political structure or machine? The division into two parts according to verb-forms and the omission of the office of the Ephors (see further below) suggest the former, the area in question being the form and nature of the decision-making process. On the other hand, the inclusion of the cult of Zeus and Athena and the 'tribing and obing', together with the specification of the precise size of the Gerousia, suggest the latter. I incline mildly to the former view: Plutarch, at any rate, introduced the text into his biography on the grounds that the creation of the Gerousia was the first and most important of Lykourgos' many political masterstrokes and that the Rhetra was an oracle dealing with the position of that body.

The details are even more baffling. The association of politics and religion is typically Greek, but the cults of Syllanian (?) Zeus and Athena are not otherwise attested in Sparta, despite the relatively rich ancient literature on Spartan cults. However, the association of Zeus (father of the Spartans' mythical progenitor Herakles) with Athena (patron deity of Sparta) is appropriate and indeed paralleled,[51] and most of the ingenious attempts to emend 'Syllanian' do not convince.[52] The next puzzle is the force of the aorist participle in 'having done the tribing and obing' (both Greek verbs are *hapax legomena*). The usual three Dorian tribes are attested for Sparta as early as Tyrtaios (fr. 19.8 West) and must have been there from the beginning. The obes are certainly local as well as kinship units and are most easily identified with what Thucydides (1.10.2) untechnically called 'villages'. There may, then, be a reference here to the incorporation of Amyklai as the fifth obe about 750 BC, although the aorist suggests, if anything, that this had already taken place.[53] So, too, the Gerousia or council of elders advising the king (as in Homer; cf. the Roman Senate) must have been as old as the kingship itself. But the specification of its size and, above all, the inclusion in it of the kings must reflect a change in the relative status of the kingship and the aristocratic council, to the advantage of the latter: it is striking that the kings do not appear independently in the Rhetra, as they do in Tyrtaios (fr. 4 West). This is surely a key aspect of the transformation of Sparta from a tribal kingship into a *polis*.

Turning to provisions (1) to (4), we may associate the provision for regular celebration of the festival of Apollo with the regular holding of a general assembly of the whole citizen body (*damos*) each month.[54] Precisely what power (*kratos*) was given to the *damos* under provision (3), if indeed that is the correct reading, is unclear; but undoubtedly the exercise of it was restricted in the first place by the fact that the *damos*' freedom of speech was also subject to the discretion of the same body under provision (4). Indeed, a likely interpretation of provisions (2) to (4) taken together is that the *damos* was allowed *no* discussion even of such proposals as the Gerousia decided to put before it, although it is of course possible that discussion of an issue *was* permitted prior to the Gerousia's putting a formal proposal to the vote. Anyway, even if we suppose that the *damos* was granted as much as formal sovereignty under provision (3), provision (4) seems to me to make it unambiguously clear that this sovereignty was of a passive or negative nature. In conclusion, it should be stressed that the text gives no hint of the nature of the issues that were liable to be discussed by the Gerousia and brought before the full assembly for its 'yea' or 'nay'.

It is not possible to advance the discussion of the Rhetra much further without appealing either to instances of the political decision-making process in operation in the fifth to third centuries or to Aristotle's comments on Sparta in the *Politics*.[55] The Rhetra was, after all, preserved as a living document, and it was the apparent congruence between later practice and the provisions of the Rhetra which made possible (though not likely) the view that the Rhetra was a fourth-century BC forgery.[56] However, if we are to understand the Rhetra's original significance, we must first try to pinpoint the specific historical context in which it may have been first produced and acted upon. This entails considering as a whole the century from *c.* 750 to 650, which has been justly dubbed 'The Age of Revolution'.[57]

This 'Revolution' had four main facets. First, relative overpopulation in Old Greece led typically to settlement overseas and stimulated at home a decisive switch from pasturage to arable farming. Second, as warfare in consequence became more frequent and organized, with each state seeking to secure the maximum utilizable and defensible cornland, the basic objectives of warfare became the menacing, temporary possession or destruction of the enemy's crops and the protection of one's own. To secure these objectives, hoplite (i.e., heavy-armed phalanx) fighting replaced open-order, ill organized and individualistic skirmishing. Third, there was a rapid growth of overseas trade, especially in slaves, metals and luxury finished goods and raw materials. Finally, political change was so swift that there occurred not only the full development of the *polis* to assume the shape outlined in Section II but also the first examples of the 'tyrannical coup'.

Sparta, predictably, was not unaffected by any of these main facets of the revolutionary century. But its handling of them did indeed set an indelible stamp of peculiarity (in both senses) on its political and social system as a whole. First, instead of dispatching settlers abroad, the Spartans preferred to satisfy their land-hunger at the expense of their immediate neighbours, initially in Lakonia, then – more remarkably – across Taygetos in Messenia. We know relatively little about the fighting in Lakonia, but, for whatever reason, the conquest and control of the Lakonian Helots posed comparatively few problems[58] – in comparison, that is, to the conquest and final subjugation of the Helots of Messenia, which occupied more than a century and required at least two sustained wars, the second in response to a revolt which nearly succeeded. Second, somewhere in the first half of the seventh century Sparta adopted the hoplite mode of warfare, possibly only after suffering the one major defeat ever inflicted by Sparta's main Peloponnesian rival, Argos.[59] Third, the archaeological evidence, especially from the sanctuary of Artemis Ortheia in Sparta, reveals a pattern of trade and manufacture not unlike that suggested by the contemporary dedications at the other important Peloponnesian sanctuaries. What, then, of the fourth, narrowly political, facet? In particular, how did Sparta avoid tyranny?

A passage in Aristotle's *Politics* (1306b29-07a5) arguably provides the key clue to the correct perspective within which to view Sparta's political development in this period and so, by extension, to interpret the Rhetra's original significance. Here, in the context of his discussion of *stasis*, he cites the no fewer than five occasions known to him on which there was a possibility of political revolution in Sparta between the late eighth and early fourth centuries. Two of these fall within the 'Age of Revolution'. First, there was an attempted coup centring on an enigmatic group called Partheniai, which led to the Partheniai emigrating to found Sparta's only

32

true overseas colony, Taras in the instep of Italy, in *c.* 706. We cannot be certain of the real motives behind the coup; but legitimacy and citizen-rights were apparently involved, implying that these had already been officially defined, and possibly too the relationship between Amyklai and the other four villages of Sparta was at issue.[60] Second, at the time of the Messenian revolt referred to above, the revolutionary demand was advanced for the redistribution of Spartiate land. (We might also add that traditionally King Polydoros was assassinated, perhaps *c.* 665, the last monarch to be so dethroned probably before the equally turbulent third century.) Since, therefore, Sparta experienced the same problems as other states over the distribution of land, civil rights and political power, the most promising way to construe the Rhetra is as a response to extreme political crisis. Can it be tied more closely to a particular stage of the crisis?

How the kings are seemingly downgraded to mere members of the Gerousia in the Rhetra has already been noted. This downgrading may perhaps be linked specifically to the establishment of a joint kingship at Sparta in *c.* 770; or, if that is thought too precise, it should unquestionably be linked to the general decline, indeed disappearance, of kingship in the Greek world as a whole during the eighth century in favour of a *polis* ruled by aristocrats.[61] Viewed in this light, the explicit inclusion of the kings in a document like the Rhetra, divinely sanctioned and guaranteed by Apollo, can be regarded as a brilliant method of guaranteeing that the kingship itself would not die completely. Certainly, a by no means titular joint kingship did survive, and it is not perhaps unreasonable to detect the hand of the kings Theopompos and Polydoros at work here. At any rate, Theopompos was later believed to have established the Ephorate precisely as a preservative of the crown (below).

However, it is provision (3) which seems to me to give us a usable *terminus post quem* for the document. *Kratos* (power) for the *damos*, however hedged about and however passive, surely presupposes the existence, in no matter how rudimentary a form, of the hoplite phalanx; in other words, of a group of Spartans outside the charmed circle of the nobility with sufficient metaphorical as well as literal muscle to compel recognition of their existence in defined political terms. We cannot date the hoplite reform in Sparta – assuming its occurrence (see Chapter 11) – more precisely than the first half of the seventh century, but a date in the first quarter is not implausible. If that is accepted, the connection of the Rhetra with Theopompos and Polydoros would receive some independent support.

The Rhetra does not, alas, spell out the issues over which the *damos* was to exercise its power of decision; but, given the postulated historical context, a say in the essential question of foreign policy, peace or war, was an obvious and minimal right for the *damos* to demand. There were, however, other no less pressing issues to be resolved, and the Rhetra could not possibly have been the sole instrument of reform introduced about this time. For example, land had to be redistributed to provide the material basis for turning all Spartan citizens into hoplite warriors (in this respect Sparta was and remained truly unique in all Greece). At some stage, too, the *agôgê* (unique for being compulsory) had to be inaugurated or regularized (see Chapter 7). What matters, however, is that the Rhetra was a successful solution to the problems it confronted. This success we infer from three facts: first, the survival of the text; second, the apparent lack of any further substantive change in the decision-making process; and, third, the avoidance of tyranny.

The resulting political system was regarded as a paradigm of 'orderliness' or 'law-abidingness' (*eunomia*), and all ancient commentators from Herodotus to Plutarch were impressed by the apparent political harmony maintained within the Spartan *polis* over a period of four or more centuries.[62] Aristotle, as we saw, painted a considerably less rosy picture, but even he could not have denied Spartan law-abidingness when it was judged by the standards of Greek civic practice as a whole. It was at least poetically just that it was into the mouth of a Spartan king – albeit an exiled and formally traitorous one – that Herodotus (7.104.4) should have placed the classic statement of the quintessentially Greek idea that the Law was above all men.

It may be thought that this political achievement at so early a date was impressive enough. Some scholars, however, have argued that Sparta went further and actually made a pioneering contribution to the technique of government.[63] One of the political powers of the third-century Gerousia, we learn from Plutarch (*Agis* 11.1), was their deliberative initiative, that is, their right of prior discussion and formulation of proposals to be voted upon by the full assembly.[64] This *probouleusis* was also a feature of the most progressive (within the framework of the individual *polis*) political experiment of ancient Greece, the Athenian democracy of the fifth and fourth centuries. It is not improbable, however, that it had been first introduced at Athens in the early sixth century by Solon; one of his poems was entitled 'Eunomia', and in this as in other respects he may therefore have been consciously following a precedent set by Sparta in the Rhetra almost a century earlier.

One corollary of this hypothesis might be that, although *kratos* for the Spartan *damos* did not of course mean democracy (*dêmokratia*) on the Athenian model, the Spartan system of oligarchy – for such it was in reality – was to some extent more open, more 'popular', than that of other oligarchical states, even in the Classical period.[65] Against that view, however, there seem to me to be at least three decisive counter-arguments. First, the political position of the Spartan Gerousia resembled, not that of the Solonian Council of 400, still less that of the Kleisthenic Council of 500, but that of the unreconstructed Athenian Areopagos, in that both these bodies were 'guardians of the laws' and politically non-responsible. Second, although we do not know in detail the sequence followed by the decision-making process in Sparta, it seems clear that the Gerousia did not merely deliberate before the assembly of the *damos* but actually in effect took decisions on its behalf. For since no discussion or at least no alternative proposals were permitted in the assembly, it is hardly likely that an assembly whose members had been trained from earliest childhood to respect and unquestioningly obey their elders (and betters) would easily reject a proposal of the Gerousia, at any rate not a unanimous one. Third, as far as the alleged openness of the Spartan oligarchy is concerned, it will be enough here to point out that votes in the assembly were taken 'by shouting and not by ballot' – there was no counting of votes, hence no notion of 'one man, one vote'; elections were conducted according to what Aristotle dismissed as 'childish' (i.e., easily manipulated) procedures; legislation was a rarity in Sparta, and such laws as were passed were anyway brief and not committed publicly to writing; finally, but by no means least, there was no popular judiciary.[66] The most, therefore, that can be said is that the Spartans had early on devised a technique whereby the hoplite *damos* might formally resolve irreconcilable conflicts within the aristocratic élite, thereby helping to forestall tyranny.

Indeed, it was precisely because the essentials of the decision-making process had been worked out so early and, perhaps above all, because they were worked out to meet a situation of military crisis that Sparta could not possibly have resembled democratic Athens. To put that same point differently, Sparta's Archaic period, in terms of the evolution of political institutions, was also its 'Classical' epoch. The reason why the decision-making process and the balance of political power were so to speak 'frozen' at this stage is to be sought outside the bounds of the citizen body itself, in the military and economic situation in which the Spartans had chosen to place themselves. They had decided to live off and base their lifestyle on the extraction of a surplus from exploited Helot labour, but in order to do so successfully for so long they were obliged to wage what was in effect a continuous war, now overt, now covert, especially against the Messenian Helots.[67]

It may perhaps be considered odd that I have not yet discussed the board of five Ephors ('Overseers'), who seem to occupy so prominent a place in Spartan politics in the Classical period. There are two reasons for the omission (not oversight). First, they happen not to be included explicitly in the terms of the Great Rhetra, although the office was allegedly created by King Theopompos or, less plausibly, by Lykourgos. Second, such political power or prominence as they later achieved (though I believe it has often been exaggerated and misconstrued) was not obtained until the middle of the sixth century, traditionally thanks to the enterprise of the legendary Chilon (Diog. Laert. 1.68.6), one of the 'Seven Sages' of ancient Greece.

As far as the origins of the office are concerned, the reason allegedly given by Theopompos himself for his creation – that the Ephorate would help to preserve the monarchy – seems to me to contain an important germ

35

of truth.[68] In other words, although the oath exchanged monthly between kings and Ephors (Xen., *LP* 15.7) did put the onus on the kings to obey the laws, and although the series of trials and banishments of kings in the fifth and fourth centuries was importantly the work of boards of Ephors,[69] yet the kingship still retained the potential for overriding *de facto* political power. Witness, for example, the reigns of Kleomenes I and Agesilaos II (Chapter 5). The Ephors, on the other hand, though elected from all the *damos*,[70] were certainly in no sense popular representatives. Rather, on attaining a position of collective eminence, the Ephorate fitted smoothly into the oligarchic hierarchy, satisfying the need for a relatively youthful and dynamic executive, while its individual members were prevented by their annual tenure of office from attaining a dangerously large amount of personal power. There was no cause to exile Ephors, and tellingly it was to the kingship (or rather monarchy) that the ambitions of a Lysander aspired.[71]

Thus the association of the Ephor Chilon with the increase of collective power for the Ephorate around the middle of the sixth century would plausibly seem to suggest that for some reason the Ephors from this point on came to play a new and important rôle in the Spartan *polis*. This rôle is not far to seek, namely, in Sparta's foreign relations. For it was precisely about this time that Sparta ceased its attempts to expand its home base by conquest and 'Helotization' and began instead to extend its power abroad – and so increase its domestic security – through diplomacy, by building up the network of alliances which culminated by 500 BC in what we know as the 'Peloponnesian League'.[72] It was as head of this alliance that Sparta naturally came to be chosen as leader of the Greeks against Persia.

VI

My final topic is Sparta's contribution to the development of inter-*polis* relations and the effect which these relations had in their turn upon the ideal type of the *polis*. Sparta had of course entered into diplomatic or military relations with other states before the mid-sixth century, but these had been either temporary, or more personal than political, or of a primarily religious character. I have in mind such aid as was rendered to Sparta by Samians in the Messenian war (Hdt. 3.47); the contribution made by Sparta (especially by its kings) to the development of the institution of *proxenia*, an extension of guest-friendship to the level of the *polis*; and Sparta's participation in the religious associations known as amphiktyonies.[73]

Around 550 BC, however, Sparta *qua polis* inaugurated a political phenomenon which has been given the modern technical title of 'hegemonic symmachy'.[74] By this is meant a series of individual military alliances between one *polis* as *hegemôn* ('leader') and *poleis* which were subordinated to the *hegemôn* in foreign policy. The English 'symmachy' renders the Greek *summachia*, which denotes an alliance both defensive and offensive expressed in Greek terms as 'having the same friends and enemies'. The essential reason for this Spartan initiative was precisely the same as for Sparta's 'peculiarity' as a *polis*, namely its fear of the Helots, towards whom, as Thucydides (4.80.3) is probably to be taken as saying, Spartan policy 'had always been based almost entirely on the idea of security'.

It does not much matter for our purposes whether the first of these alliances was concluded with Elis or, as most believe, Tegea.[75] What is important is that this innovation signalled the beginning of the demise, or at any rate the compromise, of a cardinal element of *polis*-hood, *autonomia*. It was thereafter only a matter of time before loss of *autonomia* led also to loss of *eleutheria*, since a *hegemôn* needed to be sure that the ruling classes of its subject-allies would comply semi-automatically with its wishes. Typically, as Thucydides (1.19) observed, the method chosen by Sparta to achieve this objective was to support oligarchic governments throughout its alliance. Oligarchies of the wealthy and often aristocratic few were more easily controlled than more open political systems and more inclined to approve Sparta's own selfish ultimate aim, control of the economically indispensable Helots within Sparta's own *polis*-frontiers. It was not, however, until Sparta had (with massive Persian aid) won the Peloponnesian War in 404 that the full implications of Sparta's hegemonial position for the freedom and autonomy of its subordinate allies were realized.[76] As a *locus classicus*, we might perhaps single out Sparta's treatment of Mantineia in 385. Not only was Mantineia's hitherto barely tolerated democracy replaced by an oligarchy, but through a process of *dioikismos* the Mantineians were actually compelled to pull down their city-walls and revert to living in dispersed 'villages'.[77] There, indeed, was political reaction with a vengeance.

The 'Peloponnesian League', however, was never a league in the full sense, let alone a supra-*polis* federal state like the Achaean League of the Hellenistic period (which Sparta, revealingly, had to be compelled to join).[78] Indeed, it can be said to have been a league in any sense only from the time that the subject-allies won the right of collective veto over the decisions of the *hegemôn*, probably in about 505. If asked to explain why Sparta was able to effect this remarkable transformation of inter-*polis* relations and so, ultimately, of the *polis* itself, I would point to Sparta's unique experience within its own extraordinarily large and variegated *polis*-territory. This could have served as a kind of laboratory experiment. For the relations developed by Sparta with its Perioikic 'allies' (also known loosely as '*poleis*') foreshadowed in microcosm the system of imperialistic domination Sparta later evolved, at first in the Peloponnese, then in mainland Greece, and finally in the Aegean basin as a whole, before the systems-collapse of the second quarter of the fourth century (cf. Cartledge 1987).

VII

To conclude, I offer an outline and of course highly tentative chronological sketch. It was the initial decision taken by the Spartan aristocracy, including the two kings, to turn Sparta into a *rentier* state living off Helot surplus labour that mainly determined thereafter Sparta's own development as a *polis* and the character of its relations with and effect upon other *poleis*. Sparta thereby became the most self-sufficient of all Greek *poleis* and yet at the same time not a typical *polis* at all, in the senses that the territory of the Spartan citizens was not co-extensive with that of the *polis* as a whole and the state did not possess a true urban centre.

Somewhere in the first half of the seventh century, following a political crisis both within the ruling aristocracy and between the aristocracy and the *damos*, a sort of 'social contract' was devised whereby the aristocracy (including the kings) retained ultimate political sovereignty, while the *damos* was given at least a decisive say in the matter of peace and war. Sparta had become a *polis* in the constitutional sense, although the hereditary kingship had not disappeared along with the other vestiges of the tribal state.

Finally, it was the peculiar tripartite system of Spartiates, Perioikoi and Helots elaborated within the *polis*-frontiers that both led and permitted Sparta to inaugurate the process culminating in the demise of the original *polis* as such. Appropriately, therefore, we end with the ultimate in paradox; the *polis* which was not a canonical *polis* and which did as much as any state to hasten the downfall of that mode of political organization yet survived longer than any of its major partners and rivals in something like its original political form. Thus the battle of Sellasia in 222 BC, in which Sparta was crushingly defeated by the Macedonian overlords of mainland Greece, marked far more than simply a military defeat for Sparta.[79]

4

Literacy in the Spartan Oligarchy

Introduction

The original version of this essay, like that on hoplites (Cartledge 1977), appeared first in the *JHS* and was a direct offshoot of an Appendix to my 1975 Oxford doctoral dissertation, 'Early Sparta *c.* 950-650 BC: an archaeological and historical study'. The Appendix in question focused on the 'Great Rhetra', a document in prose that was typically represented as being in some sense a law; yet according to one of the so-called 'little rhetrai' attributed to Lykourgos (as recorded in Plutarch's *Life of Lykourgos* ch. 13), the Spartans had no written laws because they had specifically outlawed them. So how was one to explain this exception, if indeed it was an exception? That raised the whole issue of the uses of writing in Sparta, both public and private, and especially for political purposes. Since the original article was published, an entire – short – monograph on Spartan literacy has appeared (Boring 1979; see my review in *CR* 30 [1980] 294), and there is forthcoming a sharp article by Ellen Millender (which the author kindly shared with me) that reopens (and seeks to close) a number of the most relevant issues. Literacy as such, in ancient Greece generally, has continued to engage a number of very good scholars, though the principal concern and focus has remained, not Sparta, but the relationship between mass (?) literacy and democracy at Athens: e.g., Harris 1989; Thomas 1992; Robb 1994. Since the teaching of literacy in my view formed a part, if a subordinate one, of the Classical Spartan *agôgê*, readers are referred also to Chapter 7, below.

*

I

Somewhere in the first half of the eighth century BC the 'graphic counterpart of speech' (David Diringer's nice expression) and a fully phonetic alphabetic script were respectively reintroduced and invented in Greek lands.[1] Thus the Greeks (apart from those of Cyprus, among whom continuity of writing may be inferred) achieved the feat, unique among European peoples, of rediscovering the literacy they had lost; and that after an interval of at least four centuries. The alphabet marked an enormous technical and practical advance on the clumsy 'Linear B' syllabic script, in the sense that it made it possible 'to write easily and read unambiguously about anything which the society can talk about'.[2] However, it is important not to misconceive or exaggerate the significance of Greek alphabetism. As Harvey's exhaustive study demonstrated (1966), even in Classical Athens, where popular literacy probably attained the highest level hitherto known in the Greek world, there were still significant areas of illiteracy or at best semi-literacy.[3] Widespread literacy must not simply be deduced from the mere availability of a phonetic alphabetic script of the Greek type.[4] Further factors must be taken into account. One of these, Harvey suggested, is the political system. For although 'democracy and literacy do not necessarily go hand in hand' (1966: 590), he suggested cautiously that the high level of literacy in Athens in the fifth and fourth centuries was perhaps 'not entirely unconnected with the fact that she was a democracy' (1966: 623).

In order to test this postulated correlation, Harvey compared the case of Classical Sparta, which he saw – rightly, as I shall argue below – as constituting the opposite political pole to Athens and for whose degree of literacy there was a fair amount of both literary and epigraphical evidence. His modestly expressed conclusion was that 'the average Athenian could read and write with greater facility than the average Spartiate' (1966: 628). Harvey's main argument seems to me to be wholly cogent; but for several reasons Spartan literacy merits thorough and constant re-examination and reassessment in its own right.

First, the claim both ancient and modern (it was entertained, for example, even by so sceptical a historian as George Grote) that the Spartans were completely illiterate must be scrutinised afresh. Second, what is probably the earliest example of Spartan writing so far discovered was published only in 1975, and it raised anew the question of Sparta's role in the development and diffusion of the alphabet in the Peloponnese and elsewhere. Third, it is only against the backdrop of the Spartans' (il)literacy that their proverbial 'laconic' speech can be properly evaluated. Finally, a just appreciation of the nature and level of literacy at Sparta can arguably make a significant contribution to the debate, also modern as well as ancient, on the correct characterization of the Classical Spartan 'constitution'.

II

In 1975, two remarkable inscribed bronze artefacts were excavated at the Menelaion sanctuary near Sparta. One was a sacrificial meat-hook, dedicated by one Deinis 'to Helen wife of Menelaos'. The other was a pointed or ovoid *aryballos* of exceptional quality, whose shape – provided it is appropriate to compare the Protocorinthian series in clay – should give it a firm approximate date of 650 BC. If (as we must assume) the *aryballos* was dedicated soon after its manufacture, the incised lettering it bears constitutes the earliest known Spartan or – to employ the conventional regional nomenclature – Lakonian writing by a quarter of a century or more.[5]

We may indeed go further. It is far harder to inscribe bronze than ivory, clay or soft limestone (the materials carrying the earliest examples of the Lakonian script known hitherto).[6] Yet the letter-forms on the *aryballos* are not merely recognizably 'Lakonian' but (given the constricted surface) remarkably clear and neat too. This one inscription, in other words, seems to presuppose a *tradition* of literacy of considerable duration. It therefore renders plausible the assumption that the alphabet had reached Lakonia within a couple of generations of the generally accepted approximate date of its invention (c. 775 BC) – well in time, that is to say, for it to have been exported to Taras by Spartan colonists in c. 700.[7] The new inscription may also have political implications; at any rate it lends weight to the view that the so-called 'Great Rhetra' (Pluk. *Lyk.* 6), whatever its precise nature or significance, was given written form as early as the first half of the seventh century.[8]

How then did the Greek alphabet reach Sparta in the first place? The possibility that it was actually invented on the island of Kythera, which lies off the Malea peninsula, was canvassed by Anne Jeffery (1961: 8). For Kythera was a known meeting-place of Greeks and Phoenicians (whose role in the invention of 'letters' even the priority-conscious Greeks did not seek to deny) and a Spartan dependency by c. 545 at the latest.[9] That possibility, however, she ruled out chiefly on the ground (not entirely cogent, see Thuc. 4.53.3) that Kythera did not lie on a regular trade-route. We can now add that the island has yielded no clear archaeological evidence of connections with mainland Lakonia before the second half of the seventh century, although Xenodamos, a Kytheran poet of the first half of the century, was said to have visited Sparta.

Instead, therefore, Dr. Jeffery suggested two potential sources whence a more or less developed alphabet of the required local or regional form might have reached Sparta, namely Rhodes or Delphi. It is hard to decide between these alternatives, but on balance I prefer Delphi: negatively, because of the almost total absence of archaeological evidence for direct contact between Lakonia and Rhodes earlier than the sixth century; positively, because of the peculiarly close contact Sparta maintained officially with the Delphic Oracle, from the eighth century onwards. We do not know when the special permanent ambassadors to Delphi known as Pythioi (below, Section III) were first appointed at Sparta by the kings, but the asserted connection of the 'Great Rhetra' with Delphi and of both with Kings Theopompos and Polydoros implies for me a *terminus ante quem* of c. 675.[10] Indeed, traditionally the first Delphic oracle given to the Spartans was delivered jointly to Kings Archelaos and Charillos, and their joint reign could on one modern reconstruction have fallen between c. 775 and

760, satisfyingly adjacent to the suggested date for the invention of the alphabet itself and for the start of the oracle.[11] Archaeological confirmation of some form of official Spartan interest in Delphi before 700 may perhaps be derived from an exemplary 'Geometric' bronze horse-figurine of undoubtedly Lakonian style (and presumably Spartan manufacture) excavated in the area of the Roman agora.[12] Thus the close similarity between the Lakonian and Phokian local scripts is consistent with Dr. Jeffery's suggestion that the Pythioi brought back from Delphi examples of alphabetic writing in the shape of oracles written perhaps on strips of leather (cf. Eur. fr. 627 Nauck).

Closely parallel literary and archaeological evidence attests an early and continuing Spartan interest in Olympia (the Oracle of Zeus as well as the Games).[13] The discus inscribed with the name of Lykourgos, which Aristotle saw at Olympia and dated (in our terms) 776/3, must of course be dismissed as a 'forgery'. But the suggestion that the alphabet was transmitted to Olympia from Sparta (Jeffery 1961: 185) is, if anything, strengthened by the new aryballos inscription.[14] In any case, the debt of Messenia to Sparta for its alphabet is not controversial, although the earliest known inscriptions from Messenia itself are not earlier than the sixth century, and diaspora Messenians (whether ex-Helots or other expatriates) are not attested epigraphically before the fifth.[15]

III

So much for what might loosely be called the 'prehistory' of Spartan literacy. Hereafter, although most of the discussion will have implications for the earliest period, and I shall return in various connections to the epigraphical evidence of the sixth century, I shall be primarily concerned to discuss Spartan literacy in the fifth and fourth centuries. By 'literacy' I shall mean simply what Trollope called 'the absolute faculty of reading' (and writing) rather than 'the adequate use of a book' or any deeper sensitivity to literary creations (although the transmission of seventh-century Spartan poetry to writers of the fifth and fourth centuries will not be excluded from consideration). Since this essay will deal exclusively with the literacy of Spartans of citizen status, and not with that of the other free inhabitants of Lakonia, evidence will be drawn solely from literary texts pertaining to Spartans and (with a few justifiable exceptions) from inscriptions found on territory directly held by the Spartan State. In this Section I shall attempt to answer the straightforward question: were the Spartans, or any Spartans, literate in the basic sense outlined above?

First, the literary sources. According to the anonymous patchwork 'Dissoi Logoi' (90 F 2.10 D-K) of *c.* 400 BC, 'Sokrates' in Plato's *Protagoras* (342a ff.), and Isokrates in his own, embittered voice (*Panath.* 209; cf. 251), all Spartans were illiterate. The author of the Platonic *Hippias Major* (285c) adds that many were also innumerate. If, moreover, a man brought onto the stage by the fourth-century comic poet Philyllios (fr. 11 Kock) was both an illiterate (which is not certain) and a Spartan (which is merely a guess), this may be further evidence at least of Athenian beliefs about Spartan (il)literacy. We should not, I suggest, take these passages *au pied de la lettre*. The *Protagoras* passage is a joke, as to some extent is the one from the *Hippias Major*. Isokrates was a rhetorician and, moreover, an Athenian cultural chauvinist.[16] The 'Dissoi Logoi', finally, spoils its intended effect by including an – easily refutable – Spartan hostility to music. What such sources are doing, in short, is producing yet another variation on the well-worn theme that, in comparison to the cultivated Athenians of the Periklean Funeral Speech (esp. Thuc. 2.40), the Spartans were unlettered philistines (cf. Plut. *Lyk.* 20.8; *Mor.* 192b, 217d, 226d, 231d, 239b).

This was of course a charge which the most rabid Athenian 'Lakonizer' of the late fifth or fourth centuries would have been hard put to it to deny, even in the unlikely event of his wishing to do so. There was no market in Sparta, as there was in Athens, for the works of such as Anaxagoras – or for any other *bibloi gegrammenai*.[17] We should not, however, misread the significance of this contrast by projecting it back into the seventh and sixth centuries, when there was no 'market' in 'books' anywhere in the Greek world, and when Sparta was a leading patron of creative literature. Besides Tyrtaios and Alkman, Spartans listened to a succession of foreign poets from Terpander of Lesbos in the early seventh century to Simonides of Keos in the early fifth, who found Sparta a congenial – and no doubt lucrative – field for the display of their talents. Whether or not this justifies the description of Archaic Sparta as in any sense 'remarkably literate' (Davison 1968) I am unclear; but it does at least raise the question of how Tyrtaios and Alkman (to ignore the practically unknown Kinaithon, Spendon and Gitiadas) acquired their familiarity with the leading literary *Kunstsprachen* of their day, and how their work was transmitted to Classical Athens. In other words, did Tyrtaios and Alkman practise their craft (if only in part) through the medium of the written text?

It should be emphasized at once that, even after the inauguration of a 'market' in 'books', most Greeks typically recited from memory or heard, rather than read, their literature – hence *ana-gignôskô* ('I recognize again' = I read) and *akroatai* ('hearers' = readers); also that the process whereby ancient Greek literature was disseminated or handed down in written form was always more akin to *samizdat* ('self-produced' in Russian) than to publication in the post-printing sense. Thus poems of Tyrtaios were sung by the Spartans on campaign (Lycurgus, *Leokr.* 107; Philochoros, *FGrHist.* 328 F 216), while those of Alkman received an annual airing at the Gymnopaidiai festival (Sosibios, *FGrHist.* 595 F 5).

By the fifth century, however, Alkman was known to the Athenian comic dramatist Eupolis (fr.139 Kock) and perhaps also Aristophanes, and in the fourth Tyrtaios could be quoted *in extenso* by the Athenian politician

Lycurgus. Hence, since 'any book that was well known at Athens in the fourth century is likely to have been known at Alexandria in the third' (West 1974: 57), it is not surprising that our earliest book-text of Tyrtaios should belong to the third century or that Alkman should have excited the scholarly curiosity of no less a critic than Aristarchos. For the seventh century, however, we are reduced to inference. Given the close verbal dependence of Tyrtaios on the *Iliad* and of Alkman on the *Odyssey* (or at least *an Odyssey*), it is quite possible – though by no means inevitable – that they had access to a text of the poems, as is implied by the story that 'Lykourgos' had Homer copied (Plut. *Lyk.* 4.4). Again, although we have no specific evidence that Alkman caused written versions of his own poems to be produced, it is at least conceivable that those most interested in their verbally faithful preservation (one or both of the Spartan royal families, for example) would have had them committed to papyrus.[18]

Nevertheless, despite this evidence for literary creativity (and perhaps literate poets) in Archaic Sparta, it must be admitted that the character of Spartan public education does nothing automatically to rule out the imputation of illiteracy to the Spartans of the Classical period. For the *agôgê* was, at best, 'educational' only in an extended sense and is more fruitfully regarded as a comprehensive means of socialisation.[19] Thus in the developed system of the fifth and fourth centuries the more orthodox musical and gymnastic exercises were combined with social institutions like age-classes and common meals and with *rites de passage* to produce tough, self-disciplined and unquestioningly obedient military men. Furthermore, Spartan supremacy abroad, which depended on repression of the Helots (and to a lesser extent the Perioikoi) at home, was not either won or significantly maintained by skills and techniques involving a developed level of popular literacy.

However, despite the contrary evidence of the 'Dissoi Logoi', Plato and Isokrates, and despite the character of Spartan education and society, the selection of the literary and epigraphical evidence set out below is sufficient to refute at any rate the charge of total illiteracy, even in the case of the humblest Spartan ranker.

1. Kings[20]

We are bound to infer from Plutarch (*Ages.* 1.4) that the heir-apparent was normally released from the universal obligation to go through the *agôgê*. This inference is apparently contradicted by Teles (fr. 3 Hense), but he is not a particularly trustworthy witness and anyway may mean only that a king's sons other than the heir-apparent were not so exempted. However, since the teaching of literacy could hardly have been an integral part of the *agôgê*, we need not in any case infer from this exemption that the kings were typically illiterate.

It is of course true that the stories and anecdotes which involve kings

4. Literacy in the Spartan Oligarchy

either sending letters (e.g. Hdt. 6.50.3; Thuc. 1.128ff.; 132.5; 133.1; Xen. *Ages.* 1.14; Plut. *Mor.* 211b, 212e, 219a, 222a-b, 225c-d) or receiving letters (Plut. *Lys.* 28.2; Athen. 7.289e) could all be interpreted in terms of dictation to or recitation by a literate person, as indeed could the political tract composed by the exiled Pausanias (*FGrHist.* 582); and we do once hear of a king (Agesilaos) being accompanied on campaign by a personal private secretary (*grapheus*: Xen. *Hell.* 4.1.39; Plut. *Ages.* 13.2).[21] On the other hand, there are three anecdotes in which literacy is attributed to a Spartan king explicitly.

In the first (Hdt. 7.239) the exiled Damaratos for reasons of secrecy and diplomacy scraped the wax off a wood-backed tablet, wrote his message to the Spartans on the wood and then re-covered the tablet with blank wax.[22] Aineias 'Tacticus' (31.14), a fan of such cryptography, would have approved of the stratagem, but the Spartans who received the tablet were baffled until Gorgo, daughter of Kleomenes I and wife of Leonidas, advised them to scrape off the wax.[23] The whole passage has in fact been suspected (probably unjustly) of being an interpolation in Herodotus, but at least its author did not find anything unusual or extraordinary about the literacy of Damaratos. It is only unfortunate that he was not more explicit about the identity of 'the Spartans' (Ephors and Gerousia?) who eventually read Damaratos' message. The two other anecdotes (Plut. *Mor.* 214e-f: writing; Ephoros *FGrHist.* 70 F 207: reading) both concern Agesilaos, who, incidentally, did participate in the *agôgê*.

Those are the only explicit pieces of evidence, but the use of the *skutalê*, whatever its exact nature, seems to demand that any king (or other commander) could write and read, unaided, at least simple messages, which would naturally be expressed as laconically as possible.[24] Finally, it seems legitimate to infer from the fact that the kings had custody of Delphic oracles (Hdt. 6.57.4) that they could read (cf. Hdt. 5.90f.; and perhaps Plut. *Lys.* 26.2).

Monarchy, even in a literate society, does not of course necessarily require or imply literacy on the part of the monarch. But the Lakonian alphabet was infinitely simpler to master than, say, the script which the Assyrian king Ashurbanipal triumphantly claimed to have learned. In any case, Ashurbanipal could rely on an elaborate scribal bureaucracy, somewhat as the mediaeval English kings could employ a literate clerical élite. Neither of these props was available to a Spartan king – although there was perhaps someone in Sparta competent to decipher *Assuria grammata* (Thuc. 4.50), i.e. Aramaic script.[25] On the whole it seems reasonable to conclude that Spartan kings could both read and write.

2. Other commanders and military officials

In some respects (dispatches, letters, *skutalê*) the remarks on the literacy of the kings apply here too. Indeed, the Spartan *epistoleus* (Vice-Admiral) may have acquired his title from his function as *epistoliaphoros* (Xen. *Hell.* 6.2.25). The bulk of the explicit evidence, however, concerns the *roi manqué* Lysander (Xen. *Hell.* 1.1.23; Plut. *Lys.* 14.6, with *Mor.* 229b, 229f [14]; *Lys.* 16.2, 19.8-12, 20.1-4, 28.3, 30.4); but note also, for example, Thuc. 8.33.3. Finally, mention should be made of the 'booty-sellers' (*laphuropôlai*: Xen. *Ages.* 1.18), who must somehow have recorded the booty they received and sold, and of which they donated a tithe to divine protectors.

3. Ephors

The five members of the annual board of Ephors were also presumably literate.[26] For apart from exercising a general supervision of the laws of Sparta, which were not written down (Section V),[27] and a particular watching brief over the conduct of royalty, they played a key role in foreign affairs, which involved the sending and receiving of dispatches and the drafting of treaties (Section V). At least by the fourth century, the Ephors were elected 'from all the *damos*' (Arist. *Pol.* 2.1265b39-40, 1270b25-8 [the selection-procedure is here stigmatised as 'extremely childish'], 1272a31-2). But unfortunately this is not quite the convincing proof we are seeking that all Spartans were functionally literate: for although numbers of eligible citizens in Aristotle's day were so low that most Spartans probably had to serve as Ephors, presumably only those who were fully qualified in all respects would have put themselves forward for election in the first place.

4. Gerousia[28]

It is doubtful whether the *gerontes*, who counted in their number the two kings *ex officio*, had to produce either their *probouleumata* or their legal judgements in writing. But since they co-operated closely with the Ephors, for example when sitting as the Spartan 'Supreme Court' to try kings, they were probably as literate as they. A fourth-century BC inscription from the oracular shrine of Ino-Pasiphaë at Perioikic Thalamai records a dedication by a member of the Spartan Gerousia (*IG* 5 1.1317); this may be thought to support that assumption.

5. Envoys

In the fifth and fourth centuries diplomacy was a relatively underdeveloped aspect of Greek statecraft.[29] Sparta, however, took more trouble than most Greek states to get its diplomacy right.[30] Since war is one expression of failed diplomacy, part of the explanation of the Spartans' diplomatic finesse is, somewhat paradoxically, their general unwillingness after the sixth century to become involved in a fight. It would be surprising if

Spartan envoys were not required to be literate (and possibly multi-lingual).[31]

As an extension of their interstate diplomacy Sparta devised a special kind of envoy, the four Pythioi, whose possible role in the introduction of the alphabet to Lakonia in the eighth century and the preservation of a text of the 'Great Rhetra' we have already noticed (Section II). The Pythioi were permanent delegates to the Oracle at Delphi, two being selected on a hereditary basis by each of the kings (Hdt. 6.57.2,4; Xen. *Lak. Pol.* 15.5; Cic. *De div.* 1.43.95; Suda *s.v.*).[32] They may also have played a wider role in Sparta. The Greeks in general did not acquire the habit of keeping documentary records until fairly late, as we shall see. But if there was ever anything like a Spartan Public Record Office, the Pythioi are possible candidates for the role of archivists. The records, however, are unlikely to have consisted of much more than Delphic (and other?) oracles, royal pedigrees, and lists of kings, Ephors and perhaps the victors at the Karneia and other festivals.[33]

6. Hupomeiones and hippeis[34]

Xenophon's account (*Hell.* 3.3.4-11) of the abortive conspiracy organized by Kinadon in *c.* 400 is remarkable in several ways, but it has not in the past been treated from the standpoint of literacy.[35] Kinadon himself, who is expressly said to have been able both to read and to write, is especially interesting as belonging to the cadre of *hupomeiones* ('Inferiors') not that of the *homoioi* ('Peers', i.e. full citizens). Thus if the 'Inferiors' were lapsed 'Peers', this might strongly suggest that the average full Spartan citizen was functionally literate, unless of course Kinadon had been specially selected and trained for his role as secret agent.

In the same Xenophontic story the eldest of the *hippagretai* (the three who chose the other 297 *hippeis*) and the 'younger men' (presumably *hippeis*) detailed to arrest Kinadon are also said to be literate. An inscribed relief in honour of a Thiokles was erected by the *hippeis* (here called *koroi*) at Sparta in the sixth century.[36]

7. Ordinary Spartans

There is a story in Justin following Trogus (*Hist. Phil.* 3.5.10-11) that during the Messenian War of the seventh century the Spartan soldiers wrote their names and patronymics on wooden plaques (*tesserae*) which they then tied to their arms. This tale cannot be disproved, at least not on purely chronological grounds, but it can never be positively verified either. Nor can we say who was responsible for drawing up the presumably written wills referred to by Aristotle (*Pol.* 2.1270a28) or the certainly written mortgage-deeds (*klaria*) mentioned in a third-century context by

Plutarch (*Agis* 13.3). In the second century BC, however, a Spartan turns up unexpectedly on a papyrus as party to a written contract.[37]

8. Women

It is well known that Spartan girls received an education equal to, though separate from, that accorded their male counterparts. Much of this was allegedly designed to produce robust mothers of sturdy male offspring, though no doubt it served also to socialize the politically disenfranchised half of the citizen population. Plato in the *Laws* (806a) speaks also of a 'compulsory education in the arts' and earlier, in the *Protagoras* (342d), had made Sokrates refer to Spartan women who were 'proud of their intellectual culture'. Plato is admittedly a tendentious witness, but Aristophanes (*Lys.* 1237) apparently mentions a female Spartan poet, Kleitagora, and Iamblichus (*Vita Pyth.* 267) lists several female Spartan Pythagoreans. We need not take as literally authentic the anecdotes in which Spartan mothers write to their warrior sons (Plut. *Mor.* 241a, d, d-e).[38]

So much for the literary evidence. Turning to the epigraphical, we find that this is not as helpful as we might have hoped, for two main reasons. First, all known private Spartan inscriptions have accrued from formal, religious contexts. The vast majority of them consists of ex-voto dedications, mainly of the type of those offered to Helen with which we began (Section II), but including also a significant quantity of victory-dedications. To these can be added a handful of inscribed gravestones and funerary reliefs.[39] Writing on perishable materials like leather, papyrus and wax has naturally not survived the Lakonian climate and soil-conditions.[40] But it is disappointing to have nothing comparable to, for example, the informal note scratched on a potsherd in sixth-century Athens, in which the author (probably a Megarian) instructs someone to 'put the saw under the threshold of the garden gate'.[41] Excavation in a settlement-area of Classical Sparta might conceivably transform our picture of Spartan literacy. To the fifth-century Athenian ostraka, however, which have figured prominently in the arguments for widespread Athenian popular literacy, there could of course be no Spartan counterpart, since the Spartans did not allow a popular say in the exiling of prominent figures.

Second, even if we adopt the useful distinction between 'formal' inscriptions executed by professionals (whether incised on stone and bronze or painted on pottery before firing) and 'informal' cursive inscriptions, we can never be sure whether the professional in any particular instance was a Spartan citizen. The point of difficulty here is the widespread belief, amounting to a dogma, that no full Spartan citizen ever practised a manual *technê*.[42] But the scholarly tendency to regard Spartan society as unique in all particulars at all periods (a legacy from antiquity) rather than as a whole in specific periods should be firmly resisted.[43] If I were to hazard a guess at a possible division of labour, I would tentatively assign at least the public (and possibly all) formal inscriptions on stone (cf. Section V) to the hands of Perioikoi, who may have organized their profession on a hereditary basis.[44]

What then are we to make of the informal cursive graffiti? Those certainly produced by craftsmen – the doodles on scrap pieces of soft limestone from the Ortheia sanctuary, the 'ossified' abecedarium on the neck of the Vix *krater* (if the alphabet is indeed Lakonian), and the masons' signatures at Amyklai[45] – involve the ambiguity just discussed. But the graffito dedications incised on fired pottery, of which there is a fair number (though fewer than those painted on before firing), could well be the work of Spartan citizens.[46] At least, the frequency of error is perhaps sufficient to exclude the possibility that they were all the work of professionals, although it may be that orthography, let alone calligraphy, was not highly esteemed in Sparta.[47] Even if, strictly speaking, such graffito inscriptions imply no more than that Spartans could read, I am prepared to take them as evidence that they could write too.[48] A remarkable graffito of *c.* 500 on a sherd from the Spartan akropolis, whose author was presumably an illiterate trying to keep up with the literate Joneses, seems to support this inference.[49]

That is pretty well the sum of evidence from literature and private epigraphy for Classical Spartan literacy, considerably eked out by inference.[50] Though rather paltry, it is still adequate to refute the imputations of total illiteracy cited at the beginning of this section. There is no reason therefore not to credit the unequivocal statement of Plutarch (*Lyk.* 16.10; *Mor.* 237a) that the Spartans – like the Cretans (Arist. fr. 611.15 Rose) – were taught as much reading and writing as was needful (cf. generally Thuc. 1.84.3-4).[51] To make sense of the evidence set out above, we need only to suppose that for most Spartans the needs were ordinarily neither many nor pressing and that public functionaries alone were called upon to perform routine acts of literacy on a day-to-day basis. The Spartans, that is to say, dwelt primarily in a world of oral discourse.

IV

This was a world in which they were well fitted to survive. For the reverse side of limited Spartan literacy is the premium placed by that society on the ability to converse in a succinct and stimulating manner, employing the *aphelês brakhulogia* (Sextus Emp. *Adv. Math.* 2.21) immortalized in the Spartans' honour as 'laconic'.[52] This was not necessarily a sign that they had nothing worthwhile to say,[53] but rather expressed a refusal to privilege rhetorical form over content. The story that the Scythian Anacharsis had found the conversation of only the Spartans to be 'sensible' was firmly rejected by Herodotus (4.77), but the fiction bespeaks a real difference of conversational style between the Spartans and the rest of the Greeks. Well was the mid-sixth century Spartan Chilon, Ephor and reputed author of memorably gnomic utterances, accounted one of the 'Seven Sages' of ancient Greece.

However, our specific information about the conversational topics covered in high and low Spartan society suggests a level well below that of these lofty dicta. In an intentionally humorous passage in a Platonic dialogue (*Hipp. Ma.* 285d) we are told that the (presumably ordinary) Spartans listened 'most readily to tales about the generations of heroes and men, the ancient foundations of cities, and in general to *arkhaiologia*', which may be translated as 'the whole range of stories about the distant past'.[54] As for the Spartan aristocracy, represented here by its most blue-blooded members, the doubtless well-informed Xenophon (*Hell.* 5.3.20) relates that 'Agesipolis was well suited to share with Agesilaos in conversation about youthful exploits, hunting, riding, and homosexual love-affairs (*paidika*)'. This tallies well with Plutarch's list (*Lyk.* 24.5) of favourite Spartan 'out-of-hours' activities: dancing, feasting, festivals, athletic exercise and ... conversation.[55]

V

Thus we come to the last of the particular problems we set out to tackle: does an understanding of the nature of literacy at Sparta help us to characterize correctly the Spartan *politeia* or 'constitution'? The study of the Spartan polity has been described as a form of 'intellectual gymnastics';[56] but an outsider might be pardoned for using a less friendly metaphor after contemplating the voluminous modern literature on Sparta's 'constitutional antiquities', much of it scarcely more than free invention, the remainder at best intelligent speculation sometimes distorted by ancient theory.[57] It could hardly have been otherwise, however; two partly overlapping and mutually reinforcing aspects of the 'Spartan mirage'[58] saw to that.

The first in point of time and significance was the 'Lykourgos-legend', which treated Sparta as the paradigm of a state that owed all its economic, social and political institutions to the enactments of a single lawgiver.[59] The ancient controversies over the historicity of Lykourgos still stir some modern imaginations; but Lykourgos the man is in the present context a side-issue.[60] Nor is this the place to enter the minefield of 'Great Rhetra' *Forschung*. Suffice it to say here (see further Chapter 3) that this document for me represents the essence of the complex political solution wrongly attributed *en bloc* to 'Lykourgos' and that it should be dated somewhere in the first half of the seventh century.

The second distorting aspect of the 'mirage' was the theory of the 'mixed constitution' (*miktê politeia*), developed perhaps in the fifth century but not apparently applied to Sparta until the fourth.[61] This theory held that the best (because the most stable) form of political system was either one which combined in a harmonious whole ingredients from each of the three basic 'constitutions' (monarchy, aristocracy/oligarchy, democracy)[62] or one in which the different elements acted as checks and balances to each other. The 'mixed constitution' theory overlaps and reinforces the 'Lykourgos-legend' most insistently in its stress on the supposed absence of *stasis* in Sparta after Lykourgos' reforms.

Happily for us, however, not all the ancient sources were equally persuaded of the truth of every aspect of the 'mirage', and, since Sparta did in fact experience severe *stasis*, the ancient explanation of its supposed absence in terms of the 'mixed' nature of its *politeia* is hardly cogent. Today, indeed, it is usually denied that such an entity as a 'mixed constitution' is practically possible, but there have been isolated modern defences of the ancient view.[63] Thus, to take a representative modern statement, A.W. Gomme described Sparta's political system as 'of a normal aristocratic type' apart from 'the anomaly of the two kings'.[64] It is unclear whether Gomme thought the anomaly consisted in their being *two* Spartan kings or in the survival of the kingship itself, but he obviously considered his description to be uncontroversial. Two decades later, however, A. Andrewes re-opened the whole question of the nature of the 'government' of classical Sparta in a powerfully succinct article. After giving what I would regard as a very acceptable picture of the Spartan political system ('an oligarchy notorious for its discipline and respect for age and authority') he concluded from the relative prominence of the Ephors and Assembly and the correspondingly low profile of the Gerousia in the period on which we are best informed (roughly the lifetime of Xenophon) that Sparta had 'in some ways a more open constitution than most oligarchies' (1966: 1).[65]

This conclusion has not passed unchallenged.[66] To the arguments against it that fall within Andrewes' own immediate frame of reference can be added those arising from the study of literacy at Sparta. To summarize the former: whatever view we take of the political competence of the *damos* under the terms of the 'Great Rhetra', it is extremely doubtful whether there was ever much debate in the Spartan Assembly. At any rate, *ho boulomenos* was almost certainly not permitted (even if he had the courage and motivation) to speak as and when he pleased. On the one occasion on which we know the Spartans held 'frequent assemblies' (Hdt. 7. 134.2: *haliês pollakis sullegomenês*) the question at issue was 'Does any Spartan wish to die for the fatherland?' The distance in atmosphere and conception between this and, for example, the Mytilene debate at Athens in 427 is absolutely unbridgeable. Voting in the Spartan Assembly was conducted according to an archaic procedure, 'by shouting and [as Thucydides was careful to add] not by ballot' (Thuc. 1.87). In other words, the Spartans did not recognize the principle of 'one man, one vote', according to which everyone counts for one and no one for more than one. Moreover, as already noted, the methods of electing Ephors and Gerontes were dismissed by

Aristotle as 'childish', presumably because they were so easily manipulated. Once elected, the members of the Gerousia were non-responsible (Arist. *Pol.* 1271a5-6), even though they together with the Ephors constituted the Spartan 'Supreme Court'. It cannot be stressed too much that there was no popular judiciary in Sparta.[67]

Add to those the arguments against 'openness' drawn from a consideration of Spartan literacy. First, there were no written rules governing the conduct of lawsuits heard before the Ephors (Arist. *Pol.* 1270b28-31). Second, and yet more importantly, legislation was not a typical feature of the ordinary Spartan's political experience,[68] and even such laws as were passed were not committed to writing (hence perhaps their 'laconic' expression: Plato *Laws* 721e). Indeed, according to a doubtless apocryphal and inevitably 'Lykourgan' *rhetra* (Plut. *Lyk.* 13.1 ff.; cf. *Mor.* 227b), it was forbidden to inscribe laws in Sparta, on the unimpeachably correct psychological ground that *paideia* (training, indoctrination) was a better teacher of obedience and discipline than external legal compulsion.[69] The same leitmotif lies behind the explanation attributed apophthegmatically to Zeuxidamos son of Latychidas II (Plut. *Mor.* 221b) for the fact that Spartan laws on bravery were unwritten. The one possible exception to or contravention of this prohibition, interpreted as a sixth- or fifth-century sacred law regulating the cult of Demeter, is of highly dubious status and value.[70] Indeed, the general prohibition of named tombstones at Sparta (Plut. *Lyk.* 27.3), at least after *c.* 500, might be taken to imply that in some areas of Spartan experience the written word was endowed with a quasi-magical potency.[71]

However that may be, a cursory survey of Spartan epigraphical evidence reveals at once a dearth of official State documents of any kind. It was known from literary sources that treaties were drafted at Sparta and publicly displayed there – or rather in the chief sanctuary of Sparta's fifth constituent village, the Apollonion at Amyklai.[72] But only one actual example on stone is known to have survived from Sparta, a fifth-century treaty of *summakhia* (offensive and defensive alliance) with the otherwise unattested Aitolian Erxadieis.[73] Since the latter were presumably not admitted to membership of what we call the 'Peloponnesian League', it is uncertain what relation the terms of this treaty bear to those of what was probably the earliest building-block of that alliance, namely the Spartans' treaty with Tegea of *c.* 550.[74] The only other extant State document known from Classical (as opposed to Hellenistic) Sparta lists contributions by various individuals and states to a war-fund.[75]

Apart from those two from Sparta itself, public inscriptions in the Lakonian script comprise only the following half-dozen: four from Olympia (a dedication of a bronze *lebês* by *toi Spartiatai*; two marble seats occupied by Spartan *proxenoi* of Elis in the sixth century; and the base of an offering to Zeus by the Spartans, probably *c.* 490/80);[76] one from Athens (polyandrion of the Spartans buried in or near the Kerameikos in 403);[77] and one

52

from Delos (stele recording a decree of protection granted to the Delians by Sparta between 403 and 399).[78]

For the sake of completeness we could perhaps add to the tally of known public inscriptions two victor-lists from Sparta, the (non-extant) stele inscribed with the name of those who fell at Thermopylai in 480 (Paus. 3.14.1; cf. Hdt. 7.224.1), the boastful epigram which Pausanias the Regent had inscribed at Delphi (perhaps on the limestone base of the Serpent Column), the (non-extant) inscribed stelai marking the site of the official reburial of the same Pausanias (Thuc. 1.134.4; Paus. 3.14.1), and five manumission-stelai from Tainaron (*IG* 5, 1.1223-32).[79] This is a poor harvest indeed, and the fact that six of them (the dedications and the funerary inscriptions) do not differ in kind from private inscriptions serves to underline the absence of documents with political implications of the sort that a law or other public ordinance would have carried.

Thus far then the contrast between Spartan and democratic Athenian practice in respect of public documentation is stark. We should not, however, magnify or otherwise distort its significance. In the first place, Athens, possibly following the example of those inveterate publishers of lawcodes, the Cretans, had published laws more than a century before the democracy was established in 508/7, the initial impetus perhaps being the growth of the coercive power of the *polis* at the expense of, and in open opposition to, the self-help justice of feuding aristocratic families.[80] Secondly, although no ancient state, democratic or otherwise, could rival democratic Athens in the publication of documents affecting the common weal, even Athens did not set up a central archive until the last decade of the fifth century (in what later became the Metroön).[81] Finally, on present evidence it is hard to draw a sharp distinction in regard to public documentation between Sparta and, say, Corinth.[82]

These are necessary qualifications. We need not, however, be so minimalist as to deny that the publication of documents by the Athenian democracy meant anything more than a claim to 'open' (rather than closed, aristocratic) government.[83] For at Athens the connection between the publication of potential documents in permanent form and the development of democratic institutions and practice is apparent, not only chronologically but also from, for example, ideological statements emphasizing the radically different underpinnings of written and unwritten lawcodes in terms of social class and political power (esp. Eur. *Supp.* 433-7; cf. Gorgias fr. 11a, 30 D-K; Diod. 12.13.1). Especially noteworthy is the insertion in published documents of a clause to the effect that *ho boulomenos* may read them.[84]

Written definition of rights and duties will not of course automatically secure their effective exercise for all alike, whether rich or poor, strong or weak. But there seems equally to be something approaching a general rule that, to paraphrase Euripides, written definition marks an indispensable step on the road towards achieving this objective. Indeed, Spartans were reportedly not permitted so much as to criticize the laws – unless that is just another democratic Athenian slur.

To conclude, the alleged 'openness' of the Spartan 'constitution' is merely apparent and stems from the peculiarly Spartan feature that the Assembly was the army of adult male hoplite warriors in civilian dress. It naturally therefore had to rubber-stamp, in an open demonstration of solidarity and token sovereignty, decisions which in practice had already been taken elsewhere.

VI

If we return finally to the broader question with which we began, the role of literacy in social organization, we must at least conclude that the Spartan evidence does not support the technological determinism implicit in the simple deduction by Goody and Watt of widespread popular literacy from the mere availability of a version of the Greek alphabet. The simplicity of the alphabet did indeed make it possible for the ordinary Spartan man (and probably woman) to acquire a rudimentary knowledge of reading and writing. Yet at the same time literacy in Sparta remained very thinly spread, and deep literacy was the preserve of an élite operating at the highest levels of state.

To say that Sparta made it 'son point d'honneur à rester une ville de semi-illettrés' (Marrou 1971: 45) is perhaps an overstatement. Rather, the nature of the development of Spartan society from the eighth century BC onwards, above all its broadly oligarchic political system and the fraught relationship of the citizen-body to the Helots, did not either necessitate or even encourage the development of those social arts the successful performance of which is dependent on a high level of popular literacy.

5

Spartan Kingship: Doubly Odd?

Introduction

This essay is published here for the first time. The original oral version was delivered on United Nations Day (24 October) 1995 at an Oxford seminar 'Empire Ancient to Modern: the Rulers' convened within the Faculty of Modern History. I have tried to retain some of the original talk's oral quality, and, with a view to keeping it accessible to a non-specialist audience, I have not supplied full references to ancient texts.

Kingship, or rather monarchy, has been very much on the collective English – or British – mind in recent years; so I began my talk by mentioning the then recent advent of Prince Charles's elder son to Eton, which had cast the spotlight once again on the education of a future English (or British) king, and by extension on the station in life for which he was being educated. That in turn raised the question of the nature of our constitution, and indeed of the United Kingdom, not to mention our position in the wider world, with special immediate reference to our position within the EU. Vernon Bogdanor's *The Monarchy and the Constitution* appeared in the month following my talk, but was hardly able to quell all discussion or silence all dissent. Tom Nairn, for example, author of a lively account of Britain and its monarchy twenty years ago, *The Enchanted Glass*, has more recently and rather pointedly looked forward to *After Britain* (1999).

In what follows my aim, like that of Carlier 1984, is to approach the Spartan kingship comparatively, trying to assess and evaluate its distinctiveness or possibly uniqueness within a wider, especially but not solely ancient Greek, framework. The most recent discussion of the Spartan kingship known to me is Miller 1998, who focuses fixedly on its dual nature. My account allows also for individual initiative.

*

I. Constituting the subject

Pretty much the same questions, *mutatis mutandis*, could be and have been asked of Sparta's 'constitution', in so far as that word applies (below), as are currently being asked of the United Kingdom's. Was it either (i) a kingship/kingdom (*basileia*, as Herodotus 7.209.4 and Xenophon *Ages*. 1.1 each once called it) in some more than purely titular sense, or (ii) a disguised collective dictatorship (that was the view of those ancients and moderns who have stressed the role of the Ephorate), or (iii) an 'aristocratic constitution of normal type – except for the anomaly of the two kings' (Gomme 1945: 129; cf. Ste. Croix 1972: 125ff., following possibly Aristotle), or (iv) an oligarchy but a distinctively open, quasi-democratic one (Andrewes 1966; Carlier 1977; 1984: 240-324), or even (v) a democracy, in some ancient Greek sense, if not of course of the same, radical kind as that of Athens; or was it, finally, (vi) a mixed constitution (as sources known to Aristotle characterized it) – if such a thing has ever really existed, or could exist (cf. Nippel 1980)?

Rather than evaluating each of these possible general classifications (all susceptible of further sub-classification and nuancing), I shall be taking a more positive, concrete approach, by focusing on the careers of two kings in particular, separated in time by a century and representing respectively the two royal houses: Kleomenes I (*c*. 520-490), the Agiads; and Agesilaos II (*c*. 400-360), the Eurypontids. To set those two admittedly exceptional careers in their immediate political and cultural context, I shall conduct my investigation under three main headings: constitutional position and power (Section II), military command (Section III), and charisma (Section IV).

But I must preface my discussion, as I would any discussion of any aspect of ancient Spartan history, with an account of the nature of our evidence. The history of ancient Sparta as a sovereign and independent Greek city may be said to have begun *c*. 700 and ended in *c*. 145 BC. Within that span of five and a half centuries, we have not a single Spartan historian, and precious few certainly authentic Spartan official written documents. The evidence of archaeology, though authentic and contemporary, is also mute and difficult to interpret politically. Thus the vast majority of our written historical evidence is non-Spartan, most of it fifth-century or later, and almost all of it subject to the systematic distortion of the 'Spartan mirage' (Ollier 1933-43; Finley 1962a; Rawson 1969; cf. Chapter 12).

Spartan history, that is, what actually happened or how it actually was in ancient Sparta, does not come to us straight (in so far as any historical information does) but is mediated to us through the reflections, variously distorted, of interested outsiders: mainly of philosophers who approved Sparta's educational regime and social arrangements, and of politicians who approved what they took Sparta's 'constitution' to be, and the policies that Sparta pursued either towards its subject populations at home or towards other Greeks and non-Greeks abroad. This multiple partiality of the evidence – both incomplete and biased – must render any positive reconstruction of how, let alone why, it actually was in ancient Sparta extremely tentative and delicate.

II. Constitutional position and power

It is a moot point whether any ancient Greek *polis* or 'citizen-state' can be said to have had a constitution, as opposed to laws (varying in precision and consistency) regulating the conduct of officials. True, they had a word, *politeia*, which we do regularly translate 'constitution', but *politeia*, besides also meaning 'citizenship', could be referred to as the 'life' and 'soul' of an ancient Greek city – hardly what we today, at any rate, would understand by 'constitution' (significantly, a word we take from the Romans, not the Greeks). In short, we are probably better advised to talk in terms, not of constitution, nor even 'government' (in the sense of 'the British government'), but 'governance'.[1]

How then are we to classify Sparta within any conventional ancient Greek scheme? The Greeks, or some Greeks, invented politics, or the political, in a strong sense, and that invention was a precondition for their further invention of political theory.[2] Thus some Greek or Greeks at some time before about 430 BC (see Hdt. 3.80-2) made the brilliantly economical discovery that all particular instances or species of governance could be subsumed under one of just three genera: rule by one, rule by some, or rule by all. Logically that tripartite classification is exhaustive; heuristically, it is enormously fruitful, since it does help wonderfully to concentrate the mind. So, in those terms, is Sparta's governance to be classified as rule by one (some form of monarchy), by some (some form of aristocracy or oligarchy), or by all (some form of democracy)? The fact that, as we have seen, different Greeks at different times classified Sparta under all three genera, and were even driven to the desperate expedient of inventing a fourth classificatory term, the 'mixed constitution', in order to find a suitable slot for Sparta, indicates how difficult they found Sparta to classify (cf. Oliva 1998).

That difficulty, as I have suggested elsewhere (see Chapter 3), arose largely because the tripartite classificatory scheme was invented and found applicable for Greek citizen-states as they had developed, evolved or mutated by the fifth century, and were continuing so to develop, evolve or mutate. Sparta's 'constitution', by contrast, had emerged (to put it neutrally) well before the fifth century and then frozen almost solid, so that fifth-century categories could not be simply and straightforwardly applied. To borrow the terminology of a German school of ancient history inspired by Christian Meier (cf. Meier 1990), fifth-century 'kratistische' language (demo-cracy, olig-archy) did not fit the actual, 'nomistische' political arrangements of Sparta – a city in which political rule or sovereign power (*kratos*) was subject to customary, rather than legalistic, interpretation, to *nomos* in the sense of custom, tradition and authority rather than *nomos* in the sense of positive law.[3]

So much for the problem of classification in general, that is, of *any* classification of Spartan governance. In specific detail, the two main sources of difficulty were and are, on the one hand, the Ephors (esp. Richer 1999), and on the other hand, the two kings, and, not least, the relations between these two offices and their holders (Richer 1999: ch. 23). The difficulties may be looked at in two different ways: first, structurally and formally; then, functionally and pragmatically. What were, first, the respective 'powers' of the two 'offices' (*arkhai*)? Second, how were these powers cashed out in terms of practical political exchange? I shall concentrate here on the kings.

The first point to settle, or at least clarify, is whether the two Spartan *basileis* 'really' were 'kings', as opposed to merely called by a word that can mean 'kings'?[4] Strictly, of course, they were not monarchs, but at most dyarchs, since Sparta had had, allegedly from time immemorial, two kings, not one, who were drawn hereditarily from two distinct and not quite equal (Hdt. 6.51) aristocratic families, each claiming descent ultimately from the 'demi-god son of Zeus' (Thuc. 5.16), that is, Herakles, a born hero who became a god. But if they were not monarchs, were they nevertheless royal? In terms of their ancestry, exhibited and buttressed by official pedigrees which also did service up to a point as king-lists, they certainly were.[5] If one were, for example, to compare and contrast them with the Greek tyrants, that is, non-legitimate sole rulers, who arose first in the seventh century, it was precisely the Spartan kings' super-aristocratic birth coupled with official recognition of their hereditary right which conferred on them unique (or almost unique) legitimacy to govern – or at any rate 'be king' (*basileuein*).

On the other hand, their power or authority was clearly not kingly or regal in the same way(s) as that of, say, an early-modern European monarch: it was not, in other words, absolute. Of course, even 'absolute' monarchs must in fact depend for the effective exercise of their authority on their court circles and on other instrumentalities beyond their constant and immediate reach. Nevertheless, those quasi-absolute early-modern monarchs could not be called to account through due legal process in the way that Spartan kings could. In this perspective, it was the Greek tyrant and the later Hellenistic monarch (Carlier 1984: 511-14; Shipley 2000: ch. 3) who were the 'absolute' rulers of ancient Greece. As for the Great King of Persia, he was the very model of an ancient absolute monarch (cf. Hall 1989: e.g. 95), as the Greeks tellingly acknowledged by the singular linguistic device of dropping the definite article when referring to him. On the other hand, a Spartan king was certainly more royal and more kingly than the 'kings' (*basileis*) referred to scornfully by the early Greek didactic poet Hesiod as 'bribe-swallowing' or 'gift-devouring': those men were what we would rather call 'lords', that is ruling aristocrats.[6] So too, *a fortiori*, a

Spartan king was certainly more royal and kingly than the annual, chiefly religious official selected by lot at Athens who really was merely called 'King'.[7]

Let us next consider, briefly, the relationship between kings and Ephors, or rather the antagonism between the kingship and the ephorate, in which many modern scholars used to see the key to the practical working of the whole Spartan system of governance.[8] Xenophon, who knew Sparta well at first hand and wrote a laudatory biography of a Spartan king (Agesilaos), wrote also a short pamphlet on some Spartan political, social and cultural institutions (the so-called *Lakedaimoniôn Politeia*). Here (*LP* 15.7), he records verbatim the oath sworn monthly between, on one hand, the two kings jointly, and, on the other, the board of five Ephors collectively, whereby the Ephors swore to uphold the kingship 'unshaken' – so long as the kings for their part abided by the laws of Sparta. Clearly, the onus was placed explicitly on the kings to obey the laws; if they did not, or if the Ephors could be persuaded or could persuade themselves that one or both had not done so, the Ephors had the power to impeach the king(s) before a Grand Jury (consisting of the Gerousia, afforced by themselves). Some kings were, we know, not only tried but also deposed in this way.[9] It was one mark of the exceptionalism of our two chosen examples that Kleomenes I, though indicted, survived such a trial, whereas Agesilaos II went out of his way, successfully, to avoid one.

However, before we rush to infer that 'the ephorate' must therefore always have had the whip hand over 'the kingship', the following complicating factors must be kept firmly under consideration. It was always one king on trial, not both, and the other king was always *ex officio*, as a member of the Gerousia, on the jury. The two kings, who came always from two separate aristocratic houses (until Kleomenes III effectively abolished the traditional kingship by installing his brother on the other throne: cf. Carlier 1984: 498 – table; Nabis, though called 'king', was in fact a tyrant: Mossé 1964; Cartledge & Spawforth 1989: ch. 5), were usually competitors, if not personal and/or political enemies. This institutional rivalry was rationalized and even sanctified in terms of a traditional enmity between the two royal houses that was underpinned by myth-history (Hdt. 6.52).

The tradition might of course be broken, or at any rate the rivalry mitigated, in particular instances, as we shall see below. But the ephorate – or rather, astute individual Ephors – might normally expect to be able to exploit this as it were traditional split between the two reigning kings to their own individual or corporate advantage. Not, however, that the Ephors, great though their formal powers undoubtedly were, always had all the best tunes, since they themselves might be split. Decisions taken by them as a board were reached by majority vote; boards were elected annually, tenure was not iterative, and one board of Ephors might take a very different, even contradictory, position from its predecessor, a switch that was likely to involve transferring allegiance from the person or policy of one king to his rival; and, finally, when it did come to an indictment of a king on a major political charge, the five Ephors were but a small minority of the Grand Jury, always formally outvoted by the twenty-eight elected members of the Gerousia and the other king.

In short, from the apparent imbalance in power between kings and ephors, or the kingship and the ephorate, we should not automatically infer that the Ephors were necessarily the linchpin of the Spartan system of governance. Nor should we infer that it was a power-struggle between kings and Ephors, or the kingship and the ephorate, that made the Spartan political mechanism tick. Of all the possible alternative loci of power I would myself again stress one above all the others put together: the Gerousia (consistently underrated, I believe, by both ancient and modern writers).[10] Sparta, my Sparta, was almost literally a gerontocracy. To become a (non-royal) member of the Gerousia, one certainly had to be aged sixty or over, that is, beyond the required period of compulsory military service, and, probably, an aristocrat by birth. Once elected, you served for life. The Nobel Prize committee for Literature is a near parallel, structurally, as was the Soviet Politburo, and as is the Chinese governmental hierarchy. Without the Gerousia, no major decision of Spartan foreign and, I suspect, domestic policy could be made. It was the Gerousia, as we have seen, that with the admixture of the Ephors constituted Sparta's supreme court. The two reigning kings, regardless of age, were members *ex officio*. The longer a king reigned, therefore, the greater his chance of determining both the composition and the political complexion of the Gerousia. Both kings could clearly expect to have supporters on that body drawn from their respective royal houses (this is the source of an apparent slip in Hdt. 6.57.5, picked up by Thuc. 1.20.3), as well as supporters won and maintained in other ways and for other reasons.

Ex officio membership of the Gerousia, therefore, was by no means the least of a king's privileges and prerogatives. My second main reason for playing down the alleged struggle of Ephors against King and playing up the importance of the kingship is derived from close study of the career of possibly the most ambitious Spartan known to history. Lysander commanded the force that decisively concluded the Peloponnesian War in Sparta's favour. But when not long afterwards he wanted to change the Spartan political system, and did everything in his power to make that happen, the office to which he aspired was that of king.[11] This was an office whose powers he was particularly well placed to appreciate, both because he had held the office of Nauarch (Admiral of the Fleet), which Aristotle later described as a sort of second kingship, and because he had suffered personal humiliation and political emasculation at the hands precisely of a Spartan king, a man with whom his relationship had been of the most intimate nature (cf. Chapter 8) – his former beloved, Agesilaos.

Moreover, had the kingship really been so unimportant, it is unlikely that Sparta would have been quite so frequently riven by succession-disputes, which recall not so much the regular infighting of political rivals for office in a Greek city but rather the harem politics of an oriental dynasty. Such disputes confirm, as Moses Finley remarked (1981a: 32), that the kings were 'a persistently disruptive force of a special kind and magnitude in classical Spartan history'. But they also suggest that the Spartans had a peculiarly high, symbolic regard for kingship – of their odd, dual kind – as such.

III. Military command

At home, a Spartan king's powers of initiative, decision and executive decision were comparatively limited – in comparison, that is, to their far greater powers when abroad on campaign at the head of an army (Herodotus and Xenophon rightly distinguish sharply their powers in war and in peace: cf. Cartledge 1987: 105) In war, they came nearest to exercising the sort of power the legalistic Romans distinguished as *imperium*, to put it bluntly, the powers of life and death, including over Spartan citizens. True, even on campaign a king had to reckon with the watchful presence of two Ephors, exercising the function their name literally signified – 'overseeing'. It was true, too, that the Spartans as a whole exercised both prospective and retrospective control over a commanding king, both because after 506 only one king at a time could command any given force, so that there might be competition for who was – or was not – to hold it, and because after returning home from campaign a king might be arraigned before a Grand Jury. Nevertheless, precisely as in Rome, military campaigning gave a Spartan king a unique chance to build up both material and symbolic capital.

One king, technically only a regent, let that power go to his head, when he commanded a united Greek force to victory over the Persian hordes at Plataea in 479. For that indiscretion Pausanias was severely reprimanded and paid eventually with his life. But as long as a militarily successful king kept his head while all around were – sometimes literally – losing theirs, he might be sure to gain some increase in *auctoritas* to set against the formal restrictions on his *potestas* (once more, the Roman parallel is illuminating). Therefore we should not take too seriously or literally Aristotle's dismissive description of the Spartan kingship as a sort of 'hereditary and perpetual generalship' (*Pol.* 1285a7, cf. 1271a40-1). First, this was no ordinary generalship, but one that could almost be described as a generalship 'with full powers' (*autokratôr*), as long as the campaigning lasted. Second, Sparta was in some important sense a military state and society, so that to hold the command of the army *ex officio* was potentially to be given access to what was considered culturally the most desirable and impressive form of power of all. Aristotle's characterization may perhaps hold water when say Leonidas, the hero of Thermopylae, is compared with a full-blooded monarch like Alexander the Great, but that would not exactly be the fairest of comparisons.[12]

IV. Charisma

Mention of Alexander leads me naturally to my third subject-heading, charisma. Alexander is, probably, the most charismatic of all ancient kings, if not the most charismatic Ancient character full stop. He is, to use another Greek-derived term, an icon. But what I want to claim here is that all Spartan kings were charismatic – by definition, regardless of their personal qualities; in other words, that the kingship as such was charismatic in a Weberian sense. Weber's concept may perhaps suffer from 'an uncertainty of referent: does it denote a cultural phenomenon or a psychological one?' (Geertz 1983: 121); and one might prefer Carlier's term 'mystique' (1984: 256, 297-301; though he does also use 'charisme', 292). But for my purposes charisma connotes both cultural and social-psychological esteem, stemming from 'the inherent sacredness of sovereign power' (Geertz 1983: 123). By calling the Spartan kingship charismatic I mean to say that it was distinguished by its perceived possession of some special grace, of ultimately divine derivation. I would emphasize that the symbolic trappings of Spartan royal rule cannot and should not be separated from its substance.

These trappings were several. There is no evidence for the Spartan kings' being blessed with the mediaeval royal touch, but we do know that other Spartans in public were not permitted to touch them. Then, there were the other body-language protocols – always taken very seriously in ancient Greece generally – of sitting, walking and running. In the presence of a king, everyone else except the king must stand; this was to take to the ultimate degree the general Spartan custom whereby juniors were expected to give up their seat to a senior. Conversely, if the Ephors summoned a king to their presence, he did not have to get up and go at the first time of asking, nor yet at the second, but only at the third, whereupon he would normally progress at a dignified walking pace. Agesilaos aroused mirth because, responding punctiliously at the first time of asking, he did not merely walk but ran – or rather, since he was lame in one leg from birth, hobbled. The Spartans, perhaps even more so than other Greeks, despised physical (or indeed any kind of) disability,[13] and Spartan laughter was typically laughter at another's expense.[14]

Second, there was the kings' already mentioned descent, ultimately divine, from great father Zeus, but more immediately heroic, from Herakles, and, more immediately still, Homeric, thanks to their connection with Menelaos, Homeric ruler of Lakedaimon, and his controversial wife Helen. Helen's twin brothers Kastor and Pollux, a.k.a. the Dioskouroi (sons of Zeus), served as the mythical representatives of the two Spartan kings, to the extent that, when the Spartans went to war, they took along with them images of one or both of the Dioskouroi as talismans. With this divine and heroic descent went what Carlier (1984: 246) calls 'une "puissance royale" transmise par le sang', crucial especially in determining the succession. Solidary with their more than human birth was their more than human ritual of death. So remarkable was this, because so extravagantly lavish by contrast with the burials of ordinary Spartans (and other Greeks by the fifth century), that Herodotus was reminded of the funeral rites of barbarian, non-Greek kings, specifically those of Scythia and Persia. For the period of his death and mourning the king symbolically became identified with the city (*l'état c'est moi*), a very 'un-Greek' state of affairs before the Hellenistic period.[15]

Nor was that the only non-Greek, specifically oriental, feature that Herodotus (6.58, 59) the acute comparative ethnographer detected in the powers, attributes, airs and graces with which Spartan kingship was hedged. Indeed, in one absolutely fundamental institutional-symbolic respect the Spartan kings were not citizens, not members of the '*homoioi*' or 'peers', as the Spartans collectively styled themselves, at all, but 'more equal' than ordinary or indeed than all other Spartans.[16] That is, the heir-apparent in each royal house was exempted from the *agôgê*, the state-imposed and state-run educational cycle, which from one point of view was a sort of trial by ordeal to see whether a Spartan boy would eventually be fitted to achieve adult Spartan warrior status (see Chapter 7). This is the extreme instance of a general feature of the Spartan kingship, what has been rather politely called its 'imperfect integration within the commonwealth' (Munson 1993: 48).

Moreover, in addition to their charisma and their unique – and charismatic – exemption from the *agôgê*, the Spartan kings, like aristocrats in most other Greek states, were by virtue of their birth high priests (of Zeus and daughter Athena). This entitled them to certain spiritual and material prerogatives in the conduct of the major Greek civic religious ritual of animal-sacrifice, both at home and abroad, and both on and off the battlefield (Carlier 1984: 256). It also gave them unique access, a sort of hot line, to the principal Greek oracular shrine of Delphi, sacred to Zeus' son Apollo.[17]

According to Spartan myth, the laws attributed sometimes to the human or part-human lawgiver Lykourgos had also received the divine sanction of approval by Delphic Apollo. Since those laws among other things guaranteed not just the continued existence of the kingship for ever but also the kingship's special place within Sparta's system of governance, it was very much in the kings' joint interests to keep the Delphic priesthood sweet. In return, moreover, they might reasonably expect to be able to use Delphic favour to further their own policies, especially if they had an enlarged view of Sparta's place in the Greek world as a whole. It is very striking in this connection that, when (as we have seen) Lysander wished to change the rules to make himself eligible for the kingship, he felt he had first to line up on his side all the other major Greek oracles (and the non-Greek oracle of Ammon in the Libyan desert) in order to try to counteract the peculiarly strong *mana* of Delphi.[18] It is very noticeable, too, that, although the Ephors had the power to use an oracular shrine to test the continuing validity of a particular king's rule, not only did they have that power only once in every eight years but in their use of it they were confined to a local oracular shrine located in a Perioikic town (Ino-Pasiphaë at Thalamai) whose authority was infinitely smaller than that of the mighty panhellenic Apollo, recipient of all the major festival honours at Sparta.[19]

V. Kleomenes I and Agesilaos II

Enough has been said, I hope, on the kingship's constitutional status, its prerogatives of and in military command, and its charisma to set the scene for my two concrete illustrations. My aim here is not of course to provide a blow-by-blow account of their reigns, but rather to select what I take to be particularly revelatory episodes, revealing of what Edward Gibbon might have called 'the nice and secret springs' of these two kings' effective power over policy, both its formulation and its execution, for long periods.

i. Kleomenes I[20]

Our main source on Kleomenes is Herodotus, but either he or his informants or both were on the whole biased against him, and he is presented mainly as a negative paradigm – of irreligion and megalomania.[21] He and his principal Eurypontid co-king, Damaratos, allegedly exemplified to perfection the traditional antagonism between the two royal houses, so much so that Kleomenes had Damaratos deposed – sacrilegiously, according to Herodotus; whereupon Damaratos 'medized', that is, went over to the Persians, becoming (allegedly – one suspects family pride and Herodotean artistry have combined to exaggerate this) one of Xerxes' most trusted advisers. Because of the deposition and medism of Damaratos, and the alleged sacrilege of Kleomenes followed by his death in suspicious circumstances, the story of Kleomenes' reign comes surrounded by a dense fog of myth-history, difficult for us to penetrate. A further obstacle is that Herodotus, unlike his successors Thucydides and Xenophon, was barely interested in mundane 'constitutional' details; at least, he never let them get in the way of telling a good story. This is a pity, because Kleomenes' long reign (c. 520-490) witnessed not just an acute domestic constitutional crisis but also two major international crises for Sparta, with Persia and with Athens, and hence with its Greek allies.

Roughly speaking, Kleomenes seems to have swung from a foreign policy of opposition to Athens to one of co-operation with Athens against the encroaching might of the Persian Empire. In between the two poles came the rise of what we call the Peloponnesian League, through which alliance Sparta claimed and expressed the status of a great Greek power. It was as head of the Peloponnesian League, most conspicuously, that Sparta led the united Greek resistance, such as it was, to Persia in 481-479. Herodotus does not explicitly associate Kleomenes with bringing the Peloponnesian League into existence, though he is usually read as at least implying that. What he does make clear is that Kleomenes, despite certain foreign policy failures, was from 506 to the late 490s in effect the key player in, if not sole ruler of, Sparta.

One factor contributing vitally to that position was the sheer length of his reign (curiously falsified by Herodotus). By 494, when he was impeached on a charge of high treason, he had been on the (Agiad) throne for some twenty-five years, so that all or most of the Gerousia will have been appointed at least under, and perhaps thanks directly to, him. It does not therefore strike me as altogether odd that, since the court trying him in 494 presumably consisted of the Gerousia and the Ephors, he should have been acquitted of that charge of high treason, especially as his defence was a blatant appeal to Sparta's dominant religious ideology (cf. Parker 1989). This was a sort of Spartan equivalent to the race card played by the defence in the notorious trial of O.J. Simpson.

ii. Agesilaos[22]

Agesilaos' even longer reign of some forty years (he was vigorously active to the end of his life, in his mid-eighties) is also unusually well documented, far better so, anyhow, than Kleomenes'. Thanks to Xenophon, above all, we can I believe begin to see what really made Sparta tick, so far as major decisions of public policymaking were concerned. To employ the useful Roman terminology, Agesilaos did indeed rule Sparta for most of his forty years because he saw that the formal deficiencies in the *potestas* of the kingship – especially at home, and thanks particularly to its dual character – would have to be and could be adequately compensated for by exploiting its potential for *auctoritas*. The two chief means he employed to maintain and increase the latter were, first, his ideological self-presentation as the quintessential good Spartan citizen, the living embodiment of all the Spartan virtues – as opposed to the sort of king Lysander might well be thought to have wanted to become; and, second, his deployment, on a massive scale, of a technique that again we tend to associate more with Rome than Greece, namely personal patronage.

Not that such a patronage model may be applied to Spartan politics in the same way or on anything like the same scale as it might be to explain the politics of the Roman Republic. For a start, Sparta was tiny by Rome's standards, and its organization of voting in elections, legislation or policymaking was utterly different.[23] But patronage does help to explain better than any other model of power-accumulation and power-dispensation how the kingship at Sparta could be used to wield decisive influence, thanks especially to its huge wealth, its prerogatives in public sacrifices, games, and feasts, and its near-exclusive pre-eminence in military commands and appointments. In particular, it is patronage that accounts for Agesilaos' capacity in 378 to deliver the vote of acquittal in the major political trial of Sphodrias.[24]

Sphodrias was a high-ranking Spartiate, who had been entrusted with the properly imperial task of governing Thespiai, a quite important city of Boiotia, whose chief city Thebes was Sparta's former ally and now principal enemy. Sphodrias was a king's man, but not one of Agesilaos': he owed his appointment to Agesilaos' fellow – or rather rival – king Kleombrotos. Moreover, the action for which he was on trial before the Gerousia (and presumably Ephors) – the invasion of Attica with a view allegedly to seizing the still ungated Peiraieus – was both a flagrant breach of an international diplomatic agreement and a flagrant violation of Agesilaos' own line of foreign policy towards Athens and Thebes. One would therefore have expected Agesilaos to vote for Sphodrias' condemnation (to death), especially as Sphodrias himself was so confident of the guilty verdict that he did not even dare return to Sparta and so in effect convicted himself. As things unexpectedly turned out, however, not only did Agesilaos vote for acquittal but, as Xenophon makes clear, it was Agesilaos' vote that swung the vote of the entire jury.

Agesilaos' motives for switching his vote interest me less than the modalities and implications of his switch (cf. Chapter 8). The Gerousia was at the time divided into three groups: Agesilaos' faction, the faction around the other king (to which Sphodrias belonged), and those members 'in between', who were not committed to either faction. A figure cannot be put on the size of any of these three groups; all we can say is that either Agesilaos' faction together with the other king's faction added up to a simple majority, or that Agesilaos' switch convinced enough of the uncommitted as well to constitute that majority for acquittal. Either way, Agesilaos' switch was a brilliant political move. His foreign policy was already seriously damaged anyhow; but against that damage Agesilaos could now offset the gain, in purely factional terms, resulting from the fact that the other king and especially Sphodrias himself would be so beholden to him that they would be likely to put up less, and less effective, resistance to his foreign policy schemes in the future.

So indeed it proved in the event. Sphodrias and Agesilaos' co-king Kleombrotos both died on the battlefield of Leuktra in 371, unlike Agesilaos himself, and they died fighting a war against Thebes that was the outcome and fulfilment of the wishes of Agesilaos above all. That battle, in retrospect, can be seen to have been the watershed of Sparta's fortunes as a great Greek power. It marked the end not only of her new-style empire but also of her old-style Peloponnesian League, and – what a tragic poet might have called the 'coping-stone of wretched ills' (*thringkos athliôn kakôn*) – the loss of half her domestic power-base, namely the territory of Messenia together with the Messenian Helots. Sparta thereby ceased, inevitably, to be a great Greek power.

VI. Aftermath

Let me conclude briefly with some mention of the *Nachleben* of the Spartan kingship, the use made of it in post-antique and sometimes very much later political debate and discourse. According to Shelley, 'we are all Greeks', in the sense that 'Our laws, our literature, our religion, our arts, have their roots in Greece'. This is at best misleading.[25] But we *are* all Greeks insofar as crucial aspects of our cultural heritage, inheritance, or legacy are Greek, in that we have chosen to appropriate these features from the Greeks, to treat the Greeks as in these vital respects our ancestors. One of these areas is politics, and the discourse that goes with it, and it is impossible to overlook the extraordinarily frequent appearance of kings and kingship, and their frequent lionization, in the story of the Spartan legacy.[26]

Times change, however, and, as Elizabeth Rawson accurately observed (1969: 170), 'No one today would think of taking Agesilaus as a model, either for himself or for his rulers'. Yet 'though both the structure and the expressions of social life change, the inner necessities that animate it do not' (Geertz 1983: 143). The relevant 'necessity' here, I suggest, would be a politics of charisma, whereby subjects (in our case) or fellow-citizens (as in Sparta) are induced to accept and internalize 'the master fictions by which that [social and political] order lives' (Geertz 1983: 146). The history of the Spartan kingship may yet have something to teach us.

6

Comparatively Equal:
A Spartan Approach

Introduction

The original version of this essay appeared in the published proceedings of a 'Democracy 2500' conference held in 1993 at Georgetown University, Washington DC, under the sponsorship of the National Endowment for the Humanities and the American School of Classical Studies at Athens (Ober & Hedrick eds 1996). It formed part of a panel on Equality, and was more specifically a response to a keynote paper delivered by Kurt Raaflaub (Raaflaub 1996). But my aim here is not only, nor indeed so much, to respond directly to Raaflaub's admirably clear, diachronically arranged essay, although I shall be taking issue with it on a couple of points. Rather, it is to give one of a number of preliminary sketches in miniature (cf. Cartledge 1996b, 1998b) of a forthcoming work entitled *Political Thought in Ancient Greece. Elite and Mass from Homer to Plutarch*, and so to stake out a slightly more ample terrain of enquiry. That work will be significantly comparative, but it is sobering to note that in the past two decades over 200 books have been published on the subject of equality in English alone, any serious selection of which would include at least Baker 1987, Beitz 1991, Green 1985, Nagel 1991, Norman 1987, Phelps Brown 1988, Roemer 1994, Sen 1992, Temkin 1994, and Westen 1990. Of published work on ancient notions of equality I have learned most from Harvey 1965.

*

> ... man
> Equal, unclassed, tribeless, and nationless,
> Exempt from awe, worship, degree, the king
> Over himself.
>
> (P.B. Shelley, *Prometheus Unbound*)

I. Aims and methods

I wish first, and very briefly, to compare ancient and modern conceptions and practices of equality, more specifically ancient Greek and post-Renais-

68

sance 'Western' conceptions. Second, and in more detail, I wish to draw some comparisons within the ancient world, between Greek and Greek. According to the structural-functional anthropologist A.R. Radcliffe-Brown, it is the aim of comparison to discover the universal.[1] For disciples of the 'Cambridge School' of 'conceptual history', on the contrary, among whom I should count myself,[2] comparison ought to emphasize difference.[3] In the present case, at all events, it is hoped that comparison will serve, first, to make us 'clearer about features of our own social and political environment, features whose very familiarity may make it harder for us to bring them into view';[4] and, second, to help us specify the peculiarities of ancient Greek constructions of equality by contrasting the set of meanings then available to political actors with that available today.

The concept of 'constructions' merits special emphasis, since all of us presumably – whether we are ancient historians, political philosophers, or just plain citizens – are mainly interested in explaining, or understanding, the twin processes of discursive negotiation and practical implementation of political concepts. Equality happens to be one of the two most funda-mental of these (the other is freedom), both in ancient and in modern democratic discourse. Since, however, language is constituted in political action, and political action in turn conditions or determines language,[5] a tension or dialectic subsists between political theory (or ideology)[6] and political praxis. This is especially likely to be so in an antagonistic, zero-sum political culture such as that (or those) of classical Greece.[7] It follows that we should expect the meanings of a core concept like equality to be especially unstable, and to become extraordinarily hotly contested in situations of civil strife or outright civil war. Thucydides' famous account of the civil war on Kerkyra does not either disappoint or confound that expectation (see further below). In short, 'there can be no histories of concepts as such; there can only be histories of their uses in argument'. In application of this methodological principle, three distinct 'uses in argu-ment' of the general term *equality* in ancient Greece are hereafter proposed for consideration: reference, criteria of application, and ap-praisive function.[8]

Use in Argument 1: reference

In the first place, we must ask what kinds of equality were at stake, and within what value-system?[9] To begin comparatively, and negatively, we are not dealing here with the – or a – liberal sense of the equality of individual rights against the State.[10] Even if the Greeks did recognize what might plausibly be called rights, they did not have the fortune to know the separately instituted 'State' in any post-Hobbesian sense, and they did not construe the individual in a modern way.[11] Nor, second, are we dealing with the equality of all humankind in the sight of God, in either some specifi-cally post-Pauline Christian or some generically eschatological, transcendent, metaphysical sense.[12] At most, the pagan Greeks would have accepted that *vis-à-vis* the immortal gods all mortals were equally powerless.[13] Nor, finally, is there any question here of sexual or gender equality, in the sense that modern feminism, according to one dictionary definition, is 'advocacy of women's rights on ground of equality of the sexes'.[14]

Instead, for classical Greece as a whole, not just classical Athens, the meanings of equality that were practically in question are threefold. First, and most broadly, there was political (or civic) equality, meaning equality of status and respect within the conceptual framework of the Greeks' normative system of polarized sociopolitical hierarchy.[15] Inasmuch as, and to the extent that, the Greek citizen was by definition male not female, free not slave, native insider not stranger or outsider, adult not child, he was in those respects and to that extent equal to all other citizens, and deserving therefore of equal respect, privilege, consideration, and treatment. However, the translation of formal citizen equality into universal equality of outcome was frequently frustrated by inequalities of birth (aristocrat against commoner, *agathos* against *kakos*) and of wealth (rich against poor, *plousios* against *penês*). Different Greek communities in practice distributed the privileges of citizenship differentially, in accordance with their divergent evaluations of these two factors, especially the latter.[16]

Second, there was theoretically the possibility of equality of welfare, that is, the good life in a sense that is not narrowly materialistic or mathematically calculated: generalized *eudaimonia*, or 'well being'.[17] This should not be confused with the allocation of precisely equal shares of some or all privately as well as publicly owned goods.[18] Third, the Greeks, especially the democratic Greeks, operated with an idea of equality of opportunity. This amounted to the notion that all relevant citizen contestants in the (often literally) life-and-death race of public, political activity should ideally start behind the same line and run across a more or less level playing-field.[19]

Use in Argument 2: criteria of application

It has been noted cross-culturally that equality has often tended to be urged as an idea or ideal against some perceived inequality, particularly in moments of revolutionary upheaval.[20] Classical Greece was no exception. In 427 the democratic revolutionaries of Kerkyra were loud in their demand for what they styled *isonomia politikê* (Thuc. 3.82.8).[21] For Thucydides, the disabused Athenian historian, this was but a specious slogan, a cloak for the selfish ambitions of a power-mad clique. The speciousness was due, however, not only to the alleged motives of its propagators but also partly to the slogan's inherent radical ambiguity, or vapidity. For what was to count in practice as an 'equal' sharing of power, and, more importantly, which (of the) 'people' were to constitute the relevant community of sharers, actual or imagined?[22]

Isonomia, that is, may have been 'the fairest of names' (Hdt. 3.80.6), but it was the beginning, not the end (in a temporal sense), of a political argument.[23] In fact, it might be appropriated just as easily by Greek oligarchs (Thuc. 3.62.3) as by Greek democrats, depending on who were judged worthy to be counted as relevantly equal, and in what respects. Aristotle was not the only oligarch to propound a theory (or ideology) of distributive, proportionate or 'geometric' equality, that is to say, a relativist notion of equality based on moral evaluation according to which some citizens were literally 'more equal' than others.[24] On the other hand, even democrats, who more honestly espoused the opposite 'arithmetical' conception, were prepared to concede that in practice equality was not everything (see further below). It was not mere accident that *isonomia* was not an official slogan of the Athenian democracy, let alone its guiding principle: contrast 'the strong principle of equality', which may justly be held to underlie the United States' dominant construction of democracy today.[25]

Use in Argument 3: appraisive function

The Greeks did of course 'have a word for' *equality*, in fact more than one: not only *isotês* but also *to ison* (the equal thing), wherein 'equal' bears its root meaning of exactly, mathematically equal, as in an *iso*-sceles triangle. But they operated and negotiated as well with a wide range of compound nouns starting with the *iso-* prefix. I cite five. *Iso-nomia*, just mentioned, stood for the most general and unspecific principle of political equality; *iso-kratia* and *is-êgoria* connoted, respectively, its oligarchic and democratic constructions.[26] *Iso-timia*, not certainly attested before the third century BC, captured the social notion of equality of consideration or respect, parity of esteem; and finally *iso-moiria* did the same for the economic idea of equal distribution of some communal goods.[27]

This verbal flexibility regarding civic equality, welfare equality and equality of opportunity may be considered to be in itself an improvement on our comparatively restricted and ambiguous vocabulary. But the Greeks went further still. They not only employed *iso-* compounds in this acutely sensitive area of political semantics. They also realistically anticipated the 'discovery' of modern political philosophy that, although equality 'does, after all, imply sameness',[28] in hard political practice the operative criterion governing equality's implementation is not sameness or identity but similitude or likeness. Hence, *isotês* was complemented pragmatically by the concept of *homoiotês*, especially in the familiar prepositional phrases meaning 'on an equal and fair basis' (*en / epi tois isois kai homoiois, epi têi isêi kai homoiâi*).[29] Equality by itself, in other words, was not considered to be in all circumstances fair or just, even in the eyes of hard-line ideological egalitarians in democratic Athens. Yet of all ancient cities Athens was surely the one that most fervently preached the gospel of equality.

II. Comparing Athens and Sparta: similars and equals

In comparing the political systems and ideologies of Athens and Sparta, it makes sense to start with Aristotle and his *Politics*, not least because it was his own basic principle of political-philosophical method to start from the received and reputable views (*ta phainomena, ta endoxa*) of the prudent (*phronimoi*) participant observers and practitioners of civic life in the Greek *polis*. For Aristotle a *polis* had to consist of similars (*homoioi*); indeed, the *polis* according to one of his definitions is 'a kind of association of similars' (*Pol.* 1328a35-36). Yet earlier in the same work, where he had been explicitly seeking to define the citizen, he had apparently said just the opposite: citizens cannot all be similars, even *qua* citizens (*Pol.* 1276b28, 40; 1277a6-7). Contradictions are by no means unknown elsewhere in the *Politics*, and this one too surely reflects the tension between the Greeks' ideal aspiration toward equality and the failure of its perfect implementation in practice. A properly Aristotelian golden mean is struck in the formulation that 'the *polis* aims at being composed, as much as possible, of similars and equals' (1295b25-6).[30]

The dyad 'similars and equals' (*homoioi kai isoi*) is crucial. It is the concrete counterpart of the abstract prepositional phrase meaning 'on a fair and equal basis' cited above. In a democratic context, such as that of Athens, the original[31] and most developed of Greek democracies, the latter phrase accurately reflected the combination of partial egalitarianism in theory with hierarchy and subordination in practice that characterized all ancient systems of direct self-rule of and for the demos. Indeed, the rhetorical negotiation of such phrases or slogans may well have been the strategic response of ideological democrats at Athens or elsewhere to one of the strongest charges pressed against ancient democracy on principle by its diehard opponents, namely that it perpetrated the manifest absurdity and injustice of treating unequals equally.[32]

Athenian democratic equality

At any rate, in democratic Athens from about 460 BC onwards, all Athenians were considered qua citizens to be officially equal on principle. That strong principle was grounded in the claim that the essence of democracy was freedom, so that all Athenian citizens were *ex hypothesi* free – both by birth and, being masters of themselves and of each other's collective destiny, by autonomous situation. On the grounds that they were all equally free in this civic sense, 'kings over themselves' in Shelley's oxymoronic phrase, they were all equal.[33] That in turn gave rise to the democratic view that use of the lottery was the most appropriate practical way of apportioning among citizens the equality of *timê*, meaning both abstract 'esteem' and concrete 'office,' to which they were theoretically entitled. Sortition of course had purely pragmatic implications and consequences too (such as the attempted prevention of bribery in the jury-courts), but its intrinsic ideological connotation of equality was no less important to underpinning the Athenians' collective sense of political self-definition and civic identity.[34]

In hard fact, however, Athenian citizens neither were, nor were considered for all purposes to be, exactly equal, identical, and the same, in all relevant respects. They were not so, most conspicuously, with respect to the allocation of executive responsibility, especially since active political capacity was in some cases deemed to depend crucially on wealth. Hence the Athenians' wholly pragmatic resort to election rather than sortition for filling the great military and financial offices of government. For the tenure of these, the privileged elite few, the seriously rich – who were likely also to be exceptionally well educated and expertly knowledgeable – were adjudged differentially well qualified. The other side of this pragmatic elitism, perhaps, is the negative ideological discrimination against Athenians of the lowest socio-economic status, the thetes.[35] In short, in democratic Athens the rules were as follows: *isotês* in basic but not indefeasible principle was to be tempered for practical purposes by *homoiotês*. Citizens who were all 'same-ish' (*homoioi*) were not necessarily or exactly 'the same' (*homoi*) and should not therefore automatically be treated as 'equals' (*isoi*) but rather 'on a basis of equality *and* similitude.'

Spartan an(ti)egalitarianism

It is all too easy to receive the impression that Athens was the whole of classical Greece. Actually, it was one of up to 1500 separate, usually radically self-differentiated political communities. In Aristotle's time, the political regimes of most of them could be classified fairly straightforwardly as variants of either democracy or oligarchy. But when it came to the classification of classical Sparta, Athens's 'other' in many respects, confusion reigned, as indeed it still does today.[36] The reason for bringing Sparta centrally into the present discussion is that the Spartans apparently identified themselves as citizens under the title of *Homoioi*.[37]

In light of what has been said above, it should now be clear why it is vital to avoid the standard English translation of *Homoioi* as 'Equals.' Despite their universal and communally enforced educational system, Spartans did not graduate into civic adulthood as assembly-line *Homoioi* counting politically as *Isoi*. Rather, unless they were revolutionaries, they did not seek *isotês* in any sense other than the ideal enjoyment of an equal lifestyle (*iso-diaitoi*: Thuc. 1.6.5).[38] Comparison and contrast of the Athenian and the Spartan methods of registering and counting legislative, electoral, and policy-making votes will enable us to make the same point substantively.

Democratic Athens, to borrow Euripides' strictly anachronistic phrase (*Supp.* 353), was an *isopsêphos polis*. In actual practice, raising the hand (*kheirotonia*) was more common than use of the secret ballot (*psêphos* means 'pebble'), and in the Athenian Assembly, to save time, votes were usually estimated rather than (as they always were in the Council and People's Court) individually counted. But the principle was egalitarian in all cases: one citizen-one vote, with everyone counting for one and no one for more than one. In sharp and obvious contrast, the Spartan method of open voting by shouting in the formally sovereign Assembly (Thuc. 1.87) implicitly denied that principle. It was entirely consistent with that denial that the Spartans abjured altogether the Athenian method of sortition for appointing to office.[39] A supposedly Spartan *bon mot* nicely reflects this essential difference between the two cities: 'In answer to the man who insisted that he establish a democracy in the *polis*, Lykourgos replied, "Do you first create a democracy in your own household" ' (Plut. *Mor.* 228cd [21]).[40] Greek male citizen democrats, in other words, inconsistently drew the line at instituting equality in their own homes, which they ruled undemocratically, whereas the Spartans consistently preached and practiced inequality both at home and in public civic space.[41]

Spartan political actuality confirms the judgement of 'Lykourgos'. Towards outsiders, all Spartan citizens turned a uniformly homogeneous and resolutely exclusive face.[42] In terms of their internal civic capacity, however, Spartan citizens were self-differentiated along four axes of hierarchical discrimination: not only by birth and wealth, but also by age and attainment (*andragathia*, 'manly virtue': Hdt. 5.42.1). It might perhaps be said that the same kinds of discrimination existed in Athens too, but there they were far less 'exciting,'[43] far less pronounced and of far smaller moment.

What made the difference between the two cities' systems was, in a word, the Spartans' Helots. Because of this servile yet native Greek, politically motivated and much more numerous underclass, Sparta had had to become an essentially military society, and, then as now, multiple hierarchization suited the military way. There was no place for genuine equality in the ordered *kosmos* that Sparta was ideally represented to be (Hdt. 1.65.4). Spartans in a real sense could not afford to practise egalitarianism, except of the pseudo-egalitarian 'geometric' variety favoured by Athenian oligarchs. In Athens, too, the citizen was by definition a warrior, but he was not, like the Spartan, a full-time professional warrior constantly in training for war against the enemy within. And he was so to speak a citizen first, and warrior second: there was more space between his military and his other civic functions than was the case institutionally, ideologically or psychologically at Sparta.[44]

III. Conclusion

I end with two very different modern writers on equality. First, there is Charles Beitz, who has identified political egalitarianism as the ideal that each of us should have an 'equal say' in the determination of policy and choice of our political leaders, and envisages this ideal as underlying the modern concept of democracy. What is this if not a modern translation of ancient Greek, and especially ancient Athenian, *isêgoria*, reminding us that the 'noble and substantial political ideal'[45] of egalitarianism is a living legacy specifically of classical Athens?

Second, and finally, there is Primo Levi, perhaps the most compelling literary witness to the Holocaust, who included the following observation in a reply to questions from readers of his *If This Is a Man* and *The Truce*: 'In every part of the world, wherever you begin by denying the fundamental liberties of mankind, and equality among people, you move toward the concentration camp system, and it is a road on which it is difficult to halt.'[46] Notwithstanding all the undeniable institutional and ideological differences between ancient Greece and the modern world, these two quotations do in their disparate ways sufficiently indicate the desirability, and I would add the possibility, of making a conscious and pragmatic connection between them.[47] The reconstruction of modern democracy (cf. Euben et al. eds 1994), aided by critical reflection on ancient political systems, is no mean goal and prize.[48]

Part III

Society, Economy and Warfare

7

A Spartan Education

Introduction

The original version of this chapter appeared in a privately printed and not easily accessible Festschrift, *Apodosis*, presented to my revered Latin schoolmaster, Dr W.W. Cruickshank of St Paul's School London, to mark his eightieth birthday in 1992. It began by quoting some words of the School's founder, the great Renaissance humanist John Colet, one of whose aims was 'the formation of good Christian life and manners', and pointing out that, although that aim had not been achieved in my case, nevertheless the title of my essay was not at all autobiographical. On the contrary, the essay owed its inspiration to the Demokritean *sententia* quoted as my epigraph below: if you think that *your* school was a regular Dothepersons Hall, then consider the Spartan alternative.

Since 1992, the major work to appear in this area is Kennell 1995, with which I have taken gentle issue in my review in *CR* n.s. 47 (1997) 97-8. Birgalias 1999, the book of a Paris doctoral thesis, with a Preface by the distinguished French historian of ancient Sparta, Claude Mossé, is a useful compendium of ancient information and modern bibliography; though Birgalias does not apparently know or at any rate cite Kennell's book. His observation (1999: 356) that, just as Athens' originality consists in its invention of democracy, so Sparta's resides in its invention of its pedagogical system is well worth pondering. Lupi 2000, the published version of a 1997 Naples doctoral thesis, is an important recent discussion of Spartan age-grades and classes.

*

> You must not seek certain things and must be content with others, comparing your own life with that of those who do worse and deeming yourself fortunate, when you reflect on what they undergo.
> (Demokritos B191, quoted in Cartledge 1998a: 48)

By most ancient Greeks' standards, and even by those of the Victorian public school (which liked to regard itself as somehow carrying on the 'Spartan tradition'), a Spartan education was pretty tough, not to say pretty gruesomely brutal.[1] Hence, in part, as we shall see, our still remark-

ably popular expressions: a 'Spartan' existence – spare, austere, self-denying mode of life; and 'laconic' speech – curt, clipped, military-style utterance. There is not, though, much profit or interest in merely cataloguing
Sparta's pedagogical brutality. Rather, I propose to address what I take to
be the three most important historical questions that Spartan education
raises. First, why and how did the Spartan educational system come to be
as it was in the Classical period[2] – that is to say, both a system, and a
publicly imposed and minutely and centrally organized system? Secondly,
what function or functions did this education serve within the wider
context of the Spartan *kosmos*, the Spartans' social and political order as
a whole? Finally, was it because of this peculiar educational system that
the mighty Spartans had come to be viewed by most other Greeks as
'other', that is, as virtually a race apart and almost a different species of
mankind – rather as we (or some of us) in the West may regard some
Oriental peoples today?[3]

I begin, almost inevitably, with possibly the most famous piece of extant
fifth-century BC Greek prose, the Periklean Epitaphios or Funeral Speech,
as re-presented by Thucydides (2.35-46). Apart from its value as testimony
to 'the invention of Athens', the fashioning of Athens' self-image as a
democratic polity, it is also a prime example of the way in which the Greeks
and especially the Athenians constructed Sparta as 'other', as a deviation
from or rather a polarized inversion of the 'Greek' norm:[4]

> [T]here is a great difference between us and our opponents ... in our educa-
> tional systems (*en tais paideiais*). The Spartans, from their earliest boyhood,
> are submitted to the most laborious training in courage (*to andreion*); we
> pass our lives without all these restrictions, and yet are just as ready to face
> the same dangers as they are ... There are certain advantages, I think, in our
> way of meeting danger voluntarily, with an easy mind, instead of with a
> laborious training (*ponôn meletê*), with natural rather than with state-
> induced (*meta nomôn*) courage ...
>
> (Thuc. 2.39.1,4, trans. R. Warner)

Whether or not 'Perikles' was right about the effects of the Spartan and
Athenian approaches to education, he was undoubtedly correct that the
Spartans' and Athenians' educational practices were not just very different
from but radically opposed to each other. Education, moreover, was something that the real Perikles perhaps took a particular interest and pride
in, for surely the description of Athenian democratic institutions and
character in the Funeral Speech (Thuc. 2.41.1) as 'a process of education
for all Greece' (*tês Hellados paideusin*) is a genuine quotation, not a
Thucydidean conceit. Its relevance for our concerns is that, although
Athens too was a highly exceptional Greek community, not least because
of the thoroughgoing democratic lifestyle hymned by Perikles, yet in its
educational system – or rather lack of one – Athens far more closely
approximated to the vast majority of Classical Greek states than did

7. A Spartan Education

Sparta. A brief and inevitably somewhat crude preliminary sketch of an average Classical Athenian education will serve, therefore, not only to bring out the difference between Athens and Sparta, but also to highlight comparatively the peculiarity of Sparta in the context of the Classical Greek world as a whole.[5]

In Classical Athens education up to the age of eighteen was entirely a private affair. It was arranged and paid for by parents who were not legally compelled by the *nomoi* to have their children formally educated at all, let alone up to our current minimum school-leaving age of sixteen. Teachers in Athens were typically men of low status and badly paid. It was, for example, one of the many unpleasant characteristics of Theophrastos' Illiberal Man (*aneleutheros*) to reduce the teacher's income by keeping his children at home and pretending they were ill (*Characters* XII.6, composed at Athens in *c.* 300); but the Illiberal Man will not have been alone in behaving like that. Poor Athenian parents, indeed, may not have been able to afford any formal education outside the home whatsoever. Such schools as existed were run from private houses or from rooms attached to a public or private *gumnasion* (training-ground for a variety of athletic sports), which could be used for physical education.

Boys normally began to attend school from the age of seven, or earlier if the family were well-to-do. Girls, however, rarely attended formal school at all. They were 'educated' at home, chiefly for the purely manual and domestic tasks that were to be their lot as married women. Thus the rich Athenian who serves as the fictional or at all events fictionalized protagonist in one of Xenophon's dialogues (the *Oeconomicus* or *Treatise on Household-management*) may have been excessively conservative in many ways (and conversely somewhat liberal in others),[6] but he was not by any means untypical of his class in deliberately marrying a girl of only fourteen from a sheltered background so that he could teach her what he considered necessary.[7] So by 'education at Athens' in the formal sense we mean the education of boys, and more specifically of prospective citizens.

This was divided into three main areas at what we would call the 'primary' level: basic literacy (and possibly numeracy), music, and physical education. Some schools offered instruction in all three, but it seems to have been usual for parents to choose different teachers for the different subject-areas. Basic literacy was easy enough to teach, thanks to the simplicity of the Greeks' fully phonetic alphabet of twenty-four to twenty-eight letters;[8] and it would seem that most Athenian citizens were functionally literate in the most rudimentary sense that they could scratch a name, at any rate their own, on a broken potsherd (*ostrakon*) or wax-tablet as public or private necessity dictated. The implication of the famous apocryphal anecdote about Aristeides – he was allegedly once asked, by an illiterate citizen from the sticks who had never so much as clapped eyes on him but was just heartily sick of hearing him called 'the just', to write his own name on a potsherd during an ostracism (Plut.

Aristeides 7) – is that only the most boorishly rustic of *agroikoi* could not manage as little as that.[9]

The music teacher taught Athenian boys pipes- or lyre-playing and singing. These were important, indeed basic, social skills in a society where music played such a large political role: for instance, every year at the Great Dionysia festival some 1200 citizen participants were required for the dithyrambic and dramatic competitions, that is, some four per cent of the total adult male citizen body, the equivalent of about a million people in the UK today.[10] Physical training involved running, long jump, javelin-throwing, boxing and wrestling. This was useful training for competition in athletic games such as those held in association with the Great Panathenaia festival every four years, but it was also essential training for warfare, at least for the richer one third to one half of the citizenry who were able to equip themselves to fight as heavy-armed infantrymen (*hoplitai*) – though it was not exactly valueless, either, for the other half, the thetes who rowed Athens' trireme warships.[11] In the Classical period, between *c.* 500 and 322, Athens was at war with someone on average three years in every four.[12]

That tripartite educational curriculum might, as I said, be described by us as 'primary'. But it could also become 'secondary', if parents wished their sons to continue within it after the age of twelve or so and could afford the fees. There did not exist, in other words, a separately defined 'secondary' curriculum at Athens. Nor, *a fortiori*, was there a third-level curriculum. However, in the course of the second half of the fifth century something that we might want to label a form of 'higher' education was introduced at Athens, though again it was available only to the sons of the rich. This novel pedagogy was that offered by the mainly non-Athenian 'Sophists', self-styled sages (*sophistês* was originally an honorific term) who offered, at a price, instruction on literally any subject under (and indeed including) the sun. But the basic skill they claimed to be able to impart was the ability to argue a case persuasively – hence Plato's impassioned denial (in the *Protagoras*) that virtue (*aretê*) could be taught, and Aristophanes' wicked parody of Sophistic debate in the *Clouds*, in which the 'Wrong' Argument (*logos*) paradoxically and thus truly sophistically triumphs over 'Right'.[13] Although the Sophists taught widely throughout the Greek world, even in Sparta, they were most at home in democratic Athens, 'the city of words', where all major political decisions were taken communally in public by several hundreds or several thousands of citizens after competitive debate in the Assembly or People's Court.[14]

So much, in brief, for Athenian formal education: hardly very extensive or organized, and not at all compulsory. In Sparta they ordered these matters as differently as could be, as the expatriate, pro-Spartan publicist Xenophon, Athenian by origin and upbringing, was at pains to stress in the short pamphlet he wrote on Spartan society in the first half of the fourth century.[15] Xenophon could assume, for instance, that outside Sparta chil-

82

dren were not normally given any formal education whatsoever after early childhood, and although (or because) he was a former pupil of Sokrates, he entirely agreed with other, less well educated 'Lakonizers' (fans of all things Spartan) that the Spartan educational system could not be surpassed. In fact, so wholeheartedly did he approve of it that he put his money where his mouth was so to speak, by actually putting his own two sons through it, at the suggestion of his patron and friend King Agesilaos II.[16]

The reasons for Xenophon's approval of Sparta included personal gratitude to the city for giving him a home during his long exile; but the warmth of his approval was due – rather oddly, given Sparta's official disdain of theoretical speculation – to loftier, philosophical considerations. First, Spartan education was comprehensive in its organization. Second, it was compulsory for all Spartan boys from the age of seven until they attained their socio-political majority (as opposed to physical maturity) at eighteen. All Classical Greek political philosophers, apart from the near-anarchist Cynics, were agreed that comprehensiveness and compulsoriness were pedagogic desiderata for the production of 'good' citizens.

The most general Classical Greek word for 'education' was *paideia* or, as used by Perikles (above), *paideiai* in the plural; this picked out the immaturity, the 'child-ishness', of those receiving it. The Spartans, however, as so often (e.g., in their homoerotic sexual vocabulary: below), preferred their own local technical terminology and invented a word specifically for their own peculiar brand of education: *agôgê*. Literally, this means a 'leading' or 'raising' and might therefore be thought by us to be more appropriate for cattle than humans. But the Spartans could not have agreed less: on the contrary, they extended the cattle-rearing metaphor to the groups and sub-groups into which the boys were divided and subdivided by age (*bouai, agelai, ilai*), and the official in immediate overall charge of the training programme as a whole was likewise called literally the 'Boy-herd', *Paidonomos*. One modern school of thought would trace the terminology, like the origins of the *agôgê* itself, back to a (yet more) primitive Sparta whose economic basis was nomadic pastoralism rather than sedentary agriculture.[17] But if we suspend judgement on ultimate or immediate origins to concentrate instead on structure and function, the terminology does by itself speak worlds for the Spartans' rigidly hierarchical attitude to the process of education and gives a peculiar twist to our jocular description of unruly boys as 'little beasts'.

The *agôgê* began for a Spartan boy at the age of seven. We are not nearly so well informed about the education of Spartan girls, but there is reason for thinking that they, uniquely in Greece, did undergo some sort of formal, communal and public educational cycle. To some extent this seems to have resembled the 'primary' education given to Athenian boys, but in other ways, especially the physical exertions, it was a carbon copy of the Spartan boys' curriculum, and that is presumably an important clue to its meaning and function. For a Spartan woman's primary social rôle was not, unlike that of her Athenian sister, the performance of strictly domestic tasks – though she was expected to be able to run a home. Rather, the goal of her life was childbearing (*teknopoiia*), so that the reason for the exceptional treatment and valuation of Spartan girls before their relatively late marriage was broadly eugenic. Manpower in Classical Sparta was, as we shall see, a particularly pressing political issue, and it was in recognition of the woman's indispensable role that her childbearing was accorded equal public status with her warrior husband's fighting in battle.[18]

To return to (and stay with hereafter) the boys: at seven they were snatched away from the possibly loving arms and the certainly not so cosy warmth of their parental homes and placed, along with their age-mates (boys born between two fixed points, probably celebrations of one of the major annual festivals – the Hyakinthia, Karneia or Gymnopaidiai) in a kind of state *crèche* or public dormitory.[19] Thenceforth, until they retired from potentially active military service at the age of sixty (supposing by some chance they had managed to survive for that long), they were the property of the Spartan state (*to koinon*, e.g. Hdt. 1.67.5) rather than masters of their own destiny.

Indeed, right from his birth – or before it, if the *agôgê* be counted as in part a eugenic device – the Spartan state had intervened in a boy's life-trajectory at the expense of parental initiative and control. For it was not the boy's father who, as in other Greek states, decided as a matter of private business whether he was fit to be reared: that was the task of 'the elders of the tribesmen' (Plut. *Lyk.* 16.1). Ancient Sparta, like China today, was formally a gerontocracy, dominated by the members of the (minimum-age 60) Gerousia or (literally) Senate; as a foreign visitor is alleged apophthegmatically to have remarked, 'Only in Sparta does it pay to grow old' (Plut. *Mor.* 235f [60]).[20] If, moreover, the tribal elders' decision was negative, the infant's fate was to be hurled, as an un-person, a non-entity, debarred a priori from the civic community, into the mountain chasm known euphemistically as the 'Deposits' (*Apothetai*). That, though, was just the first of an endless series of official measures illustrating another general feature of Spartan social organization, namely the concerted and determined effort to minimize the importance of the family – or, to be more accurate, family life – and to emphasize rather the cardinal and overriding significance of communal ties.[21]

Some modern historians, abandoning their proper function perhaps, have condemned this Spartan approach to social engineering as 'totalitarian', as if ancient Sparta were Stalinist Russia, Hitler's Germany or present-day China.[22] But such an implied (and sometimes explicit) comparison is, I think, misleading in one crucial respect. For all Classical Greeks typically assumed that the interests of the state – or, as they saw it, the *koinônia* of the citizens, since there was no State (with a capital 'S') in a post-Hobbesian sense in Classical Greece[23] – overrode the interests of the individual; indeed, there is no ancient Greek word for 'individual' in that privatized sense.[24] Sparta, in other words, merely held an extreme version of the general ancient Greek view of the collectivity's prior claims, a difference of degree, not of kind. (Although differences of degree, if sufficiently extreme, can turn into differences of quality, I do not believe that to have been the case here.) Extremism, too, is arguably a key to all Sparta's extra-ordinary social practices, including its educational system. For the Spartans pursued their social objectives with a single-mindedly ruthless determination that either enthralled or appalled other Greeks.

It has been denied by Kennell (1995) that we can know anything very much about the details of a Classical Spartan boy's educational cycle. His grounds are that our mainly non-contemporary evidence, from the Hellenistic and Roman periods, reflects only the altered, post-Classical conditions, after Sparta had ceased to be a great power and had re-created, that is, invented anew, its educational system. That is too extreme and severe. There are sufficient fits between what we learn from Plutarch and what we have in Xenophon to justify the hypothesis of significant continuities, or at any rate the accuracy and extensiveness of Plutarch's reading in Classical sources.[25]

Between the ages of seven and twelve a Spartan boy 'studied' pretty much the same subjects as his Athenian counterpart (cf. Beck 1993): reading and writing, music and dancing, and physical exercise. But the Spartan boy studied them compulsorily, because successful passage through all the stages of the *agôgê* was a precondition, a sort of trial by ordeal, for his eventually qualifying for admission to full citizenship *via* election to a common mess (Singor 1999) at the age of twenty. Some Classical Greek commentators considered the *agôgê* to be, like the common messes, a 'democratic' feature of the Spartan system, precisely because it was equally compulsory for all (with the sole exception of the heirs-apparent to the two Spartan thrones); but since it was of the essence of a genuine Greek democracy that there should be no qualifications, let alone qualifying tests, for citizenship other than legitimate citizen birth, this would seem to be straining the sense of 'democratic' unduly.[26] Moreover, the conditions under which a Spartan boy 'studied' were inordinately tougher than those imposed on an Athenian of the same age. In particular, they included a rich variety of imaginatively nasty punishments, such as having his thumb bitten by the young adult 'teacher' for failing to answer a question sufficiently 'laconically' (i.e., snappily and wittily).[27] Then again, rather than going to a private 'school' (*didaskaleion*) the Spartan boy was taught his lessons in a kind of communal 'brat pack', in which he lived all his life away from home.

A final major difference between the 'primary' education of Athenian and Spartan boys was that for the latter the physical element of the regimen, which placed the emphasis on endurance, was far and away the most important. The Spartan boys were required to go barefoot in all weathers and terrains, wearing just a single homespun garment against the sometimes bitter cold of a Spartan winter. They had to cut reeds from the banks of the River Eurotas, with their bare hands, to serve as beds. They were kept on short rations from the public food-stores, so short, in fact, that in order to survive they had to, indeed were officially encouraged to, steal extra food – provided that they were not caught red-handed. If they were caught, they were punished severely, and corporally, not for stealing, but for being caught. Hence the apocryphal tale of the boy who stole a fox and rather than confess allowed it to gnaw through his entrails until he dropped down dead in front of a senior (Plut. *Lyk*. 18.1). The tale is of course literally untrue, even fantastic (how does one steal a wild animal?), but emblematically, mythically, it carries conviction. For if there were one member of the animal kingdom on which a Spartan boy's lifestyle could be said to be modelled, it was the fox, and *phouaddein* (a verb meaning to exercise the body) and *phouaxir* (noun denoting a late adolescent about to undergo the ritual whipping ceremony) were technical terms of the *agôgê* derived from the epichoric word for 'fox' (*phoua*, elsewhere in Greece *alôpêx*).[28]

After the age of twelve the boys' training regimen is said, almost incredibly, to have become even tougher. From now on, surveillance (the appropriate term, with its military and police connotations) of the boys by their seniors was made constant. The adolescent boys were subjected to the strict, quasi-military discipline that led Plato and Isokrates among others to speak of Sparta as a kind of barracks or armed camp. Each year-class was given its own name, and progress from one class to the next was made conditional upon undergoing and successfully surviving certain specified competitive tests, usually linked to the performance of some religious ritual. A well-known instance is the braving of whip-lashing seniors in order to steal the largest possible number of cheeses from the altar of (Artemis) Ortheia, a goddess of vegetation and fertility, and the patroller of the boundary between youth and adulthood.[29] Spartan education at this second stage thus resembled nothing so much as a paramilitary assault course. Music and dancing were not dropped from the curriculum, because they had religious associations and military applications, encouraging fitness and a sense of rhythm vital for successful hoplite warfare. But it took the Spartans to transform the joyous social activity of dancing into a parade-ground endurance test, as they did in the annual festival of the Gymnopaidiai (probably meaning Festival of 'Unarmed Dancing') celebrated at the height of Sparta's exceptionally hot summers.[30] Paramilitary physical exercises were the order of the day for the Spartan male pre-citizen youth.

This intensified period of training extended between the ages of twelve and eighteen, up to the threshold of manhood. It was thus principally as a manhood-ritual that the Spartans, like some other better documented, non-state societies, institutionalized the practice of pederasty. The *agôgê* provided a hospitable framework.[31] From the age of twelve, that is to say, a Spartan boy became eligible, or rather was officially obliged, to take a lover, an older male lover, usually a man who belonged to the youngest grade of adult male warrior citizens (the *eirenes*) and was not yet married. What might be considered child-abuse and legally actionable behaviour in our society was thereby not only officially approved but legally enforced in Classical Sparta. Precisely how the boys and young men paired off, we do not know, although there is good evidence that at least the sons of the Spartan elite did not have total freedom of choice. Nor do we know, because the sources are riddled with *arrière-pensée*, exactly what was the nature of the physical-sexual element in these relationships, although I am now more than ever convinced that Erich Bethe's original hypothesis of anal copulation (Bethe 1907) was right. In Athens it was counted degrading for the younger partner to be submitted to such supposedly bestial treatment; but a central motif of the latter stages of the Spartan *agôgê*, as Vernant (1991) has brilliantly demonstrated, was precisely the inversion or subversion of adult norms, and this method of sexual intercourse both inverted the norm of adult equality and subverted the sharp normative distinction drawn by all other Greeks between men and beasts. The overall aim of this ritualized pederasty is, however, clear, namely to foster the initiation and ease the incorporation of the youths into adult Spartan society as fully-fledged citizen warriors.

The older partner was supposed therefore to serve for the junior partner as a kind of substitute father and more generally as a rôle-model, the ideally courageous, resolute and loyal warrior, a paragon of what the Spartans called *andragathia* or 'manly virtue' (e.g., Hdt. 5.42.1). One anecdote (Plut. *Lyk.* 18.8), subject to the usual historiographical reservations, brings out this special educational significance of the pederastic pairing relationship particularly neatly. In one of the gruelling physical contests that were *de rigueur* for the adolescents a youth reportedly made the mistake of crying out in pain; but in contrast to the situation when one of the younger boys was caught in the act of stealing, it was not the clamant youth himself who was punished – but rather his older lover, for having failed to 'inspire' in his 'hearer' (these are the technical Spartan homoerotic terms) a properly Spartan *karteria* (endurance) and *enkrateia* (self-control).

When – and if (fatal accidents in the *agôgê* are easily predictable and in fact attested: Xen. *Anab.* 4.8.25-6) – a Spartan boy eventually reached the age of eighteen, the formal educational cycle came to an end and he entered the liminal phase of his life during which he was classified technically as 'boy-ish' (*paidiskos*), that is, between a 'boy' (*pais*) and a man (*anêr*). The majority of the *paidiskoi* now underwent, like their Athenian coevals known as *ephêboi* (those on the threshold of *hêbê*), a period of 'national service', as it were, preparing them for entry at the age of twenty (provided they passed the next test, election to a common mess) into the standing army of adult citizen warriors. However, apparently an élite few of the eighteen-year-olds were specially selected (again, we know not how nor by whom) to join a corps dubbed rather sinisterly the Krypteia or 'Secret Service Brigade'. On the one hand, in a manner characteristic of rituals of adult initiation, this period of service continued and indeed reinforced the inversion of adult norms that we have already detected in the second stage of the *agôgê*: the Kryptoi lived away from Sparta (whereas adult Spartans most of the time lived concentrated in the central place, unlike, say, the citizens of Athens, who resided in demes scattered throughout Attica, most of them outside the Athens Peiraieus 'City' area: see Chapter 2, above); they lived as isolated individuals, not as corporate members of a solidary band; they were armed only with a knife (not strictly a piece of military equipment), and they were obliged to fend and forage for themselves (whereas as adult members of a common mess in Sparta or as soldiers on campaign they had their material wants met from their common mess-fund or by the state's elaborately organized commissariat). They were, in short, as Vidal-Naquet has brilliantly described them, 'anti-hoplites'.[32]

But there is also an 'on the other hand'. A clandestine survival exercise superficially similar to the Krypteia is, I understand, prescribed today in the Western Isles of Scotland for recruits to Her Majesty's Marines. With this, rather crucial, difference: that trainee Marines are not also expected or required to go around intimidating or murdering the local population, without provocation. For the Kryptoi, however, that was the main and immediate object of the exercise: to kill, after dark, any of the Spartans' enslaved Greek population of Helots whom they should accidentally-on-purpose come upon in either Lakonia or more especially Messenia. The humane and philosophic Plutarch (*Lyk.* 28.4) could not bring himself to believe that the wise and gentle Lykourgos had instituted such a barbaric practice and preferred to ascribe it to Spartan paranoia following the great earthquake and subsequent Helot revolt of the mid-460s. But we, who perhaps do not even believe in the historicity of Lykourgos the man, let alone in 'his' singlehanded authorship of the Classical Spartan social, economic, military and political regime, need not be so squeamish. For the Krypteia's Helot-culling can be given a 'logical' explanation as an integral part of the aim and functions of the *agôgê* as a whole, and there is no reason not to suppose that it had been so interpreted and integrated from the very inauguration of the *agôgê* (somewhere in the mid-seventh century, as I should suppose).[33]

Which brings me back, finally, to the questions I asked at the start. Without wishing to appear reductionist, I suggest the answer to all three lies in a famous Thucydidean parenthesis: *aiei gar ta polla Lakedaimoniois pros tous Heilôtas tês phulakês peri malista katheistêkei* (Thuc. 4.80.3). Even if we read this, as the word-order may suggest we should, to mean 'So far as the Helots were concerned, most Spartan institutions had always been designed primarily with a view to security' (rather than 'Most Spartan institutions had always been designed with a view to security against the Helots'), and even if we take it that it was the Helots of Messenia rather than Lakonia who solely or mainly determined the Spartans' precautionary attitude, I would still want to insist, against a recent 'revisionist' trend of interpretation, on the absolutely fundamental causal role being ascribed here by Thucydides to the Helots.[34]

For if I may explicate that suitably laconic parenthesis (as Thucydides himself had no need to do), it was the Helots who constituted the Spartans' principal agricultural workforce and therefore enabled a Spartan citizen to pay the mess-dues on which his continued citizenship depended. More generally, it was the Helots who, by freeing the Spartan citizens *en bloc* from all productive labour (other than warfare), enabled their masters to develop their uniquely military society, a workshop of war. But at the same time it was also the Helots who so outnumbered the Spartan citizen population that the latter gave a unique spin to the normal Greek concern with legitimate procreation and developed a remarkably (and for many Greeks unacceptably) high public valuation of mothers. More especially, it was the Helots who, as the enemy within, 'lying in wait for their masters' disasters' in the striking phrase of Aristotle (*Pol.* 1269a37-9), necessitated as well as enabled the Spartans' military mode of life, and their unique transformation of a *polis* into a military-police state.[35] Within Sparta's elaborately and minutely organized machinery of prophylaxis against the Helots the *agôgê* fitted as smoothly and as noiselessly as any other moving part. For its principal aim and function, admirably served by the climactic Helot-culling, was to initiate Spartan boys and youths into Spartan manhood in such a way that they internalized the values of the adult citizen warriorhood.

So, indeed, it would seem to have operated successfully enough until 370/69, when for reasons that it would take – indeed, has taken me – a whole book (Cartledge 1987) to try to explain, the larger part of the Helots finally revolted successfully into not just personal freedom but full political autonomy and statehood, becoming citizens of the new – or, as the Messenians' own myth-history had it, reborn – *polis* of Messene. Sparta, the real historical city of Sparta, never recovered fully from that blow and remained a relatively minor, though none the less fascinating, state for the rest of antiquity.

However, by a sort of ideological compensation the idea(l) of Sparta, first propagated in literary form by radical Athenian conservatives such as Kritias (leader of the 'Thirty Tyrants' junta of 404-3) and Xenophon, has survived and flourished right down to our own day.[36] Not the least stirring element in the tradition of that ideal, or mirage, of Sparta has been its educational system, the *agôgê*, though in more recent times it has of course been cauterized, in Plutarchan fashion, of such monstrous carbuncles as Helot-culling. If, however, you accept the thesis of this essay, to remove

89

that feature would be to void the *agôgê* of its ultimate rationale and *raison d'être*. In contemporary political terms, therefore, it would be an unusually insensitive educationalist who followed in the footsteps of Kritias and Xenophon and seriously contemplated adopting the Spartan alternative.

8

The Politics of Spartan Pederasty

Introduction

The original published version of this essay (1981a) was a revised version of a talk delivered to the Cambridge Philological Society in 1980 under the title 'Sodom in Sparta'; the chairman introduced it as 'Sodomy in Sparta', which was only partly inaccurate. Since then, it has been reprinted as such, without authorization, in W.R. Dynes and S. Donaldson (eds) *Homosexuality in the Ancient World* (Garland: N.Y., 1992) and, with permission and addenda, in A.K. Siems (ed.) *Sexualität und Erotik in der Antike* (WdF 605: Darmstadt, 1988) 385-412, 413-15. The following version incorporates those addenda and includes further updates, but the argument remains substantially the same. It is rather homosexuality and pederasty in Classical Athens that have undergone the more substantial scholarly revision during the past two decades. Two major issues have been raised. First, granted that ancient Athenian homosexuality was not in all respects merely an earlier version of the homosexuality (or homosexualities) of contemporary Western societies, was it yet something fundamentally different? To put that rather crudely, were there 'gays' in Classical Athens? Second, was sex between Athenian males, and characteristically that means between a young adult citizen man and an adolescent pre-citizen boy or youth, conceptualized exclusively or predominantly in terms of power, or might the pleasure principle be equally or at any rate significantly in play also? The opposing positions are represented, with vim as well as some animus, respectively by Winkler 1990 and Davidson 1997.

There has, moreover, been something of a sea-change in conceptualization of the whole field during that same period, that is, not only in ancient history but in all historiography to do with sexual and other relations between and within the two sexes. To put it very briefly, histories of sexuality and 'women's history' have tended to be superseded by histories of gender: see, e.g., Larmour et al. eds 1997. Masculinity – ideas of what it is to 'be a man' – is now every bit as lively an issue as 'the position of women' or 'the woman question'. For simplicity's sake I cite here in illustration only two collective volumes, to one of which I was myself a contributor: Foxhall & Salmon eds 1998, 1999. I hope that my own approach to Spartan pederasty in 1980/1981 will be considered sufficiently compatible with these later approaches.

*

I

Homosexuality tends now to claim the same amount of space in the public prints that was not long ago lavished on the 'woman question'.[1] The incidence of AIDS and concern over the homosexual content of sex-education in schools have continued to make it a major news item. Its prominence in contemporary life is reflected in art. There are some sixty current journals dealing with the subject in all its multifarious manifestations. The experience of homosexuals in the Third Reich concentration camps and the rôle of the homosexual as hero in contemporary fiction have lately provided matter for book-length studies. Biographies of Havelock Ellis, Edward Carpenter and W.H. Auden and the memoirs of John Addington Symonds have discussed their subjects' writings on or practice of homosexual behaviour. The sexological team of Masters and Johnson have applied their peculiar quantitative approach to homoerotic physical response. Christian attitudes to homosexuality, notably in mediaeval Europe, have been extensively canvassed. In a less scholarly vein Edmund White has written of his travels in gay America; he is much concerned, as are Jeffrey Weeks and other members of the British Gay Left Collective, with the politics and political vocabulary of homosexuality. 'Homophobia' has entered the language. Many other illustrations could be given. In short, 'the love that dared not speak its name has become ... insistently communicative'.[2]

Thus the scholarly books devoted by K.J. Dover and F. Buffière to ancient Greek homosexuality represented the specifically ancient Greek fall-out of a veritable publishing explosion.[3] But they also made plain enough the gulf that separates prevalent western conceptions and practice of homosexuality from those of the Greeks.[4] In sharp contrast to our generally observed social and psychological norms, the Greeks did not see themselves as presented with an either/or choice between being 'a heterosexual' and being 'a homosexual'. They applied the same range of words, including both primary and metaphorical obscenities, with the same explicit and implicit meanings to both heterosexual and homosexual behaviour. Anyone – at least anyone in Classical Athens, which provides a disproportionate amount of our evidence – was free to declare openly the intensity of his homosexual response.[5] The Greeks did inevitably recognize that a very small minority of individuals might be predominantly or exclusively homosexual in orientation. But in so far as adult males practised homosexuality, this typically took the form of pederasty with an adolescent junior partner and occupied a defined, and transient, phase and place in the masculine life-cycle. For 'homosexuality' in ancient Greece, therefore, we can normally read 'pederasty', although – a useful reminder of the dangers of etymology – ancient Greek *paiderastia* was not the equivalent of our 'homosexuality'. For the latter, the Greeks did not have a word.[6] Finally, and this is in some ways the most important cultural difference of all, the Greeks did not labour under the incubus of a doctrinal tradition reinforced by ponderous temporal authority which holds that homosexual relations in whatever guise or context, or undertaken from whatever motives, are essentially diabolical or, on a slightly more charitable view, the manifestation of a shameful disease.[7]

The modern scholarly study of Greek homosexuality, which goes back well over a century and a half,[8] has inevitably had to wage a constant struggle to avoid importing extraneous moral judgements.[9] The other major obstacle to enlightenment is the state of the available evidence, which is such that recreating a picture of Greek pederasty has been well likened (by Buffière) to the problem of restoring a Minoan fresco. The five most important written sources are late Archaic and early Classical poetry; Attic comedy; Plato; Aeschines I (*Against Timarchos*); and Hellenistic homosexual poetry. Only two of these five, Attic comedy and Plato, inform directly on Spartan pederasty, and there is good reason to question the unvarnished truth of their testimony. Our fullest sources of information, Xenophon and Plutarch, are hardly more unimpeachable, chiefly because they are both purveyors of the 'Spartan mirage' – the partly distorted, partly imaginary picture of Sparta that its non-Spartan admirers needed and wanted to believe represented the reality. None the less, I hope to show that the evidence on the nature of Spartan pederasty, taken all together, can be made to yield further information and insights without being unduly tortured.

My other main aim is to elucidate the development and specify the functions of pederasty in Sparta between about the seventh and fourth centuries BC, the period of Sparta's greatest power and widest influence in the Greek world. Having established its nature with the degree of precision permitted by our inadequate ancient sources, I shall attempt to illuminate its social functions by locating it firmly within what has been called broadly the Spartan 'ritual system'; this is the strand of Spartan social organization comprising the *rites de passage*, the *agôgê* or compulsory and comprehensive educational cycle, the age-sets and the *syssitia* or common messes.[10] There is nothing novel in locating pederasty here: Xenophon and Plutarch both made the connection between pederasty and the *agôgê*, and recent scholarship has gone some way towards what I consider a plausible explanation of the connection by using, if not always appropriately, comparative ethnographic material.[11] No previous student, however, has fully brought out the crucial element in Spartan pederasty that may quite precisely be called homosexual politics.

II

Xenophon was a participant observer of Spartan society towards the end of the period under special investigation here. But he was far from a disinterested observer. Politically speaking, he was a 'lakonizer', and few would dispute that his pamphlet on the Spartan *politeia* (*Lak. Pol.*) is mainly apologetic, if not actually encomiastic. Xenophon was, moreover, a client of the powerful Spartan king Agesilaos II, on whose death in *c.* 360 he felt obligated to publish a eulogy trumpeting his hero as a 'thoroughly and completely good man' (*Ages.* 1.1, 10.1). In the eulogy Xenophon (*Ages.* 5.4-7; cf. 8.8, 10.2, 11.10) does not disguise his subject's strong homoerotic proclivities but seeks rather to make a virtue of them by stressing Agesilaos' exceptional *enkrateia*, his repression of the urge to indulge his inclinations physically.[12] The suspicion arises that what Xenophon retrojects into the distant past as the ideal of homosexual chastity prescribed by the notional lawgiver 'Lykourgos' may in fact be the present programme or official propaganda of the reactionary and homophile Agesilaos.[13] A final reason to doubt the objectivity of Xenophon's testimony is the fact that, wearing his philosophical hat, he in his *Symposium* (esp. 8.12) no less than Plato in his advocated the eschewal of physical gratification in sexual relations.[14]

The first chapter of the *Lak. Pol.* deals with *teknopoiia* (reproduction), the second with *paideia*, the education of those whom Xenophon refers to generically as *paides* (boys).The aims of this *paideia*, he says, are to produce adult men who are, obedient, respectful, and self-controlled; and he believes it to be a truth universally acknowledged that in respect of these qualities the men of Sparta surpass other Greeks. It is in this context that Xenophon felt constrained to comment on *paidikoi erôtes*, 'intimacy with boys', as the Loeb translator rather coyly renders the phrase.[15]

For 'Lykourgos', according to Xenophon, deemed it 'a very fine form of *paideia*' if an honourable or respectable man who was enamoured of the *psychê* (character) of a boy should try to make of him a friend in all innocence and spend time in his company. On the other hand, in total contrast to the practice in Boiotia and Elis, 'Lykourgos' had branded physical lust as highly shameful and so ensured that there was no more copulation (*aphrodisia*) between *erastai* and their *paidika* than there was between parents and their children or between brothers. 'I am not, however, surprised', Xenophon concludes, 'that some people find it impossible to credit this (*sc.* rule of physical chastity). For many states tolerate sensual gratification with boys'.

This brief account is hardly satisfactory. It is defensive and polemical in tone, elliptical in content, and one-sided in its emphasis on the physical element – or rather the alleged absence of same.[16] Xenophon does not say whether, other things being equal, every Spartan *pais* was expected, encouraged or required to enter into such a pederastic relationship. He uses the standard Greek terms for older lover, *erastês*, and younger beloved, *paidika*,[17] without even a hint that in Sparta as in Crete pederasty had generated a local technical vocabulary.[18] He sets the relationship in the context of Spartan education, but he does not specify at what stage of the *agôgê* a *pais* became eligible to act as *paidika* nor, beyond saying that the *erastês* should be *hoion dei* (honourable or respectable), does he indicate how this pederasty might help to produce obedience, respectfulness and self-control in the *paidika*. He says nothing about the age and social (as opposed to moral) status of the *erastês* or the duration of the relationship. Finally, Xenophon leaves it doubtful how rigorously the allegedly prescribed norm of physical chastity was in fact observed. For although he represents the taboo on physical gratification as equivalent to an incest taboo, he does not state that it was actually illegal; and even if it was, as later sources allege,[19] we have to allow for Xenophon's bitter observation in the appended fourteenth chapter of the *Lak. Pol.* that the Spartans now 'obviously do not obey ... the laws of Lykourgos'.

None of these many deficiencies is entirely made good either by our other directly preserved fourth-century sources, Plato and Aristotle, or by our most detailed single source on Spartan pederasty, Plutarch, who though writing around AD 100 drew directly or indirectly on fourth-century material among much else. According to the MSS of Plato *Smp.* 182a-c, the Athenian speaker Pausanias there contrasts Elis, Boiotia and other states where men are inarticulate and homosexual *erôs* receives unqualified approval with, on the one hand, states that give it their unqualified disapproval and, on the other hand, Athens and Sparta where the *nomos* is 'complicated' (*poikilos*). Yet in the later *Laws* (1.636b, 8.836a-c) Plato's mouthpiece, the anonymous Athenian interlocutor, twice emphasizes that in Sparta as in Crete male homosexual intercourse is not only tolerated but widely if not universally practised.

This seeming contradiction could be removed by the drastic expedient of tampering with the text of *Smp.* 182a-c.[20] Alternatively, and preferably, the contradiction could be treated as merely apparent. That is, the 'complication' of the *nomos* could be taken as a reference to the coexistence of official tolerance of state-sanctioned pederasty with condemnation of physical gratification therein, while Plato's Athenian could be read as either referring to homosexual acts outside approved pederastic relationships or implying that the *nomos* on pederastic chastity was not in practice observed. At any rate, Plato was the last person to have swallowed uncritically the anti-Spartan calumnies (if they are calumnies) of the Athenian comic stage.[21]

So far as Cretan practice is concerned, Plato's Athenian is explicitly supported by Aristotle.[22] But in the case of Sparta Aristotle's evidence may tend in the opposite direction, towards corroborating the picture drawn by Xenophon. In the course of a lengthy critique of the Spartan *politeia*, also in the second book of the *Politics* (cf. Herrmann-Otto 1998), Aristotle cites as one of its chief defects the fact that Spartan men are ruled by the women (*gunaikokratoumenoi*). This situation he considers typical of all military and bellicose peoples, except those like the Celts and some others who 'openly place a high social value on male homosexual intercourse'. The clear implication is that the Spartans did not so value it. However, Aristotle may of course have been referring only to intercourse between adult males and not to pederasty; and in any case his imputation of gynecocracy to Spartan society is not at all well founded (see Chapter 9).

Plutarch, especially in his 'biography' of Lykourgos, provides the most detailed information. On the whole, he follows Xenophon's general line on Sparta, but Xenophon's work was clearly not his sole source for his account of relations between Spartan *erastai* and their *paidika*, since his is appreciably more extensive. In describing the *agôgê* (*Lyk.* 16-21) Plutarch notes that, once the boys had turned twelve, their training was intensified. This change is implied too by late glosses on passages of Herodotus and Strabo which preserve the names given, from the thirteenth year on, to the age-sets into which the boys were divided between the ages of seven and seventeen inclusive.[23] It was at this stage of intensified training, says Plutarch (*Lyk.* 17.1), that '*erastai* began to frequent the company of those of the reputable (*eudokimoi*) boys who had reached that age'.[24]

Plutarch next describes how the supervision of the boys was so stepped up that it became impossible for a miscreant to escape detection and punishment. In this heightened surveillance the role of the boy's *erastês* was so important, according to Plutarch, that he shared in the good or bad reputation of his *erômenos* (beloved). On one occasion, so it was said, an *erastês* was actually punished for an ignoble cry emitted by his *erômenos* in some boys' combat. However, Plutarch continues, competition for the exclusive love of a particular boy did not exist in Sparta. To the contrary, those who conceived *erôs* for the same boy regarded this as an occasion for starting mutual friendships and would thenceforth strive tirelessly and in common to improve their shared *erômenos* to the utmost.

It would not, I think, be unreasonable to doubt this uplifting vision of philerastic co-operation, especially as Plutarch himself elsewhere insists, rightly, on portraying Sparta as a society shot through with officially sponsored competitiveness at all levels. It is hard to see why in practice pederasty should have been an exception to this rule, however desirable that might have been in theory. Rather more problematic, and important, is the restriction implied by Plutarch's claim that would-be *erastai* confined their attentions to 'reputable' boys. Does this mean that not all Spartan boys would expect or be expected to find an *erastês*? Or is this just another moralizing gloss by Plutarch designed to repudiate the charge of sensual gratification and so to represent Spartan customs in their most admirable light?

The fullest evidence bearing on this problem is to be found in Aelian's *Varia Historia* (3.10,12), written later in the second century AD, but the quality of this work is as variable as its subject-matter. Like his contemporary, Maximus of Tyre,[25] Aelian repeats the Xenophon-Plutarch line on Spartan pederastic chastity;[26] but he adds further information which if true would be highly significant. A fine and upstanding (*kaloskagathos*) Spartan, Aelian says, who did not act as *erastês* to boys of fine character (*kalôs pephukotes*) would be fined by the Ephors. This supports, indeed formally corroborates the public and official character of Spartan pederasty as it is presented by Xenophon and Plutarch. But again the specification of moral probity as a necessary condition of participation smacks of special pleading.[27] On balance, therefore, I am inclined to believe that for a Spartan boy to enter into a pederastic relationship after his twelfth year was the norm, whether or not he was strictly *eudokimos* or *kalôs pephukôs*. This hypothesis is at least consistent with the location of pederasty within the *agôgê*, which indisputably was compulsory for all Spartan boys (with one exception to be discussed later).

A strong supporting argument may be drawn from a characteristic feature of Spartan society as a whole, namely its general attempt to de-emphasize family life as opposed to communal life. Consistently with this, authority over boys was not the exclusive prerogative of their biological fathers but was transferred to the community as a whole as represented by the older age-grades. Xenophon (*Lak. Pol.* 6.1-2) speaks only of other fathers playing this authoritative role, but Plutarch quite clearly implies that *erastai*, who would not normally be fathers in the biological sense, acted as surrogate fathers to their *erômenoi*. This is a procedure familiar to anthropologists and psychologists, who classify it as displaced fathering.[28] It would, I think, be odd in this social context if only some, let alone a minority of, Spartan boys acquired such surrogate fathers after their twelfth year. In short, I have no doubt that the evidence of Xenophon and Plutarch is sufficient to establish the important conclusion that pederasty in Sparta was institutionalized and compulsory.[29] Whether or not sensual gratification, specifically sodomy, was a structural feature of institutionalized pederasty we cannot say for certain, though I would expect it to have been a widely prevalent feature.

I return to that point later. First, one final aspect of the nature of Spartan pederasty may usefully be examined through the literary sources, namely the possible duration of the pederastic relationship. In Plutarch's main discussion (*Lyk.* 17-18) there is no question but that, as in Xenophon, the *erômenos* or *paidika* is a *pais*, that is, below military age. Since Plutarch (like Xenophon) does not even glance at the age of the *erastês*, it seems legitimate to assume from their silence that in this respect at least Sparta conformed to general Greek practice and that Spartan *erastai* were normally unmarried young adults aged between about twenty and thirty.[30] However, in a relatively unnoticed passage a little further on (*Lyk.* 25.1), where Plutarch is talking about the Spartans' everyday activities, he says that those under the age of thirty 'absolutely never went to market but had

97

the transactions necessary for the management of their households carried out for them by their kinsmen and *erastai*'. A Spartan, in other words, might still be an *erômenos* after becoming a fully adult warrior and member of a common mess at the age of twenty, when he would grow his hair long and grow a beard.[31] Whether he would normally have had the same 'steady' *erastês* since his early teens we do not know. But we do learn from Xenophon's *Symposium* (8.35) that, in contrast to Theban and Eleian practice, it was not a feature of Sparta's military organization deliberately to post all *erômenoi* beside their *erastai* in line of battle.[32]

That exhausts the usable testimony of the partial (in both senses) literary sources on the nature of Spartan pederasty.[33] There are to my knowledge no relevant Spartan inscriptions to compare with the rock-cut graffiti from Thera and Thasos or the *kalos*-inscriptions from Athens.[34] The archaeological evidence from Sparta is only slightly less exiguous and is almost entirely confined to the sixth century BC. A series of bronze figurines of nude girls or young women with decidedly masculine physique could somehow reflect the taste in adolescent youths of the average Spartan *erastês*.[35] A drinking-cup depicting heterosexual (?) anal copulation apparently in a ritual context might be perhaps indirect evidence for the corresponding homosexual mode.[36] The terracotta votive masks depicting unbearded 'Youths' and bearded adult 'Warriors' found in the sanctuary of Ortheia cannot be connected with any religious dance of which we have specific knowledge;[37] it is therefore conceivable that some at least of these may have been dedicated by *erômenoi* and *erastai* in a sanctuary that had special connections with the *agôgê*. Finally, it may be worth mentioning a crudely made terracotta figurine of a man in the notably gymnastic act of fellating himself, though I hasten to add that the ancients saw nothing peculiarly homosexual in fellation as such.[38]

III

I turn now from the nature of Spartan pederasty in the fourth century BC to its possible origins, development and social functions in the seventh to fourth centuries. Any discussion should still begin from a celebrated article by Erich Bethe, almost a century old though it is.[39] Emboldened by the upsurge in the scientific study of homosexuality,[40] and strongly influenced by the not unconnected growth of anthropology,[41] Bethe proposed a strikingly novel interpretation of Spartan – or, as he loosely and misleadingly called it, Dorian – pederasty. He was far from being the first modern scholar to question its alleged chastity.[42] But he was the first to argue that the physical element, which he took to be anal copulation, was fundamental to the relationship between *erastês* and *erômenos*.

He suggested, on what were then the flimsiest of comparative ethnographic grounds, that the Dorians could have regarded semen as (in Edward Carpenter's somewhat fanciful formulation) 'the vehicle and special condensation of the soul'[43] and the injection of semen *per anum* as a means whereby the excellence (*aretê*) of the *erastês*, specifically his military excellence, might be transmitted in a quasi-magical way to the *erômenos*. This, Bethe proposed, was the earthy physical reality behind the idealization of the pederastic relationship purveyed by the extant literary sources, sources who were reflecting an increased civility and growing distaste for homosexual anal intercourse.

Further, Bethe affirmed that for the Dorians of the seventh, sixth and most of the fifth centuries pederasty was institutionalized: it was 'ein öffentlich anerkanntes, heiliges, Grund legendes und Leben bestimmendes Element'. So far as its origins were concerned, Bethe toyed with the hypothesis that the pederastic sexual act might have developed spontaneously as an initiation rite in the men's associations, that is as a *rite de passage* qualifying the initiate for entry as a full member into the adult male warrior community.

Reactions to this heady cocktail of comparative ethnography, philology and social history have been mixed.[44] My own – leaving aside the obviously false implications of the epithet 'Dorian'[45] – is generally favourable; but two stipulations regarding any use of comparative ethnographic evidence must be added. First, through the ignorance, reticence, indifference or distaste of western travellers, missionaries and anthropologists we are far less well informed cross-culturally on homosexuality than we could ideally wish.[46] Fortunately, though, we are not concerned here with the statistical incidence of homosexuality in global perspective, but with its form, location and functions in specific societies. In these respects the comparative approach, which cannot of course supply the primary evidence we lack, throws up enough of the right kind of material to suggest possibilities of explanation for the evidence we do have.

The second point of method has been well expressed by Finley: 'What anthropology illuminates about Sparta, paradoxically, are certain aspects of her lost early history rather than the Sparta from which the fossilized evidence comes'.[47] That is to say, even in the seventh century BC the Spartans were far from being a *Naturvolk* or 'primitive' people; and Sparta was not technically a 'smallscale' or 'pre-state' society. We cannot therefore treat Sparta and the communities studied by modern ethnographers and anthropologists as strictly analogous entities. If the evidence from the latter can shed light on the former, what will be illuminated are the origins or prehistory of certain Spartan customs or customary complexes. Comparative ethnography, in other words, may be used only as a kind of geological tool to lay bare the strata of cultural deposit below those exposed for us by the surviving literary sources.[48] It is the task of properly historical source-analysis to explain the functions of these customs or customary complexes within the society as a whole at different periods and to suggest why and how they might have been re-institutionalized or re-adapted to serve new functions.

Three contemporary 'primitive' societies – none of them known to Bethe, incidentally – seem particularly helpful for comparative purposes.[49] The first is that of the Aranda and neighbouring aborigines of central Australia. Among these tribesmen pederasty, as reported by a German missionary, was institutionalized within an initiatory framework.[50] An unmarried but fully initiated (i.e. circumcised and subincised) young adult male was allocated a youth aged between twelve and fourteen, who had to belong to a prescribed kinship category. The couple would then cohabit, often for several years, until the older partner married a woman. The junior partner meanwhile would be neither circumcised nor subincised, and he would be 'used as a woman', that is, required to play the passive role in anal copulation.

Among the Keraki Indians of Papua pederasty also occurred within the context of pubertal initiation.[51] A youth from the previous batch of initiates was privileged to sodomize the initiand for the first time. Thereafter, during some months of seclusion, the novice was freely available for this purpose to his seniors of the opposite moiety, always taking the passive role. Come the next round of initiation, the newly-initiated could now take the active role in his turn. Full adult status was acquired subsequently on heterosexual marriage. Williams presumed (in classically culture-bound fashion) that the real motive of the anal copulation was simple gratification, but the Keraki themselves believed that it was conducive to desirably rapid physical growth.[52]

The final and most extensively documented society is that of the Marind-Anim in what was Dutch New Guinea.[53] This is a sex-segregated, male-dominated society, once warlike, which divides the male youth into age-grades, prescribes elaborate rites to mark the passage from one grade to another and makes male homosexual anal copulation an integral part of initiation into full adult status. Sex segregation begins between the ages of five and eight, and from the onset of puberty the adolescent boy is placed under the tutelage of a surrogate father. The latter acts as master of ceremonies in the rituals symbolizing the boy's promotion from one age-grade to another and copulates anally with him in the men's house – a form of intercourse that the Marind, like the Keraki, link with physical growth. This actively sexual relationship between boy and surrogate father persists until the former's marriage at the age of nineteen or twenty, and the sexual act is considered to strengthen the bond between them. Even after adulthood and marriage homosexuality continues to occupy an unusually large slice of the sexual life of Marind males, and its general social approbation is reflected in their mythology. Marind women, on the other hand, have no separate or autonomous culture of their own, and emotional and physical relations between the sexes were judged to be unsatisfactory by van Baal.

We cannot, for the reasons stated, simply substitute 'Spartans' for 'Marind-Anim', despite the apparent formal similarities between their socio-sexual arrangements. This in effect is the error of Brelich.[54] He took the view that the developed Spartan *agôgê* of Classical times was not just somehow derived from an initiatory cycle of primitive type but actually was such a cycle. He therefore argued, since he rightly located the pederastic relationship within the *agôgê*, that pederasty was precisely an initiatory *rite de passage* in Sparta, although he accepted from Xenophon that – unlike the rites of the Marind and so on – the relationship was a non-sexual one.[55] I prefer to suggest that the comparative ethnographic evidence does not illuminate directly the Classical Spartan *agôgê* but should rather be taken to reveal a cultural horizon below, though not necessarily immediately below, that portrayed, with some bias, by Xenophon.

We do not know whether the ancestors of the Classical Spartans had anything approaching an initiatory-cum-educational cycle of age-sets and *rites de passage* when they first settled permanently in the south-east Peloponnese, probably in the tenth century BC.[56] But we do know that at some point or points thereafter the *agôgê* was minutely organized and that successful passage through it was made one of the requirements for admission to the ranks of the *Homoioi* or Spartiates, the adult male citizens of full status. This comprehensive and competitive *agôgê*, though it contained overtly religious elements and associations, was an essentially secular institution. It fulfilled the twin functions of socialization and education, and its character and objectives were overridingly military.[57] The historical question therefore to be addressed is this: how and why did this bundle of customs of disparate origins and purposes become institutionalized so as to perform the secular, pedagogical and military functions described or implied by the sources?

Certainty is of course impossible. On the principle of economy of hypotheses it would be easiest to suppose that at least the fundamentals of this social reorganization coincided with the pivotal economic and military reform that transmogrified all Spartiates into professional heavy-armed infantrymen. That reform, I have argued elsewhere, should belong in the first half of the seventh century.[58] The militarization of Spartan society inevitably embraced matters erotic;[59] and in the time of Xenophon, if our earlier discussion is on the right lines, pederasty was incorporated in the militaristic ritual-educational package that was the *agôgê*. But had it been institutionalized there from the start, *ex hypothesi* from the first half of the seventh century, or was it not introduced until later?

Again, the available sources reduce us to speculation. The earliest usable evidence for homosexuality in Sparta (I exclude Diod. 8.21) is provided by the Partheneia (Maiden Songs) of Alkman, who flourished around 600 BC.[60] But these were sung in a female and aristocratic ambience; and although there is reason to suggest that the education of Spartan girls was in some respects modelled on that of the boys, Alkman's evidence is insufficient to justify the inference that pederasty was universal and institutionalized in his Sparta.[61] Indeed, some lines of the rather earlier Spartan poet Tyrtaios (fr. 10.27-30 West) have been taken to point in the opposite direction, though I do not think they can be so pressed.[62] In short, there is no unambiguously positive evidence, literary or otherwise, for pederasty of any kind in Sparta before the late fifth century.[63] However, consideration of the conditions potentially favouring the incidence of male homosexuality there may suggest that pederasty could have been institutionalized within the developed *agôgê* sooner rather than later.[64]

In general terms the variables conditioning the incidence of homosexuality in different societies have been found to include the following: mode of child-rearing, segregation of the sexes, availability of partners of the opposite sex, age of marriage, polygamy, concepts of chastity and of sexuality, institutionalization of sexual activity, and concepts of status-role.[65] In the reorganized warrior community of Sparta from the seventh century onwards the emulation generated by the 'Greek contest-system' reached a pitch of intensity rarely paralleled elsewhere.[66] I return to the 'politics' of Spartan pederasty in my final section; but in this connection it is worth noting here what ethologists call the 'rank-demonstrating significance' of the pederastic sexual act.[67] The next relevant variable is the gap in time between the onset of puberty in the average Spartan male, probably at about the age of fourteen,[68] and his usual age of marriage, at about twenty-five. During this interval there was no absolutely rigid segregation of the sexes, it is true, and Spartan girls and women did enjoy certain freedoms denied to other Greek females.[69] But if all Greek cities were in a sense 'men's clubs', in Sparta probably the 'atmosphere of masculine exclusiveness was even more intense' than elsewhere.[70]

Next, there is the point insisted upon by Plato's Athenian in the *Laws* (1.636b; cf. *Theaet.* 162b, 169ab), namely the role played by gymnasia as hotbeds of homosexuality. The Spartans put a premium on gymnastic exercise; and, if Thucydides (1.6.5) is to be believed, it was they who invented the universal Greek customs of exercising stark naked and rubbing down with olive oil. In Sparta therefore the cult of the nude male body is likely to have been pushed to extremes, as it is known to have been in other less gymnastic Greek cities;[71] the festival of the Gymnopaidiai, instituted in 668 BC (Pettersson 1992), would seem to confirm this presumption. Finally, it is certainly the case that would-be Spartan *erastai*, freed from the daily round of productive toil, had the leisure required for the observation and courtship of potential *erômenoi*.

None of these conditions favouring the incidence of homosexuality and its early institutionalization in the form of a pederastic code is wholly peculiar to Spartan society, but their presence in combination suggests that the integration of institutionalized pederasty into the *agôgê*, whenever precisely it occurred, will at any rate not have been awkward.

IV

In this final section I turn from the nature of Spartan pederasty as
reported by the sources (Section II) and from its possible origins and
development within Spartan society (Section III) to the functions it may
have fulfilled in its institutionalized form. I concentrate on what may for
convenience be called 'the age of Xenophon', the later fifth and earlier
fourth centuries, both because this is in general the best documented
period of Spartan history and because it is only from this period that we
have detailed information on specific pederastic relationships between
Spartiates.[72] Both involve King Agesilaos II, before and after his accession,
who was an exceptional figure in many respects but not wholly so in this
regard.

If we are to believe Plutarch (*Ages.* 2.1, *Lys.* 22.6), Agesilaos in his youth
had become the *erômenos* of no less a figure than Lysander. There was
admittedly a tendency in antiquity to invent homosexual ties between
great men;[73] and Plutarch is our only source. On the other hand, Plutarch
was unusually interested in Agesilaos and proudly advertised the original
research he had done into a detail of his subject's life (*Ages.* 19.10). His
account, moreover, is circumstantial. For he tells us that it was when
Agesilaos was 'in the so-called *agelai*' (the 'troops' or 'herds' into which
Spartan boys were organized in the *agôgê*) that Lysander took him for his
erômenos; and Plutarch informs us, again uniquely but plausibly, that
Agesilaos was exceptional for a Spartan king in having gone through the
agôgê (since he had not been expected to succeed to the Eurypontid throne)
(*Ages.* 1.4).[74]

How should we interpret the significance of this pederastic relationship
between two members of the Spartiate elite? Plutarch is naturally anxious
on principle to deny any physical element to it whatsoever and alleges that
Lysander had been 'struck' (*ekplageis*) by the propriety of Agesilaos' nature. But Lysander was in any case unlikely to have been smitten with the
physical beauty of the congenitally lame and (for a Spartan) unusually
short Agesilaos; so even if it is accepted that Lysander's motives in
pursuing the royal prince were chaste and high-minded, physical consummation of the relationship once it had been established is not to be ruled
out.[75] However, ought we to take Plutarch's account of Lysander's motive
at its face value? I suggest rather that the relationship is best explained
in the context of the Spartan 'contest-system'.

Sparta was a quintessentially agonal society, permeated with ambition,
envy and distrust. Even citizenship, synonymous with membership of the
hoplite army, was the prize of long years of competitive struggle and came
only with the satisfaction of conditions above and beyond legitimate
citizen birth, including election to a common mess. It would be remarkable, to say the least, if institutionalized pederasty had not been somehow
linked to and expressive of the Spartan contest-system.

103

Xenophon gives pride of emphasis to the tutelary and educative function of Spartan pederasty, representing the older *erastês* by implication as a model and guide to his younger *paidika*. This is undoubtedly an important part of the truth. But he also speaks, if in idealized terms, of a friendship between the two, and this may be a significant clue. For in the ultra-competitive environment of Sparta pederasty could have been a way of enabling men 'to resolve their ambivalent orientation to men and to establish close relationships with some of them'.[76] The bond thus created could have been strengthened by physical consummation.

That seems to me a plausible account of how pederasty was linked through the nexus of friendship to the contest-system, and the longer the pederastic relationship lasted the more plausible it becomes. However, Spartan pederasty will also have been expressive of the contest-system. Despite Plutarch, competition between would-be *erastai* cannot have been eliminated, and the status of the successful *erastês* will have been enhanced in proportion to that of his *erômenos*. There were few bigger fish in the Spartan sea than the adolescent Agesilaos, and there can be little doubt that it was because he was such an outstanding catch that Lysander courted him.

In the late 430s, when their relationship will have begun, Lysander for all his cunning is perhaps unlikely to have anticipated his later rôle as kingmaker for Agesilaos (Xen. *Hell.* 3.3.14). But the potential utility to his future career of becoming the closest *philos* of Agesilaos and so linked intimately to the Eurypontid royal house will not have been lost on the exceptionally ambitious man who proverbially knew how to piece out the lion-skin of Herakles with the skin of the fox (Plut. *Mor.* 190e, 229b). Indeed, the connection will have recommended itself particularly, if, as seems to have been the case, Lysander had himself started life in somewhat reduced circumstances.[77] Pederasty, in other words, could have acted at Sparta in the age of Xenophon, as it certainly did in fourth-century Crete,[78] as a means of recruiting the political elite, the inner circle of those Spartans whom Herodotus (7.134.2) characterizes as 'the first in birth and wealth'.

That would be one aspect of the politics of Spartan pederasty in a narrow sense. Another, I believe, is to be detected in the *locus classicus* for all Spartan sexual politics, Xen. *Hell.* 5.4.20-33. In 378 BC the high-ranking Spartiate Sphodrias was arraigned on a capital charge before Sparta's supreme court. There was no doubt of his guilt, and Sphodrias in effect condemned himself by disobeying the Ephors' summons to stand trial. Yet Sphodrias was acquitted, thanks to the decisive vote of Agesilaos who at first and for good personal reasons had favoured condemnation. What caused his change of mind? Xenophon's unusually detailed narrative of the episode reveals that Sphodrias' son was the *erômenos* of Agesilaos' son Archidamos (the future Archidamos III) and vividly describes how Archidamos eventually plucked up the courage to intercede with his father on behalf of his beloved.[79] However, Xenophon is at pains to make clear that it was not because of his son's intercession that Agesilaos relented but because of Agesilaos' own fixed conception of the national interest: Sparta could not afford, in his view, to lose soldiers of Sphodrias' calibre.

This momentous and far-reaching decision of Agesilaos admirably expresses his influence in Sparta and nicely reflects the shortage of Spartiate manpower that was becoming critical.[80] But it has another, less immediately apparent significance too. For Sphodrias was not just an outstanding Spartan soldier but also a member of the Spartan political elite and, even more to the point, a member of the entourage of the other Spartan king, Kleombrotos. Now, Xenophon tells us in his post-mortem encomium of Agesilaos (*Ages.* 7.3) that it was his hero's studied policy to behave towards his political opponents in the city like a father towards his children. If we translate that pious simile into the language of practical political reality, it means that Agesilaos sought to nullify domestic political opposition (of which there was a good deal throughout his long reign), and if possible to turn opponents into friends, through the dispensation of patronage (cf. Cartledge 1987: ch. 9).

I therefore find it hard to believe that it was merely a coincidence that his son should have been the *erastês* of Sphodrias' son, even if the latter really was 'the most handsome and reputable of his age-group'. Agesilaos will surely not have squandered the opportunity to make the pederastic system work to his own political advantage by fostering this relationship, as I imagine Agesilaos' father Archidamos II had fostered his son's with Lysander. For it gave him an intimate line of communication to the opposing royal circle and, through his decisive role in the acquittal of Sphodrias, a hold over it that was to be put to excellent effect in the increasingly bitter struggle to control and direct Sparta's foreign policy during the 370s. Earlier in the *Hellenika* (5.3.20) Xenophon had related that Agesilaos, by then aged at least fifty, had enjoyed engaging in *paidikoi logoi* with Kleombrotos' predecessor: I doubt very much that this was just idle chit-chat.[81]

To conclude: much of this essay, especially in the final section, has been speculative. The nature of the ancient evidence makes that inevitable. But I hope readers will at least agree that Spartan pederasty is a topic whose significance is by no means to be confined to the erogenous zones.[82]

9

Spartan Wives:
Liberation or Licence?

Introduction

The ultimate source of this chapter is a paper delivered before the Oxford Philological Society in November 1976. I received helpful comments from members of the large audience, in particular Pierre Vidal-Naquet (the origins of a lasting friendship) and the late Simon Pembroke. The published version of that paper appeared in 1981, soon enough to provide a target for an entire American doctoral thesis: Kunstler 1983 (summarized in Kunstler 1987). What divided us chiefly, and divides scholars still, is the issue of the extent to which adult Spartan women (to all intents and purposes, wives) were – if the phrase may be excused – masters of their own destiny. We are all now today even more aware than some of us were twenty years ago of the extent to which Classical Sparta is a construct, or fabrication, of our Athenian or Athenian-influenced literary sources. A key part of that construct was the 'liberated' Spartan woman, both liberated, that is, from 'normal' male controls and liberated in her lifestyle within and yet more strikingly outside the household ('home' doesn't seem quite the right word): see recently Millender 1999. In gender terms, as we should now more easily put it (cf. Introduction to the previous chapter), the Spartan women were seen as 'natural' women, allowed by the curiously uxorious men of Sparta to indulge freely their innate female emotions and passions to such an extent as to overturn the equally 'natural' hierarchy of male sexual and social domination. This constructed Sparta of the non-Spartan imagination was a reversed world, with the women on top, fulfilling in fact a Delphic prophecy delivered jointly to the Argives and Milesians that was intended surely as counterfactual: 'when female conquers male and expels him ...' (Hdt. 6.77, trans. R. Waterfield).

I tried to suggest in 1981, what I still believe today, that it is necessary to correct significantly this misleading impression given by the sources: in my view, Spartan women did indeed enjoy certain freedoms, including legal freedoms, that were denied to their Athenian counterparts, but they were not, to put it mildly, as liberated as all that. Broadly speaking, Zweig 1993 prefers to follow Kunstler – and before him Pomeroy 1976 (see esp. n. 112, below) – in allowing for greater female initiative than I would, whereas Dettenhofer 1993 inclines more to my position. Thommen 1999 is a useful recent review, adding little but providing a very helpfully up-to-date bibliography.

*

I

A quarter of a century ago, the neologism 'sexist' gained entry to an Oxford Dictionary, *The Advanced Learner's Dictionary of Current English*, third edition (1974); it was glossed as 'derisive of the female sex and expressive of masculine superiority'. Thus 'sex kitten', which is still defined in exclusively female terms in the latest, tenth edition of *The Concise Oxford Dictionary* (1998), finally met its lexicographical match.

This point about current English usage has of course a serious, and general, application. For language reflects, when it does not direct, prevailing social conceptions. It is not accidental, for instance, that there is no masculine counterpart to the word 'feminism'. 'Male chauvinism', the nearest we have come to coining one, is more emotive than descriptive and so involves ambiguity; while 'sexism', even when it is given an exclusively masculine connotation, is still, formally, sexually neutral. 'Feminism', by contrast, unequivocally denotes the striving to raise women to an equality of rights and status with men – or should do, anyhow.[1]

It has been suggested that there were inchoate feminist movements or tendencies in the ancient Greek world, for example in the Classical Athens of Aristophanes and Plato (where, as we shall see, they would certainly not have been out of place).[2] But feminism in the contemporary sense did not really emerge before the eighteenth century; and in Britain, for instance, it was only with the passage in 1975 of the Employment Protection, Equal Pay and Sex Discrimination Acts that women raised themselves on to an all but equal footing with their male fellows – at any rate in the technical, juridical sense.[3]

Despite such advances, there is obviously still ample room for controversy over precisely what counts as sexual equality, and over the ideas and practices consistent with its achievement or maintenance. What is not controversial, on the other hand, is that scholarly interest in all sorts and conditions of women has run at unprecedentedly high levels since the 1960s. Predictably, if somewhat belatedly, some of this interest rubbed off on students of the ancient world. In 1970 Ste. Croix could still legitimately complain that 'ancient historians, one may think, too readily forget that women are, after all, half the human race'.[4] But since then the steady trickle of studies on women in Graeco-Roman antiquity turned into a small flood,[5] and in 1976 there first appeared a scholarly work which ventured to cover and summarize the whole field.[6]

The women of ancient Sparta, however, form something of an exception

107

to the rule of oblivion suggested by Ste. Croix. The reason for this is, I think, fairly straightforward. As Winwood Reade nicely expressed it in the high Victorian era, 'In Greece a lady could only enter society by adopting a mode of life which in England usually facilitates her exit'.[7] In other words, the female citizen population of Sparta were not Victorian 'ladies'. They enjoyed the extraordinary and perhaps unique distinction of both being 'in society' and yet behaving in a socially unacceptable manner. Or so it seemed to non-Spartan males from at least as early as the sixth century BC, though the particular aspects of female Spartan behaviour which have excited hostile comment over the centuries thereafter have varied greatly according to the epoch and outlook of the individual contributors to the far from moribund 'Spartan tradition'.[8]

On the other side of the fence, however, from at least the late fifth century BC onwards there have been male 'Lakonizers', admirers of all things Spartan, who have found Spartan sexual mores and institutions worthy of both praise and imitation.[9] Indeed, following the rise of modern feminism, the ideal of female emancipation has joined the ranks of 'the most diverse ideas ... formulated or recommended with Spartan aid'.[10] Thus, what to the sixth-century BC Sicilian Greek poet Ibykos and his like-minded successors had seemed outrageous or at least unseemly in the behaviour of the Spartan 'fair' or 'gentle' sex has also been portrayed in recent times as a shining example of women's liberation in practice.[11] The main aim of this chapter will be to try to strike a balance between these extreme attitudes – so far, that is, as this is possible for a male ancient historian largely dependent in the end on exclusively male literary sources.[12]

My secondary aim is to provide, space permitting, a complete and accurate account of what we can (and cannot) know, or reasonably assert, about the social and economic position of adult Spartan women of citizen status in the sixth to fourth centuries BC – or, what comes to the same thing, about the position of those of them who entered the estate of matrimony.[13] For although they have earned a regular place in the scholarly literature on Greek women as a whole and on Spartan history in general, justice is rarely done, it seems to me, either to the importance of the subject[14] or to the complexity, variety and, not least, the fragility of the evidence.

One final preliminary point of method: in a stimulating Inaugural Lecture delivered before Oxford University the distinguished Americanist Carl Degler asked whether there was a 'history of women'.[15] He was responding to a certain 'political and polemical' feminism that was then prominent, and by his question he meant to ask whether there was a history of women in the same sense that there is a history of, say, blacks in America or of any other 'minority' group.[16] That is, can a purely sexual difference be regarded as in and of itself historically significant, or are women, for all important purposes, so inextricably tied to men that 'women's history' cannot be conceived of as a separate and autonomous subject of study? Degler's own answer went as follows (1974: 31):

> Women are different from men, both in the roles they have been assigned or have assumed historically and in their biological make-up. History, in short, affects them differently from men, just as they affect history differently. Their past cannot be subsumed under the history of men. What we need to recognize is not that women and men are the same – as certain political and polemical goals might suggest – but that they are different. For it is that difference that justifies, indeed requires, a history of women.

The extant evidence for the women of ancient Sparta regrettably does not allow us to consider in much detail the factor of 'biological make-up' on which Degler rightly places great emphasis. However, although I think I agree in principle that there could be a history of women such as Degler delineates, I would argue that even women's biology may be conditioned if not determined by their society's existing gender-power relations (cf. Scott 1986) – anatomy is not always, quite, destiny; and so I am far more concerned than perhaps he would be to show that the real significance of the Spartan women under study here flows from their integral place within the structure and ideology of Spartan society as a whole.

II

I select as a map and compass the views on Spartan women expressed in the third quarter of the fourth century BC by Aristotle in the *Politics* (1269a29-1271b19), for three main reasons. First, Aristotle was unquestionably the greatest sociological thinker of Antiquity.[17] Second, despite his attendance at Plato's Academy, he was singularly free from that 'Lakonomania' which infected certain upper-class circles in democratic Athens.[18] Third, however, he fully shared the dominant Greek male conception of women as inferior in his society; and, as Theodore Besterman has remarked of Voltaire in a different connection, his language 'was the language of his time, and we must not expect even the greatest of men always to rise above their environment'.[19]

Following an examination of the ideal states proposed by Plato and two others, Aristotle turns in Book II to the three polities which had generally been accounted the best of those actually existing – Sparta, Crete (treated as a political unit for theoretical purposes) and Carthage. He prefaces his discussion of Sparta with the observation that all polities must be evaluated in accordance with two different kinds of criterion. According to the first, any positive law shall be adjudged good or bad in the light of the laws of the ideal state – Aristotle's own version of which is exposed later, in the seventh and eighth Books. According to the second, a law shall be adjudged good or bad according as it is, or is not, consonant with the idea or postulate (*hupothesis*) and character of the constitution (*politeia*) set before the citizens (or, following a variant MS reading, himself) by the lawgiver.

As for the first type of criterion, Aristotle self-confessedly follows the Plato of the *Laws* (1.625c-638b; contrast *Rep.* 8.544c) in adjudging the *hupothesis* of the Spartan lawgiver reprehensible on the grounds that it is one-dimensional and deals with only a part of virtue, the military part (1271a41-71b10).[20] How well, then, does Sparta measure up when evaluated according to the second kind of criterion? Poorly, is Aristotle's categorical answer – a judgement he seeks to substantiate by discussing in turn the seven main areas in which he finds it especially faulty, viz the Helots, the women, the Ephorate, the Gerousia, the common meals, the system of naval command, and public finance. (His aspersions on the dual kingship seem to me to fall rather under the first type of criterion: see Chapter 5.) I shall restrict myself to the second item, the prominent placing of which cannot be accidental, and scrutinize Aristotle's seven specific criticisms of the Spartan women.

The first of these is addressed to *hê peri tas gunaikas anesis*, which could mean either 'the licence permitted to the women' or 'the licentiousness of the women' (the Greek is formally ambiguous). Such licence or indiscipline (*anesis*) is deemed deleterious both to the general intention of the constitution and to the happiness or well-being of the state. Since women constitute half the citizen population of any state (cf. *Rhet.* 1361a10-12), in *politeiai* where their condition is degenerate half the state must be considered unregulated by law – an exaggerated conclusion hardly entailed by the premises, but one that, again, accords with the views of the Plato of the *Laws* (1.637c, 6.781a, 7.806c). In what, then, does this degeneracy consist? Whereas the state is hardy as far as the male citizens are concerned, the women abandon themselves utterly to every sort of intemperance and luxury.[21] Once more, this is at the very least a sweeping generalization, perhaps to be read in light of Simone de Beauvoir's plausible claim that 'fear is always mixed with the blame attached to woman's licentious conduct'.[22]

The consequence of the women's intemperate luxury affords Aristotle his second ground for criticism, namely that in Sparta wealth is (too) highly valued.[23] The damage this caused was aggravated by the third ground of complaint, the fact (as he sees it) that the Spartan men were ruled by their women. Aristotle takes this (unnatural) state of affairs to be typical of all military and warlike peoples, with the exception of the Celts and a few others who openly place a high value on male homosexual intercourse. Then, after some further general remarks, Aristotle comments vaguely that at the time of Sparta's domination – that is, before 370 BC and perhaps specifically from 404 to 371 – many things were managed by the women.[24]

Another consequence of the women's intemperance (*akolasia*), and Aristotle's fourth ground for criticism, is that they exercised an extremely harmful influence even over the daring of the state. For example, during the Theban-led invasion of Lakonia (370/69 BC) they were not merely useless, like women in other states,[25] but actually produced more confusion than the enemy – yet again, somewhat of an overstatement, although the women's poor showing is attested by the well-informed and usually pro-Spartan Xenophon (*Hell.* 6.5.28; cf. Plut. *Ages.* 31.5-6).

Aristotle now pauses to consider how the indiscipline of the women came to be. It was, he says, only to be expected. For during a series of wars against their Peloponnesian neighbours the men were away from home for long periods and were made ready for the lawgiver, Lykourgos, by their military mode of life. The women, by contrast, traditionally succeeded in resisting the attempt of Lykourgos to submit them to the laws.[26]

It is the women themselves, therefore, according to Aristotle, who are responsible for their indiscipline, though he implies that the men and their lawgiver deserve the blame for it. Apparently recapitulating what he has just said, he then states that the degenerate condition of the women not only gives the constitution an air of indecorum but also engenders material avarice. Actually, that is by no means a straightforward résumé of his immediately preceding remarks. The charge of avarice may indeed be regarded as specifying the general statement that wealth is highly valued in Sparta. But the accusation of indecorum is entailed only if a crucial hidden premise is interpolated. This premise is the view expressed earlier in the *Politics* (1254b13-16; cf. *Poet.* 1454a20-2), that women as a sex are by nature inferior to men and marked out from birth for subordination to and rule by them.[27] Hence, the indecorum of the Spartan polity follows from the fact that the men are ruled by the women (*gunaikokratoumenoi*), since the latter have stolen the men's birthright. For in Aristotle's thoroughly conventional masculine opinion, as expressed in his *Rhetoric* (1361a6-8), female excellence was not properly political but consisted (merely) in bodily beauty and physique, sexual self-control and modesty, and liberal industriousness.

Mention of avarice leads Aristotle understandably to his fifth ground for criticism: the unevenness of the distribution of private landed property in Sparta. The women's contribution to this was that by the time Aristotle was composing the *Politics*, around the 330s,[28] almost two-fifths of the whole country (that is, Lakonia, since Messenia had been lost to Sparta in 369) was in their control. In fact, for three reasons, ownership of real property was concentrated in a few Spartan hands (cf. 1307a34-6): first, the laws did not prevent the gift or bequest of land; secondly, there were many heiresses (*epiklêroi*), who might be married off at the discretion of their father or his nearest male relative; finally, dowries were large.

This apparently dominant position of rich women in the Spartan land-tenure regime occasioned Aristotle's sixth criticism, which was directed against the critical shortage of male Spartan military manpower (*oliganthrôpia*). In a country capable in his view of supporting 1,500 cavalrymen and 30,000 hoplites – he must now be thinking not only of Lakonia but also of adjacent Messenia, which the Spartans had controlled from *c.* 650 to 370 BC – the adult male citizen body sank to less than one thousand. As a result the state could not withstand a single blow, the defeat by the Thebans at Leuktra in 371. Sparta, to put it laconically, was destroyed through *oliganthrôpia.*

Aristotle next reports a tradition that in the days of 'the ancient kings' citizen numbers had been maintained by extending the citizenship to foreigners; allegedly, the citizen body had once numbered as many as 10,000. But the correct way to have ensured adequate manpower, in his view, would have been to keep landed property more evenly distributed. Instead – and this is Aristotle's seventh and final criticism of the women, although he does not spell out what their active role in this may have been – the Spartans had a law designed to stimulate the production of (male) children (*teknopoiia*). Under its provisions the father of three sons was exempted from military service, the father of four[29] from all state burdens. However, given the unequal distribution of landed property and – what Aristotle tacitly assumes – the normal Greek system of equal patrimonial inheritance by sons, many sons inevitably fell into poverty. That is, they became too poor to fulfil the condition of full Spartan citizenship which Aristotle faults a little later on (1271a26-37), the contribution of a minimum quantity of natural produce to a common mess.

III

Just how accurate or apposite these criticisms are, and to what period (if any) in the development of Spartan society they are peculiarly applicable – these are perhaps the two most important questions under consideration here. First, however, it must in fairness be pointed out that Aristotle's seemingly devastating critique would not have, or did not in fact, cut much ice with two authors on whose work, *faute de mieux*, we are bound to lean heavily.

Aristotle need not have read Xenophon's selective and mistitled essay on the Spartan constitution, the *Lakedaimoniôn Politeia*.[30] But Xenophon, if hardly objective, was at least a 'participant observer' of Spartan society in the first half of the fourth century, and his essay very likely offers a representative sample of the kind of pro-Spartan arguments Aristotle may have been seeking to rebut. The indefatigable Plutarch, on the other hand, who was writing in about AD 100, follows Xenophon's general 'line' on Sparta, at least as he conceived Sparta to have been down to *c.* 400 BC. He had certainly read not only the *Politics* but also the Aristotelian *Constitution of the Spartans*;[31] and in his biography – or rather hagiography – of Lykourgos he felt constrained to reply explicitly to what he regarded as Aristotle's unfair or misplaced criticisms.[32] Clearly, the moralizing apologists Xenophon and Plutarch are far from unimpeachable witnesses to the

112

truth about Spartan women, but, as will be seen, their testimony can at least be used to modify and supplement that of the (in some respects) more scientific and objective Aristotle.

IV

I propose now to discuss the many controversial issues in developmental terms, that is, by tracing the lives of Spartan women in the sixth to fourth centuries BC from the womb to (in some cases) the tomb. I use the vague term 'Spartan women' advisedly. The available evidence does not permit inferences of a statistical nature about the experience of a 'typical' Spartan woman, although in some contexts it will be necessary and possible to distinguish that of rich women. Besides, the literary sources who provide the fullest pictures are, as I hope has already been made clear, highly, and consciously, selective, and they are all non-Spartan and male. Their selectivity and bias may, however, be offset to some extent by tapping sources of evidence, in particular inscriptions and material objects, which they themselves did not see fit, or had not devised the techniques, to utilize.

The evidence for the weaning and rearing of Spartan girls is scanty and not worth discussing in detail.[33] But an objection must at least be lodged against a modern inference drawn from an anecdote in Plutarch's *Lykourgos* (3.1-6), that all girl-babies in Sparta were normally reared.[34] This would have been extraordinary, I think, in terms of general Greek practice at all periods,[35] quite apart from the evidence suggesting that in Sparta the exposing of neonates was fairly frequent and that women were, if anything, in relatively short supply.[36] But we are not in any case bound to attribute a universal validity to the passage in question nor indeed to accept the construction placed upon it by (e.g.) Lacey and Pomeroy.[37]

It is necessary, however, to dwell rather longer on two cardinal aspects of the childhood and adolescence of Spartan women. First, whereas the Spartan boy left the parental household for good at the age of seven to embark upon the gruelling system of state education known as the *agôgê*, the Spartan girl – like her counterparts in other Greek states (cf. Hesiod, *Op.* 520) – resided with her parent(s) until marriage. More specifically, she continued to reside with her mother, for the matricentric character of a Spartan girl's domestic life was heavily accentuated by the fact that her father was expected to spend most of his time living communally and in public with his male peers – indeed, all of his time, should he have become a father before the age of thirty (below, Section VII). This may help to explain the alleged incidence of female homosexuality involving an older woman and an adolescent girl reported by Plutarch (*Lyk.* 18.9).[38]

Second, however, unlike girls in all other Greek states, Spartan girls were also given some form of public education. Whether or not we accept the attractive suggestion of Nilsson[39] that they underwent a course of training parallel to the boys' *agôgê*, Spartan girls undoubtedly were edu-

113

cated in a sense other than trained to perform sedentary, and in ancient Greece exclusively feminine, tasks like weaving (Xen. *LP* 1.3-4; Plato, *Laws* 7.806a) and baking (Herakl. Lembos 373.13).[40] The running races mentioned in Xenophon (*LP* 1.4) and Plutarch (*Lyk.* 14.3; *Mor.* 227d) and paralleled in other sources (Theokr. 18.22; Paus. 3.13.7; Hesych. *s.v.* *'en Driônas'*) very likely had a ritual significance,[41] as certainly did the choral dancing in which Spartan maidens participated both in Sparta and at sanctuaries elsewhere in Lakonia and Messenia.[42] But the throwing of the discus and javelin, and the trials of strength or wrestling also attested by Xenophon and Plutarch, presumably had a mainly secular character. It is, though, a little hard to credit the evidence of Euripides in his *Andromache* (597-600) that the girls wrestled naked with the boys.[43] This looks too much like a deliberate travesty in line with the view of Euripides – or strictly of Peleus, father of Achilles – (595-6) that it was impossible for a Spartan maiden to be sexually modest (*sôphrôn*).[44]

Such an accusation does, on the other hand, appear to have some basis in Spartan actuality. For both total nudity in public (at religious processions: Plut. *Lyk.* 14.4-7) and the wearing of a revealingly slit mini-chiton (Pollux 7.54-5)[45] – hence the opprobrious epithet 'thigh-showers' first known from Ibykos (fr. 58 Page)[46] – are strikingly confirmed by a series of Spartan bronzes, mostly of the sixth century.[47] These figurines and mirror-handles portray girls or young women with underdeveloped or de-emphasized secondary sex characteristics. It is not, I think, fanciful to associate this feature with the strongly homosexual orientation of the average Spartan male.[48] But what is most significant is that in Greek art generally the nude female figure is not at all frequent before the fifth century and is then normally reserved for women of low social status. The shock felt by non-Spartan, and especially perhaps Athenian, males at such uninhibited – indeed, indecent because almost masculine – exposure may be comprehended the more readily if, as I believe possible, Spartan girls appeared publicly before males in the nude (or at least scantily clad) even after reaching puberty.[49]

According to Xenophon and Plutarch, the Spartan girl's education was confined to physical exertions and designed to serve exclusively eugenic ends, that is, to produce strong mothers of healthy infants and to alleviate the pangs of childbirth (in which, we infer, maternal mortality was not infrequent).[50] No doubt, eugenic considerations were important, particularly perhaps after *c.* 500 when, as we shall see, official steps were taken to further citizen procreativity. But there is also evidence to suggest that the things of the mind were not entirely neglected.

According to Plato in the *Protagoras* (342d), there were Spartan women who prided themselves on their learning and culture (*paideusis*). He refers specifically to their attainment in speech (*logoi*) – notoriously, Spartan women did have something to say and were reputedly not afraid to say it publicly[51] – and singles out their contribution to quintessentially Spartan brachylogy. But he also mentions their *philosophia* in this passage and, in the *Laws* (7. 806a; cf. *Rep.* 5. 452a), their participation in high culture (*mousikê*). Not much weight can be placed on the testimony of Plato, the philo-Lakonian or at least unorthodox Greek educationalist, and at any rate in the *Protagoras* passage irony is to be suspected.[52] But Aristophanes seems to refer in the *Lysistrata* (1237; cf. *Vesp.* 1245-7) to a Spartan poetess called Kleitagora;[53] and the late antique writer Iamblichos (*Vita Pyth.* 267) names several female Spartan Pythagoreans. Finally, the epigraphical evidence, though formally ambiguous, at least does not contradict the view that at any rate some Spartan women were basically literate.[54] Basic literacy, after all, was the most that the ordinary Spartan man was expected to acquire, inside or outside the *agôgê*.[55]

The real significance of this education, in both its physical and its intellectual aspects, is that it reflects an official attempt to maintain some form or degree of parity between the sexes. The chief political function of this apparent equality of treatment, however, was not one that a modern feminist would necessarily approve, but rather to socialize the non-military half of the population in the values of a peculiarly masculine warrior culture.[56] At all events, it was certainly not designed to promote companionship or partnership in marriage; as we have seen, Aristotle attributed what he took to be the indiscipline of the women, not to the equality of their education, but to the (surely genuine) separateness of Spartan married life. On balance, therefore, I incline to think that the introduction or general enforcement of the male *agôgê*, in the course of the seventh and sixth centuries, diminished the status of women in Sparta.[57] Thereafter, much as elsewhere in Greece though in a peculiarly singleminded way, the primary emphasis in the upbringing of girls was on preparing them for their future subordinate roles as wives and mothers of warriors.

V

The ostensible purpose of the physical side of a Spartan girl's education may, then, have been to cultivate eugenic strength. It might also be argued, however, that a by-product of her vigorous open-air existence in the demanding Spartan climate was the far-famed beauty of Spartan women.[58] Lysistrata, the eponymous Athenian heroine of Aristophanes' play (*Lys.* 79-83), marvels with considerable comic hyperbole at Lampito's muscular virility; but she praises also the Spartan woman's skin and her wondrously developed breasts.[59] The other facets of Spartan feminine beauty singled out, for example, by the Spartan poet Alkman in his maiden-songs of *c.* 600 BC[60] are less recondite, indeed conventionally aristocratic: above-average height, slim, well-turned ankles, and long, flowing, fair hair.[61] But even the latter has a special point in the Spartan context (below, Section VII). In fact, feminine beauty *per se* may have had an important function to perform in my next pair of topics, the timing and purposes of marriage.

We are quite well informed about the precise though diverse ideas held by the Greeks on the proper age for a girl to get married.[62] This diversity is of course only to be expected. Marriage was the most crucial *rite de passage* in any Greek girl's life,[63] and different states and thinkers enjoined or advocated different norms in accordance with their evaluation of the status and functions of women. As far as Sparta is concerned, however, our information is disappointingly imprecise.

Lykourgos, according to Plutarch (*Mor.* 228a) set limits to the age of marriage. The existence of an upper age-limit is apparently confirmed by references to a Spartan law against late marriage (Plut. *Lys.* 30.7; Pollux 3.48, 8.40); and Plutarch (*Kleom.* 1) provides evidence for a minimum age too. But these regulations, like the law enforcing marriage itself (below), almost certainly applied only to the men.[64] No source gives an absolute figure for the age when a Spartan girl in Herodotus's phrase 'reached the season of marriage' (6.61.5), and Plutarch (*Lyk.* 15.4) merely says she would not marry before her body had reached its acme. Did her diet, which was allegedly superior, presumably in quantity, to that of other Greek girls (Xen. *LP* 1.3-4; cf. Plato *Rep.* 5.451e), ensure that she attained puberty earlier than the age of thirteen or fourteen, which seems to have been the norm in Greece generally?[65] Or, alternatively, did her vigorously athletic childhood delay the onset of menstruation?[66]

To give Plutarch his due, he does at least make it clear that Spartan girls married relatively late; and, besides adducing the inevitable eugenic motive also proposed irrelevantly for the men by Xenophon (*LP* 1.6; cf. *Mem.* 4.4.23), he reasonably claims that older brides made for happier marriages. If we tentatively adopt Nilsson's hypothesis of a female educational curriculum running in tandem with the male *agôgê*, then the lower age-limit for a girl's marriage might be set at eighteen.[67] If we also take account of what may have been the normal Spartan male practice of getting married at about twenty-five[68] and the general Greek view that the husband should be older than his wife, the upper limit for a bride should float around the twenty mark. Indeed, if we were to press the suggested parallel between male and female education, we might argue that girls normally married at the age when their brothers became fully adult warriors, probably at twenty.

One fact, however, is not in doubt. At least after *c.* 500 BC all Spartan men were obliged by law to marry (Plut. *Lys.* 30.7; cf. *Lyk.* 15.1; Stob. *Flor.* 67.16 Meineke; Pollux 3.48, 8.40);[69] and the sanctions of the law were reinforced by an elaborate ritual and customary apparatus (Xen. *LP* 9.4-5; Klearchos fr. 73 Wehrli; Plut. *Lyk.* 15.2-3; *Mor.* 227ef). On the one hand, there was nothing peculiarly Spartan about this. The 'making of children' (*teknopoiia*) in marriage could be accounted a form of state liturgy or public service elsewhere in ancient Greece too.[70] Thus there need not be anything

116

out of the ordinary in, for instance, the Spartan marble statue of *c.* 600 or the terrracottas of the sixth century which celebrate fertility and child-birth in a ritual context.[71] On the other hand, the *de facto* (and perhaps also *de iure*) exemption by *c.* 500 of women who died in childbed from the Spartan prohibition on named tombstones;[72] the celebrity of the Spartan mother; and the eye-catching insistence of Kritias (88 F 32 D-K) in the late fifth century, followed by Xenophon (*LP* 1.3) in the fourth, on the primacy of *teknopoiia* in Sparta – all these do seem to betoken an exceptional Spartan preoccupation with human reproduction, an impression that is amply corroborated by Spartan marital practices (below, Section VIII).

It could be argued that this preoccupation was an inevitable function of the special position the Spartans had placed themselves in since the mid-seventh century *vis-à-vis* their subordinate but vastly more numerous serf population, the Helots. We might then compare the practice in the Mani peninsula of southern Lakonia in more recent times of referring to male infants as 'guns'.[73] But the emphasis of Kritias and Xenophon at least could also be a reflection of the extraordinary and critical decline in the male citizen population during the fifth and early fourth centuries (the *oliganthrôpia* criticized by Aristotle, above, Section II). In other words, what deserves particular attention, and requires careful handling, is the question how far, for whom, and at what periods, other reasons for entering upon a marriage besides *teknopoiia* were operationally or affec-tively significant.

The sources do not allow us to discuss personal sentiment with confi-dence, although Bickerman has rightly noted that our evidence concerning (hetero)sexual affection in Greece begins with the (probably seventh-century) *Hymn to Aphrodite.*[74] But they do suggest that other motives than *teknopoiia* may sometimes have been paramount. There is, first of all, the feminine beauty discussed above, the role of which is most colourfully conspicuous in the Herodotean story (6.61-3) of the deceitful third mar-riage of King Ariston (reigned *c.* 550-515) to which we shall return. The difficulty of interpretation here is that, apart from a dubious Plutarchan apophthegm (*Mor.* 232c), the evidence concerns only kings or the *roi manqué* Lysander (Hermippos fr. 87 Wehrli). What we cannot judge is whether feminine beauty was as it were the icing on the matrimonial cake or one of its essential ingredients – unless of course 'beauty' may also be interpreted figuratively as equivalent to ripeness for marriage, as some of Alkman's poems suggest.[75]

We do, however, know of two other ingredients which in some cases at least certainly were essential. The first of these is specific to the inner core of Spartan families distinguished from the rest by birth. This core em-braced above all the two royal houses, the Agiadai and Eurypontidai. But it also included the wider category of 'the descendants of Herakles', from which alone the royals were permitted to select their consorts (Plut. *Agis* 11.2); and I suspect that it extended to other 'privileged families' too.[76]

What these upper-class Spartans had in common was the desire to contract marriages amongst themselves from considerations of high politics (e.g., Hdt. 5.39-41; Plut. *Kleom.* 1). Parallels from the Homeric epics or the real world of Archaic Greek dynasts are not inapposite.[77]

The second ingredient, on the other hand, was not necessarily thus restricted in its operation, although its connection with the first was intimate. For wealth, as the saying goes, marries wealth. In ancient Greece generally, political power and privilege connoted the possession of considerable inherited landed property. This was not absolutely necessarily the case in Sparta, where manly virtue (*andragathia*) displayed in the *agôgê*, on the training-ground and on the battlefield, and good connections, provided they were backed by the minimum of wealth needed to ensure citizen rights, could take a man like Lysander to the top.[78] Lysander, however, was very much the exception that proved the validity in Sparta of the general Greek rule about political power and privilege.[79] That rich Spartans behaved like rich Greeks generally in the matrimonial field, indeed aggressively so, is strongly suggested by the existence of a probably unenforceable Spartan law against 'bad' marriage (Pollux 3.48, 8.40), which Plutarch tells us (*Lys.* 30.7) was principally designed to deter them from contracting marriages for reasons of economic gain.

By the time of Aristotle, and I suspect for at least a century before that, this law was a dead letter; and, as we saw, a crucial part of Aristotle's critique of Spartan women was also a critique of the Spartan property-regime as a whole. Since the latter is a problem of massive proportions, it is impossible to broach it usefully here beyond stating dogmatically my belief that all the land of which Spartan citizens had the usufruct was possessed in the form of private and legally alienable property from at least the mid-seventh century.[80] It is, however, necessary to attempt to assess the active role of the Spartan women in a property system the defectiveness of which was in Aristotle's view ultimately responsible for the downfall of Sparta as a great power.

VI

By Aristotle's day the distribution of land in Lakonia was massively unequal. In itself this was not very remarkable: the situation could be paralleled in many other Greek states. What was remarkable, however, or so it struck Aristotle, was that almost two-fifths of the whole country – by which can only be meant the land in Lakonia owned by Spartan citizens – was in the hands of women. We do not know how Aristotle came by this figure, but undoubtedly to his (sexist) eyes it was in itself a reprehensible fact. Certainly, too, it presupposed a stark contrast between the property laws of Sparta and those of Athens, in which he spent a considerable amount of his adult life as a resident alien (and so, incidentally, as one technically debarred from owning real property). It becomes less extra-ordinary, however, in a broader, comparative perspective.

As Ste. Croix has emphasized,[81] Athenian women of post-Classical times eventually became considerably better off in respect of property ownership than their oppressed forebears of the fifth and fourth centuries had been (below). But if a more direct comparison and contrast be sought, then we may point to the fact that in Aristotle's own day there were maternal inheritances (*matrôia*) as well as patrimonies (*patrôia*) in, for example, Arkadian (and so non-Dorian) Tegea[82] and, most relevantly, Dorian Gortyn on Crete. Cretan parallels have been too often used as a substitute for the evidence we lack for Sparta. But a case can be made for, if not a direct relationship, at least a parallelism of development between some aspects of the Cretan and Spartan social systems.[83] And in the case of women's property rights, the comparative material from Gortyn does seem peculiarly informative, even though it relates to conditions officially in force *c.* 450 BC, a century or more before Aristotle was composing the *Politics*.[84]

Aristotle noted, in the passage considered in Section II, that there were many *epiklêroi* in Sparta and that *proikes* (dowries) were large. I believe he was seriously mistaken or at least misleading on both counts. In the first place, he was almost certainly technically incorrect to use the Athenian term *epiklêros* to describe the Spartan heiress.[85] His error, however, may be more than merely one of vocabulary. For in Classical Athens women could not hold and dispose of more than a trifling amount of property in their own right, and the brotherless heiress, who as an *epi-klêros* literally 'went with the estate', was bound to marry her nearest male relative in order to keep the estate within the descent-group of her father. Herodotus (6.57.4), by contrast, calls the Spartan heiress *patroukhos* (literally 'holder of the patrimony'), and this apparently corresponds to the Gortynian term *patrôiôkos*. Now in Gortyn, unlike Athens, women could own property in their own right (*Lex Gort.* 2.46-7, 49-50, 3.25, 32-3, 36, 42-3, 4.26., 5.1-9, 17-22, 7.52-8.30, 9.8-9), and daughters automatically inherited a (smaller) portion of the family estate alongside their brothers (4.46-5.9). So it seems that here Herodotus is the witness to the – verbal and substantial – truth and that in Sparta *patroukhos* meant something like what we understand in our society by 'heiress'.

As to dowries, the evidence from Gortyn suggests that Aristotle is guilty of a similar terminological and semantic confusion. For there is no trace of the dowry at Gortyn, and there is a compelling consensus among our sources, other than Aristotle and a rogue passage in the Plutarchan *Moralia* (775c-e), that there was no dowry at Sparta either.[86] One of these sources, the third-century BC grammarian Hermippos, paints a fantastic picture of Spartan men and girls of marriageable age being shut up together in a dark room for the men to take pot luck and grab a wife. This flatly contradicts our more sober evidence for the manner in which a

Spartan maiden was taken for a wife (below, Section VII). But the kernel of fact could be Hermippos' unequivocal statement that the captive girl was led away by her prospective husband without a dowry (*aproikos*).

In other words, what Aristotle calls 'large dowries' were really, I suggest, a form of anticipatory inheritance, that is, marriage-settlements consisting of landed property together with any movables that a – rich – father (or mother) saw fit to bestow on a daughter. If a daughter had no father, or brother of the same father, then she would inherit in her own right as *patroukhos* and as such was a particularly desirable catch. It is thus not difficult to see how, given a decreasing number of legitimate male heirs of full citizen status, landed property could have become concentrated in the hands of women.

Daughter-inheritance, incidentally, would also give particular point to the information conveyed only by Philo, the Jewish scholar of the first century AD (*De leg. spec.* 3.4.22), that in Sparta uterine siblings (*homomatrioi*) were permitted to marry each other.[87] We know of no actual examples of such a marriage, but we know of no specific Spartan incest-taboo against them either;[88] and there is evidence that the Spartans, like so many other peoples before the nineteenth century, attributed the active role in reproduction solely to the 'childmaking seed' (Hdt. 6.68.3, with 61.2) of the father.[89] If we were tentatively to accept the accuracy of Philo's evidence, we would have another, though small, contributory cause of the concentration of Spartan landed property in a few hands.

According to Herodotus (6.57.4), however, the Spartan kings in his day, the mid-fifth century, had jurisdiction over the allocation of *patroukhoi*, in cases where the father had not made express provision for their marriage before his death. A second royal prerogative he mentions was that of witnessing adoptions – which, in view of the alleged Spartan hostility to what we call 'the family', it is not irrelevant to note are 'characteristic of a … society which thinks in terms of inheritance through the family'.[90] Yet by the second half of the fourth century both of these prerogatives had been forfeited to the discretion of private individuals, and Aristotle was either unaware of their former existence or perfectly aware that they had not served, even if they had been designed, to even out the distribution of private landed property and maintain male citizen numbers.

Indeed, the kings themselves, despite their monthly oath to obey the laws (Xen. *LP* 15.7), did not a little to further the process of property-concentration. (Here we recall those motives for marriage other than *teknopoiia* considered above in Section V.) Anaxandridas II (reigned *c.* 560-520), Leonidas I (*c.* 491-480) and Archidamos II (*c.* 469-427) all married close consanguineous kin (Hdt. 5.39; 7.239; 6.71); while Kleomenes III (236-222) was married off to Agiatis, the widow of Agis IV (*c.* 244-241), precisely because she was a *patroukhos* (Plut. *Kleom.* 1; Plutarch, however, naturally calls Agiatis an *epiklêros*). What endows these royal marriages with special significance is that in the mid-third century the mother and grandmother of Agis were accounted the richest of all Spartans. In fact, by the time of Agis' accession the proportion of land owned by women in Sparta had reportedly increased from almost two-fifths to an absolute majority (Plut. *Agis* 7.4; cf. McQueen 1990; Mossé 1991).

However, it is of course a separate question whether the ownership of property by rich Spartan women automatically entailed property-power exercised in the political sphere, or (if they are distinct) the 'gynecocracy' criticized by Aristotle. If we are to make a judgement on this and so on the responsibility of the women themselves for the concentration of property in their hands, we must now turn from the theory to the practice of Spartan marriage.[91]

VII

Herodotus, we suggested, was probably precise in his use of the term *patroukhos*. But was he also technically correct to employ in the Spartan context the normal Athenian word for 'betroth' (*enguô*), and were all Spartan daughters (whether *patroukhoi* or not) 'betrothed' by their father or his male heir acting in the capacity of legal guardian (*kyrios*), as Aristotle apparently believed?[92] In other words, did a Spartan daughter have no more say in the choice of her husband or the terms of the marriage-contract than an Athenian girl, or did she have the room for manoeuvre (to put it no higher) enjoyed by her counterpart at Gortyn, where the *kyrieia* (legal guardianship of a female by her nearest male relative, usually her father in the first instance and then her husband) did not exist? The evidence is slight and not clearcut.[93] However, one passage – Xen. *Lak. Pol.* 9.5, which seems to say that no Spartan would ask a Spartan legally adjudged to be a coward (literally 'trembler', *tresas*) for the hand of any unmarried female in his household – tilts the balance in favour of the existence of the *kyrieia*.[94] If that is so, then we cannot automatically infer that ownership of property conferred on Spartan women personal independence, let alone political power.

Another well-known Herodotean story (6.65.2) provides less equivocal evidence for the next stage of the nuptial process. Damaratos (reigned *c.* 515-491) is said to have frustrated the marriage plans of his relative (second cousin?) and royal successor, Latychidas II (*c.* 491-469), by (literally) anticipating him in seizing the girl to whom Latychidas was 'engaged' and 'having' her as a wife.[95] Not surprisingly, perhaps, it is at this juncture that the already powerful temptation to introduce comparative anthropological evidence from 'primitive' or 'non-state' societies is often found irresistible.[96] It is therefore necessary to state briefly why comparison of this kind involves additional dangers here, over and above those attendant on the use of any form of comparative material.

In the case even of Archaic Greece, we are dealing with societies sensibly more complex, not least politically, than most of those studied by social anthropologists. Thus it is simply begging the question to label each seemingly 'primitive' feature of the historical Greek world a 'survival' from an earlier stage of culture. The correct principle, it seems to me, was well expressed long ago by Starcke:[97] 'If we are able to trace the cause of a custom in existing circumstances, we must abide by that cause, and nothing but a definite historical account of the prior existence of the custom can induce us to seek for another explanation.'[98]

As to 'marriage by capture' in Sparta, we lack the evidence to construct a 'definite historical account' of its prior existence. All we can say for certain is that a capture like the one effected by Damaratos is not incompatible either with a previous 'engagement' or with the non-existence of the dowry and that, at least in Plutarch's version (*Lyk.* 15.4-5), the capture had a purely symbolic significance.[99] None the less, the symbolism is in itself not insignificant – quite apart from its being peculiarly appropriate to a military society.[100] For, if the sources can be believed, the girl who was 'seized' played decidedly the passive role. Furthermore, although marriage at Sparta began, as at Athens, when the bride entered the house of the groom (or his parents), a Spartan marriage seems to have been conceived, not as the bilateral 'living together' or 'founding a household together' (*sunoikein*) of Athens, but rather as a one-sided 'having' of the wife by the husband (Hdt. 5.39.2; 6.57.4, 65.2; Xen. *LP* 1.8; Plut. *Kleom.* 29.3).

The wedding-night involved a strikingly bleak ritual.[101] First, the bride's hair was cropped by a (presumably married) female bridal attendant (Plut. *Lyk.* 15.5). This haircut or shave was, I am sure, intended to signal the bride's irrevocable transition from the status of virgin (*parthenos*) or girl (*korê*) to that of woman and wife (*gunê*), since she was not again permitted to wear her hair long.[102] Thus the capillary experience of the new bride offers a perfectly symmetrical antithesis to that of the newly adult male warrior, who on achieving manhood was required to grow his hair long (in so far as that was within his control).[103]

To reinforce the inverted quality of the ritual, the bride was then dressed up in a man's cloak and sandals and laid on a pallet in an unlit room to await the nocturnal attentions of her 'captor' (Plut. *Lyk.* 15.5-7). This masculine get-up, which is somewhat paralleled by the donning of a false beard by brides at Argos (Plut. *Mor.* 245f), has been explained as apotropaic cross-dressing.[104] But it is also worth pondering the suggestion that the bride's appearance was designed to ease the transition for the groom from his all-male and actively homosexual *agôgê* and common mess to full heterosexual intercourse.[105] Let us, however, consider also the feelings of the bride. Even if we should prefer not to believe that Spartan maidens enjoyed tutelary homosexual relations with older women (Plut. *Lyk.* 18.9), the bride had undoubtedly been reared and raised in an almost exclusively female domestic environment. The shock of sexual violation by an older and probably already battle-scarred man cannot have been greatly diminished by the chill and unfamiliar scenario into which she had been forcibly thrust.

If the husband was under thirty when he 'took' a wife – as he perhaps usually would be (above and n. 68) – he was not allowed to cohabit with her, and his infrequent home visits were supposed to be conducted under cover of darkness, in conspiratorial secrecy from his messmates and even from the rest of his own household.[106] Indeed, if we can trust Plutarch (*Lyk.* 15.9), several children might issue from this clandestine 'affair' before a man had seen his wife in daylight. I do not myself believe that an attempt was made, as has been argued, to keep the marriage itself secret; at any rate, aristocratic brides seem to have been hymned on the morning after their wedding-night;[107] and Pausanias (3.13.9) records that mothers made sacrificial offerings to a venerable wooden cult-image of Aphrodite-Hera on the occasion of a daughter's marriage. But it is possible that the Spartans customarily practised a kind of 'trial marriage', which was not necessarily counted as official and binding until the wife had conceived or possibly even safely given birth.[108] We should note, though, that King Anaxandridas II at least did not repudiate a barren wife (Hdt. 5.39-40). However, for him and his elite peers *teknopoiia* could have been subordinated to other considerations. It could not have been so as a rule, and this has to be kept in the forefront of the mind as we turn to what appeared to some non-Spartan contemporaries to be extraordinary, and even immoral, marital practices.

VIII

It is noteworthy that Aristotle reserved his criticisms of Spartan females for those who had crossed the threshold of matrimony. But at least he austerely restricted himself to disparaging their luxury-loving avarice, the power they wielded over their menfolk, and their disproportionate ownership of real property – and this despite his declared abhorrence of adultery (*Nic. Eth.* 1107a10ff., *Pol.* 1335b38-36a2). Rather less self-denying were his inferior successors, who indulged in wild flights of journalistic fantasy. For example, the late lexicographers defined 'the Spartan way' alternatively as buggery and pederasty or as the practice whereby the women, who were not closely guarded (cf. Cic. *de rep.* 4.6.6; Dion. Hal. *Ant. Rom.* 2.24.6), offered themselves sexually to guests or strangers (*xenoi*; cf. perhaps Nik. Dam. *FGrHist.* 90 F 103z.6).[109]

The factual basis of these allegations appears to have been the various forms of what might be described as plural marriage and polykoity that are attested by Herodotus, Xenophon, Polybius and Plutarch, and are paralleled somewhat in both the ancient and the modern worlds.[110] Herodotus was firmly convinced that the bigamy of Anaxandridas II was 'totally un-Spartan' (5.40.2; cf. Paus. 3.3.7), and that may indeed be so.[111] However, according to Polybius (12.6b.8), writing in the later second century BC, it was an 'ancestral custom' and a 'current practice' for three or four men (or more if brothers) to share one wife and for their children to be counted as belonging equally to all. Polybius then makes the apparently separate point that, when a man had produced enough children, it was both honourable and customary for him to pass his wife on to a friend.[112]

Now, the best friend of King Ariston was at first blissfully unaware of this second custom (Hdt. 6.62), and the alleged custom of adelphic polyandry may have been but a temporary expedient in a crisis.[113] But Polybius' evidence still seems to me valuable for two reasons: first, it makes explicit the notion of female passivity that we saw embedded in the marriage transactions; second, it serves as a reminder that 'the institutions commonly described as marriage do not all have the same legal and social concomitants'.[114] To put that another way, monogamy within what we call the 'nuclear family' is only one among many possible pairing relationships contrived for the procreation of legitimate offspring and so for the transmission of hereditary private property.[115]

This potential variety emerges clearly from a passage in Xenophon (*LP* 1.7-9), which is expanded, though with revealing divergences, by Plutarch (*Lyk*. 15.11-18). It might happen, says Xenophon, that an old man had a young wife.[116] Lykourgos, therefore, in order to abolish jealousy – glossed as 'womanish' jealousy by Plutarch – made it legal for such an elderly husband to introduce into his house a younger man whose physique and character he admired, for the latter to beget children by his wife (in a kind of anticipation of our A.I.D. system). Xenophon does not say for whom the children are to be begotten, but one assumes (with Plutarch) that it is for the older man, since Xenophon then cites the reverse situation of a man who does not wish to marry and yet does wish to discharge his procreative duty to the state. Such a man – more likely a widower than a confirmed bachelor – was permitted by Lykourgos to select a fertile and distinguished woman, by whom, if he could persuade her husband (literally 'him who had her'), he might have children.[117]

Xenophon's explanation of the latter arrangement is that the wives wish to possess or run (*katechein*) two households, while the husbands wish to obtain for their existing sons brothers who will have no claim on the paternal inheritance.[118] It is also, however, worth noting a modern suggestion, that these practices are based on the idea attested elsewhere that the 'noble seed' (Plut. *Lyk*. 15.12) of the warriors should be distributed as widely as possible throughout the community.[119] This suggestion is at any rate not contradicted by Xenophon's tantalising claim to know of many similar – but undescribed – pairing arrangements in Sparta. All these would of course have been in keeping with the seemingly concerted effort to depreciate family life in Sparta. But, to repeat, depreciation of family life was far from tantamount to depreciation of the family *tout court*.[120] And the overriding consideration behind these arrangements was reproduction, in particular of legitimate male children, in line with the legal compulsion placed on male citizens to marry (above, Section V).

It is perhaps significant that Xenophon makes no reference to adultery in Sparta.[121] By contrast, Plutarch (*Lyk*. 15.16; *Mor*. 228bc) felt bound explicitly to deny its occurrence. As far as sexual relationships between citizens are concerned, Plutarch seems to have been technically correct, and this is a remarkable comment on the emphasis laid on the extramarital maintenance of the male citizen population at Sparta. None the less, it is certain that adultery in the sense of sexual intercourse between a citizen and a non-citizen who were not married to each other did occur.

The alleged paternity of the evanescent hero Astrabakos (Hdt. 6.63-9) and that of the distinctly corporeal and mortal Alkibiades,[122] in each case involving the wife of a king, do not particularly concern us here. The complex and confused evidence for the so-called Partheniai illuminates Greek attitudes to the proper relationship between the sexes, and between the free and the unfree;[123] but this mysterious group is attested only in connection with the foundation of Taras (modern Taranto) in *c*. 706. There is, on the other hand, good evidence for other specially named categories of men in Sparta which undoubtedly is relevant to the position of Spartan wives in our period. Xenophon (*Hell*. 5.3.9) refers in a context of 380 BC to bastards (*nothoi*). Later sources (Phylarchos *FGrHist*. 81 F 43; Plutarch, *Kleom*. 8.1; Aelian, *VH* 12.43) mention the category *mothakes*, to which lexicographers and scholiasts add that of the possibly identical *mothônes*.

These disparate sources have been collected and well discussed, and the identification of at least some members of these categories as the offspring of Spartan fathers and Helot mothers seems virtually certain.[124] Such liaisons are at any rate a more cogent explanation for the lack of evidence for female prostitutes in Sparta (at least before the third century)[125] than alleged 'free love' among the Spartans. We cannot, however, say how frequent such liaisons may have been nor what psychological effect they may have had on Spartan wives – a salutary reminder of the inadequacy of the ancient evidence.

IX

It will be noticed, finally, that very little has been said directly on the subject of gynecocracy (and nothing about 'matriarchal survivals'). My silence is the measure of my disagreement with Aristotle (and Bachofen)[126] – tempting though it would have been to cite as a perfect illustration of Aristotle's view the huge, probably Spartan-made bronze mixing-bowl and lid of the sixth century found at Vix in France.[127] To a quintessential sexist like him, however, anything remotely approaching sexual equality, let alone female emancipation, both of which he thought he detected in Sparta, must indeed have seemed like the world turned upside down.

Moreover, his criticisms really apply only to rich Spartan women, who were of course a minority of the women under study here.

But if for once it is easy to set aside the opinions of Aristotle, it is far harder to 'hold the balance with a steady and equal hand' (an expression of Edward Gibbon) in the longstanding controversy over the general social position of Spartan wives in the sixth to fourth centuries BC – not least, as has been shown, because of the nature of the ancient evidence. To be consciously anachronistic, a modern feminist might perhaps approve their equal though separate education, which may have included an intellectual element; their frankness of utterance; their liberating attire; their freedom from sedentary and stultifying domestic chores; their control and management of their household(s); their public valuation; and above all their property rights. On the other side, however, the modern feminist is unlikely to be over-impressed by the way in which they were 'seized' and 'had' as wives in the domicile of their husbands, who could 'lend' them for extra-marital procreation and probably had at least a say in the management and disposition of their property; finally, and perhaps least of all, by the overriding emphasis placed upon the women's child-bearing potential and maternal roles by the men who monopolized the political direction of a peculiarly masculine society.

For what it is worth, my own view coincides roughly, and for rather different reasons, with that of Simone de Beauvoir: 'such examples as Sparta and the Nazi regime prove that [woman] can be none the less oppressed by the males, for all her direct attachment to the State'.[128] At all events, I hope that I may at least have made readers hesitate before seeking to enlist the women of ancient Sparta as allies in the just cause of feminism.

10

Rebels and *Sambos* in Classical Greece: A Comparative View

Introduction

The original version of this chapter was published in a Festschrift (Cartledge & Harvey eds 1985) which I co-edited for the late G.E.M. de Ste. Croix, one of the most distinguished students of ancient Greek and Roman slavery in the past half-century. For him, slavery and other forms of unfree labour constituted the basis, in a marxist sense, of Graeco-Roman civilization and culture, and he had devoted his powerful mind to studying them in all their manifestations, ideological as well as material, since his undergraduate days in the late 1940s as a pupil of A.H.M. Jones at University College London.

Slave revolt, or rather its apparent absence from the world of chattel slavery in Classical Greece, which is this chapter's theme, is just one aspect of a vast subject, the importance of which remains in my view still somewhat underappreciated, or at any rate understudied, by historians of ancient Greece. Hunt 1998 is a shining recent exception to that general neglect.

My chapter was also an evangelistical exercise in comparative method (cf. now Golden 1992), owing most in its original form to the work of Eugene Genovese (1979) on slave revolt in the Americas and something to that of Orlando Patterson (1982). Since 1985 an important study has appeared on the three slave revolts that occurred during the Late Roman Republic (Bradley 1989), and the theses of Genovese and others have been subjected to renewed scrutiny (Williams Myers 1996), providing further opportunities for reviewing my essay. I have not attempted systematically to incorporate references to the most recent literature on slavery in the Americas, which is vast, but see Berlin 1998 and, bibliographically, Miller ed. 1993-8.

This chapter is divided into two parts. In the first and longer part I attempt to apply systematically to Classical Greece those of the criteria for successful servile revolt elaborated by Genovese that I deem relevantly applicable. Here I am attempting to account for a null case, the *non-*occurrence of servile revolt – as opposed to servile *resistance*, which is to be assumed and can be documented. In the second part of the chapter I apply those same criteria of Genovese's to the Helots of Sparta, both those of Lakonia and those of Messenia. As was notorious in antiquity and is still a matter for rightful preoccupation today, this servile group – or rather groups – did actually manage to revolt, more than once, and indeed not merely to revolt but, with a lot of help from their friends (or at any rate their Spartan masters' enemies), actually revolt into full civic freedom (for the adult males of the new *polis* of Messene) as well as personal liberty.

An important part of what is at stake for modern scholars who wish to explain as well as understand this near-unique historical phenomenon is the general question of how important the Helots were to the entire Spartan political and social and cultural regime, and especially how much of a threat they posed to that regime on a regular, everyday basis – as opposed to the searingly manifest moments of concerted and open revolt. Much hangs, in this debate, on one's reading of Thucydides 4.80.2, which is irritatingly not unambiguous. Either Thucydides is saying that as a general principle of governance 'Spartan policy had *always* been determined by the necessity of taking precautions against the Helots', or he is making a more restricted claim and saying something like 'in the Spartans' relations with the Helots the central issue had *always* been to keep them under surveillance' (my emphasis – the Greek word *aiei* appears first in its sentence). Whichever of those readings is correct, it is in this same passage that Thucydides goes on to relate an instance of extreme Spartan surveillance involving the calculatedly duplicitous slaughter of 2000 Helots that the historian believed to be and presented as an illustration of a general rule – 'always', as – e.g. – in this particular instance. Those modern scholars who wish to play down the importance of the Helot 'danger' to Sparta or the determining influence of that perceived danger on the whole Spartan regime (e.g., Roobaert 1977; Talbert 1989; Whitby 1994) tend to favour the second, more minimal translation of Thuc. 4.80.2 given above and are even willing – some of them – to deny the factual veracity of that reported massacre. So not only is the nature of the Spartan regime at scholarly stake here but so also are Thucydides' reputation and standing.

Now, the testimony of Thucydides is no longer read today as it once was as the equivalent of holy writ, and more and more attention has been devoted to unmasking the powerful passions, even prejudices, by which he was moved both to write history and in the writing of his history. That is in my view quite proper and fair. It is therefore perfectly correct and legitimate to ask, first, what Thucydides' source for this story might have been (as usual, he doesn't tell us explicitly), and, second, whether there might have been any ideological or other motive that might have led him to abandon in this case what seem to have been his usual high standards of verification and authentication and so to believe a contrived and malicious fiction. As for the first issue, that of Thucydides' sources, I note that it is in connection with a centrally important aspect of Sparta's behaviour, their performance at the battle of Mantineia in 418, and with a matter involving knowledge of numbers that Thucydides declares (5.68.2) – very honestly but still somewhat surprisingly, since such confessions of ignorance are very rare indeed – that he could not estimate the Spartans' casualties in 418 with any accuracy on account of 'the secrecy of their *politeia*' – the last word is ambiguous: it could mean either the Spartan state authorities specifically in 418 or the Spartans' whole way of life in general. I infer that he did not feel such qualms in the case of the Helot massacre, even though that had been accomplished in total secrecy ('no one ever knew how each of them perished' – 4.80.4). From what, to him, reliable witness could he have received such a report? What could have been his reason(s) for believing, or wanting to believe, the report?

Since Spartan or Perioikic deserters or defectors were probably thin on the ground or non-existent and in any case deeply untrustworthy on principle, the likeliest potential Lakonian source is a fugitive Helot, though presumably not one of the 2000 supposedly being liberated for services to Sparta only to discover that by volunteering for freedom they had volunteered for their own death-sentence. Such fugitive Helots had two possible main routes of escape from Sparta's own home territory: *via* the position occupied by the Athenians at Pylos in Messenia since 425 (it was the capture of this that provoked the Spartans to extreme fear of Helot *skaiotês*, 'obstinacy', and Helot numbers in 424, according to Thuc. 4.80.3) or *via* the 'sort of isthmus' in the Malea peninsula in Lakonia opposite the island of Kythera that the Athenians occupied and fortified in 413, precisely as a place 'to which the Helots might desert' (Thuc. 7.26.2). There are other possibilities too. In both those occupations of Spartan territory the key Athenian commander had been Demosthenes, who had established special relations with the ex-Helot Messenians settled by the Athenians in *c.* 460 at Naupaktos and used them profitably both during and after the Pylos success. Thucydides' source might therefore have been a Naupaktos Messenian as well as a Lakonian or Messenian Helot deserter. Or indeed Demosthenes himself.

Why then, finally, did Thucydides choose to believe the story? Why did he find the witness or witnesses reliable and believable? Was his favourable reception of the story dictated by some more or less hidden agenda? Pro-Athenian patriotic prejudice on big issues such as war-guilt has been alleged against Thucydides, but not in my view sustainably. It is, moreover, implausible in the highest degree that as a non-democratic exile from democratic Athens he shared such fellow-feeling for slaves and Helots (who not only were unfree but Greek) as Athenian ideological democrats may – perhaps – have held. His general under-emphasis in his work on the importance of Helot dissidence and revolt is at any rate in line with an under-emphasis by all major Greek historians on the role of slaves and the unfree in Greek warfare that has been convincingly detected by Hunt (1998).

The most economical explanation would therefore seem to me to be that the reported massacre of some 2000 Helots some time before 424 fitted into a pattern already in the eyes of Thucydides firmly established and rigorously tested, a pattern of Spartan precaution to the point of paranoia towards the Helots that might entail exemplary punishments of outstanding brutality. Thucydides does not mention the Spartan Krypteia, though it undoubtedly existed in his day, nor does he cite the annual declaration of war on the Helots by the Ephors, which also has a good chance of being in force in the late fifth century (for both of these, and all other relevant, testimonia, see Ducat 1990). But if he knew of them, as he surely did, they will have been part and parcel of this reassuringly consistent picture. (He does cite a number of telling instances of Spartan murder of free Greeks: 2.67.3, the Spartans' murder of neutrals as well as Athenian and allied traders at the outset of the war; 3.68.2, their massacre of at least 200 Plataians in 427; and 5.83, their killing of all available freemen of Hysiai in 419. An *a fortiori* inference so far as Spartan treatment of Helots was concerned would therefore seem justifiable.)

One last, historiographical argument: Thucydides' overall method of presentation was paradigmatic. The chilling description of the massacre of 2000 Helots in 4.80 should therefore be read in my view as his paradigm case of the Spartans' regular treatment of the Helots. I see no reason in conclusion not to believe the authenticity of the report and every reason to regard it as powerful evidence of at least the Spartans' all too vivid perception of a Helot 'danger'.

*

I

Thirty years ago Eric Hobsbawm observed that 'the slave-societies of antiquity appear to be in recession'.[1] He was not of course referring to chronic overproduction or mass unemployment in Graeco-Roman antiquity but passing an adverse judgement on the quality and quantity of current research then being published on Greek and Roman slavery.[2] Taken from the standpoint of the long run, this observation was not strictly just; the real recession in ancient slave studies had occurred between the later nineteenth century and the end of the Second World War.[3] Thereafter there had been a considerable reawakening of interest and the beginnings of a more sophisticated reappraisal.[4] That progressive momentum has been maintained, if fitfully, since Hobsbawm wrote, though J.C. Miller (1993-8, vol. II: xii) has recently again noted a 'relative decline' in ancient slave studies.[5] Much, therefore, remains to be done, and it is the object of this essay to suggest that slave revolts in Classical Greece (*c.* 500-300 BC) – or rather their seemingly total absence[6] – constitute just one area due for further illumination by a rigorous and systematic application of the comparative method. The following quotation may serve as an appropriate starting point:

130

10. Rebels and Sambos in Classical Greece

It is not my intention to give anything like a complete account, even in outline, of slavery in the ancient Greek world ... But I think I ought at least to explain why at Athens and in the other Greek cities where slavery was already highly developed in the Classical period we never hear of slave revolts ... The reason is simple and obvious: the slaves in each city (and even in many cases within single families and farms and workshops) were largely imported 'barbarians' and very heterogeneous in character, coming from areas as far apart as Thrace, South Russia, Lydia and Caria and other parts of Asia Minor, Egypt, Libya and Sicily, and sharing no common language or culture.

One hesitates to take issue with so formidable and normally inexpugnable an interpreter of ancient social history as Geoffrey de Ste. Croix, particularly in a field where he was unusually expert.[7] But nothing in the area of human social history is without qualification 'simple and obvious', and, as I shall hope to show, the absence of slave revolts was an integral feature of the deeply complex phenomenon that he identified as 'the class struggle in the ancient Greek world'.[8]

To return to the original Hobsbawm quotation, two further preliminary comments are in order. Despite the post-war renascence of scholarship on ancient slavery, his observation (echoed by Miller) was justified from the perspective within which it was made. There was and remains a recession in ancient slave studies by comparison with the remarkable work then (and still) being done on other slave systems, above all that of the American Old or Ante-Bellum South. For in the decades since the publication of Kenneth Stampp's seminal *The Peculiar Institution* (Stampp 1956) there has been 'an outpouring of books and articles on American slavery that can probably not be matched in any other historical field, not only for volume but also for the quality and sophistication of the analysis, the innovatory techniques of inquiry and the fever-tone of the polemic'.[9]

The other necessary comment concerns Hobsbawm's definite use of the term 'slave-societies'. For this implies a judgement that the societies of Greece and Rome were indeed 'slave' societies properly so called and therefore that Greek and Roman civilization at their zenith were in some sense 'based on' slave labour. When does a society that employs (chattel) slave labour become one that is usefully classified as a slave society? Hopkins has suggested a quantitative criterion, a notional minimum cut-off figure of twenty per cent for slaves as a proportion of the labour force.[10] But it is not simply a quantitative factor, the proportion of slaves, that makes slave societies. Rather, these are societies with an institution-alized system of largescale employment of slave labour in the basic productive sectors by a ruling class which depends for the major portion of its surplus extraction – and so for its continued existence as a ruling class – on the exploitation of slave labour; and which therefore goes to great lengths to justify that surplus extraction ideologically; societies, in short, where chattel slavery is an institution integral to their production, repro-

131

duction and lifestyle.[11] Classical Athens at least would certainly qualify as a slave society on this definition, and there is good reason to think that other Classical Greek societies – Corinth, for instance (see n. 60, below) – might be similarly classified if the relevant evidence were available.

Given the unassailable and uninflatable importance of slavery in the ancient world, how are we to explain the relative recession in ancient slave studies? One part of the explanation is, surely, that most ancient historians are less sensitive than their Americanist counterparts to the 'coercions of the times'.[12] Marxist ancient historians such as Ste. Croix are of course peculiarly concerned to locate slavery in relation to the ancient and modern class struggle. But most ancient historians, strange to tell, are not Marxists, and of those who are not it is perhaps only the professing Christians among them who ought to lose sleep contemplating the evils of Greek and Roman slavery.[13] For Americanists, by contrast, the effects of the poison of slavery are still all too apparent in contemporary society, and memories can be uncomfortably jogged by the life-history of someone like Mary Duckworth who was born a slave in Mississippi on 4 June 1861, two months after the outbreak of the Civil War, and yet died as recently as April 1983.[14] The 'fever-tone of the polemic', like the rhythms and intensity of scholarly research, has much to do with the burning desire to find an antidote.

However, even if the changing times do not coerce historians of ancient Greece, the comparative dearth of good contemporary evidence for ancient slavery, especially new and quantifiable data, certainly does. It is sad but true that the fourteenth and fifteenth *Discourses* of the Stoic Dio Chrysostom, some fifteen pages of text, represent the longest surviving connected treatment of the topic; and one of the most informative passages on Classical Greek slavery consists of twelve pages of an encyclopaedic *potpourri* entitled 'The Banqueting Sophists' (*Deipnosophistai*) compiled about AD 200 by Athenaeus of Naukratis in Egypt.[15] Not that a mere increase in the quantity of evidence would automatically lead to a scholarly consensus on the main issues of interpretation. This is just one of the many lessons to be learned from the remarkable outflow of major studies on slavery in the Old South.[16] It is also one of the many reasons why the comparative approach to ancient slavery recommends itself with particular force.

The writing of comparative history, it has been well remarked, is rather like belling the cat: everyone (now) agrees that it would be a marvellous thing to do, but it is fiendishly difficult. The difficulties, broadly speaking, can all be reduced to one, that of ensuring that like is being compared to like. In the case of ancient Greek slavery the evidence is so sparse that there is a constant risk of arguing in a circle, that is, of using comparative evidence from better documented slave systems to establish a model of ancient slavery and then employing comparative details to put flesh on the model's skeleton. This risk, like all others attendant on comparative analysis, can be avoided by sticking firmly to the principle that comparison cannot supply the primary evidence we lack but rather can serve only to provoke hypotheses to explain the evidence we have.

The advantages, moreover, greatly outweigh the difficulties. Indeed, the alternatives to employing the comparative method are to relapse into mere antiquarianism or practise a form of naive inductivism.[17] For systematic comparison, apart from suggesting explanatory hypotheses, helps remove the blinkers of the obvious and the parochial. It reveals more sharply than any other approach what is unique to or characteristic of the society under study. Conversely, it brings into clear focus what differentiates ancient slavery from its African, oriental or New World counterparts.[18] Finally, perhaps comparison's most important potential contribution to historical studies is to pre-empt the assumption that what happened in history was somehow in the nature of things. It may be the case that the dominion and dependency of the master-slave relationship tend to gravitate towards universal norms. But geography, ecology, population distribution and economic organization are just some of the variables specific to different slave systems.

Comparison, like charity, should begin at home. One of the many inbuilt advantages of studying ancient Greek and Roman history is that the ancient historian who wishes to move beyond descriptive antiquarianism is virtually compelled to become a comparativist, comparing one Greek society with another (there were some 1500 in all) or some ideal type of the Greek *polis* with an ideal type of Roman society and politics and so on. The concern of the present essay is to throw light upon the problem of the non-occurrence of slave revolts in Classical Greece. The contrast with the history of 'Classical' Rome in the Late Republican period could scarcely be greater. The Romans had a proverb – proverbial at any rate by the time of the younger Seneca in the mid-first century AD – that every slave was an enemy: *quot servi, tot hostes* (Seneca *Ep.* 47.5; cf. Festus 314L; Macrobius, *Sat.* 1.11.13). Between 140 and 70 BC there were three major slave revolts which, if they did not actually inspire, certainly vividly illustrated and confirmed that proverb.[19] Indeed, there has only ever been one other slave revolt to compare with these in scale, namely the successful revolt on Haiti at the turn of the eighteenth and nineteenth centuries led by Toussaint L'Ouverture.[20] How is the contrast to be explained?

This is where comparative analysis begins to demonstrate its utility, in two main ways. First, when looked at in comparative perspective, what is really striking and seemingly crying out for explanation is not so much the (apparent) absence of chattel slave revolts in Classical Greece as the occurrence of three major revolts in Classical Italy and Sicily. It is true that the number of genuine slave societies as defined above is very small, perhaps only five or six in all (counting 'Classical Greece' as one). But between them these five spanned some six centuries of existence, and four major revolts (including that on Haiti) is hardly an enormous figure.

The second and related principal way in which comparative analysis is helpful for approaching our problem is that the scarcity and low intensity of revolts have also been a classic problem for dozens of recent historians of the Old South. If comparison is restricted to slavery in the New World, ultimately the outcome of the African slave-trade, then a contrast in this respect somewhat similar to that between Greece and Rome becomes apparent as between the Old South and the noticeably more revolt-prone Caribbean or Brazilian slave societies.[21] This, together with 'the coercions of the times', the superior documentation, and the sophisticated and innovative techniques devised for analysing it, explain why far more and far more illuminating studies have been addressed hitherto to resistance and rebellion in the Old South[22] than to this important ingredient of slavery in Classical Greece or even Republican Rome. Hence my choice of Eugene Genovese's recent synthetic study of slave resistance and rebellion in the Old South as the focus for my foray into comparative history.[23] For this incorporates all the best features of this impressive body of research and thus provides a suitably broad, differentiated and solid basis for comparative purposes.

II

From Rebellion to Revolution (*FRR*) grew out of a series of lectures delivered at Louisiana State University in 1973. That was the year before the appearance of Genovese's *magnum opus, Roll, Jordan, Roll* (*RJR*), and *FRR* as promised develops the dozen or so pages devoted specifically to slave revolts in *RJR*.[24] The first three-fifths of *FRR* are addressed to the problem of the relative scarcity of slave uprisings or outbreaks in the Old South when these are viewed within the perspective of the entire western hemisphere. The remainder, which is of less immediate and direct relevance to my present concerns, deals with what the subtitle calls 'the making of the modern world', taking the great Haitian revolt as the turning-point between slave revolts that were 'restorationist' and those that may be called 'revolutionary'. (I shall return to this distinction in Section III.)

Towards the beginning of *FRR* Genovese lists eight factors 'without regard for the presumed importance of one relative to another', factors the presence of which in a slave society 'would suggest a higher probability of slave revolt' (11). These are the eight factors as expressed in the author's own special terminology (11-12):

(1) The master-slave relationship had developed in the context of absenteeism and depersonalization as well as greater cultural estrangement of whites and blacks;
(2) economic distress and famine occurred;

134

(3) slaveholding units approached the average of 100 to 200 slaves, as in the sugar colonies, rather than twenty or so, as in the Old South;

(4) the ruling class frequently split either in warfare between slaveholding countries or in bitter struggles within a particular slaveholding country;

(5) blacks heavily outnumbered whites;

(6) African-born slaves outnumbered those born into American slavery;

(7) the social structure of the slaveholding regime permitted the emergence of an autonomous black leadership; and

(8) the geographical, social and political environment provided terrain and opportunity for the formation of colonies of runaways strong enough to threaten the plantation regime.

As Genovese at once adds, this list 'may be extended, refined, and subdivided'; and reviewers, though on the whole very sympathetic, have added two further factors favouring the probability of revolt (the high status of mulattoes, and the nature of the crops cultivated by the slaves) and have criticized his factor (7) for being too broad and oversimplified and overlapping with some of the other factors. None the less, Genovese's list can still be used profitably as a working basis for comparison, *mutatis* of course, the obvious *mutandis*[25] and provided that the sin of 'homogenization' – the perception-dulling comparison merely of broad parallels and similarities – is rigorously avoided.[26] Any artificiality that this procedure may involve should be outweighed by the gain in clarity of exposition.

(1) The master-slave relationship

We are plunged straight into the fundamental but predictably contentious area of slave ideology and psychology. For the ancient historian this is also a frankly embarrassing area from the evidentiary standpoint. Over against the mass of slave and ex-slave materials available for the study of the Old South[27] we have to set practically nothing: 'we do not possess a single work composed by a slave while in slavery. When you consider the enormous ratio of slaves in the ancient world and the talent that must have existed among them, you begin to realize the tragedy, the horror, of this datum'.[28] Horrible and tragic it may well be, but the fact remains that virtually our only guides to the ideology and psychology of the slaves owned in Classical Greece are, on the one hand, what their masters chose to write about these topics (or rather what happens to have survived from such writings) and, on the other, the slaves' overt behaviour, again as recorded in the literature composed by and for the slaveholder class. Not surprisingly, this kind of one-sided evidence tells far more about the ideology and psychology of the masters than it does about those of the slaves, but it should not be dismissed out of hand all the same.[29]

There may be a hint of resistance in the animal fables attributed to

Aesop, reputedly once a slave on the island of Samos. But even if he was not himself fabulous, he would have lived well before the Classical era, and we can only guess that similar though less polished moral tales circulated in the fifth and fourth centuries. The evidence from the slaveholders' side is ambiguous. The belief that slaves were by nature inferior to free men seems to have been generally held, although only a philosopher would feel obliged to argue the case in favour of it 'logically'; and that case, as Aristotle's philosophically deficient version makes abundantly plain, was pitifully weak.[30] Indeed, the belief seems to have been a psychologically necessary one for slaveholders to entertain. Finley suggested rightly on more than one occasion that a story preserved in Herodotus (4.1-4) is paradigmatic.[31] Here, in a notionally 'barbarian' (Scythian) context, masters and slaves find themselves engaged in open warfare, the masters employing their usual weapons of war, bows and javelins. But without success, until one Scythian master points out the error of their ways. Using bows and javelins, he says, gives the slaves the idea that they are our equals; let us rather take up our whips and so demonstrate to them our natural superiority and fitness to rule. The ploy was wholly successful, and the view of the anonymous Scythian would have been wholeheartedly endorsed by a Southern planter who in 1866 wrote, nostalgically, of the whip that 'the great secret of our success was the great motive power contained in that little instrument'.[32]

Force by itself though, or the constant more or less open threat of it, has rarely been a sufficient means of control, and few ruling classes in history have survived long merely through terror and retributive punishment. The lashings of slaves that reverberate through the comic plays of Aristophanes (e.g. *Wasps* 1292-6, where a slave congratulates tortoises on their shells) without doubt signify more than just comic business. But on the other side we have to place the paternalistic views of a thinking slaveholder like Xenophon, who taught that one should not punish in anger even a slave (*Hell.* 5.3.7, an *obiter dictum* all the more revealing for its implication that such angry chastisement was perfectly normal) and who elsewhere (*Hiero* 4.3, 10.4) wrote as if he believed there to be a perpetual state of potentially open antagonism between masters and slaves (cf. Lys. 7.35; Dem. 21.49). It is important, though, to be clear what could be meant by 'paternalism' in the context of Classical Greece.

One version of the concept is that developed at length by Genovese as the informing idea of *RJR*. This does not denote straightforward benevolence but rather an attitude motivated by 'the necessity to discipline and morally justify a system of exploitation. It did encourage kindness and affection but it simultaneously encouraged cruelty and hatred' (*RJR* 4; cf. 84, for the 'white man's burden' view of slavery). The contradiction arose from the impossibility of realizing in everyday practice the ideal legal definition of the slave as a chattel, a mere depersonalized thing. The slave's humanity had to be recognized willy-nilly, but recognition brought to the slave a consciousness of his or her personal worth. Under paternalism, therefore, the master-slave relationship was dialectical, not unidirectional. It was also symbiotic. Such a form of paternalism was fostered by the fact that in the Old South typically plantations were not vast and masters not absentees (below). They were visible, close at hand in the big house. From the viewpoint of preventing revolt – an outlook close to the surface of many free Southerners' daily consciousness, apparently[33] – not the least of paternalism's advantages was its capacity to undermine any solidarity that the exploited slaves might have developed among themselves, since it tied them individually to their masters (or mistresses) by a thousand threads.

Apart from the dearth of comparable evidence, one major obstacle prevents us from simply applying this conception of paternalism (which is anyway a matter for dispute among Americanists) to the master-slave relationship in Classical Greece. Greek slavery depended on a constant external supply of new slaves. But at the time when the supposed paternalist regime was in full swing, the slave population of the Old South was reproducing itself internally by breeding rather than being replenished or replaced by African imports. It has been estimated that only about 4.5 per cent of the ten million or so Africans traded to the New World between 1500 and 1850 ended up as slaves in the Old South (as opposed to the Caribbean or Latin America); and importation had effectively stopped in almost all the American States well before the trade was closed by federal decree in 1808.[34] No doubt, the stability of the slave nuclear family and of slave family life in the Old South can be exaggerated.[35] But this self-reproduction unquestionably gave Southern slaves a stake in the system and a disincentive to rock the boat that were not present in the same way to the chattel slaves of Classical Greece. For the latter were outsiders in the fullest possible sense: the overwhelming majority were non-Greeks (see below under factor [6]), who had been forcibly torn from their native environment with its buttressing of kinship and community ties that would have provided mutual solidarity and familiarity.[36]

Yet, despite these restrictions and qualifications, Genovese's paternalist model may not be wholly inapplicable to the slave societies of Classical Greece. What little we know about the masters' pattern of residence (chiefly, as always, related to Athenian slavery) suggests that characteristically they were not absentee landlords and indeed that at the lower social levels at any rate it was not rare for masters to work side by side with their slaves in the field, the workshop or the building site. Moreover, although slaves were regarded and treated as naturally inferior – calling an adult slave *pais*, 'child', was only the most obvious outward and visible sign of this literally paternalistic attitude – some recognition of their humanity was nevertheless accorded them institutionally (if in a limited way) as members of an *oikos* or household, chiefly through its religious observances.[37] Religion may indeed have played a crucial part in the slaves' accommodation to their unsought lot, as it certainly did in the Old South.[38] Finally, if we may accept at face value the scenes in Aristophanes where masters and slaves exchange confidences with remarkable freedom, and if we may read between the lines of the complaint voiced at about the same time by the so-called 'Old Oligarch' (Ps.-Xen. *Ath. Pol.* 1.10-12; cf. Plato. *Rep.* 563b) against the intolerably free lifestyle of urban slaves in Athens, there seems to have been give and take at least between the more privileged slaves and their masters.

Before leaving the first of Genovese's eight favouring conditions I must mention the 'personality-type' controversy that has bedevilled American slave studies since Stanley Elkins produced his one-sided portrait of the typical field-hand as a 'Sambo' – the lazy, grinning, docile, sluggish and deceitful slave of the planters' wish-fulfilment dreams.[39] There is nowhere near enough comparable evidence from Classical Greece to reconstruct a parallel composite portrait, even if one should wish to do so. But in any case, as the critics of Elkins' thesis have justly observed, what such a one-dimensional personality-type theory signally fails to explain is how 'Sambo' could also on occasion turn out to be or turn into a rebel.[40] For there were after all at least three revolts of some considerable significance in the Old South as late as the first third of the nineteenth century; and since revolt – as opposed to flight or other kinds of individual resistance (below) – was tantamount to suicide in those political and geographical conditions, these outbreaks prove at the very least that not all slaves had internalized fully the roles their masters desired them to play.

Striking confirmation of this essential point comes from a lesson that study of the Old South can surely teach students of all slave systems, namely that absence of outright revolts is not at all the same thing as absence of any kind of slave resistance to slavery. Had Westermann and Vogt taken the measure of this point, they might not have been so quick to ascribe the absence of revolts in Classical Greece to the alleged mildness of the Greek slave system.[41] Stampp and others[42] have collected an enormous amount of evidence on the various kinds of individual slave resistance practised in the Old South, ranging from malingering, complaints, tool-breaking, mistreatment of draught animals and livestock, work-slowdowns and theft, through apologetic and fantasy folklore, religion and exorcism to arson, self-mutilation, flight and occasionally acts of violence against masters – in one word, sabotage of one type or another, which 'ultimately decreases the rate of exploitation'.[43]

The Classical Greek evidence is inevitably much thinner, but it too suggests that flight and theft were the two commonest slave 'crimes'. We shall return in other connections to the 'more than 20,000' slaves who seized the exceptional opportunity provided by the closing phase of the Peloponnesian War to flee from their servitude in Attica (Thuc. 7.27.5). What was unusual about their flight was its mass character rather than the fact that they had tried (probably without success in the end: cf. Hell.

Ox. 17.4) to register their judgement on their bondage by voting with their feet. We even hear (*ap.* Athen. 4.161d) of a fourth-century comedy by Antiphanes entitled 'The Runaway-catcher' (*ho Drapetagôgos*), which strongly suggests the ubiquity of the phenomenon. *Drapetês*, meaning literally 'a runaway' of any kind, significantly came to denote specifically a runaway slave.

As for theft, two passages may suffice to illustrate the point, one generalizing, one specific. 'Everyone', wrote the longlived and very wealthy Athenian pamphleteer Isokrates (12.214) in about 340, 'considers to be the worst slaves those who behave wickedly and steal'; as a spokesman for the outlook of the slaveowning class, Isokrates is an unimpeachable witness. In detail, we learn from Demosthenes (53.16; cf. Ps.-Xen. *Ath. Pol.* 1.10), another very wealthy Athenian slaveowner, that an Athenian farmer was legally entitled to beat a slave belonging to another man if he caught him stealing his produce. This, however, was a recognized exception to the general rule in Athens (but by no means universal in Classical Greece) that persons other than the owner might not inflict personal injury upon a slave. This and other prohibitions against injuring a slave have been plausibly explained as based upon 'the owner's right of protection for his property, the need of preserving order and educating the citizens in moral excellence, and the continual fear of revolt'.[44]

No doubt, the first of these considerations was paramount: careful and solicitous treatment of one's slaves has been nicely compared (by Dover 1974: 286) to similarly motivated treatment of one's car(s) today. But – despite Vogt and Westermann – fear of slave revolt should not be neglected or entirely discounted. The slave boy not yet twelve years old who set upon his Athenian master with a knife (Antiph. 5.69) was no doubt an exceptional case, but passages of Lysias (7.35) and Demosthenes (21.49) speak of a natural enmity between masters and slaves; Xenophon (*Hiero* 10.4) asserts in a philosophical rather than rhetorical context that 'masters have often died violently at the hands of their slaves' and graphically describes citizens as 'unpaid bodyguards of each other against their slaves' (*Hiero* 4.3); and Plato in a famous passage (*Rep.* 578d-9a), the import of which has been admirably conveyed by Ste. Croix (1983: 147), conjures up the unpleasant and threatening vision of a rich slaveowner with a holding of over fifty slaves (explicitly said to be a large number) wafted with his family 'to some desert place where there would be no other free man to help him' and thereby placed in mortal danger. It would be excessive to describe such visions as betraying a neurotic fear of slave revolt, but they do at least counteract some of the more fantastic modern pictures of Classical Greek slavery as an essentially harmonious, co-operative and humane system. They remind us, too, that slaveowners were engaged in a constant struggle, ideological as well as practical, to prevent the balance of power shifting in favour of the slaves.

In short, although most slaves in most Classical Greek states apparently did somehow or other accommodate themselves to their fate, the possibility of what has been neatly called 'subversive accommodation' should never be ruled out *a priori*.[45]

(2) The occurrence of economic distress and famine

Greece and Poverty, as Herodotus' Damaratos tells the Persian Great King Xerxes, had ever been foster-sisters (Hdt. 7.102.1), and Greece's natural poverty was exacerbated by an exceptionally long war like the Peloponnesian War of 431-404, whose historian Thucydides (1.23.3) remarked upon the unusual famines and diseases that it had engendered. But it seems that it was only in the early 320s that economic distress may have bordered on general famine in Classical Greece.[46] No doubt peculiarly severe economic difficulties exacerbated the splits within the Greek ruling classes discussed below under item (7) and so in turn affected the involvement of slaves in those intestine struggles, but there is no evidence for a direct correlation between economic distress and/or famine and servile unrest, unless mass flight of slaves (as from Attica towards the end of the Peloponnesian War: Thuc. 7.27.5) be counted as servile unrest.

(3) Size of slaveholding units

In the Old South, for which more or less reliable census statistics are available, fewer than one quarter of families owned a single slave, let alone a gang of them, when slavery was at its peak in the middle three decades of the nineteenth century. Half of the slaves worked on 'farms' rather than 'plantations', that is, on units with fewer than twenty slaves. Fewer than three per cent of slaveholders – just over half a percentage point of all Southern families – owned more than fifty slaves; put another way, only one quarter of slaves worked on such large plantation-units.[47] The contrast within the New World with the situation in contemporary Brazil and the pre-1834 situation in the Caribbean countries was marked: there the production of sugar, unlike that of cotton, tobacco, rice or coffee, encouraged economies of scale, and units of more than 500 slaves were not uncommon. Hence Genovese's suggestion that units approaching the average of one to two hundred slaves conduced to revolt.

As ever, we are lamentably short of comparable evidence for Classical Greece. The one figure that has been handed down as if it were an authoritative statistic purports to record the number of slaves registered in the census taken at Athens by Demetrios of Phaleron in the penultimate decade of the fourth century (Ktesikles *ap.* Athen. 6.272c). However, like the figures attributed to Corinth and Aigina, this is ludicrously hyperbolic, as we shall see when discussing items (5) and (6). The positive evidence for individual holdings is rather more credible but, equally clearly, highly untypical: more than 1000 were reportedly owned by an associate of Aristotle, Mnason of Phokis (Athen. 6.264cd), and in the previous century 1000 by Nikias (Xen. *Por.* 4.14; Athen. 6.272c,e.), 600 by Hipponikos, and 300 by Philemonides (Xen. *Por.* 4.15) – these last three being exceptionally opulent Athenians who hired out some or all of their slaves for the often literally killing work in the state-owned silver-mines at Laureion.[48] Lysias and Polemarchos, wealthy and probably privileged metics (resident aliens) at Athens, owned 120 slaves in the late fifth century, and most of these may have been employed regularly in the brothers' shield manufactory (Lys. 12.8,19).[49] But if so, the number engaged in this single enterprise had been uniquely inflated by the demands and opportunities of the arms trade in the wholly exceptional Peloponnesian War (431-404), and in fact we hear of no other comparably large slave manufacturing unit in the whole of Greek antiquity. The orator Demosthenes' homonymous father, who owned in two batches fifty-two or fifty-three manufacturing slaves (Dem. 27.9; cf. Pasion's fifty *plus*: Dem. 36.11) is the next largest slaveholder on attestation for Classical Greece, a useful corroboration of Plato's choice of the figure of over fifty slaves to represent a notably large and in certain circumstances potentially fearsome holding; see above under (1).

At the other end of the scale of wealth, the ancient evidence again clusters around Athens. The 5000 or so citizens who at the close of the fifth century owned no land in Attica (Dion. Hal. *Lys.* 32-33 = Lys. 34) no doubt for the most part owned no slaves either. But several passages indicate or imply that the ownership of slaves here by families above the pauper line was really quite widespread, at least by contrast with the concentration of ownership in the Old South (e.g., Thuc. 3.17.4, 7.75.5; Lys. 5.5, 24.6; Isaios 5.11; Xen. *Mem.* 2.3.3; Dem. 45.86, 54.4; Theophr. 25.4).[50] Such passages are corroborated by the seemingly low (in terms of amortization) purchase-price of even skilled slaves.[51] It is, moreover, worth stressing, in contradiction of the once prevalent view to the contrary, that slaves were widely employed in Greek agriculture – the basic productive sector of antiquity – as well as in domestic service and mining. 'For poor men', Aristotle (*Pol.* 1252b12) noted, 'the ox takes the place of a slave'; or, as a leading modern student has put it, 'If we have trouble identifying [a special category of] "agricultural slaves" in Athens, it may be in part because they are everywhere'.[52] *A fortiori* this would be even more true of states (the majority) in which craft manufacture was of slighter economic significance – Mnason's Phokis, for instance, Kerkyra, Elis or Chios.[53] However, Mediterranean dry-farming of the staple dietary triad of cereals, olives and vines did not call for economies of scale, and the intensification in farming of which Jameson and others have well written need have involved only small numbers of additional, slave hands – slave for preference because, as Xenophon (*Mem.* 2.7.6) remarked, the point about owning foreign slaves was that one could 'compel them to do whatever work is convenient'. We do hear of bailiffs or overseers (*epitropoi*), themselves

141

typically slaves or freedmen. But supervision of agricultural slaves would on the whole have been simple and direct, and Classical Greece clearly belongs at the Old Southern rather than the Brazilian/Caribbean end of the spectrum in respect of slave-unit size.[54]

(4) Frequent splits within the ruling class

By such splits Genovese understood situations in which either two or more slaveholding countries frequently war with each other or there are frequent bitter struggles within a slaveholding country. He had in mind specifically the situation in the Caribbean, where 'the French incited the slaves of the British, who incited the slaves of the Spanish, who incited the slaves of the French' (*FRR*, 22). A priori one might have expected both situations to obtain in Classical Greece, a congeries of many independent and often mutually antagonistic states where splits within the slaveholding class of individual cities and splits between slaveholding states were virtually endemic, particularly in the fourth century.[55]

As it happens, though, the specific evidence is virtually confined to the civil war on the island of Kerkyra (Corfu) in 427: both sides appealed to the slaves for support by offering manumission as a reward, and the slaves, interestingly, decided for the democrats against the oligarchs – presumably because as prospective freedmen they anticipated a better future in a democratic than in an oligarchic *polis* (Thuc. 3.73). This example is, however, unlikely to be unique, since Thucydides treats the Kerkyra civil war as a model of the kind of civil wars that broke out almost universally in the course of the Peloponnesian War. Moreover, one of the clauses of the Peace imposed on the subjugated Greek states in 338/7 by Philip of Macedon would seem to offer corroboration: this outlawed the tactic of liberating slaves for the purpose of furthering political revolution (Ps.-Dem. 17.15; cf. Hypereides fr. 18 Blass). On the other hand, the known examples of successful incitement to servile revolt by outside agitators are confined to the serf-like populations of Thessaly (Xen. *Hell.* 2.3.36) and Messenia (below, Section III).

(5) Proportion of slave and free and of (6) imported to home-bred slaves

Revolts were more likely, Genovese observes, where blacks heavily outnumbered whites and where African-born slaves outnumbered those born into slavery in the Americas. I take these numerical factors together. For 'blacks' we can read 'slaves', since from the late seventeenth century onwards after an experiment with white bondage[56] blacks were exclusively preferred for slavery in the Old South and were always so preferred in the Caribbean and Brazil. Translating this into Greeks terms, for 'blacks' we may read 'barbarians' (non-Greek *barbaroi*), towards whom the attitude of

142

virtually all free Greeks – not excluding those like Aristotle who might have been expected to do better – was a mixture of something akin to modern racism and nationalism.[57] For 'African-born' we should understand primarily those slaves in Greece who had been born in Phrygia, Thrace or Scythia – the *terres d'élection* as sources of slaves so far at least as those held in Athens and Attica were concerned.[58]

The preserved figures for total slave numbers in the various states of Classical Greece are notoriously unreliable, or rather unusable. The alleged census-figure of 400,000 from late-fourth-century Athens referred to above under item (3) turns out on closer inspection to be laughably exaggerated, as David Hume long ago demonstrated.[59] *A fortiori* our other two figures, which do not have even spuriously statistical value and relate to states with far smaller carrying capacities and total capital assets, are even less likely to be anywhere near the mark: 460,000 in Corinth, 470,000 on the island of Aigina (Athen. 6.272b,d, the latter quoted on the supposed 'authority' of Aristotle). True, chattel slavery could well have been quite highly developed in Corinth, in the manufacturing sector as well as in agriculture;[60] but merely to point out that 460,000 *in toto* would have given a ratio of some 500 slaves per square kilometre is sufficient to make any further argument superfluous. Only for Athens is there perhaps enough of the right kind of evidence to start talking about orders of magnitude, and the more cautious modern estimates (or 'guesstimates') yield a range of between 60,000 and 100,000 slaves, between one half and one third of whom could have been employed in the Laureion silver mines at their peak.[61] This would mean that slaves – again, on the more cautious modern estimates – accounted for between a quarter and a third of the total population of Attica at that time or, put another way, were in a ratio to the free population of about 1:2.[62] These proportions roughly correspond to those obtaining in the Old South as a whole in the mid-nineteenth century, at least as they were recorded in the 1860 census.

Athens and Attica, however, as can be inferred from a passage of Thucydides (8.40.2), did not have the highest density of slaveownership in Classical Greece; that dubious honour, so far as chattel slaves (as opposed to serf-like bondsmen) were concerned, apparently belonged to the slaveowners of the island of Chios. Independent corroboration of that inference may perhaps be found in the view first attested in the mid-fourth century (and no doubt a product of reflection consequent upon the recent mass liberation of the serf-like Helots of Messenia) that the Chians had pioneered the introduction of chattel slavery among the Greeks.[63] On Chios, then, slaves may at times have constituted as much as half the total population (as in Mississippi and South Carolina); and it is not irrelevant to add that most of these must have been at least part of the time employed in agriculture (the skilled ones in viticulture). This high ratio may also be somehow connected to the conspicuous but unfortunately undated slave troubles on the island reported by a Syracusan historian of the third century (Nymphodoros, *FGrHist.* 572 F 4); see further below under (8).

As for the ratio of foreign-born to home-born (*oikogeneis*) slaves, there can be no doubt but that in Classical Greece the former seriously outnumbered the latter, chiefly perhaps because of the relative cheapness of foreign imports (n. 51, above). The expressed preference of the author of the Aristotelian *Oeconomica* (1.5.6) for allowing slaves to breed – on the prudential grounds that their children would be hostages for their parents' good behaviour – is surely as eccentric as his advocacy of manumission as the prize for good conduct. Even this author, though, regards purchase of slaves as the normal mode of acquisition.

In this respect, then, Classical Greece stood nearer to Brazil, where the slave trade persisted until late in the nineteenth century, than to the Old South, in which breeding had become the norm by the beginning of that century (when the trade was abolished by Federal decree). Yet in contrast to the Brazilian experience and more markedly to that of Sicily in the last third of the second century, Classical Greece did not apparently experience slave revolts. This example does not, however, necessarily undermine Genovese's general proposition concerning the ratio of foreign to home-bred slaves, since the high ratio in Classical Greece was offset by two other factors, one quantitative, the other qualitative. The first is the usually overwhelming proportion of free to slave just noted. The second is a function of the ancient Greek class struggle. For whereas the free (whether slaveowners or not) would typically be united in opposition to the slaves as a group (cf. Xen. *Hiero* 4.3), the slaves owned by any individual or by the slaveholders of a state collectively would tend of their masters' set purpose (cf. Plat. *Laws* 777cd; Arist. *Pol.* 1330a25-8) to be a heterogeneous, polyglot mass with no shared cultural background or other focus of social solidarity and unable to communicate with each other except in their masters' language.[64] This was not, though, the sole or even necessarily the determining reason why there appear to have been no largescale revolts of chattel slaves in Classical Greece. For Brazilian masters employed the same technique of class warfare but without the same result.

(7) Emergence of an autonomous black leadership

No one will deny the importance of (a) leadership. That is a truism. The crucial question, rather, concerns its nature, and how it is to arise and become effective. In the Old South, slave revolts were few and none really major, but those that did occur were all led by artisans and industrial slaves, that is, by men from the privileged minority (never more than thirty per cent) constituted by the skilled and semi-skilled.[65] A South Carolinan Senator is on record as regarding industrial (as opposed to agricultural) slaves as already 'more than half freed'.[66] This was typical planter's hyperbole, but it captures the essential point about the connections between conditions of work and capacity to lead a revolt. Slaves who were not subjected to the crushing routine and daily punishments involved in organized, driven fieldwork were freer to contemplate making a revolt and might carve out for themselves the necessary spiritual and ideological space to dare the almost suicidal.

In Classical Athens (relevant evidence is unavailable for other states) we might antecedently expect leadership in revolt to have come from the comparably privileged strata of artisan slaves who lived apart (*douloi chôris oikountes*), running small businesses funded initially by their masters to whom they paid a fixed percentage of the proceeds from selling their products; or from the slaves who were hired out by their masters for seasonal agricultural work or other purposes (*andrapoda mistho-phorounta*); or from the most privileged stratum of all, the public slaves (*dêmosioi*) owned by the Athenian state.[67] But their capacity to organize revolt was of course hampered by the objective conditions already discussed, and their will to revolt will have been sapped by their superior conditions of life, which in some cases really may have amounted to their being more than half free. For it was of privileged slaves such as these that the 'Old Oligarch' (Ps.-Xen. *Ath. Pol.* 1.10-12) complained, perhaps in the 420s, that slaves could not be distinguished from (poor) free men by their dress and demeanour on the streets of Athens; and it was they alone who stood any realistic chance of achieving manumission under economically tolerable circumstances.

For, generally speaking, manumission in Classical Greece, as in the Old South, seems to have been infrequent, at least by comparison with Roman practice.[68] Aristotle, it is true, and a follower of his went out of their way to recommend the prospect of manumission as a general principle of slave-management (*Pol.* 1330a32-3; cf. Ps.-Arist. *Oec.* 1.5.6); but that probably means this was a principle not yet widely accepted, despite its obvious utility in encouraging exertion and loyalty on the part of the slaves. Presumably, therefore, the economic and political consequences of manumission were not as a rule felt to be especially desirable by Classical Greek slaveowners. Westermann's belief that manumission was a straightforward procedure and widely practised was based on the shakiest of evidence.[69] His further inference that it was 'an astonishing fluidity of status ... which, in large measure, explains the absence of slave revolts in the Greek classical period' was therefore not only false in fact but also, and not incidentally, seriously weakened by comparative Brazilian evidence.[70]

(8) Colonies of runaways

There is no shortage of evidence for runaways (*drapetai*) in Classical Greece, as we have seen. But I know of no such permanent colony of runaways as the seventeenth-century Palmares *quilombo* of Brazil nor any equivalents to the late-seventeenth- and early-eighteenth-century maroon (*marron*) settlements of Jamaica.[71] Possibly relevant, however, is the unique ancient account of the runaway slave Drimakos who, perhaps in the early third century BC, took to the mountains of Chios and organized a band of runaways to carry out guerrilla operations against the landed property of their former masters.[72] Having failed to subdue Drimakos militarily, the owners came to an agreement under the terms of which Drimakos would receive only grossly maltreated runaways and return all others to their masters. This agreement is closely paralleled in the treaty signed by the Governor of Jamaica with the maroon leader 'Captain' Cudjoe in 1738.[73] Since Chios was by no means the only Greek state to afford suitably rugged and forested mountains for strong points of refuge and resistance, the successful establishment of Drimakos' colony should probably be somehow linked to the unusually high ratio of slave to free on Chios and (more tentatively) to the reported brutality or at least misman-agement on the part of the Chian slaveholders. Thucydides (8.40.2) had been struck by the large numbers of slaves who deserted to the Athenians in 411.

III

In the previous section Genovese's eight factors favouring chattel slave revolt were applied comparatively to Classical Greece. Only two – (4) and (6) – were found to be present to any significant degree, and they were counteracted by other factors. Genovese did not claim to have ranked the factors he isolated in order of importance, partly no doubt because the most difficult aspect of attempting to explain complex social phenomena is precisely the relative weighting to be attributed to the relevant condition-ing and contributory variables. But I think he would not be unwilling to accept that (1) – the factor that may be shortly summarized as slave ideology – was at bottom the most decisive of them all. This at any rate would help to explain why peasants in comparably difficult material circumstances have been able to revolt more frequently and more success-fully than slaves, even though, as Barrington Moore has soberly noted, 'peasant revolts have been repressed far more often than they have succeeded'.[74]

However, in case any reader should still be tempted to hold fast to the notion that it is easy to draw up an order of priority for any given servile population, let alone for all servile populations at all times and in every place, let me consider briefly and in outline the one servile population in Classical Greece that did revolt more than once, and the majority of which eventually revolted successfully into full political as well as purely per-sonal freedom: the Helots of Lakonia and Messenia.[75] Their unique experience may further illuminate the problem of why the other servile populations of Greece apart from the Penestai of Thessaly (Xen. *Hell.* 2.3.36; Arist. *Pol.* 1269a37-8) did not apparently revolt either regularly or

146

successfully.[76] Again, I shall take Genovese's list of favouring factors (where relevant) as a series of working hypotheses, only in this case to see whether they are verified rather than falsified, bearing in mind throughout that the evidence, though more abundant than for any other Greek servile group, is presented to us by largely hostile sources and never by the Helots themselves.

(1) The master-slave relationship

First, on a point of definition, the Helots were in Greek parlance *douloi* (the commonest term for the unfree), no less than were the chattel slaves of, say, Athens. To take two telling illustrations: the collective noun *douleia*, 'servile population' or 'slave class', appears in the terms of the treaty of defensive alliance between Sparta and Athens in 421 (Thuc. 5.23.3), and the pro-Spartan Athenian oligarch Kritias, writing for a non-Spartan public, went so far as to describe the Helots as being *douloi* to a greater extent or degree than any other *douloi* in Greece (88 B 37 D-K). If we have regard solely to the Helots' economic function as involuntary and exploited producers of the Spartans' surplus, their designation as *douloi* is indeed perfectly correct.[77] But legally, socially, even politically, they differed markedly from chattel slaves. They were not foreigners bought and sold on the market, outsiders wrenched from native ties of kin and religion. Nor were they wholly owned by and totally at the disposal of individual Spartan masters. Rather, they were Greeks, enslaved collectively upon and tied to the land their ancestors had once tilled as free men, and they were held in subjection by explicit and repeated acts of the Spartan political community, the *polis* of the Spartans. They had, moreover, some kind of family life, which is part of the reason they were able to reproduce themselves as a servile population over many generations. Finally, in the case at least of the more numerous (Thuc. 1.101.2) Messenian Helots, they had a sense of common identity that may fairly be called political. Legally, that is to say, they were a kind of state-serfs.[78] Socially and politically, they were a people, almost a nation.

Turning from definition to practice, we find absenteeism, depersonalization and cultural estrangement all relevantly present in the master-slave relationship. Precisely how production was organized on a Helot-run estate (*klaros*, literally 'allotment') we shall never know. But the Spartan *klaros*-owners were for most of the year necessarily absentee landlords, at least until they were exempted from active military service at the age of sixty (cf. Xen. *Hell.* 5.4.13). The *klaroi* in Lakonia, however, were far more accessible than those in ultramontane Messenia, and it was doubtless in Lakonia that rich Spartans kept ready their supplies of horses, dogs and provisions with a view to indulging in their favourite pursuit of hunting boar and other wild game (Xen. *LP* 6.3-4; Plut. *Lyk.* 12.4; cf. David 1993). It is possible that organization of labour and distribution of its products were left immediately in the hands of the Helot equivalent of an overseer (*epitropos*; cf. the Spartan dialect word *monomoïtos* glossed as 'leader of Helots' in the lexicon of Hesychios); but it is doubtful whether there were Helot equivalents of slave-drivers, and if there was any Helot-breaking to be done, that could be arranged by the notorious Spartan 'Secret Service' (Krypteia: Arist. fr. 538; cf. Jeanmaire 1913; above, Chapter 7).

Depersonalization and cultural estrangement are harder factors to assess. In this, as indeed in all respects except the strictly legal and economic, it makes sense to distinguish more or less sharply between the Helots of Messenia and those of Lakonia. The Messenians lived further away from their collective master, on the far side of a formidable (2407m) mountain barrier. This physical separation will have done nothing to attenuate the psychological alienation they felt and expressed in the shared consciousness of having once been 'the Messenians', members of their own independent *polis* of Messene (reconstituted as such after 369). It was immaterial to the efficacy of this 'nationalist' myth that their ancestors had not in fact travelled far, if at all, along the road to *polis*-status before the Spartan conquest and annexation began in the latter part of the eighth century. Thus it was no doubt more particularly against the Messenian Helots that the Spartans' remarkable, and to my knowledge unparalleled, annual declaration of war on the Helots (Arist. fr. 538) was directed.

The Lakonian Helots, on the other hand, though they too were Greeks, seem to have been subjugated earlier and were more immediately within the reach of the long arm of Spartan physical and psychological repression. They were therefore perhaps more likely to have had their kinship and community solidarity undermined in any case, but a further contributory factor towards this end seems to have been that their ancestors had been enslaved before any shoot of 'national' or *polis* consciousness had had time to grow. By the fifth century, anyhow, if not long before they had seemingly lost any notion of an anterior political independence. When the Theban Epameinondas led the first-ever invasion of Sparta's territory (370/69), we are told (Plut. *Lyk.* 28.10) that he found Lakonian Helots so successfully indoctrinated that they refused to sing verses by various poets since these had been declared taboo by their masters. Yet at that very moment the Helots of Messenia were in revolt *en masse* and about to achieve permanent liberation.

However, even this apparently telling example should not be taken to mean that all Lakonian Helots were at all times entirely passive and submissive. Following the massive earthquake of *c.* 464 which directly affected Sparta town (Thuc. 1.101.2; Diod. 11.63.1-3, 65.4), some of them certainly joined in the revolt that ensued. Indeed, I would venture to suggest that it may well have been they who began the revolt, in apparent contradiction of their normal passivity. For exactly this contradiction between 'Sambos' and rebels has been observed in the Old South, notably in the person of Nat Turner who led a slave rebellion in 1831.[79] Paternalism in Genovese's sense, however heavy-handed, can cut in more than one way.

Undoubtedly, though, the great revolt of *c.* 464, which lasted several years, was essentially a Messenian affair (esp. Thuc. 1.101.2-103.3; Diod. 11.63-4). Like the successful revolt of 370/69, it perfectly exemplifies the observation of Aristotle (*Pol.* 1269a37-b5) that the Helots were 'like an enemy constantly sitting in wait for the disasters of the Spartans'.[80] These revolts should, moreover, be classified as slave revolts (using 'slave' loosely), notwithstanding the fact that in servile revolts the participants typically aim at purely individual liberation rather than social transformation. For the essence of slave revolts, before the thoroughly 'modern' one led by Toussaint L'Ouverture in the wake of the French Revolution, was that they were 'restorationist'.[81] In the sense that the Messenians were aiming to restore themselves to what they took to be their anterior political and social condition, their revolts were precisely that; and if their aim was a collective rather than individual transformation, this was because they were collective, not individual, *douloi* of Spartans.

(2) The occurrence of economic distress and famine

Only two famines are attested in all Spartan history, neither of them in the Classical era; and Sparta, even when stripped of Messenia, was (probably significantly) not among the states in Greece to receive grain from Cyrene during the shortage of the early 320s.[82] A Spartan public regulation (Plut. *Mor.* 239e) imposed a religious curse upon any *klaros*-holder who exacted more than the maximum stipulated rent (or tribute) payable by the Helots working his land; but this regulation may not antedate the reform of Kings Agis IV and Kleomenes III in the 240s and 230s. It is therefore possible that some Helots found themselves squeezed economically, whether by more powerful Helots or by their Spartan masters, especially perhaps in the late fifth and early fourth centuries, when some rich Spartans were displaying a countercultural propensity to self-differentiation that included consumption at a higher level than the officially recognized norm (e.g. Xen. *LP* 5.3). Specific evidence is lacking, however, and this was probably not a major factor influencing Helots to revolt.[83]

(3) Size of slaveholding units

We know nothing precise about the numbers of Helots working on any one *klaros*, but an important passage of Xenophon (*Hell.* 3.3.5) recounting an abortive conspiracy among the lower orders of Spartan society led by one Kinadon (a lapsed Spartan) virtually proves that there were more than one Helot family on each – and probably many more than one on the holdings of the richest Spartans (women as well as men). Again, though, this will have been by itself a relatively insignificant revolt-producing factor, especially if the Helots lived dispersed in their individual families among the several *klaroi* rather than grouped into hamlets or villages. Livy's phrase *castellani* (34.27.9, in a context of *c.* 200 BC) could mean either 'villagers' or 'farm-dwellers', and Thucydides' Helos (4.54.4) was probably a centre of occasional religious cult rather than permanent Helot habitation.

(4) Frequent splits within the ruling class

According to the Spartan 'mirage', the myth of Sparta promoted initially by the Spartans themselves but given wide currency and sustained by pro-Spartan oligarchs and philosophers in other states (esp. Kritias 88 B 6-9, 32-7 D-K),[84] one of the distinguishing features of developed Spartan society was the harmony and unanimity (*homonoia* or same-mindedness) that prevailed among the full Spartan citizens, who styled themselves *Homoioi* or 'Peers'. In reality, disharmony on occasion reached such a pitch that Aristotle (*Pol.* 1306b31-6) felt justified in treating two outbreaks at the turn of the fifth and fourth centuries, including Kinadon's abortive conspiracy (Xen. *Hell.* 3.3.4-11), as cases of potential *stasis* or open civil strife. To these may be added the Pausanias affair of the later 470s or early 460s, in which Regent Pausanias was accused – no doubt falsely in fact – of promising not just to free Helots but actually to make them into Spartan citizens (Thuc. 1.132.4).[85] A causal connection may be postulated between this affair and the great Helot revolt of *c.* 464, as between the succession crisis of *c.* 400 and Kinadon's conspiracy.[86]

As for splits between slaveholding states, Aristotle (*Pol.* 1269a37-b5) attributed the absence of servile revolt on Crete to deliberate abstention by the Cretan states from mutually inciting each other's servile under-classes (here called *perioikoi*). The contrast he had in mind particularly was with the attitude of Sparta's enemies to the Helots, which became blatant in the early fourth century.[87] The liberation of the Messenian Helots and the reconstitution of the *polis* of Messene could not have been accomplished without outside, especially Theban, material aid. And not just material but also moral aid. There are no Classical Greek abolitionists on record, it is true, but the Sophist Alkidamas need not have been alone in justifying the liberation of the Messenian Helots on the (strictly non-Aristotelian) ground that 'God has left all men free; nature has made no man a slave' (Schol. in Arist. *Rhet.* 1373b6).

(5) Proportion of slave to free and of (6) imported to home-bred slaves

Factor (6) does not apply as such, since the Spartans owned few if any chattel slaves, and the Helots were self-reproducing. But unlike slaves in the Old South, they also reproduced themselves as members of a homogeneous ethnic group who spoke the same ancestral language as their masters. Plato (*Laws* 777bc) and Aristotle (*Pol.* 1330a25-8) rightly linked these shared characteristics with the Helots' propensity to revolt. Factor (5), on the other hand, could hardly be more relevant and significant.

Whatever the precise numbers may have been on either side, there is no doubt but that the Helots collectively grossly outnumbered the Spartans (Hdt. 9.10.1, 28.2, 29.1; Thuc. 8.40.2), and that this gross and indeed growing numerical disparity was a vital factor governing relations between the two antagonistic classes. The Peloponnesian War (431-404) seems to have marked a turning-point in this regard. The felt disparity encouraged the Spartans, on the one hand, to create privileged ex-Helot statuses (Thuc. 5.34; cf. Myron, *FGrHist.* 106 F 1), thereby furthering the traditional ruling class aim of dividing and ruling their subjects, and, on the other, to conduct a savage exemplary massacre of those Helots thought most likely to prove rebellious (Thuc. 4.80.2-4; cf. Jordan 1990).

(7) Emergence of an autonomous black leadership

Given the technologically undeveloped, agrarian character of the Spartan economy, potential rebel leaders cannot be sought among an urban and privileged artisan section of Helots. Indeed, it is hard to see where such leaders could emerge from within the Helot population itself, unless it be from a postulated 'kulak' stratum of richer Helots – the kind who were eventually in a position to pay the not inconsiderable cash sum of five *minai* required by Kleomenes III to buy their freedom in 223 or 222 BC (Plut. *Kleom.* 23.1). The only rebel leader known to us by name, the Messenian Aristomenes (Paus. 4.6.3, 14.7 etc.), has been transmitted to posterity under a halo of legend and propaganda assiduously polished in the aftermath of the 370/69 liberation. Even his date is uncertain, though more likely to be mid-seventh century than early-fifth. Otherwise, it is revealing that leaders are offered, or put themselves forward, from within the ranks of the master class – a Pausanias, a Kinadon. The Helots were in a sense insiders as well as deliberately excluded outsiders in this peculiar society.

(8) Colonies of runaways

For a slave revolt to be sustained for any length of time a 'maroon dimension', so it has been argued from the comparative Brazilian and Caribbean evidence (n. 73, above), is indispensable: the establishment, that is, of a more or less autonomous and self-sufficient colony of runaways. Naupaktos (Thuc. 1.103.1-3; Diod. 11.84.7-8) was in a sense such a colony after *c.* 460, but the parallel is not close, not least because the Naupaktian Messenians were too distant from the homeland to offer continuous succour to their enslaved brethren in revolt (but see Thuc. 4.41.2).

However, during the revolt following the great earthquake of *c.* 464 some considerable number of Messenian Helots was able to subsist and withstand siege on Mount Ithome for an appreciable period in the 460s and perhaps into the 450s, which argues the establishment of semi-permanent communal institutions. Resort to Ithome was facilitated by the great distance separating it from Sparta, not to mention the 2407m Taygetos massif running between the two sites. It was probably not just at times of generalized revolt that the sanctuary of the mountain was sought, although it was apparently only at Poseidon's shrine at Tainaron in southern Lakonia that Helots might legitimately seek asylum (Thuc. 1.128.1).

IV

To conclude: the underlying cause of the revolts of the Helots, as of servile revolts everywhere, was the simple fact that they wanted to be free. But the Helots were only *able* to revolt outright because their ethnic and political solidarity provided the Messenians with the appropriate ideological inspiration and organizational cohesion, and because their numerical, geographical and international situation gave them (and Sparta's enemies) the requisite room for manoeuvre and ultimately justified hope of success.

These conditions did not obtain for the chattel slaves of Classical Greece. That they did not to our knowledge revolt is not therefore a sign that they were mostly happy with their unsought lot but rather a mark of the success with which their owners conducted a conscious and unremitting class struggle against them. That struggle was not a simple phenomenon: by employing a comparative approach, I hope to have been able to demonstrate that the factors potentially relevant to explaining servile revolt are many and complex and that the absence of slave revolts in Classical Greece cannot be fully explained in terms of just one of them.[88]

The Birth of the Hoplite: Sparta's Contribution to Early Greek Military Organization

Introduction

This chapter represents a reworking of the English original of an article which appeared in Italian translation as 'La nascita degli opliti e l'organizzazione militare', in S. Settis ed. *I Greci* Vol. II, Part 1 (Turin 1996) ch. 23. (I am most grateful to Einaudi Editore for permission to re-use the material in this way.) The Italian translation was illustrated and contained an Appendix entitled 'The Nature of Hoplite Battle'. Both the illustrations and the Appendix have been cut from the present version, though some material from the latter has been redeployed here.

The chapter forms part of a debate, still (I hope) ongoing, about the causes, effects and meanings of the development of the hoplite style of phalanx fighting, which became almost *de rigueur* among the more important Greek states during the course of the seventh and sixth centuries. The Spartans were the acknowledged pastmasters of this hoplite art, and I used a discussion of their experience as the focus of an earlier contribution to the debate: Cartledge 1977. If I seem merely reactionary in questioning Kurt Raaflaub's recent assertion that 'The evidence of Homeric and early Greek warfare leaves no space for a "hoplite revolution"' (Raaflaub 1999: 140), then so it must be. Besides the excellent Raaflaub 1999, the second edition of Hanson 1989 (published 2000) also contains exceptionally useful supplementary bibliography.

*

War for Shakespeare was the 'great corrector of enormous times'. The advent of so-called 'total' war in the twentieth century provided a horribly prosaic confirmation of that poetic definition. Yet in a sense total war is not a complete novelty in the Western tradition. For the ancient Greeks, too, the wider mobilization of society rather than the outcome of any particular battle was usually the decisive factor in their monotonously regular inter-city military conflict. There is, too, in any society a reciprocal relationship between the way it performs in war and the nature of the culture that supports it, and in the societies of ancient Greece war was an integral part of their way of life, part of the air the Greeks breathed.[1] So the general renewal of military sociology that is evident in the contemporary historiography of war, placing less emphasis on battlefield manoeuvres than on the relationship between war and society, is especially appropriate for the history of ancient Greece. The 'polemology' now practised by both ancient historians and historical sociologists of ancient Greece deserves the warmest welcome.[2]

The ancients themselves, however, wrote the history of Greek warfare very differently. The Greeks' chosen topics were invariably specific wars rather than war in general; and there is a marked contradiction between the general explanations for warfare offered by the political philosophers Plato (competition for territory, riches and slaves) and Aristotle (war seen chiefly as a process of enslaving those who deserve to be so enslaved) and the more narrowly 'political' factors urged in explanation by the historians Thucydides and Polybius.[3] Here I shall follow the lead of the ancient political philosophers, drawing on the enlarged sense of 'the political' that I have developed elsewhere.[4]

For the study of Greek warfare, or the polemology of ancient Greece, cannot be separated from the project of a general, very broadly 'political' history of ancient Greek civic mentality, social structure and economic organization. Any adequate account of Greek warfare must relate battle experience to its social presuppositions, ideological projections and its value (effective or imaginary) as an instrument of political action. More specifically, since for these Greek thinkers politics (or the political) crucially embraced also economics, and since warfare was seen importantly as a mode of economic acquisition, they found it quite natural to treat warfare – whether inter-state (*polemos*), civil (*stasis*) or irregular (*lêisteia*) – as an integral part of the 'political art' (*politikê tekhnê*). I shall treat the birth of hoplite warfare and early Greek military organization likewise.

However, the state of the available evidence poses major difficulties for any historian of ancient Greece, especially in its earliest historic or protohistoric phases. (The period covered in this chapter will extend from approximately 800 to 500 BC, with special attention to the century or so from 750 to 650.) One unfortunate effect of the general lack of good contemporary evidence has been to encourage an unstable and often indefensible use (or abuse) of absolutely every surviving scrap of literary, epigraphical or archaeological data, especially Homer and the early elegiac poets (Kallinos, Tyrtaios), and figural representations in a variety of media.[5] It is worth recalling at the outset that they were not intended as faithful historical documents by their creators, that they are open to widely divergent interpretations, and that they are rarely probative. Instead, therefore, in this chapter almost as much attention and interpretative emphasis will be given to the formulation of appropriate models, and to what has been called 'the logic of contextual analysis' (Bryant 1990: 486) familiar in the discourse of sociological history since Marx and Weber.[6]

Given the congruence of war and politics in ancient Greece, and the importance of ancient Greek politics in the Western cultural and political tradition, it is not surprising that the hoplite phenomenon has for long been the focus of acute interest. All scholars are agreed that by 500 BC hoplites dominated most Greek battlefields: that is, heavy-armed and heavily protected infantrymen bearing a large double-handled shield on their left arm and wielding a thrusting spear in their right hand, massed in a tightly organized and drilled phalanx several ranks deep.[7] Even after the rise of new arms and new forces in the following century and a half, hoplite mentality continued to dominate Greek civic ideology (see further below). Tradition, as often in the history of war and society, tended to reign supreme in the military sphere.[8] On the other hand, the twin issues of what a typical hoplite battle might have been like[9] and of what any one particular hoplite battle was actually like[10] remain fiercely contested scholarly battlegrounds, for ideological as well as technical reasons. Xenophon, for example, knew the military situation of his day as intimately as anyone, and knew what he was saying when he described the hoplite battle of Koroneia in 394, in which he himself fought, as 'unlike any other' in his time (*Hell.* 4.3.16; *Ages.* 2.9: cf. Cartledge 1987: 220; and generally Anderson 1970), but unfortunately he did not pass on his first-hand knowledge unambiguously to us.[11]

Here, however, I shall confine myself to yet another scholarly battleground, namely the origins and early development of the hoplite phenomenon. Interpretation of these processes over the past sixty or so years has spanned the entire spectrum of logical possibility: from the claim that at any rate the most important Greek cities experienced a full-blooded 'hoplite revolution', through belief in the occurrence of a more or less sudden 'hoplite reform' at different times in different parts of the Greek world somewhere between about 750 and 600 BC, to the view that there was no significant change at all, or at most a gradual evolution, in military tactics and organization in recorded post-Bronze Age Greek history. Why, or rather how, can such sharp differences of opinion exist?

To put it simply, they hinge partly on matters of fact (were hoplite arms, armour and tactics so very different from pre-hoplite? in so far as there were technical, tactical and organizational changes, how quickly did they occur, and how universally?), but mainly on the construction that is placed upon the (relatively few) agreed facts. To schematize, there is, on the one hand, the 'old orthodoxy'. This maintains broadly speaking that there was, if not an outright revolution, at least a very significant tactical reform, the outcome and implications of which were both a developed form of hoplite phalanx fighting on the battlefield and significant political change off it.[12] On the polar opposite side are lined up those 'revisionists' who deny that within the historical era – that is, beginning with the period of real Greek history from which the Homeric poems issued or to which they chiefly referred – there was any significant tactical change in (massed infantry) fighting whatsoever, and who therefore minimize the role of the military factor in the unquestionable political changes that may be summed up in the phrase 'the rise of the *polis*'.[13] A middle position is occupied by those such as Van Wees, who believe there was a change from pre-hoplite mass fighting to hoplite mass*ed* warfare but that this did not constitute a 'reform', let alone a 'revolution'.[14]

It would take longer, and be a more speculative exercise, to enquire why revisionism emerged in this field of ancient history, and why it has been so widely successful. Part of the explanation no doubt is normal, cyclical, endogenous change, as a new generation of historians inevitably seeks to make 'progress' in understanding and explaining the past by rejecting the dominant paradigms of its mentors. Another, and I would guess a larger, part of the answer is to do with the widespread repugnance of the late 1970s and 1980s against structuralist, social-determinist, and especially Marxist theories of historical change – an externalist interpretation that accords well with Benedetto Croce's dictum that all history is contemporary history. The account that follows is written by a former combatant in this murderous scholarly warfare who has retired from the fray and is content to look on in relative safety from the sidelines.

Homer is often said to have been the Greeks' equivalent of the Jewish or Christian Bible, at any rate in the extended metaphorical sense that the epics continued to function for centuries throughout the Greek world as an icon of ethnic and cultural self-definition and as a normative benchmark.[15] But to the Greeks the epics were also a sort of history book – if a rather bad one in the view of the more enlightened critics (e.g., Thucydides). And not only to the ancient Greeks: Heinrich Schliemann's archaeological achievements at Hissarlik, Mycenae, Tiryns and elsewhere were arguably due not least to his conviction that Homer was as much a historian as an epic poet. But the loose analogy with the Bible remains in my view more persuasive.

Like the Bible (whether in its Hebrew, Greek or Vulgate versions), Homer was culturally authoritative for later generations despite the fact that the society or societies whose behaviour and norms the epics describe or presuppose was or were almost unimaginably different from those experienced by their later hearers and readers. Besides, just as Homer got the real world of Mycenaean Bronze Age Greek palace societies very wrong, as we now know from a combination of archaeology and palaeography, so later Greeks perpetrated a no less confused and confusing conflation of their 'heroes' – whether ruling aristocrats, hereditary monarchs, or popularly chosen democratic leaders – with the heroes of epic. Alexander the Great is perhaps the *ne plus ultra* of the heroizing phenomenon. The fact that later Greeks were able to identify themselves with the

156

supposed world or society of Homer should not be taken as evidence of significant continuity, let alone identity, of actual political, social or – what concerns us here – military organization and ideology.

A further difficulty for the historian of ancient Greece who wishes to make use of the epics as evidence are the circumstances of their creation. They were the products of a centuries-long oral tradition unconstrained by properly historical attention to accuracy, authenticity, and consistency – indeed, of a tradition constrained rather to mutate and evolve in accordance with the changing circumstances and expectations of the poets' audiences. If it is indeed the case that no imaginative poet can be expected to be as consistent and authentically realistic as the historian might wish or demand, then this is true to the ultimate degree of the poets of the Homeric tradition of oral epic.[16] In short, arguments for the existence of a genuinely historical, single and uniform Homeric 'society' or 'period' or more vaguely 'world' seem monumentally unpersuasive.[17] My own view, which the mountain of recent investigation has merely reinforced, is that Homer's fictive universe remains immortal precisely because it never existed as such outside the poet's or poets' fertile imagination(s) – in much the same way as Homeric language was a *Kunstsprache* never actually spoken outside the context of an epic recital.

That does not of course mean, however, that every detail of the *Realien* in Homer must necessarily have been wholly invented or significantly falsified.[18] Comparative study of traditional oral heroic epic poetry, indeed, would suggest that the era in which the tradition attains its narrative crystallization, as in the *Iliad* and *Odyssey*, is the one that contributes most in the way of historical actuality to the finished product.[19] And that era, the experts are generally agreed, spans roughly the century from 750 to 650. But what betrays the artificiality of the construction as a whole is its unreal or unrealistic combination of details – social practices, metals technology, political ideology and so on – not to mention the divine interference in or control over the affairs of mortal men. That composite artifice is as apparent in the vital details of warfare in the *Iliad* as it is in other fundamental spheres of collective activity.

To give the revisionists their due, however, they have at all events put paid for good to the old idea that the ordinary, non-heroic Greeks at Troy had merely walk-on parts in the unfolding military drama. Excepting the climactic duel of Achilles and Hector, such *monomakhiai* are not militarily decisive, and normally Homeric battles are fought and settled mainly by mass action.[20] The seemingly critical importance of heroic duels is an illusion created by the poets' almost cinematographic device of zooming in on their individual engagements for the sake of dramatic narrative effect.[21] However, contrary to revisionist orthodoxy, there is all the difference in the world between mass military action, even decisive mass military action, and regular engagements between massed ranks of hoplite phalanxes.

Thus, whereas it is perfectly legitimate to point out that a Homeric battle-description according to which the proximity of one's neighbour's shield is considered an asset rather than a liability implies or assumes the practice of close-order combat, it is quite illegitimate to extrapolate from that to (knowledge of or familiarity with) the existence of developed hoplite phalanx warfare.[22] Moreover, 'a constant scattering and rallying of troops is incompatible with maintaining a tight formation', and 'the repeated ebb and flow of battle' such as we find in Homer militates likewise against the inference of regular, massed infantry fighting.[23] Then, there is the further problem of the use of chariots in Homer, for which no straightforwardly 'realist' reading has yet been (or ever will be) able adequately to account.[24]

How one interprets Homeric inconsistency or ambivalence of battle-description is of course another matter. Narrative artistry, as suggested above, must be one part of the answer. The cumulative nature of the oral epic tradition might be another. Yet more crucial than either of these, I would argue, is the influence of political ideology. For 'the heroic form of mobile, open-field combat' with its 'individualistic hero-ecstasy' enabled the heroes literally to stand out (*ek-stasis*) from the crowd as champions (*promakhoi*),[25] and thus to provide suitable political (not necessarily military) role-models for the elites of the contemporary Greek world of *c.* 750 to 650.[26]

We shall return later to the properly political dimension of Homeric representation. First, it must be added that a modified revisionist interpretation or re-interpretation of Homer, which allows for implicit or explicit reference there to heavy-armed mass fighting, does have the further merit of being perfectly consistent with the extant contemporary archaeological evidence – both actual finds of arms and armour and representations of them borne by warriors on and off the battlefield.[27] This evidence tells us that the one absolutely crucial innovation in equipment – the convex, two-handled body-shield made of wood and with an offset rim of bronze – had been made, possibly first in Argos, by 700. Clearly, such a shield was inappropriate, if not a positive hazard, in any other than massed phalanx fighting, and the most economical explanatory hypothesis is that it was invented precisely to improve the offensive but more especially the defensive efficiency of the already vital infantry warriors.[28] So too the invention and adoption of the bronze cuirass and greaves, and of the characteristically hoplite 'Corinthian' helmet, also in the years around 700, point in the same direction. Absolute and total uniformity of equipment either within any one Greek hoplite army or across the entire Greek world is not, however, to be expected and was not achieved all at one go.

Technical innovations have been likened to genetic mutations of microorganisms in the sense that they may open new geographic zones for exploitation or break down older limits on the exercise of force within the host community. But the Greeks were not especially noted for technical innovation, the reception of which is typically due as much to culture as to technical invention; and they were no exception to the general rule that military men prefer manageable evolution within stable functional categories to revolutionary breakthroughs in weaponry. So some special explanation seems to be required for this apparent outburst of technical innovation in the military sphere towards 700 BC. Since what demands explanation is not so much the availability of the requisite raw materials and of craftsmen with the appropriate skills as their decisive practical employment, we seem, again, to be being forced to look for broader social and political explanations of the changing military phenomena. Given the absence of good contemporary evidence, it is here above all that modelling and 'situational logic' will have to be called up for duty.

It is comparatively easy to establish a direct connection between hoplite warfare and the rise of particular Greek states. One thinks automatically of those 'conquest'-states and permanent overseas settlements (*apoikiai*) which owed their existence, or their size, shape and nature, in whole or in part to the force of hoplite arms.[29] Of the former, Sparta is the classic instance; of the latter, Sparta's only genuine *apoikia* Taras, founded in south Italy at the end of the eighth century in the teeth of native hostility, may serve to illustrate the point.[30] It is the indirect connection between hoplite warfare and the rise of the Greek state as such that is far harder to ground empirically, partly because there is enormous scope for controversy over the very definition of 'state', partly because of the condition of the extant evidence.[31] If I find Aristotle's *Politics* especially helpful in this debate, this is not because I regard him as a reliable historian of early Greece, but because on the basis of his deep reflection upon and analytical understanding of the *polis* of his own day he found it 'natural' and useful to formulate a model of its early historical development in precisely military terms.[32] That his model was demonstrably false in certain empirical respects should not be regarded as fatally weakening the value of the model as a tool of historical understanding.

The essential difference for Aristotle between the *polis* and pre-*polis* or non-*polis* societies was that the *polis* was a strong community of (adult male) citizens with defined rights and privileges (especially those of holding office and passing legal judgement).[33] Being a citizen in Aristotelian terms meant among other things being a warrior, a member of the citizen militia, and what sort of warrior you were typically determined in its turn what sort of citizenship you exercised, whether first- or second-class. There was, in other words, in Aristotle's model a strict isomorphism between political power and military function, such that a state in which the dominant military force was cavalry would be ruled by a small landed aristocracy of noble birth and (ideally ancient) wealth, whereas a state which depended chiefly on hoplites would be in Aristotle's terms some form of oligarchy – still ruled by the few (*oligoi*) rather than by the masses, but by the significantly larger percentage of the citizenry who were *hopla parekhomenoi*, that is, able to afford their own relatively expensive hoplite equipment (as the majority of citizens in any Greek city at all periods never could).[34] Let us now try to situate that model in historical context, to relate it to the hypothetical concrete actualities.

The most general context of all is the transitional epoch sometimes known as the 'Greek Renaissance' that definitively put an end to the Dark Age (or Ages) in all but a few remote regions or districts of the Greek world.[35] Darkness is no doubt to some extent in the eye of the beholder, and there has been a revisionist tendency to deny the existence of any genuinely Dark epoch between say the twelfth and the eighth centuries.[36] But even the most ardently revisionist critic is bound to admit that in several fundamental respects the Greek world of 700 BC was radically different from the Greek world of 1000 BC. Above all, beginning in about 750 there is clearly visible a quite remarkable growth or expansion, both demographic and geographic.[37] This was fostered by and fostered in its turn a palpable increase in the long-distance exchange of raw materials and finished goods as well as human beings, including specialized artisans, and possibly some shift from pastoralism to agriculture or agro-pastoral economy.[38] The combination of demographic, geographic, and commercial expansion and beneficial interaction with non-Greek cultures impacted on both the economic and the political structures of the leading communities of old Greece.[39] It somehow led to the self-conscious crystallization of an ideally autonomous and autarkic *polis* identity;[40] and that new consciousness in turn expressed itself militarily in a 'veritable epidemic of border wars', as neighbouring communities fought either to gain or to retain adequate civic *Lebensraum*.[41]

Hoplites were not well adapted to the broken or mountainous country of which much of mainland Greece consists, nor were they especially well suited to the plundering of mobile property.[42] However, for the ravaging and more especially the protection of the relatively few level-plain croplands appropriated as their principal economic basis by the newly crystallized *poleis* they were without peer, and that presumably is just exactly why hoplite phalanx fighting was developed, and developed when it was.[43] At any rate, as is made crystal clear by the *skolion* (drinking-song) of the Cretan Hybrias among much other evidence, there was a perceived homology between agriculture and warfare, in that the productive functions of the warrior were defined in agricultural terms.[44] Hoplite warfare was indeed typically conducted for the sake of and indeed physically on top of agricultural territory.[45]

How precisely hoplite phalanx warfare was introduced and developed is another matter. The role played by tyrants, for example, who in several states usurped autocratic power outside or in defiance of the established political order but wielded it somehow with the active or passive support of the majority of hoplites, has been the subject of particularly intense yet inconclusive speculation.[46] One state no doubt took the lead in one technological or organizational aspect, another in another; but in due course a process of 'peer polity interaction' ensured that the hoplite phenomenon was generalized to much if not most of the Greek world by 500.[47] It is probably significant, however, that non-*polis* Greek communities of the less centralized, less politicized *ethnos* type did not either experience tyrants or develop hoplite forces until later.[48]

In conclusion, it is salutary to revert to the economic dimension of the process in order to recall and emphasize that there would have been no militarily effective forces of hoplites anywhere in Greece – and little or no incentive to create them – but for the existence of a sufficient number of citizens possessing both the economic means and the political will and capacity so to equip themselves. This principle of citizen self-equipment was – with one possible exception (see below) – at the heart of the Greek hoplite achievement, differentiating it radically from the military reforms of patrimonial monarchies like the Assyrian that also depended on the creation and regular deployment of massed infantry armies.[49] Here, in other words, is one more confirmation of the general rule that the nature of warfare and of the army that conducts it is a reflection of the society from which they spring. However, the change that resulted in citizen-hoplites becoming the determining force of a Greek *polis* was a complex compound of not only technological and tactical but also ideological and above all socio-political factors. It is therefore necessary now to examine those two latter kinds of factors more closely and, where possible, more individually.

Hoplite language – and actuality – were always heavily focused on war's symbolic functions in the construction of identities, borders and boundaries.[50] Ritualization was of course hardly peculiar to hoplite warfare; compare the mediaeval 'age of chivalry'. But the Greeks do seem to have taken hoplite ritualization to extremes both on and off the battlefield. Age-class organization, rites of passage, male bonding, and pederasty (to name but a few) were all either institutionalized or re-adapted to suit the new hoplite context.[51] Hoplite battle, which was regularly preceded and accompanied by animal sacrifice and other forms of religious devotion, has even been described as 'more ritualistic than rational in its set forms'.[52] Its ritual challenge to honour certainly allowed full play to the Greeks' ludic, agonistic mentality;[53] and the Theban 'Sacred Band' formed in the 370s was but a particularly explicit instance of the engrained tendency of hoplite warfare to regard the hoplite armed force as a sworn and consecrated body, conducting war as a special form of public self-sacrifice.[54]

A specifically hoplite value-system and code of honour were necessarily devised to accompany and reinforce the ritualization of hoplite militarism. Self-discipline and self-control (*sôphrosunê, enkrateia*) and all the other qualities that went towards the construction and maintenance of military *taxis* or order (such as rhythmic co-ordination, cohesion, self-sacrifice, collective uniformity and relative egalitarianism) were deliberately fostered. The hoplite's supreme test was to remain 'in rank' or 'in his proper station' (*en taxei*). This hoplite martial code symbolized the disciplined solidarity of the civic community. Its more narrowly political expression went under the name of *eunomia*, that is, orderly obedience to the agreed rules. That was the title ascribed to poems by both the Spartan hortatory elegist Tyrtaios and the Athenian lawgiver Solon; the latter's vivid use of a shield-metaphor also nicely captures the hoplite value system.[55]

On top of, or rather running right through, all these other hoplite qualities was that of gendered masculinity. Bravery or courage (*andreia*, *andragathia*, literally 'manliness', 'manly virtue') was construed as identical with the sort of innately masculine pugnacity that was demanded by fighting in the hoplite phalanx. The Spartans indeed went as far (too far, in the censorious view of Aristotle) as to identify hoplite virtues with Virtue itself. A revelatory anecdote preserved by Thucydides (4.40) concerns those Spartan hoplites who, to general Greek astonishment, surrendered on Sphakteria in 424. The reason they gave for their surrender was that they had been struck down at a distance by arrows, weapons which were incapable of distinguishing the truly virtuous warriors (*kaloikagathoi*) from the cowards, and which the Spartans therefore dismissed derogatorily as 'spindles' (*atraktoi*) – typically feminine, domestic implements. Had they been fighting face-to-face in phalanx formation against truly brave warriors wielding the manly hoplite spear, then of course (they implied) they would not have surrendered but fought on.

In their attitude to archers these Spartans were typical of Greek hoplite mentality and ideology in general. In actual fact, however, archers and other light-armed troops had by no means been made entirely redundant by the advent of hoplite fighting – indeed, they were probably more useful and used in that style of war than the dominant ideology cared to reveal.[56] But according to the dominant military ideology, all troops other than hoplites were precisely 'the "Other" warrior' – *l'autre guerrier*, in Lissarrague's apt phrase.[57] The hoplite was the norm and standard.

Archaeology adds telling confirmation to the literary sources for the hoplite code, both negatively and positively. Negatively, it would appear that soon after 700 individual warrior-graves were abandoned as a cultural form in the Greek hoplite world.[58] Thereafter when arms and armour were removed permanently from the utilitarian sphere, they were thesaurized by being dedicated to the gods in the more appropriately public communal space of religious sanctuaries, alongside miniature copies of the genuine articles and miniature representations of the hoplites themselves, such as the lead examples dedicated at Sparta to Ortheia.[59] Some surviving examples of hoplite equipment are remarkable artistic as well as technical achievements. The helmet rescued from the Giglio Island shipwreck off Elba is a conspicuous instance. With its engraving of wild boars and snakes, symbolizing respectively hunting and death, this helmet serves also as a peculiarly concentrated graphic representation of hoplite culture and ideology.[60] No less symbolically expressive was the use of painted pottery to depict hoplite ideology; indeed, some of the most powerful scenes in all Greek vase painting are those depicting a woman handing his emblematic shield to her hoplite warrior husband as he departs for the battleground.[61] 'With your shield – or on it', as Spartan wives were supposed to have intoned.

To summarize the argument so far, let us consider an illustrative tale from Herodotus (1.82). In about 545 BC the so-called 'Battle of the Champions' – an agonal, ritualized combat between 300 selected 'champions' on each side – was fought on and for the sake of borderland won some time earlier from the Argives by Sparta. At the end of the fighting just three men remained alive, two Argives and one Spartan. But whereas the Argive survivors quitted the field to report their 'victory' (the egalitarianism of the hoplite ideology is neatly transparent) to their fellow-citizens at home in Argos, the sole Spartan survivor, Othryadas, remained on the battlefield and 'in his proper station' (*en taxei*). He therefore claimed the victory for Sparta and set up a battlefield trophy.[62] Not surprisingly, however, the Battle of the Champions was not at the time considered decisive either militarily or politically, and it was soon followed by an all-out battle which the Spartans conclusively won. But so deeply symbolic was the original battle felt to be by both sides that it caused the Spartans either to institute new or to modify existing religious rituals, and it induced the Argives to ask for a return match – 125 years later (Thuc. 5.41). In fact, despite such crucial later developments as the rise of the trireme warship (dependent on the musclepower and teamwork of sub-hoplite citizens and hired non-citizens) and peltast mercenaries (hired non-hoplite foreigners), the whole complex of hoplite ideology and values was so deeply entrenched in Greek mentality by 500 that the citizen-militia hoplite model continued to dominate the ideology even of democratic Athens, where the power-holding majority of citizens rowed the militarily crucial warships.[63]

The precise nature of rule in the early Greek polities, both pre- and post-*polis*, is yet another topic of huge controversy, complicated in this case by the potential availability of the *Odyssey* as well as the *Iliad*.[64] Later Greek writers, who clearly had few qualms about using Homeric evidence as history, seem mostly to have envisaged the existence of a traditional monarchy 'on fixed conditions' (Thuc. 1.13), hereditary but not absolute, with kings ruling only as long as their fellow aristocrats (who collectively controlled effective military power) were prepared to support them. These monarchies were thought to have somehow given way to republican regimes of an oligarchic type, either more or less narrow aristocracies in the strict sense, or oligarchies of wealth and merit rather than just noble birth. Aristotle, for instance, as we saw above, correlated the evolutionary phase of aristocratic government with the predominance of cavalry warfare.

Modern scholars in their usual sceptical way have questioned the existence in early Greece not only of kings in the sense of genuine monarchs but also of a true hereditary aristocracy, although few if any have gone so far as to deny the early existence of a developed ideology of aristocracy – 'always to be the best and among the first' (*Iliad* 6.208), connoting a combination of birth, wealth, intelligence and skill in council and war.[65] They have also doubted, more cogently, whether there was ever a stage at which true cavalry warfare was the dominant military mode. The mounted hoplite makes an early appearance in Greek art, but he, like the elite Hippeis of Sparta later on, is plausibly thought to have fought on foot.[66]

Controversy over the use of Homer for political reconstruction has centred in particular on the question whether the epics presuppose, imply or at any rate betray the existence of the *polis* (however defined). According to what was for long the most influential interpretation, the 'world of Odysseus' was one in which a Greek's primary loyalty was to his household (*oikos*) rather than to the community as such; social stratification was vertical (*oikos* against *oikos*) rather than horizontal by class (rich against poor); and the rulers ruled by might and tradition rather than by defined right. But that interpretation, too, has been questioned in the current upsurge of revisionism, in both its sociological and its political aspects.[67] For my part, I would not presume to endorse any strong view, but my reading of the Homeric epics (virtually the only strictly contemporary written evidence available) does suggest that, if the *polis* is present therein, it is so at most intermittently, and in a latent and undeveloped form. Signally lacking in Homer, it seems to me, is one crucially defining characteristic of the *polis* – the (or a) concept of citizenship. A kind of Homeric patriotism is detectable, no doubt, but not the notion of publicly defined membership in a civic corporation within properly political space.

The case of Hesiod (*c.* 700 BC) seems to me to be rather different, although it is of course a separate question whether the seemingly more parochial *Works and Days* can be given a 'panhellenic' application in the same way as the *Iliad* and *Odyssey*. Hesiod does apparently address an immediate, concrete, contemporary historical situation, that is, the abuse of political power, as he sees it, by the 'bribe-swallowing' or 'gift-devouring' *basileis* ('kings' or 'lords') of little Askra in Boiotia. But the properly political basis of these local rulers' power is not specified by Hesiod, and it may not have been clearly specified in actuality. What does emerge clearly from the poem, however, is that Hesiod can envisage significant political change happening only when – and if – there should occur a change of heart and mind on the part of the rulers, against whom he urges religious or moral rather than secular political or military sanctions. In this respect Hesiod 'crystallizes the "moral economy" of a *dêmos* in dependency'.[68] This is not all that far removed from the dichotomous socio-political situation assumed and endorsed by Homer's Odysseus in the second book of the *Iliad*: on the one hand, there are the kings or lords; on the other, the *dêmos* – a useless mass, not to be taken into account in either war or council. The only important difference from the situation implied in Homer is that

Hesiod appears to be giving shape and voice to an inchoate anti-aristo-cratic, or at any rate oppositional, political ideology, which in Homer was either suppressed or (in the person of Thersites) savagely caricatured.

Such a dependent and powerless and uniform *dêmos* surely precludes the existence of any significant number of hoplites in Hesiod's Askra, let alone a fully developed hoplite phalanx. For the viability of the phalanx presupposes some further differentiation of the powerless Homeric *dêmos* into hoplites and sub-hoplites. The former, the *hopla parekhomenoi*, are those who can afford to serve as hoplites, and the hoplite style of fighting implied and required the existence of a sizeable proportion of the citizenry with that economic capacity. And not just with the economic capacity, but also with the political will for self-enrolment. However precisely that will was engendered, it is difficult to separate it from the rise of the *polis* with its basic notion of membership in a civic corporation and its apportionment of political prerogatives in accordance with military function (along the lines of the Aristotelian model).

Rather than add my speculation to that of others on the possible role of Pheidon at Argos or Kypselos at Corinth in either introducing the hoplite phalanx or exploiting the hoplites to usurp sole power, I shall consider briefly the relationship between hoplite military organization and socio-political structure in the two most important *poleis* of early Greece, Sparta and Athens, the comparison and contrast of which will also be instruc-tive.[69]

Sparta was in most respects the classic example of the early Greek 'hoplite state'. Both in detail and in overall structure Sparta's military organization was at the earliest possible date made solidary with its social structure and political power-system.[70] Spartan culture, too, acquired a definitely military cast, evident most notably in Spartan religion and in the martial elegy of Tyrtaios.[71] Yet in two and perhaps three respects Sparta, paradoxically, could not be called a typical or normal hoplite state, for reasons mainly connected with the need to suppress an unfree popula-tion (see Chapter 10). First, it turned itself into a fully military society, almost an armed camp, on permanent red alert. Second, all Spartan citizens, not merely as elsewhere the wealthiest 30-50 per cent, became hoplites. Third, though this cannot be demonstrated, it seems likely that hoplite arms and armour were not procured privately by individual Spartan citizens, but were supplied to them centrally from the civic arsenal.[72]

Athens, in contrast, seems to have been relatively slow to develop a hoplite military organization. The situation here was complicated by the difficulty of effecting the synoecism of the territory of Attica as a whole; warfare between Athens and Eleusis seems to have been ongoing when Sparta had already expanded out of Lakonia into neighbouring Messenia, and control of the island of Salamis was still an issue between Athens and Megara in Solon's day around 600. However, when the change to hoplitism was effected, it was politically decisive. The 'constitution' attributed to Solon as extraordinary legislator in 594 distributed political power essentially in accordance with military function, the chief beneficiaries being economically defined census-groups called Hippeis ('Cavalrymen') and Zeugitai ('Yoke-men', i.e. hoplites). Likewise in 508/7, when Kleisthenes' reforms 'established the tribes and the democracy for the Athenians' (Hdt. 6.131), his new tribes formed the basic units of the politically re-empowered hoplite army.[73]

In other words, despite the many differences of historical circumstances and social structure between Athens and Sparta, there was in both states a strict parallelism between the properly political subdivisions of the citizen body and the constitution of military units – precisely as postulated by Aristotle's model.[74]

I conclude by looking yet more briefly at the relationship between warfare and politics in a narrower sense.[75] Armed violence makes sense, if the Prussian theoretician von Clausewitz is right, only if it serves political ends. That was at any rate especially true in a world such as that of the early Greeks, where the political was considered primary, warfare was very frequent, and the 'Military Participation Ratio' was high – where, indeed, it was above all through the collective action of warfare that the community of citizens reasserted itself as such again and again.[76] In these circumstances early Greek hoplite warfare could hardly be anything other than quite literally 'the continuation of state policy, or of political intercourse, with the admixture of other means' (von Clausewitz's famous if often misunderstood dictum).

How, then, might the rise of hoplite phalanx warfare have particularly affected the conduct of Greek foreign policy, of what the Greeks called 'matters of war and peace'? Probably the neatest illustration is the multi-state military alliance formed by Sparta in the second half of the sixth century, which moderns call the Peloponnesian League.[77] The principal forces of this alliance were the hoplite armies composed mainly by the member-states' *autourgoi*, that is, typically, the self-employed, self-supporting citizen farmers. Members of this novel interstate grouping bound themselves under oath to support each other militarily 'with all strength and in accordance with their capacity' (*panti sthenei katto dunaton*) – and that meant the capacity of the hoplites' strong right arms. But they also bound themselves to 'follow the Spartans wherever they might lead'. To ensure compliance with their wishes, the Spartans saw to it that their allies were governed by compliant oligarchies (Thuc. 1.19). That the allies' compliance was relatively easy to secure followed from the socio-economic fact that the hoplites, the *hopla parekhomenoi*, were the wealthiest 30-50 per cent or so of the citizenry who both could afford and were willing to incur the expense of hoplite equipment and training. Being wealthy and relatively few, they naturally favoured oligarchy, the rule of the few rich. Aristotle would have understood (cf. Cartledge 1977: 12).[78]

166

Part IV

The Mirage Re-Viewed

12

The Mirage of Lykourgan Sparta:
Some Brazen Reflections

Introduction

Earlier versions of this paper have been delivered as undergraduate lectures in Cambridge, and as invited lectures to undergraduates in Oxford and at the Antiquité et Image conference of C.N.A.R.E.L.A. (Coordination Nationale des Associations Régionales des Enseignants de Langues Anciennes) held at Nîmes in 1991. The decision to concentrate, in this pubished version, on bronze artefacts as illustrations was taken mainly for the following four reasons. First, as Snodgrass 1971 has observed, metals take one close to the heart of the functional basis of an ancient society. Second, bronzeworking in particular raises in acute form the issue of who – full Spartan citizens, degraded or otherwise inferior Spartans, Perioikoi or Helots? – made Lakonian artefacts, in what quantities, and for what purposes: see also Hodkinson 1998. Third, some small bronze Lakonian figurines will stand scrutiny as works of art (cf. Dickins 1908) in any context, and many Lakonian bronze artefacts of the sixth century were very widely distributed (from Hungary to Aden: see most recently Stibbe 2000), both of which archaeologically certain facts do at least offer a challenge to both ancient and modern constructions of ancient Sparta. Finally, small bronze figurines, beginning with the Late Geometric bronze horse-figurines which are now widely scattered in public and private collections on both sides of the Atlantic (Zimmermann 1989: 171-5), happen to be my favourite category of Spartan objects.

*

The useful expression the Spartan mirage (*le mirage spartiate*) was invented in the 1930s by the French scholar François Ollier (Ollier 1933-43). He coined it to describe the idealization of Sparta in Greek antiquity, that is, the distorted or entirely imaginary literary tradition about ancient Sparta – what Sparta was, what it had achieved, what it stood for. This false image, or series of images, was of course projected originally by the Spartans themselves, for their own internal purposes, and it was constantly revisited and revised by them. Yet, so far as our written evidence (the sole interest of Ollier) is concerned, the mirage has been handed down almost exclusively by non-Spartans: from the bloodstained Athenian oligarch Kritias, writing towards the close of the fifth century BC, to Nazi propagandists in the twentieth century (Losemann 1977), and indeed beyond.[1] The mirage can, however, be given a wider definition, to include material artefacts as well as literary confections. Sparta, as Anton Powell (1989) has rightly stressed, was peculiarly preoccupied with and peculiarly adept at visual propaganda.

More harmlessly, and more accurately indeed, spartan is now frequently used as an epithet meaning tough, rigorous, disciplined, austere, self-denying, spare, minimally comfortable or comfort-seeking. One example is the Exeter Spartan Club (I owe the reference to David Harvey), although probably the men and women devotees of wrestling who disport themselves there would be shocked to learn that ancient Spartan girls and Spartan boys – allegedly – wrestled against each other, stark naked.[2] Another is the Spartan brand of chocolates – hard-centre, of course – manufactured in this country by Terry's. The box-designer had the happy thought of illustrating the theme with a representation of an ancient Greek temple – but, alas, he or she chose to depict the no doubt evocative but scarcely relevant remains of the sixth-century Doric Temple of Apollo at Corinth. At least it was a Doric temple. A third I have culled from a recent newspaper headline that speaks for itself: 'Spartan prison makes violent inmates worse'. But the most remarkable recent illustration of all has featured already in my Preface to this book, so eye-catching is it: an advertisement for the Hyatt Regency hotel chain that seeks to promote custom by reassuring potential guests that its accommodations are anything but spartan.

The ancient version of the literary mirage had three main components. First, it maintained that time out of mind the Spartan polity had been uniquely free from internal disorder and civil strife (*stasis*). Second, it claimed that this utopian situation was owed mainly to the fact that since time immemorial Spartan citizens had dutifully obeyed the laws laid down for them by their wondrously omniprovident lawgiver Lykourgos.[3] Third, it promoted the idea that these laws, which were held to differ in strikingly important ways from those of all other Greek states, affected absolutely every aspect of Spartan life, private no less than public.[4] That was the agreed minimum content of the mirage. Thereafter all was disagreement – as to who, or what, and even how many, Lykourgos had been, when he had lived, and precisely what he had done and why. For present purposes, the question of Lykourgos the man, if he ever was a real human being, is strictly a side-issue. What does concern me, rather, are those aspects of the mirage of Lykourgan Sparta which archaeological (including art-historical) evidence might in principle be expected to confirm, refute, or at least clarify. This essay, in other words, is an exercise in historical archaeology or archaeological history.[5]

12. The Mirage of Lykourgan Sparta: Some Brazen Reflections

The foundation-legend of historical Sparta is a myth, or part of a myth, known as 'The Return of the Descendants of Herakles'. This myth is a nice example of the standard type that the anthropologist Bronislaw Malinowski dubbed charter myth, and was intended to justify retrospectively the Dorian Spartans' forcible occupation of first the south-east, then the whole southern, Peloponnese. Needless to say, there is no obligation to believe in the literal authenticity of any such Return. I do myself believe, however, though many do not, that archaeology can be used to confirm the ancient view held by the Spartans themselves that the Dorians were recent, in their terms post-Trojan War, immigrants to the Peloponnese (Cartledge 1992b; Eder 1998: esp. 136-9; but see Margreiter 1988). I am also of the view that archaeology, in the form of detailed stylistic analysis of the earliest Dark Age (sometimes called Protogeometric) Lakonian ceramics, can be made congruent with the literary evidence indicating that the Dorians who eventually became Spartans entered the Peloponnese from the north-west. The pottery evidence from Sparta and elsewhere in Lakonia, furthermore, may arguably be taken as showing that they settled the site of historical Sparta not later than the end of the tenth century BC.[6]

When the wanderings of these and other peoples, both Doric-speakers and speakers of other Greek dialects, were at an end, by about 800 in round figures, the dialect map of the Aegean Greek world had reached pretty much its final shape – before the next great Greek phase of Völkerwanderung, which is conventionally if misleadingly referred to as the age of colonization, saw Greeks permanently established by 500 BC from the Pillars of Herakles (the straits of Gibraltar) in the west to Phasis in Georgia at the far eastern end of the Black Sea. Sparta, as we shall see, was not to be a major player in this latter movement, preferring other, geographically more insular means of expansion. By 700, at all events, she was securely in control of at least the central Eurotas valley of Lakonia, securely enough anyhow to have embarked already on the conquest of the river valley of the Pamisos in neighbouring Messenia (south-west Peloponnese).

The aim of this essay is to consider the bearing of archaeology and art-history on Spartan society and economy mainly as they were constituted during the succeeding seventh and sixth centuries. Had Sparta always been the cultural desert projected by the later mirage? Did Spartan citizens never participate directly in manual crafts? These are just two of the more significant and more basic questions to which answers will be sought. In the process of answering them, relying largely on objects made from bronze, I shall seek to provide also a brief outline conspectus of the development of Spartan – or Lakonian – visual art from the eighth century to the fifth, together with a certain amount of necessary background historical detail.[7]

We begin with the settlement of Sparta, that is, with its physical manifestation. Readers of Pausanias' second-century AD travelogue might gain a very different impression of the urban centre of Sparta from that conveyed by Thucydides in the late fifth century BC (see above, Chapter 2). At any rate, rather a large number of buildings were described or mentioned by the later traveller, with the clear implication that they were for the most part really ancient constructions, a legacy of Sparta's Classical greatness. I was once fortunate enough to buy in modern Sparta a black-and-white picture postcard bearing an artistic reconstruction purporting to show the Agora of Ancient Sparta; this clearly owed more to Pausanias than to Thucydides. Yet it is not the least of the paradoxes of the modern study of Sparta that we do not yet know for sure where the Classical Spartan Agora actually was located. So that artistic reconstruction was, quite literally, a modern mirage.

From fantasy we move to fact, or as near as archaeologically derived data can come to providing that. Our knowledge of Spartan art and archaeology and their chronological development remains far from perfect. But it would be very much more imperfect than it is were it not for two ancient archaeological accidents, and for the careful excavations of the British School at Athens at the start of the twentieth century, at the sanctuary of Ortheia, later surnamed and identified with Artemis, located on the right (west) bank of the Eurotas at the eastern limit of Sparta town in the ancient village (*kômê*) of Limnai.

The first ancient accident occurred in the following way. The original, rather primitive temple of Ortheia was constructed, according to the best modern reckoning (Boardman 1963), in about 700 BC. A century or so later, following a destructive Eurotas flood, a new temple was built on a fresh layer of sand, at least 1.5 metres deep, with which the whole sanctuary area (*temenos*) was now strewn. This sand-layer had the happy effect of sealing in, and so leaving largely undisturbed, the rich early deposits of votive dedications.[8] The second accident was that in the later third century AD, perhaps following a no less destructive raid by the Germanic Heruli in 267, a semicircular quasi-amphitheatre was built in the sanctuary.[9] Its purpose was to enable spectators, including foreign tourists, to sit in some comfort while they watched Spartan youths undergoing the (long established, in some form) *diamastigôsis* ritual, that is, being flogged, preferably to death, in front of the altar of Ortheia Artemis. A side-benefit, for us, of constructing this monument to sado-tourism was the protection of many of the offerings made to Ortheia between *c.* 550 BC and the third century AD from the ravages of men and the elements. It would be comforting to believe that the youths did not give their lives entirely in vain.

At the height of Sparta's power, between *c.* 550 and the early fourth century BC, the sanctuary of Ortheia thus contained a limestone temple in the Doric order, rather simple but making at least some gesture at architectural decoration; a large, stone-faced altar; and several other buildings which presumably housed religious officials, ritual equipment, and perhaps surplus offerings.

This area, a natural hollow by the Eurotas, had first been sanctified in the tenth century, probably when the Dorians first settled Sparta. At least, there is no question here – as there is at Amyklai a few kilometres further south – of continuity of worship from the Late Bronze Age into the Early Iron Age. Cultic activity seems at first to have been restricted to animal-sacrifice and the pouring of libations (oil or wine) around a very basic, oblong earthen altar. These humble beginnings no doubt reflected accurately enough the reduced circumstances and the impoverished quality of life in this era, truly the Dark Age (cf. Chapter 11) of Lakonia. We cannot however comment on that with any confidence, as there is hardly a trace extant of the contemporary settlement, just a few house-walls and graves. What we can say, though, is that the focus of settlement in this part of the south-east Peloponnese had shifted definitively to Sparta and away from the earlier, Bronze Age or Mycenaean central place some distance to the east, on the other side of the Eurotas.

Over the next two centuries or so, say from 900 to 700 in round figures, the picture becomes considerably brighter and more variegated. Dorian Sparta was then extending its influence and power over the entire Eurotas valley of what became known as Lakedaimôn or Lakônikê in Greek times and Laconia in the Roman period. Indeed, the push to the west, across or rather around the massif of Taygetos, so as to occupy at least part of the even more fertile Pamisos valley, had already begun well before 700. In the process Sparta transformed some of the hitherto peasant occupiers into Helots, a kind of state-serfs, others into Perioikoi, dwellers round about, who were a by-product of the annexation of the riverine valleys. They, like the Helots, were also Greeks and spoke the Lakonian and Messenian varieties of Doric Greek; but, although subordinated to the Spartans politically, they unlike the Helots remained personally free.[10] By 700, therefore, we mean by the Spartan state the *polis* of the Lakedaimonioi or Spartiatai (cf. Chapters 2-3).

Thanks to their newly increased agriculturally-derived wealth, and further enriched by the spoils of war, the Spartan ruling elite of kings and aristocracy were able as well as willing to build for Ortheia her first temple within a newly defined *temenos*. Indeed, it is the building of this temple, together with those for the city-goddess Athena on what passed for the akropolis of Sparta and for Menelaos and Helen jointly at the Menelaion site a little way east across the Eurotas, that signalled both materially and spiritually the emergence of the Spartan *polis*.[11]

Unfortunately for the archaeologist and historian of Sparta, the first Ortheia temple consisted largely of perishable materials. So, too, the cult-statue was probably a primitive wooden cylinder of the *xoanon* type, virtually aniconic. But thanks to the sand-layer, and to the British excavators' unusual care, we have preserved a good selection of the earliest votive offerings to Ortheia, which can be classified and, no less importantly, dated with some precision. All excavation is of course in one sense destruction, but R.C. Bosanquet and R.M. Dawkins, successively directors of the Ortheia dig, were pioneers in digging and recording a Classical Greek site stratigraphically. The excavators' published accounts can still be checked, as I have myself done, against the dig notebooks preserved in the British School archives at Athens, and Professor L. Marangou (now of Ioannina) above all has demonstrated how the recorded pottery associations may be used to yield a generally accurate guide to the dating of individual artefacts (Marangou 1969, an admirable account of the Archaic ivory and bone objects). It was, however, Boardman (1963) who in recent times first stimulated the proper awareness of the School's archaeological achievement at Sparta.

The potters and vasepainters of Protogeometric (or Dark Age) and Geometric Sparta, operating between *c.* 950 and 700 BC, were fairly backward, both technically and artistically.[12] The local Late Geometric style of pottery of the second half of the eighth century is recognizably Lakonian, and may therefore indirectly speak to the emergence of the early Spartan state, since its geographical limits coincide neatly with what we know of Sparta's later political borders; but artistically speaking it was almost wholly indebted to the workshops of Argos and Corinth for its baggy shapes and its repetitive linear or figural motifs and can therefore safely be passed quickly over. By contrast, the bronzeworkers of Lakonia in the eighth century were leaders in their respective fields in the Greek world as a whole.

A figure like that illustrated in Plate 1 cannot be dated precisely on stylistic grounds, and the stratigraphic evidence of the associated pottery would allow a date anywhere between 750 and 650.[13] If the individual elements of the body are looked at separately, it is clear that the artist-craftsman (*kheirotekhnês* is the later word; in Homer such skilled workers are called *dêmiourgoi*) was working within wholly Geometric conventions. But though the overall composition is static, appropriately enough for a seated figure, it does at least mark an attempt to represent the 3-D quality of the original model or real subject. A date in the region of 700 would therefore be acceptable enough, which would make it roughly contemporary with the construction of Ortheia's first temple. Indeed, this figurine and the other, more expensive votives like it were part of the reason why the temple was built, namely to protect them from speedy decay in the open air in a low-lying marshy (hence Limnai) environment. Even more important factors, though, were the desire to display wealth and to symbolize *polis* unification. What exactly this figurine is supposed to represent is not clear: a drinker, some have suggested (and the Spartans, at any rate later, are known to have liked their wine), or, more flatteringly, a thinker (one wit has even identified him as Lykourgos pondering his laws ...).

Rather earlier, perhaps, than our member of the thinking or drinking classes is the 10cm-high bronze horse-figurine illustrated in Plate **2**. A special feature is the depiction of Siamese twins cut in intaglio into the base, possibly representing the brothers of Helen, the Dioskouroi Kastor and Polydeukes (Castor and Pollux), who had peculiarly Spartan associations (cf. Hdt. 5.75). If anything, this figurine is even finer in technique and artistic conception; and that may help to explain why it was not found in Sparta itself but had been reckoned a suitable export for dedication in a sanctuary at Phigaleia (near Bassai) in south-west Arkadia. Despite its provenance, it can be assigned quite confidently on stylistic grounds to a Lakonian workshop (Zimmermann 1989: 129, no. 93; cf. Herrmann 1964), though one cannot be quite so certain that this shop was operating exclusively in Sparta, rather than, say, Olympia, from where by far the largest number of such Lakonian horse-figurines have been recovered (Heilmeyer 1979).

In Sparta horse-figurines such as this – solid-cast by the lost-wax method, highly stylised, on a rectangular, often openwork stand – formed the largest class of bronze figurines dedicated to Ortheia in the eighth century.[14] This was only to be expected, from one point of view. The period around 700 was the great age of the conquering Spartan aristocracy, and the horse was then and remained thereafter the aristocratic symbol *par excellence*. Still in the fifth and fourth centuries the descendants of Herakles, not least the two kings, owned a great many horses, some of which they used in battle, while others they raced competitively both inside and outside Lakonia.[15] Nevertheless, the quantity, quality and – not least – distribution of these Lakonian bronze horse-figurines bespeak much more than aristocratic values.

They have been found in contexts both dedicatory and funerary all over the Peloponnese, in central Greece, and as far west as Taras (where the Spartans established their only true *apoikia* in c. 700) and as far east as Samos (an island with which Spartan contacts were unusually early, extensive and enduring – see Cartledge 1982b; and cf. Plate **3**). This wide but thin distribution is not to be explained anachronistically in terms of trade and commerce (cf. Cartledge 1983), but rather for the most part as evidence of personal contacts and gift-exchange between Spartan and other Greek (and possibly non-Greek?) aristocrats, typically men who were bound together by ties of *xenia*, or what Herman (1987) has called ritualized friendship. The finds at Olympia, however, constitute a class apart.

What would have been the largest and finest of all Lakonian Geometric bronze horse-figurines was excavated here. It would have been – only it was miscast, thereby demonstrating that as early as 775 or so (on Heilmeyer's admittedly rather high dating) a craftsman working in the Lakonian stylistic idiom and so doubtless trained in Sparta was operating from a workshop at Olympia, on either a long-term or, more plausibly, a short-term basis. This is a sure sign of the increasing complexity of artistic and social organization in Sparta, but it may also be more than that. For, so I would argue, it is Olympia that holds the key to the precocious accomplishment of Lakonian bronzeworkers.

Traditionally – though the tradition is attested no earlier than the late fifth century – the Olympic festival was established first on a regular basis in what we call 776 BC. Aristotle had no good warrant for believing that Lykourgos was a co-signatory of the Olympic truce, but Spartans certainly took a keen interest in the festival from early on, probably to begin with as individuals (both competitors and spectators) rather than as representatives or delegates of their community. Between 720 and 576 BC no fewer than forty-six of the eighty-one known victors were Spartans. The craftsmen of a community whose citizens were so conspicuously successful in the Games naturally benefited from commissions of objects that competitors and spectators (who came to be regarded officially as *theôroi*, sacred ambassadors) could dedicate to Zeus either before or after the events. Rubbing shoulders with fellow-craftsmen from other Greek communities in this increasingly panhellenic centre (cf. Morgan 1990) can only have sharpened the Lakonian craftsmen's aesthetic sensitivity and stimulated their technical proficiency. In its turn their Olympia experience would have had a positive feedback effect on production in Sparta itself. The identity and social status of the craftsmen, an issue to which we shall return, are unknown, but the patrons were unquestionably for the most part Spartan citizens.

The other craft in which Lakonia excelled in the late eighth and more especially in the seventh century was ivory-carving. Marangou (1969) has published, admirably, most of the excavated finds.[16] The repertoire includes, besides the undoubted circular seals, both human and animal figures in the round, often on a rectangular base, which could possibly also have served as seals – marks of individuation and ownership of private property. The carvers' forte, however, was work done in relief, whether carved from square or rectangular plaques or from the semi-lunate grips of elaborate combs.

Historically and art-historically, what is most absorbing and significant about this plethora of ivory work is the revelation of an almost totally unexpected Sparta, one which – contrary to the literary mirage – was open both physically and spiritually to the outside world, and especially to the non-Greek Orient. The raw material itself probably had to come ultimately from outside the Mediterranean area and be brought to an entrepôt such as Al Mina in Syria for transshipment thence by sea, perhaps *via* Samos, to Sparta. The motifs and scenes depicted by Lakonian craftsmen, though handled competently and sometimes superbly in a Greek manner from the outset, were often originally of oriental inspiration or derivation. It was all very far away from the crisis of political and economic confidence that we think we see gripping Sparta during the first half of the seventh century, of which a definitively military (but also socio-economic and political) solution was eventually achieved. This is reflected, visually, in the mass dedication to Ortheia of cheap lead figurines depicting hoplite warriors from about 650 onwards (see Chapter 11, n. 59), though the hoplite type never predominated among the lead votives. This is a useful reminder that archaeology may not always be a very sensitive indicator of political change. For native Spartan handicrafts suffered no obviously detectable setback at this time, but rather kept pace with the great flowering of poetry and music attested in the written sources.

The second half of the seventh century was the golden age of Spartan creative writing, the epoch of the elegist Tyrtaios and the lyric poet Alkman, both in my view Spartans born and bred. Literary tradition records too that leading poet-singers from other parts of the Greek world then visited Sparta, either because they found conditions in Sparta conducive to highflown inspiration or amenable to their skills of conciliation (cf. Van Wees 1999: 5-6), or, more sordidly, because their rich Spartan patrons – living now off the fat of Messenia 'good to plant and good to plough' (Tyrtaios) as well as Lakonia – made it well worth their while. Poetry of this sort was not normally produced for mass consumption, but in Sparta, an abnormal Greek *polis* in many ways, military and religious conditions conspired to ensure that the martial and marching songs of Tyrtaios and the maiden-songs of Alkman regularly reached a large citizen audience. As for the humbler, local traditions of singing and choral dancing, we may detect material traces of them both in the animal-bone flutes inscribed with dedications to Ortheia in the local Lakonian alphabet (Jeffery 1961) and in the series of terracotta masks that are such a distinctive feature of the Ortheia deposits (Carter 1988).

Such masks were first dedicated to Ortheia at the end of the seventh century, but their mass-production from moulds and their equally mass-dedication fall rather in the sixth. Late lexicographers have preserved the weird and wonderful-sounding names of Spartan masked dances, part religious rituals, part communal exercises. The preserved masks are possibly durable versions of the wooden, non-dedicable originals. A Spartan existence, in other words, had its moments of relaxed abandon, even though great emphasis was placed not surprisingly on the dances of an overtly martial aspect such as the *Pyrrhikhê*. For the youths undergoing the rigorously organized communal training (see Chapter 7) these complemented the more directly utilitarian physical exercises. For the adult men they were a way of enhancing the rhythmic sense so crucial in hoplite phalanx warfare.

The Gymnopaidiai, one of Sparta's most important festivals, held as usual in honour of Apollo, was traditionally supposed to have been organized first in the second quarter of the seventh century. It pitted choruses of youths against those of older male age-groups. At its kernel, probably, lay a ritual of unarmed (*gumnos*) dancing (*paizein*).[17] The abnormality of the ritualized avoidance of arms reinforced the normality of the state of war, or siege, in which the Spartans habitually existed, surrounded as they were by the many times more numerous Helot population who from being apparently loyal workers and servants might at any time turn – again: the Messenian revolt of the mid-seventh century was an awful warning – into outright enemies (cf. Chapter 10).

By the beginning of the sixth century Sparta at last had the conquest and pacification of Messenia behind her. But she seemed still hellbent on further expansion by conquest and subjugation – of Arkadia to the north and north-west (whence Plate **2**). Here, however, the Spartans' efforts to secure yet more land and yet more Helots were defeated, twice; the fetters they had sought to impose on Arkadians were on one occasion placed on themselves, pending their ransom – a classic case of being hoist with one's own petard. Where the mailed fist would not serve, the velvet glove must be donned. The eventual outcome was the formation of what we call the Peloponnesian League (Gschnitzer 1978; cf. Chapters 3, 11).

Sparta's foreign policy, at any rate down to the mid-century, remained thus outward-looking, but is it possible yet to detect in the archaeological record – or non-record – any marks of the domestic austerity (cf. Holladay 1977) that featured so prominently in the literary mirage? For some scholars, a telltale sign is the Spartan authorities' negative decision, taken for the first time at some point soon after 600, not to follow the lead of Aigina and some other Greek cities in minting silver coins. Sparta, however, was not by any means alone in this; her later ally Megara, for example, also did not choose to coin, or perhaps chose not to, and in fact only about half the 1500 or so attested Greek states are known to have coined. Nor were the relevant Spartan officials debarred from using coins minted by other states. The alleged Spartan law banning the private possession of silver coin must be dismissed as invented tradition (cf. Hodkinson 2000: ch. 5). But non-coining did rule out a convenient and prestigious method of locally estimating and storing private wealth, and allegedly it stimulated bribery (of Spartans rather than by them: see Noethlichs 1987) both at home and especially abroad. Nevertheless, it would be anachronistic in the extreme to infer that the Spartans were thereby consciously debarring themselves from foreign trade, let alone domestic exchanges. Coinage and trade came closer to being synonymous only with the issuing of fractional silver coinage in the later sixth century, and more particularly with the widespread issuing of bronze coinages in the late fifth century and fourth centuries. Hence, any post-550 austerity that may be perceived in the archaeological record cannot be laid at the door of the decision to retain a money – currency does not seem quite the right word, despite Xen. *LP* 7.5-6 – of iron spits.

As it is, far from revealing cultural barrenness and social austerity, the archaeology indicates instead a marked increase in the production and circulation of Lakonian-made goods, precisely from the second quarter of the sixth century onwards. It was then, for example, that Ortheia received her first, all-stone temple, to be followed shortly by comparably elaborate edifices for Athena on the Akropolis (the interior of which was faced with bronze plaques and thus gave rise to the patron goddess's new epithet Chalkioikos, of the Brazen House) and for Menelaos and Helen at Therapnai. It was also from about 575 that the major export of Lakonian painted pottery and fine bronze figurines and vessels began.

At least fourteen different black-figure vasepainters, some with their followers, have been identified by Conrad Stibbe (1972) and others as active in Lakonia, presumably in Sparta, during the apogee of local production between 575 and 525. The pots, mainly kylikes (drinking-cups for the symposion), kraters (mixing-bowls, often painted almost entirely black) and aryballoi (small oil-flasks), have a remarkably broad, if thin, distribution. They have been found all round the east Mediterranean basin and up into the Black Sea, and as far west as Spain, by way of Egypt, Cyrenaica, Sicily, Italy and Provence. Within this broad horizon three unusually heavy concentrations have been observed: Taras, Cyrenaica, and Samos.

The Taras concentration might be simply explained by the fact that Taras was a colony of Sparta, since ties of kinship and sentiment would have ensured constant intercommunication. But Taras was also a convenient way-station and entrepôt for goods travelling further north and west, especially to the wealthy Etruscans who liked to deposit and exhibit imported Greek luxury goods in their massive tombs at Vulci and elsewhere. Cyrenaica, again, conjures up a sentimental tie, since Cyrene was reckoned a grand-daughter city of Sparta *via* its mother-city Thera. But once more, harder economic and social realities cannot be excluded from the picture. Cyrene was famous for its horses, and from the mid-sixth century (but more conspicuously still from the mid-fifth) Spartans began a run of successes in the most prestigious Olympic event, the four-horse chariot-race (above, n. 15). Also possibly relevant is the scene depicted on the name vase of the Arkesilas Painter: a king of Cyrene labelled Arkesilas, probably Arkesilas III since he reigned at the right time, the 560s, is here shown supervising the weighing and storage of a white commodity, either the specifically local but now extinct medicinal plant called silphium or possibly wool. The Spartan painter's local Cyrenaican knowledge is undeniable and remarkable, however we interpret the scene. It betrays an interest in foreign relations and connections beyond anything that could have been inferred from the introverted, xenophobic, austerity-laden Sparta of the mirage.

The Samos concentration is the hardest of the three to account for, and I have devoted a whole article to that particular problem (Cartledge 1982b). Probably the explanation of the connection is mainly commercial, but there were perhaps also political and social dimensions to it as well. Certainly, there is direct attestation of at least one direct personal connection. From the comparatively rich archaeological documentation I pick out a rather charming attachment in the form of a lion, which was originally part of a large bronze vessel dedicated to Samian Hera in her principal shrine on the island. Around the lion's rather comical mane the dedicator has proudly had inscribed both his name, Eumnastos, and his political or ethnic affiliation, Spartiate (see Plate **3**).

This is just one example of the mass of fine Spartan bronzework that also achieved its maximum external distribution between about 575 and 525. Among the figurines two classes are particularly eye-catching: the hoplite warriors, as male as they could be, and the no less feminine female figures who serve as the handles of mirrors. Hoplite figurines have been found as far afield as Samos in the east Aegean, Dodona in north-west Greece and, in the most intriguing case of all, Aden in – from a Greek standpoint – the deepest south. The provenance of the latter is as sure – or rather as unsure – as these things can be, since this is a chance find not an object recovered in a controlled excavation. It was sold at auction for a princely sum by Sotheby's of London not so long ago and resides currently in the sometimes dubiously provenanced private collection of George Ortiz. If only it could speak, and tell us how it came to (be found in) south Arabia! Trade connections are presumably somehow or other the main explanation.

That will not work so easily, however, for the example I illustrate next (Plate **4**), which comes more prosaically from Longa in Messenia, where it was dedicated to Apollo. A mechanism more like that which accounts for the discovery of our bronze horse-figurine from Phigaleia should surely be envisaged. That the aristocratic horse had been forced to make way for the more bourgeois hoplite was entirely in keeping with the more egalitarian political spirit and military realities of the age. In this instance, I would even be prepared to countenance the suggestion that the Spartan state, the hoplite state *par excellence*, somehow arranged for or encouraged their export as a form of political propaganda. The shrine at Longa presumably belonged normally to Messenian Perioikoi, members of the crucial third force between the Spartiates and the Helots on whom the Spartans came to rely more and more as their own numbers dwindled in the course of the fifth and early fourth centuries. Not that they were always reliable: in the third Messenian War of the 460s two Perioikic *poleis* joined the revolted Messenian Helots (Thuc. 1.101.2), and it was probably in connection with this rebellious activity that the Messenians chose the Longa shrine for trophy dedications (Bauslaugh 1990).

The female half of the Spartan citizen population was notoriously not as backward in coming forward as women in Greece were ideally supposed to be (see Chapter 9). In Lakonian visual art, as well as in the literary mirage, they occupy a strikingly distinctive place. I illustrate two representatives of the class of Archaic bronze mirror-handles, one naked and one clothed (Plates **5** and **6**). The clothed example, which was found at Leonidhion (ancient Prasiai), a Perioikic *polis* within Sparta's own home territory, is extremely well preserved. The girl or young woman depicted

1. Late Geometric (*c.* 700 BC?) bronze figurine from the Ortheia sanctuary. Sparta Museum.

2. Phigaleia Horse: late Geometric (second half of the eighth century) bronze figurine from Phigaleia, of Lakonian style, with, in intaglio under the solid base, a depiction of Siamese twins (the Dioskouroi?). British Museum, London

3. Eumnastos lion: protome attachment to (lost) bronze bowl. Lakonian, *c.* 550 BC, dedicated to Hera on Samos by Eumnastos the Spartiate. Samos Museum.

4. Hoplite from Longa: Lakonian
style bronze figurine, *c.* 550 BC,
depicting a hoplite in parade
armour accompanied by his hunting dog (partially preserved).
National Museum, Athens.

5. Bronze mirror with handle in the form of a nude woman. Lakonian style, from Lousoi. Staatliche Antikensammlungen und Glyptothek München.

6. Bronze mirror with handle in the form of a clothed woman, from Leonidhion. National Museum, Athens.

7. Dodona runner: bronze figurine of a young girl athlete. National Museum, Athens

8. *Above & right:* Kosmas bronze depicting a youth, *c.* 490 BC. National Museum, Athens.

9. Arkado-Lakonian ram: attachment to (lost) bronze bowl (?), with inscribed base. Fitzwilliam Museum, Cambridge.

10. Shield from the Athenian Agora: bronze facing of shield taken as trophy from one of the 292 Lakedaimonians captured and held hostage in Athens in 425 BC. Athens, Agora Museum.

is decorously attired and would not bring a blush to the most conservative Greek male cheek. Not so the flagrantly naked – or nude – female of the mirror from Lousoi in Arkadia, and her likewise unclad sisters. They would confirm a non- or anti-Spartan's direst suspicions of Spartan female unchastity. Looked at with Spartan eyes, however, they were another matter altogether: Spartan women and their daughters could quite literally identify with these naked girls as they gazed at their own reflections in the disks they supported (Stewart 1997: 116). For they fitted comfortably into a whole range of ritualized social practices preparing Spartan girls for the office and tasks of womanhood.

Straddling the categories of independent figurines and bronze vessels were the figures created as attachments to be cast or riveted onto the Lakonian bronze kraters and hydriai (water-jars) that enjoyed almost as wide a distribution as the painted pottery. For once, there is a near-exact coincidence of literary and archaeological evidence: Herodotus (1.70) tells a bracing tale of a bronze krater sent by the Spartans as an official diplomatic gift to the king of Lydia but which, thanks to an act of Samian piracy, never reached its intended destination. Its description recalls uncannily those attested kraters of which the undoubted champion is the one unearthed at Vix in southern France, in the grave of a Hallstatt princess. This stood 1.64 metres high and had a capacity of 1200 litres (about 318 gallons). Atop the lid, serving as its handle, was a primly clothed woman. But along the rim of some such vessels were fixed partially naked or skimpily clad girl runners, such as the example from Dodona illustrated here (Plate **7**). They too, arguably, were distinctively ethnic representations, almost unthinkable as creations of any community other than Sparta.

One final illustration of the nature and complexity of Sparta's external relations in the third quarter of the sixth century is the recently published ram shown in Plate **9** (Cartledge 2000). It too was originally attached to some other support, perhaps a vessel of some kind. But its main interest for us resides in its inscription: To Poseidon the driver (i.e., charioteer) Xenokleês dedicated (this). The name and most of the lettering are Lakonian, the ram is of either Lakonian or southern Arkadian style, but the findspot was somewhere in south-western Arkadia, and there are traces of Arkadian influence on the script; so possibly its place of manufacture was, say, Tegea rather than Sparta. Cultural interaction on the borders of Lakonia and Arkadia was very much alive and well as late as *c.* 525, when this figurine was made and dedicated.

The expansion of production during the sixth century indicated by the distribution of bronzes (and pottery) outside Lakonia is mirrored in the increased quantity and quality of the local finds in Lakonian and Messenian centres outside Sparta. A particularly fine example is the miniature kouros figure dedicated to Apollo at modern Kosmas in east-central Lakonia, a Perioikic site, and now resplendently on display in the National

Museum, Athens (Plate **8**). It was made at around the time of Marathon in 490. Finds like these demonstrate the existence of local workshops among the Perioikoi serving the major sanctuaries, besides the shops in Sparta itself. So now at last is perhaps the time to raise – if not finally answer – the question of the possible role of Perioikoi in Spartan or Lakonian craftsmanship.[18]

According to the mirage, the only manual art or craft-skill (*tekhnê*) that a Spartan citizen had ever legally been permitted to practise was the art of war. Indeed, the Spartans were called precisely craftsmen of military affairs (Cartledge 1976a). On that view the role of craftsmen must have been filled by Perioikoi and perhaps some Helots, perhaps even some declassed Spartans, at any rate from about 650 BC on. I would not wish to minimize the role of the Perioikoi in this sphere, or in those of trade and mining, for example. But a fresh light was apparently thrown by the publication in the 1960s of a funerary tumulus excavated in the centre of Sparta town (Christou 1964).

Apart from the four inhumed skeletons, two adult male, one adult female, and a child, there were found the remains of a house and a potter's kiln. The family, for such they presumably were, must have been of citizen status, and perhaps quite exalted status, to qualify for such honorific burial in the centre of Sparta, where – exceptionally – intramural burial was practised as a normal ritual. At any rate, there does seem to be demonstrated here some sort of close connection between Spartans and craftsmanship – a connection that the mirage would prima facie rule out. One product of that kiln, so Christou argued, might have been the moulded terracotta amphora depicting a hunting-scene in relief (see David 1993 for the Spartans' passion for hunting) that was found in the tumulus and could therefore have served as the original grave-marker. The date of the amphora, and so Christou presumed the burials, is somewhere around 600 BC. Subsequent research has, however, failed to confirm the association of the amphora with the burials, which may well be much later (cf. Hodkinson 2000: ch. 8).

By the time of the manufacture of our handsome kouros figurine (Plate **8**), a century or so later, however, the distinctive local Lakonian tradition of Archaic visual art was coming to an end (cf. Rolley 1977b). The condition of Lakonian artistic production was by then but a wan shadow of its robust former self, and Lakonian craftsmen were provincial in the fullest sense. Locally made household items such as chairs, tables and shoes were still, reportedly, serviceable and satisfying. But neither ivory nor even local animal-bone was carved any longer for dedications to be made in any Lakonian sanctuary. Fine painted pottery and decorative bronzework were no longer made for export; local potters and bronzeworkers imitated Attic styles and produced types common throughout mainland Greece. Rich Spartans – and there were some seriously rich Spartans – unlike their social peers in other Greek cities imported very little Attic red-figure pottery, which was by then the dominant luxury tableware in the entire Greek world.

As for the native poetic tradition, that was all but extinct; Tyrtaios and Alkman had no cause to fear posthumous rivals. The one leading poet whom Sparta did manage to attract from abroad in the fifth century was the praise-singer Simonides of Keos, most famed of course for his wholly functional couplet on the Spartan dead at Thermopylai in 480 but now known to have composed also a neo-epic laudation of the Spartans' yet greater military achievement at Plataia in 479. Even the wonderful over-lifesize marble carving popularly known as Leonidas (Boardman 1978: fig. 124), which has been widely appropriated as the emblem of Spartan heroic militarism, was almost certainly executed by a foreign sculptor. Besides, its subject was anyway more likely a god or hero than a mortal man, and it is in any case probably too early to be a portrait in any strict sense of the hero of Thermopylai.

All the same, this sculpture does nicely emblematize the military style of life that had by then come to characterize Sparta. To call it a mere barracks bereft of high culture, as did certain Athenian propagandists, was probably going too far – but not all that much too far. The historical question for us therefore is why the open, progressive – or at any rate progressing – Kulturstadt of the mid-sixth century had become so meta-morphosized. There is a one-word answer, suitably laconic, namely *oliganthrôpia* or shortage of citizen military manpower. Between 480 and 371, by which time the shortage had become critical, numbers of adult Spartan warriors had dropped from perhaps as many as 8000 to little over 1000. Of course, the earthquake that hit Sparta directly in 464 will have had something to do with it. But as Hodkinson (esp. 1983, 1996) and others (e.g., Cartledge 1987) have tried to show, the malaise was not opportunistic but structural, a function ultimately of the Spartans' insufficiently well controlled system of land-tenure.

It was during this period of a hundred years, as relations between Spartans and Helots, and between Sparta and the outside world, deterio-rated, that the mirage was born – or rather manufactured, at first by the nervous Spartans themselves. It was then taken up, for their own domestic purposes, by aggressively oligarchic, especially Athenian, propagandists. In its cultural aspect the mirage was not entirely devoid of correspondence with the Spartan reality, but its pseudo-historical underpinning in terms of Lykourgan prohibitions was of course just so much gossamer and gossip.

I end therefore on an appropriately military note, with what is, rather surprisingly, the sole extant example of a full-size Spartan shield from all antiquity (Plate **10**). Even that is not a wholly accurate statement, since all that survives of this characteristically hoplite shield with its offset rim is the bronze facing, not the probably wooden core and its no less charac-teristic two handles. Shields like these are impossible to date on internal grounds, since the hoplite shield assumed a pretty constant form between about 700 and 300. But the findspot – a well dug in the Athenian Agora that had been closed by 300 – gives a *terminus ante quem*, and the inscription punched on the outside clinches the precise identification. It reads: 'The Athenians from the Lakedaimonians at Pylos'. The shield, that is, was a battle trophy, taken from one of the 292 Lakedaimonians, including 120 Spartiates, captured in 425 by Kleon and Demosthenes on the islet of Sphakteria (to be strictly accurate). The well-known story is told in full in Thucydides Book 4.

Such by then was the Spartans' *oliganthrôpia* and such their perception of it that they were prepared to sue for peace at once in order to retrieve these few hostages. As Aristotle saw with the blinding clarity of hindsight a century later, the Spartans were absolutely right to be so concerned. Sparta was, as he put it, destroyed through *oliganthrôpia*. They could not endure the single blow of the defeat at Leuktra in 371 – the ancient defeat so charmingly commemorated in the very un-Spartan Hyatt Regency's utterly modern advertisement.[19]

13

The Importance of Being Dorian:
An Onomastic Gloss on the
Hellenism of Oscar Wilde

To the memory of Bedell Stanford

Introduction

Oscar Wilde's first centenary – in 1998, marking his release from Reading Gaol – witnessed his firm establishment in the Western canon of letters, not to mention his extraordinary rehabilitation in Westminster Abbey. His second centenary – of his early death aged 46 in 1900 – is upon us as I write. His time as an undergraduate at Magdalen College, Oxford, is well documented and indeed celebrated. The essay that follows is an attempt both to recall the far less well known but even more crucial role played in his intellectual formation by his classical studies at Trinity College Dublin (which is also Dublin University, and referred to for short below as 'T.C.D.' or 'Trinity'), and to reposition him firmly within the 'Spartan tradition in European thought' (Rawson 1969).

Since the original version of this chapter was published, in *Hermathena*, the house journal of T.C.D. (now once again a dedicated Classical journal, as it was originally conceived), a major work on 'Hellenism and homosexuality in Victorian Oxford' has appeared: Dowling 1994; see my review in *Hermathena* 161 (Winter 1996) 105-8; cf. my 'Getting/After Foucault: two post-antique responses to postmodern challenges' in M. Wyke (ed.) *Gender and the Body in the Ancient Mediterranean* (Oxford, 1998) 194-8. Dowling's interesting earlier article on Dorianism in one of Wilde's major modern sources, Walter Pater, came out in the same year (1989) as my original essay on 'Dorian' Gray.

*

Oscar Wilde was a brilliant classicist, 'perhaps the best educated in the Classics of all the major figures in the Anglo-Irish tradition'.[1] He received his Classical education first at the Portora Royal School, Enniskillen, then at Trinity College Dublin (1871-4), where he came under the guidance and particular influence of the inimitable J.P. Mahaffy (with consequences to

185

be further explored in this paper), and finally at Magdalen College, Oxford (1874-8), where he took a Double First in Greats and won the enormously prestigious Newdigate Prize.[2]

Wilde did not lose touch with the world of Trinity Classics after his translation across the water to England. He travelled to Classical lands with Mahaffy, for example, and he contributed to the lightheartedly learned Dublin University journal *Kottabos* (founded under the editorship of R.Y. Tyrrell in 1869). Nor did he disavow his Classical affiliations on going down from Oxford. The curious reader of the inaugural issue of the *Journal of Hellenic Studies* will discover that in 1880 one 'Mr Oscar Wilde' was a member of the first Council of that journal's parent body, the Society for the Promotion of Hellenic Studies.[3] For the remaining twenty years – almost half – of his unhappily abbreviated life he participated fully in and indeed gave impetus, shape and direction to the disparate and somewhat nebulous literary-aesthetic tendencies that were and are lumped under the catch-all rubric of 'Hellenism'.[4] It is just one, apparently minor and hitherto entirely overlooked or misunderstood aspect of Wilde's contribution to the Classical tradition – and more specifically to the 'Spartan tradition in European thought'[5] – that I wish to discuss briefly here.

It was in the July 1890 edition of *Lippincott's Monthly Magazine* of Philadelphia that Wilde published the first version of his only novel, *The Picture of Dorian Gray*. This was reissued as a book, in an expanded, revised and (artistically) improved form, in April of the following year.[6] Ever since then, the work has exercised almost as much fascination over its readers as the fictional 'golden book' presented to its eponymous anti-hero by his evil genius Lord Henry Wotton. Yet only one of its myriad scholarly commentators has to my knowledge seen fit to remark on the significance of Wilde's choice of 'Christian' name for his eponym, and he, understandably, was not entirely at home in Classical Greek literature and history.[7]

Is there anything (much) in a name? Despite the instantly negative response given in *Romeo and Juliet*, the exceptionally large number of other 'name' entries in the *Oxford Dictionary of Quotations*, and the obsession of philosophers and anthropologists with nominalism and nomenclature, not to mention all those 'Naming Your Baby' manuals, would seem to suggest that there is, or is widely thought to be. As for creative writers, they as a tribe have a professional preoccupation with the matter, and in 1978 a diligent librarian was able to compile a substantial bibliography devoted solely to the study of names in literature.[8]

Thus for a marvellously creative author, who was himself extravagantly christened Oscar Fingal O'Flahertie Wills, a concern for personal nomenclature must have been almost second nature, and there is plenty of evidence that Wilde was indeed mightily interested in both his own and his created characters' names.[9] Yet still, for all the Holmesian effort that scholars have put into tracking down the possible sources of the names of the three main characters in Dorian Gray – Basil Hallward (was there or was there not a real portrait painter called Basil Ward for whom Wilde sat?), Lord Henry Wotton (intentional homonym, surely, of the Elizabethan grandee who in 1604 penned the immortally cynical definition of an ambassador as 'an honest man sent to lie abroad for the good of his country'), and Dorian Gray himself (was it, as Wilde later publicly denied, John Gray, the poet of decadence and decadent poet, or the fictional Sylvester Gray, suicidal subject of Edward Heron-Allen's 1888 novel *Ashes of the Future*, or even Disraeli's equally fictional eponym Vivien Grey [1826], who also had a brush with a portrait?) – seemingly only one scholar, as already mentioned, has addressed himself, at any rate in print, to the quiddity of 'Dorian'.

Before we consider his interpretation in any detail, two further preliminary remarks are necessary, in order to establish that this is indeed an aspect of the novel worth pursuing further. First, Wilde does seem to make heavy weather of names and naming at more than one significant juncture in the development of what may loosely be called the plot of *Dorian Gray*. At the very outset Basil (whose name, like that of Sibyl, Dorian's first female object of passion, is of Greek origin) makes a song and dance about Dorian Gray's name, emphasising the essential relationship of belonging between names and their owners. In chapter eight (of the revised version) Dorian reveals that he had vouchsafed to Sibyl only his Christian and not his last name. And towards the end of the book (chapter seventeen), in response to Lord Harry's 'plan for rechristening everything', the Duchess of Monmouth rejoins 'I am quite satisfied with my own name, and I am sure Mr Gray should be satisfied with his'; whereupon Lord Harry himself comments 'From a label there is no escape'. But what sort of a label was 'Dorian'?

The last essential preliminary observation is that it was emphatically not a Christian one, even in the loose sense in which 'Christian' may be applied to any forename that appeared on a late-nineteenth-century baptismal certificate. For 'Dorian' will be sought in vain either in E.G. Withycombe's standard *The Oxford Dictionary of English Christian Names* (now in its third, revised edition of 1977) or – since Dorian Gray was first published in the United States – in G.R. Stewart's equally scholarly and standard *American Given Names: their Origin and History in the Context of the English Language* (New York, 1979). In short, if 'Dorian' does now today make an appearance in popular naming manuals as a boy's name alongside its female near-equivalent Doris, that is due solely to the fertile genius of Oscar Wilde. Or rather to the exercise of that genius on his inherited conglomerate of Classical Greek learning. For 'Dorian' is of course unquestionably and unambiguously *d'origine grecque*, being the English adjective and substantive used to refer to one of the main ethnic or, more precisely, linguistic and cultural groupings of the ancient Greek people, the Dorians. But why, apart from reasons of euphony and possibly literary allusion, did Wilde choose to tap that particular onomastic root?

Modern scholarly opinion on the overall 'message' and sociocultural location of *Dorian Gray* would seem to be rather evenly divided into the 'aesthetic' and the 'homosexual' camps. For C.S. Nassaar, for instance, it is 'primarily an examination of the decadent movement'.[10] But for Jeffrey Meyers, on the other hand, it is 'the *locus classicus* of the modern homosexual novel'.[11] The late Richard Ellmann, as ever, held the balance with a steady and equal hand in his magisterial biography of 1987: '*Dorian Gray*, besides being about aestheticism, is also one of the first attempts to bring homosexuality into the English novel'.[12] Since any attempt to inject homosexuality into the mainstream (rather than the pullulating Victorian underground) of English fiction in 1890 had necessarily to employ 'a language of reticence and evasion, obliqueness and indirection' (Meyers 1977: 1), to avoid falling foul of the Criminal Law Amendment Act of 1885, one might expect to find a covert reference to homosexuality in the name of the novel's eponym. 'Dorian', as we shall soon see, fitted the bill nicely in this regard.

All due credit must therefore go to Meyers, who was at least groping in the right direction when he wrote:

> Though he is more elaborately Corinthian than austerely Dorian, he takes his name from a race whom John Addington Symonds calls 'those martial founders of the institution of Greek love'.[13]

What Meyers, as a professor of English, did not realize was that the ancient Corinthians were themselves Dorians, so that his contrast between 'Corinthian' and 'Dorian' is a factitious one. And what he did not choose to discover or at least to point out in his otherwise excellent study of homosexual literature was that beneath Symonds' – and Wilde's – determination to create an aesthetic tradition for the homosexual ideal within the currently fashionable framework of (especially Pateresque) 'Hellenism' there lay a solid bedrock of Classical scholarship.[14]

Just as Wilde was probably the best-trained classicist within the Anglo-Irish, and certainly the best within the Decadent, tradition of English literature, so Shelley had been (with the exception of W.S. Landor) 'the best classicist of all the Romantic writers'.[15] His 'Discourse on the Manners of the Ancient Greeks Relative to the Subject of Love', written in 1818 as a preface to his translation of Plato's *Symposium*, had dealt frankly if critically with Platonic homosexuality – far more critically, one might add, than his friend Byron would have done. A heavily edited version of the *Discourse* at last appeared posthumously in his *Complete Works* of 1840.[16] But ten years before that, Byron's publisher John Murray had sponsored the appearance of the first scholarly work of ancient history in English (translation) to deal among much else with what it coyly called *paiderastia*

188

– resorting to the obscurity of a learned language, partly because the bastard English word 'homosexuality' had yet to be coined.[17] That work of K.-O. Müller was devoted, significantly, to precisely 'The Dorians', and the 'connexion' or 'relation' of pederasty was considered by its author, as it has often though wrongly been since, to be a peculiarly Dorian Greek social custom.[18]

Just over forty years later Wilde's former teacher at Trinity, Mahaffy ('the scholar who showed me how to love Greek things', as Wilde perhaps ambiguously put it in a letter of 1895), published the first edition of his blockbuster *Social Life in Greece from Homer to Menander* (1874). In his preface, dated 4 November, the author duly acknowledged the aid of 'Mr Oscar Wilde of Magdalen College, Oxford' in both correcting and improving the entire manuscript. In retrospect, however, – and not, I think, merely in anachronistic hindsight – the most spectacularly seminal pages of the manuscript (305-11 of the published edition) were those given over to a 'notably frank' but (no less than Shelley's) studiously derogatory discussion of Classical Greek homosexuality.[19]

In Wilde's surviving writings the first reference to homosexuality cannot be traced earlier than 1876, and it was probably not for another ten years that in his own personal behaviour and outlook he opted decisively for the homosexual over the heterosexual component of his bisexual orientation.[20] But in view of his deep Classical learning, which was allied to a phenomenal memory and a capacity for absorbing the most voluminous and diverse reading matter with almost incredible rapidity, it is highly probable that he too had both read and stored for future use the primary sources on which Mahaffy had based his account of homosexuality in Greece. Those sources will have taken Wilde to ancient Athens, of course, the location of Plato's *Symposium*, and also through Plato's work to Elis and Thebes, where – as Mahaffy observed with barely stifled astonishment – the law actually licensed physical homosexuality and not only an idealized spiritual intimacy between males. But, above all, the sources will have guided Wilde to Sparta, the Dorian state *par excellence*, which was shortly to form the chief pole of attraction in the essay he wrote on (ancient) 'Hellenism' at Oxford after returning from his grand tour with Mahaffy in 1877.[21]

In that short essay, which is a sort of extended commentary on Herodotus' famous definition of Hellenism (8.144.2), there is no reference to homosexuality in Sparta, despite Wilde's insistence on Sparta's 'strong individuality' and his concern with its 'mode of life'. Indeed, the manuscript ends with the comment that to judge from the poetry of Alkman the Spartans would appear to have been 'exceedingly fond of ... the society of women' in his day. But since Alkman, as Wilde well knew, lived long before the time of Plato, there would seem to be a deliberate aposiopesis here. What Wilde did not go on to say was that it was for their exceeding fondness for the society of men or rather adolescent boys, and more particularly their addiction to buggery, that the Spartans of Plato's age were famous, if not notorious, in Greece – as Wilde would quickly have learned from reading his favourite Aristophanes.[22]

Sparta, however, together with Athens, was an essential ingredient in the myth of Hellenism with which so many eminent Victorians liked to envelop their immediate political, social and cultural concerns and aspirations, and it would not have done to dwell on the sordidly carnal side of a Spartan education. Fortunately, though, the very ancient sources that discoursed most fully on Spartan pederasty, Plato and Xenophon, provided such Victorians with the perfect alibi and compromise. As Mahaffy so usefully phrased it, 'all the higher classes in both Sparta and Athens would agree in reprobating [these pederastic intimacies], when they exceeded mere sentimental friendships'.[23] Or, as Müller had put it, drawing on a wider range of ancient evidence: 'At Sparta the party loving was called *eispnêlas*, and his affection was termed a *breathing in*, or *inspiring* (*eispnein*); which expresses the pure and mental connexion between the two persons ...'.[24] From there to what Richard Ellmann (1987: 301) paraphrased as Lord Harry Wotton's 'attempt to inseminate his friend spiritually' is a short and, I suggest, a direct step.

In general, the first, magazine version of *Dorian Gray* (1890) was more perceptibly homosexual than the second, book version of 1891; in the latter, Wilde responded to vitriolic criticism of its alleged gross immorality, at a time when he was still posing towards the general public as a family man, by deliberately and painstakingly toning down or excising the more suggestively homosexual references.[25] However, Wilde was not the man or writer to hide, let alone snuff out, his light under a bushel, and in the newly-added third chapter the worldly and sophisticated reader was treated to the following, 'at least ambiguous' (Ellmann) rumination of Lord Harry's:

> There was something terribly enthralling in the exercise of influence. No other activity was like it. *To project one's soul into some gracious form, and let it tarry there a moment ... to convey one's temperament into another as though it were a subtle fluid* or a strange perfume: there was a real joy in that – perhaps the most satisfying joy left to us in ... an age grossly carnal in its pleasures ... [my emphases].

Then, just in case the *cognoscenti* should be unusually slow on the uptake, Wilde added this clinching sentence: 'Grace was his [Dorian's], and the white purity of boyhood, and beauty such as old Greek marbles kept for us'. This was much more piquant stuff than the rather tame 'to influence a person is to give him one's own soul' retained from the original chapter two. It is here, therefore, that Wilde's thoroughly characteristic contribution to the Spartan tradition or, as it may more properly be labelled, *le mirage spartiate*, should in my view be identified.[26]

As principal witness for the defence of my interpretation of the associations and innuendoes of the name 'Dorian' I call in evidence finally ... the author himself. To Ralph Payne, in an often quoted but never yet fully explicated letter postmarked 12 February 1894, Wilde wrote: 'Basil Hallward is what I think I am: Lord Henry what the world thinks me: Dorian what I would like to be – in other ages, perhaps'. To be more exact, in the idealized Platonic age of Greece, as wishfully interpreted by John Addington Symonds, Edward Carpenter and other such late Victorian, neo-Hellenist progressives of actively homosexual proclivities.[27] The significance of the fact that 'Dorian' is a pagan name should not be overlooked.

Wilde, however, had kept one last literary card up his richly caparisoned sleeve. The ancient Dorians, in the estimation both of non-Dorian ancient Greeks and of nineteenth-century Victorians alike, were a rugged, earthy, solemn and generally uncultivated lot, doers rather than thinkers.[28] But Wilde's Dorian, Dorian Gray, was an effete, self-obsessed, dandiacal exquisite placed at the centre of 'a novel of sensibilities rather than a novel of action'.[29] Thus the paradoxically discordant onomastic juxtaposition, whereby the novel's most prominent *nomen* proved to be the reverse of a reliable omen, was a masterpiece of indirection very much to Wilde's aesthetic and sexual tastes. Dorian Gray, would-be Faustian moral exemplar and barely disguised avatar of Wilde's own repressed homosexual guilt, would simply by any other name have smelled far too sweet.[30]

Notes

1. 'Sparta-watching': general introduction

1. Rawson 1969; cf. my review of the 1991 paperback reprint in *JACT Ancient History Bureau Bulletin* (Nov. 1991) 15-17.

2. Cartledge 1975; 'Foreword' to Powell ed. 1989: x-xiv; and see further the following Sparta-related reviews of mine:

J.T. Hooker *The Ancient Spartans* (1980): *TLS* 7 Nov. 1980, 1266

C.D. Hamilton *Agesilaus and the Failure of Spartan Hegemony* (1991): *CR* 42 (1992) 367-9

L.F. Fitzhardinge *The Spartans* (1980): *TLS* 4 April 1980

M. Pipili *Laconian Iconography of the Sixth Century* BC (1987) & M. Herfort-Koch *Archaische Bronzeplastik Lakoniens* (1986): *CR* 38 (1988) 342-5

T.A. Boring *Literacy in Ancient Sparta* (1979): *CR* 30 (1980) 294

F. Gschnitzer *Ein neuer spartanische Staatsvertrag* (1978): *CR* 30 (1980) 295-6

W.T. Loomis *The Spartan War Fund: IG V 1,1 and a New Fragment* (1992): *CR* 43 (1993) 403-4

D.M. MacDowell *Spartan Law* (1986): *LCM* 11 (1986) 142-4

S. Link *Der Kosmos Sparta. Recht und Sitte in klassischer Zeit* (1994): *CR* 45 (1995) 188-9*

N.M. Kennell *The Gymnasium of Virtue: Education and Culture in Ancient Sparta* (1995): *CR* 47 (1997) 97-8

*My review of Link 1994 touched, controversially, on the Nazification – not, of course, by Link – of Spartan history. On that ugly topic, see Losemann 1977 and further bibliography in Christ ed. 1986: 502-3.

2. City and *chora* in Sparta: Archaic to Hellenistic

1. Cartledge 1996b; cf. Snodgrass 1977; Runciman 1982; Morris 1987; Runciman 1990; Hansen 1998; Hansen ed. 1993.

2. Kirsten 1956; cf. Kirsten 1984; Murray & Price eds 1990; Gschnitzer 1991.

3. Shipley 1996: 4.

4. e.g. Rich & Wallace-Hadrill eds 1991; Shipley & Salmon eds 1996.

5. de Polignac 1995.

6. Cavanagh et al. 1996-7; cf. Cavanagh & Crouwel 1988.

7. Jameson et al. 1994/1995; cf. Cavanagh 1991; Snodgrass 1991.

8. Cartledge 1997.

9. Leontis 1995; cf. Hirsch & O'Hanlon eds 1995; von Reden 1998.

10. Cartledge 1996c.

11. Meier 1990; Finley 1983.

12. Walbank 1985; Cartledge 1995b.

13. Sakellariou 1989; Hansen ed. 1993; Hansen & Raaflaub eds 1995.

14. Finley 1977a; 1985d; Morris 1987; Osborne 1987, 1991, 1996; Snodgrass 1993b.

15. Runciman 1990; Hansen ed. 1993; Hansen 1998.

16. Cf. Hansen 1995: 52-3, 53-4.

17. Travlos 1971; Wycherley 1978.

18. Stibbe 1989; *pace* Hansen 1995: 54.

19. Kennell 1995. See further Chapter 7, below.

20. Finley 1983: 61-4; cf. Cartledge 1992.

21. Shipley 1992; Lotze 1994.

22. Ducat 1990.

23. Alcock & Osborne eds 1994; Cartledge 1996c.

24. Malkin 1994.

25. Cf. Sartre 1979; Daverio-Rocchi 1998.

26. Lakonia Survey, GG 84.

27. Lakonia Survey, GG 95.

28. Lakonia Survey, N405; cf. Catling 1990a, 1990b.

29. Dover 1978: 105.

30. Lakonia Survey, GG 88, cf. 92.

31. *Pace* Kennell 1995: 162-9; see rather Tausend 1992: 103ff.; Thommen 1996: 15 and n. 38.

32. Cartledge 1979; Cartledge & Spawforth 1989.

33. Whitehead 1986.

34. Hansen 1987.

35. Bruit-Zaidman & Schmitt-Pantel 1992.

36. de Polignac 1995.

37. de Polignac 1994.

38. Cartledge 1985a; Robertson 1992.

39. Neils et al. 1992.

40. Loraux 1993; cf. 1986.

41. Piccirilli 1984.

42. Pettersson 1992.

43. Thanks are due especially to Susan Walker, both for inviting me to participate in the B.M. Colloquium and for organizing it so skilfully, and to Bill Cavanagh for overseeing the editorial side of the original publication. I am also indebted to Hector Catling and Joost Crouwel for helpful comments.

3. The peculiar position of Sparta in the development of the Greek city-state

1. Ehrenberg 1969: 22.

2. Pollitt 1972: 1-2.

3. Ehrenberg 1969: 12.

4. Newman 1887: 89-90. For Aristotle's distinctive contribution to ancient political theory, see Huxley 1979; Cartledge 1997: esp. 107-14; and *The Cambridge History of Greek and Roman Political Thought*, ed. C. Rowe & M. Schofield, Cambridge 2000, chs 15-19.

5. Bölte 1929: coll. 1291-2. The earliest known occurrence of *Spartiatai* is probably in a poem of Tyrtaios preserved on papyrus and published only quite recently (*P. Oxy.* 3316).

6. Cartledge 1979: 178-87; Shipley 1997; Mertens 1999; Hall 2000.

7. Bickerman 1958; cf. Hansen 1998: esp. 77-83.
8. Finley 1985a: ch. 1; Cartledge 1998b.
9. Finley 1959: esp. 164.
10. Lotze 1959; Finley 1963-4; Garlan 1988: 87; Ducat 1990.
11. Cartledge 1979: 160-77; Ste. Croix 1983: 149.
12. Cartledge 1977: esp. 16.
13. Morpurgo 1963.
14. Hammond 1972: 8, 148, 346; Finley 1977a.
15. Wycherley 1962; Martin 1974.
16. Moggi ed. 1976: no. 6, writes with justice of a 'situazione pre-sinecistica' at Sparta. See further Chapter 2 in this collection.
17. Wace 1906-7: 5-16; cf. Steinhauer 1972, Chron. 242. A wall of the late fourth century BC was excavated more recently, but its original identification as a city-wall has been abandoned: *Arch. Delt.* 21 (1966) Chron. 154-5; 24 (1969) Chron. 137.
18. Ehrenberg 1924: 28-9. On all this see further Chapter 2.
19. Andreev 1975.
20. Burn 1960: 244. See further Cartledge 1998b.
21. Momigliano 1966b; cf. Cartledge 1997: ch. 2.
22. McCarter, Jr. 1975: 65-104, 118-26; Coldstream 1977: ch. 11; Powell 1991.
23. Jeffery 1961: 183-202 (the Lakonian script).
24. Finley 1986c: ch. 5.
25. Starr 1965.
26. Shey 1976: 5-28; a full bibliography on Alkman is given by Calame 1977 (vol. I, rev. ed. 1997).
27. Ollier 1933-43.
28. Ferguson 1975: chs. 4, 15.
29. See the edition by Ollier 1948; translation with commentary in Moore 1983.
30. The sources used for the *Life* are discussed by Kessler 1910.
31. de Laix 1974.
32. We do have a continuous archaeological record for Sparta from *c.* 750; but archaeology, to repeat, is an unsure guide to politics. For example, most modern attempts to situate historically the idealized austerity so beloved of the 'mirage spartiate' have been disastrous. An exception is Holladay 1977. See further Chapter 12.
33. I am not concerned here with the wider question 'when did the *polis* rise?'; but it may be worth noting that this continuing controversy stems partly from differential weighting of the criteria of *polis*-hood. See Lepore 1978, esp. 183-253; Hansen 1998.
34. For the downfall of the Mycenaean civilization, see Greenhalgh 1978. For the period *c.* 1100-800 see Snodgrass 1971; Desborough 1972; Coldstream 1977; Eder, B., ed. 1990; Eder 1998.
35. Kiechle 1966; Hiersche 1970: 80-106; and for the Dorian settlement of Lakonia, see Cartledge 1979: ch. 7; 1992; Eder 1998.
36. Kirsten 1956: 103 ff.
37. Catling 1976-77.
38. According to, e.g., Thucydides (1.12.3), eighty years after the Fall of Troy, on the ancient dates for which see Forsdyke 1957: 62; Snodgrass 1971: 12-14.
39. Cartledge 1979: 341-6. See further Chapter 5, below.
40. Forrest 1968: 21; Jeffery 1976: 114.
41. See above, n. 18.

42. Sakellariou ed. 1975: 57.

43. The most important earlier literature is cited in Lévy 1977. This article is probably as sensible a discussion as the evidence will allow, although I cannot follow several of Lévy's conclusions, in particular his temporal separation of Rhetra and Rider; more recently see Ogden 1994; Thommen 1996; Ruzé 1997: 129-40; Meier 1998; Richer 1999; van Wees 1999.

44. Jeffery 1976: 117.

45. Forrest 1968: 21.

46. Aristotle fr. 533 Rose, with Huxley 1973: 281-2.

47. Forrest 1963: 158-9, 166-8.

48. Quass 1971: 7-11.

49. See further Lévy 1977: 88, n. 13.

50. West 1974: 184-6. For the preservation of oracles at Sparta, see Cartledge 1978: 30. On the historical development of the early Delphi sanctuary, see Rolley 1977a: 131-46; Morgan 1990: chs 4-5.

51. Agoraios/Agoraia: Paus. 3.11.9-10; Xenios/Xenia: Paus. 3.11.11. Cf. Wide 1893: 54.

52. The exception perhaps is 'Hyllanios/Hyllania' proposed by Ziehen, *RE* IIIA (1929) col. 1489 and accepted by Lévy 1977: 90 ('1484' is a slip).

53. Alternatively, a change in the political function of the tribes and obes is in question. For example, it is conceivable that reference is being made implicitly here to the supersession of the kinship principle by the locality principle of organization for military purposes. At any rate, this relatively advanced step is most easily associated with the transformation of the entire *damos* into a hoplite army: see following text. For yet another view, see the acute discussion in Roussel 1976: 233-45.

54. It may be, however, that initially regular meetings were held only once a year: Lévy 1977: 96.

55. Andrewes 1966. For Aristotle see above, n. 31.

56. Meyer 1892: 261-9; followed apparently by Sealey 1976: 74-8.

57. For the 'Age of Revolution' in general, see Starr 1961b: part III; Snodgrass 1980; 1987; cf. Starr 1977. For early Greek tyranny see Andrewes 1956: esp. ch. 6; Berve 1967.

58. Cartledge 1979: 96-7.

59. See Cartledge 1977: 25; 1987. See also Chapter 11.

60. It was presumably the Partheniai who introduced to Taras the Amyklaian cult of Apollo Hyakinthios (Polyb. 8.30.2).

61. Starr 1961a.

62. Andrewes 1938; Ehrenberg 1946b.

63. Andrewes 1954.

64. On the functions of the Gerousia, see Ste. Croix 1972: 126-8, 131-7, 349-52; Cartledge 1987: esp. 121-5.

65. Andrewes 1966.

66. References may be found in Chapter 4, below [Cartledge 1978: 34-5]; see further Cartledge 1987: ch. 8.

67. The most important sources are Thuc. 4.80.2-4 and Aristotle fr. 538 Rose; these are discussed in Cartledge 1979: 175-7, 246-7.

68. Aristotle, *Pol.* 1313a25ff.; see now Richer 1999.

69. Ste. Croix 1972: 350-3.

70. Aristotle, *Pol.* 1265b39-40, 1270b25-8, 1272a31-2. The method of selection is not specified, but I believe that it was election by acclamation in open assembly (on which see Flaig 1993).

71. Cartledge 1987: 94-6 and Index s.v. 'Lysander ... proposed reform of Spartan kingship'. See also Chapter 5, below.

72. Ste. Croix 1972: ch. 4; Gschnitzer 1978, esp. 33-9; Cartledge 1987: ch. 13; Baltrusch 1994.

73. See generally Mosley 1979; on Sparta's relations with Samos in the Archaic period, see Cartledge 1982b.

74. Ehrenberg 1969: 112-20; Bickerman 1950.

75. Bengtson ed. 1975: no. 112.

76. Parke 1930.

77. Moggi ed. 1976: no. 24; cf. Cartledge 1987: 257-62.

78. Walbank 1970: 13-27. For relations between Sparta and the Achaean League, see Larsen 1968: 443-6; Cartledge & Spawforth 1989: esp. 143-5. On Hellenistic political institutions generally, see Ehrenberg 1969: pt. II; Will 1979-82.

79. Cartledge & Spawforth 1989: 57, 59, 61, 67, 95.

4. Literacy in the Spartan oligarchy

1. The finest discussion of the possible occasion and probable date of the invention of the Greek alphabet is Jeffery 1961: 1-42; cf. Jeffery 1967. For discussion from a technological standpoint, see Havelock 1982: ch. 4. See also below, n. 9.

2. Goody & Watt 1968: 39.

3. Harvey 1966; see also Harris 1989; Robb 1994.

4. As it is by Goody & Watt 1968.

5. Catling & Cavanagh 1976.

6. Casson 1935.

7. On the Tarentine alphabet see Jeffery 1961: 279-82 (the only serious divergence from Lakonian is the absence of the multi-limbed *sigma*); equally close dependence on the metropolis is visible in religion and (other forms of) material culture.

8. Jeffery 1976: 177, raises the possibility of 'the inscribing of a *rhetra*, perhaps on a bronze plaque like the sixth-century examples of *rhetrai* found at Olympia' (cf. 1976: 42, 169). But see below, n. 69.

9. Jeffery 1961: 8. On the connections of the Phoenicians with Kythera, see Coldstream & Huxley 1972: 36. On the transmission of 'letters' to the Greeks by the Phoenicians, see Jeffery 1967: 152-4. See also below, n. 80.

10. Cf. Forrest 1963: 158-9, 166-8; West 1974: 184-6.

11. Parke & Wormell 1956: I. 83-4; II, no. 539. For the suggested dates of Archelaos and Charillos, see Forrest 1968: 21.

12. Rolley 1969: 61-2, no. 61; Zimmermann 1989: 134, no. 153. See further Chapter 12. For a possible dedication at Delphi by a Pythios, see below, n. 32.

13. Hönle 1968: 19-24.

14. Discus: Huxley 1973: 281-2. Transmission of alphabet to Olympia: Jeffery 1961: 185. For Lykourgos' alleged literacy see also below, n. 50.

15. Jeffery 1961: 202-6; add Bauslaugh 1990 (probably 460s).

16. Grote 1888: 390 n. 2 argued that Isokrates should be taken literally, since the second passage cited contains 'an expression dropt almost unconsciously which confirms it. "The most rational Spartans (he says) will appreciate this discourse, *if they find any one to read it to them*" ' (Grote's italics). I do not see why this expression should be exempted from the charge generally accepted as valid by

Grote, that Isokrates preferred rhetoric to factual accuracy; cf. Welles 1966; and, for Isokrates' take on Sparta specifically, Gray 1994.

17. Harvey 1966: 633-5. Compare the alleged banning of Sophists from Sparta (Plut. *Mor.* 226d); but see Harvey 1966: 627 n. 29.

18. On the transmission of Archaic Greek poetry in general, see Davison 1968: 86-128 (my quotation, however, is from 184); the *samizdat* simile is borrowed from Finley 1985c (1977): 146; cf. Havelock 1982: 16ff., chs 7, 12. Alexandrian commentaries on Alkman include the papyri listed as Pack 1965: nos. 81, 1950. On the language of Tyrtaios, see Snell 1969; on that of Alkman, Risch 1954: 20-37.

19. The standard modern treatment is Marrou 1971: 45-60; but see also Bolgar 1969: 23-49, esp. 30-5; see further below, Chapter 7.

20. See in general Gilbert 1895: 42-7.

21. Idaios is not otherwise mentioned, and his name may indicate that he was an Asiatic Greek or even a hellenized oriental.

22. For the kind of tablet Damaratos would have used, see Birt 1913: 259-63.

23. It is not stated whether Gorgo herself was literate, but, if I am right about Spartan women in general (see below, and Chapter 9), she probably was; see further n. 38, below.

24. The evidence for the *skutalê* is collected in Jeffery 1961: 57-8; and discussed thoroughly by Kelly 1985, who has demonstrated that it could not have been a cryptograph; cf. West 1988: 45-6 and n. 20.

25. The old view (that 'Assyrian letters' meant Persian cuneiform) was refuted by Nylander 1968: 119-36, esp. 123-4.

26. See generally Gilbert 1895: 52-9; and now Richer 1999. The Chief Ephor is explicitly credited with the ability to read in the second of the anecdotes involving Agesilaos quoted above; the same goes for Ephors as a whole in Plut. *Lys.* 20; cf. Thuc. 1.128 ff. (supposed letter of Pausanias the Regent to the Great King of Persia); Xenophon, *Hell.* 3.3.4-11 (further discussed below), and Theophrastos (fragment perhaps from his *Nomoi* on the use of *skutalê* in connection with *anakrisis*: Kelly 1985: 155 and nn. 46-7; Richer 1999: 433), which strongly suggest but do not state that the Ephors were literate.

27. It was presumably in this connection that the *Politeia* of Dikaiarchos (fr. 1 Wehrli) was allegedly read out annually to the youngest warriors in (or by) the Ephors' *archeion*.

28. Gilbert 1895: 47-9. Aristotle (*Pol.* 1271a9-10) found the method of their election 'childish' too; presumably the marks scratched on *grammateia* by the election 'jury' did not call for any greater degree of literacy than those made by Athenian jurors in *dikai timêtoi*.

29. Adcock & Mosley 1975; cf. my review in *TLS* 14 November 1975, 1348; Mosley 1979. For diplomacy in the Hellenistic and Roman periods, see Kienast 1973.

30. See in general Adcock 1948: 1-12, esp. 5; cf. Adcock 1924: 92-116, esp. 113. Of the 232 treaties collected in Bengtson ed. 1975, nearly one fifth involve Sparta or Spartans. In fifth-century Sparta heralds constituted one of the three hereditary professions (Hdt. 6.60).

31. See below p. 153.

32. Jeffery 1961: 190, suggested that the '-das, son of Dexippos' who dedicated a bronze *lebês* at Delphi in the first half of the sixth century (199, no. 11) may have been a Pythios.

33. Plutarch (*Ages.* 19.6) refers to the *anagraphai* in which he discovered the names of Agesilaos' wife and two daughters. The list of victors at the Karneia was 'published' by Hellanikos of Lesbos (*FGrHist.* 4 F 85-6; cf. Jeffery 1961: 59-60, 195).

Private inscriptions commemorating Spartan Olympic victors are *IG* 5, 1.649, 708; note also the victor-lists on stone cited below, n. 79.

34. *Hupomeiones*: Gilbert 1895: 39-40; Hippeis (an élite corps of 300 drawn from the younger adult warriors): Gilbert 1895: 60-1.

35. See now Oliva 1971: 192-3; Austin & Vidal-Naquet 1972: 106-7, 270-82, no. 59; Cartledge 1987: e.g. 170.

36. *IG* 5, 1.457, discussed by Bourguet 1927: 35-6.

37. *P. Berl.* 5883 + 5853: see Ste. Croix 1974: 53-4; Cartledge & Spawforth 1989: 71 and n. 19.

38. None of the more recent discussions of Spartan women raises the question of their literacy, but see briefly Harvey 1966: 625; and on the general issue of whether Greek women could read and write, Cole 1981.

39. Victory-dedications: Jeffery 1961: 199-201, nos. 22, 23 (?), 28, 31, 41, 42, 48, 50, 51, 52 (stele of Damonon). Grave-stones and funerary reliefs: *IG* 5, 1.699, 713, 824 (?); Jeffery 1961: 200-1, nos. 26, 29, 57, 59. Cf. below, n. 71.

40. Leather: Birt 1913: 254-6. Papyrus: Lewis 1974, esp. 84-8. Wax: Birt 1913: 259-63.

41. Lang 1974: no. 18. For Athenian writing in private life, see Harvey 1966: 615-17; Lang 1974.

42. Cartledge 1976a. The useful remarks of Jeffery 1961: 31-2 apply chiefly to international star craftsmen rather than to the anonymous members of the supporting cast.

43. Cf. Finley 1968: 145.

44. Jeffery 1961: 187.

45. Limestone doodles: Jeffery 1961: 188, 198, no. 6. Vix abecedarium: Jeffery 1961: 183, 191-2, 202, no. 66, 375; but see Rolley 1963: 483 n. 1. Masons' graffiti: Jeffery 1961: 194, 200, no. 32 (one at least may not have been a Lakonian: Jeffery 1961: 183).

46. Spartan akropolis: Woodward 1928/9: 241-52. Ortheia sanctuary: A.M. Woodward in Dawkins ed. 1929: 371-4. Eleusinion south of Sparta: Nicholls 1950: 297, nos. 53-4. Note also the inscribed bone flutes at the Ortheia sanctuary, appropriate offerings for contemporaries of Alkman: Jeffery 1961: 188, 198, no. 3.

47. Spartan epigraphic orthography moved Bourguet (1927: 8) to exclaim 'je crois que nulle part n'est attesté un usage aussi peu tyrannique'; cf. Bourguet 1927: 19-20, 27, 140 ('la fantaisie de l'écriture').

48. It is probably true that in all societies more people have been able to read than write. As is noted by Turner 1971: 7, representations of people reading were far commoner in Greek art than those of people writing.

49. Woodward 1928/9: 247, no. 5, fig. 4 ('presumably a votive inscription by an illiterate person'). The late Dr Jeffery, however, suggested to me that this may be a trial piece.

50. For the sake of completeness I note that 'Lykourgos', besides having had the Homeric poems copied (Plut. *Lyk.* 4.4), was reported to have transcribed personally a final Delphic oracle sanctioning the 'Great Rhetra' (*Lyk.* 29.4).

51. The process of instruction need not have taken long: see Plato *Laws* 809e-810a for the distinction between functional literacy and fluent calligraphy. For the further distinction between 'slow' and 'retarded' hands at the level of functional literacy in Ptolemaic Egypt, see Youtie 1971: 239-61, esp. 252-3, 256 n. 78 (repr. in 1973: 611-27).

52. The earliest source is either Ion of Chios (fr. 107 von Blumenthal) or Herodotus (3.48, dramatic date *c.* 525). For a curious (and painful) method of inculcating laconic brevity, see Den Boer 1954: 274-81. Spartan letters (epistles) were said to be comparably brief (*fr. com. adesp.* 417-19 Kock). The quintessentially Spartan apophthegms are of course of highly dubious authenticity: see Tigerstedt 1965-78 vol. II (1974): 16-30.

53. Finley 1975: 83. For the view expressed in the text, see Sakellariou ed. 1975: 275.

54. As suggested by Norden 1913: 372-3, the word *arkhaiologia* could be a Sophistic invention.

55. For the meaning of *paidikoi logoi* (Xen. *Hell.* 5.3.20) adopted here ('homosexual love-affairs'), see Chapter 8, n. 81. On the role of conversation in education, cf. Sosikrates, *FGrHist.* 461 F 1 (Crete).

56. Ehrenberg 1973: 389.

57. The earlier literature is assembled in Busolt 1893: 510-79; add Gilbert 1895. More recent studies are amassed in the footnotes to Oliva 1971: 71-102; and in Richer 1999.

58. Ollier 1933-43; for its continuation to the present century see Rawson 1969. See further Chapter 12.

59. Cf. Aristotle *Pol.* 1274a29 for some others (though Solon of course is substantially a historical figure).

60. On the historicity of Lykourgos (as opposed to 'his' laws), see Toynbee 1969: 274-83; Oliva 1971: 63-70.

61. Aalders 1968; Rawson 1969, Index, s.v. 'Mixed Constitution'; Nippel 1980.

62. de Romilly 1959: 81-99; Lasserre 1976: 65-84.

63. For example, Greenidge 1896: 74-107; but even he ends by adopting a position not dissimilar from that of Andrewes 1966 (see further n. 65, below).

64. Gomme 1945: 129 (*ad* Thuc. 1.18.1).

65. The comparison with the Athenian democracy is broached at Andrewes 1966: 16.

66. Ste. Croix 1972: 125 ff.; Cartledge 1987: esp. chs. 7-9.

67. No *isêgoria*: Finley 1976: 9. Voting and elections: Ste. Croix 1972: 348-9 (on Thuc. 1.87); Staveley 1972: 73-6. No popular judiciary: Ste. Croix 1972: 133, 349-50; cf. generally Bonner & Smith 1942: 113-29; Ruzé 1997: 129-240.

68. Müller 1839: 91; cf. 87 for his correct description of 'the aristocratical spirit of the constitution, which feared nothing so much as the passionate and turbulent haste of the populace in decreeing and deciding'.

69. For the range of meanings of *rhêtra*, see Quass 1971: 7-11. If it meant 'law' in the case of the 'Great Rhetra', then *ex hypothesi* this document was never inscribed in Sparta. The *Spartiatês graptos kurbis* (Achaios ap. Athen. 3.68b) is a mystery.

70. *IG* 5, 1.722 = Sokolowski ed. 1962: no. 28. This may, however, have been inscribed for the benefit of Perioikoi, whose literacy need carry no implications for Spartan literacy.

71. According to the MSS of Plutarch, *loc. cit.*, there were two classes of Spartans exempted from the prohibition on named gravestones: men who died in war and priestesses who died in office. For the former, see Jeffery 1961: 197, 201, nos. 57, 59; for the latter, perhaps *IG* 5, 1.824 (all three cited above, n. 39). Flacelière 1948: 403-5, following K. Latte, argued from *IG* 5 1.713 that the text for the latter exemption should be emended to read 'women in childbed'; cf. Garland 1989: 14 n. 54.

72. Thuc. 5.77, 79; 18.10 = Bengtson ed. 1975: nos. 188, 194. For some illuminating remarks on their transcription and dialect, see Bourguet 1927: 148-50. Note also Thuc. 4.118.1-10, with Bickerman 1952 (armistice of 423); and Thuc. 5.41.3 =

Bengtson ed. 1975: no. 192 (unratified treaty of 420 between Argos and Sparta, which the Spartans *xunegrapsanto*).

73. Peek 1974: 3-15; cf., however, Cartledge 1976b.

74. Bengtson ed. 1975: no. 112; we should probably distinguish the stele set up 'on the (banks of the) Alpheios' (Aristotle fr. 592 Rose) from the treaty of alliance. Such a stele, with its injunction to the Tegeans (probably) not to make Messenian Helot asylum-seekers into Tegean citizens, does not of course say anything about the literacy of Messenian Helots in the mid-sixth century.

75. Meiggs & Lewis eds 1989: no. 67; Fornara 1983: no. 132.

76. *Lebês*: Jeffery 1961: 190, 199, no. 10 (*c*. 600-550?). Seats: (i) Jeffery 1961: 190, no. 15 (*c*. 600-550? – perhaps too high); (ii) Mallwitz 1976: 275, pl. 212a (*c*. 500). Offering: Jeffery 1961: 195-6, 201, no. 49 (repr. in Meiggs & Lewis eds 1989: no. 22; cf. Fornara ed. 1983: no. 38).

77. Tod 1933; Jeffery 1961: 198, 202, no. 61.

78. Jeffery 1961: 202, no. 62; used as cover-photograph of Richer 1999.

79. Victor-lists: Jeffery 1961: 195, 201, nos. 44, 47 (the precise nature of no. 44 is unclear, and the last of the four pairs of names is written in a different hand from the others). The Thermopylai list is discussed in connection with the relevant poem(s) of Simonides by Podlecki 1968: 257-75, esp. 257-62, 274-5. Pausanias' epigram: Meiggs & Lewis eds 1989: 60, no. 27. The stelai marking his official reburial presumably fell outside the scope of the prohibition discussed in n. 71, above. Manumission-stelai: the sanctuary of Pohoidan (Poseidon) is known to have been an asylum for fugitive Helots (Thuc. 1.13.1), but, despite the use of Ephor-dates, it is uncertain whether the manumittees are Helots or private slaves (whether of Spartans or Perioikoi): see Ducat 1990: 25-6 (agnostic); Richer 1999: 281-2 (chronology only).

80. Stroud 1968. Cretan precedent: Meiggs & Lewis eds 1989: no. 2; cf. Jeffery 1961: 43, 194; Whitley 1997; Boardman 1999: 60; Hölkeskamp 1999.

81. Boegehold 1972; Boffo 1995; Sickinger 1996; cf. Welles 1966: 6, n. 16. But see below, n. 84.

82. Using Jeffery's catalogues as rough samples, we find that in the Corinthian alphabet there are 7 public inscriptions out of the 40, in the Lakonian (counting only those from Sparta and Amyklai) 1 out of the 32, or (counting them all wherever found) 6 out of the 67; Dow 1942 had suggested a political explanation – oligarchy might have influenced illiteracy.

83. Finley 1985a (1977): 156.

84. Harvey 1966: 600-1. This implies that the absence of a central archive need not have prevented persons from perusing any document in which they were particularly interested.

85. Marrou 1971: 45.

86. David Harvey, George Huxley, Peter Parsons, and the late Robert Bolgar and Anne Jeffery made illuminating comments on earlier drafts of the original version of this chapter.

5. The Spartan kingship: doubly odd?

1. Bordes 1982; Cartledge 1996b. A. Andrewes' generally admirable article 'The Government of Classical Sparta' (1966) would, I am sure, have been better entitled 'The Governance ...', to avoid any possible ambiguity or misapprehension. Earlier discussions of the Spartan kingship/dyarchy, or aspects of it, include: Adcock 1953; Carlier 1977; Cloché 1949; David 1985; Gilbert 1895; Greenidge 1896; Munson 1993; Ste. Croix 1972; and Thomas 1974, 1983. Far and away the most comprehensive and incisive is Carlier 1984: 240-324, with further bibliography at 519-20.

2. Cartledge 1996b; Finley 1983; Farrar 1988.

3. Link 1994; with my review in *CR* 45 (1995) 188-9. On *nomos, nomima*, see Ostwald 1969; van Effenterre & Ruzé eds 1994-5. On the birth of political theory, Cartledge 1996b.

4. Runciman 1989: 51-2 raises the general semantic point.

5. Cartledge 1979: App. 3.

6. Drews 1983.

7. Carlier 1984: 325ff. The same goes, presumably, for the 'king' of Argos mentioned at Hdt. 7.149.2: Carlier 1984: 381.

8. Ste. Croix 1972: 125ff. was one of the first to question this received view seriously; cf. Carlier 1984: 314-15; full discussion: Richer 1999: ch. 23.

9. Parke 1945; David 1985.

10. Cartledge 1987: esp. 121-5.

11. Bommelaer 1977; cf. Cartledge 1987: 94-6.

12. See Adcock 1953 and Thomas 1983 for comparative discussions.

13. Garland 1995.

14. David 1989; Richer 1999: Index s.v. 'Gelôs'.

15. Cartledge 1987: ch. 16; Toher 1991, 1999; cf. Flower 1988. For a mainly Athenian comparison, with special reference to post-mortem civic egalitarianism, see Morris 1994, 1996, 1998, 2000.

16. Herodotus' contrast (5.39.1) between the *genos* of Kleomenes I and the *andragathiê* (manly virtue) of Damaratos, perhaps shown first in the *agôgê*, may imply it.

17. There is a nice tale in Xenophon (*Hell.* 4.7.2-5) that shows Agesipolis I, co-king of Agesilaos, cleverly manipulating Delphic authority to suit his purposes; see Cartledge 1987: 239. On kings as 'founders' (*arkhagetai*: already in the Great Rhetra), see Malkin 1994: chs 5-6.

18. Cartledge 1987: 96.

19. Ino-Pasiphaë: Richer 1999: ch. 12. Apolline festivals: Pettersson 1992.

20. See esp. Carlier 1977; cf. Cawkwell 1993.

21. Griffiths 1989. He was by no means as mad as all that: see e.g. Nafissi 1991: 140-4 for effective exploitation of a 'philo-Achaian' policy, one effect of which was to grant him, and other Spartan kings, legitimacy both at home and abroad; cf. Hall 2000: 88 n. 86.

22. Cartledge 1987; Hamilton 1991; Shipley, D.R. 1997.

23. Staveley 1972.

24. So important was it that it had to be dealt with in two separate chapters of Cartledge 1987: chs 8 and 9.

25. Cartledge 1997: esp. Epilogue.

26. See, however, Bayle 1992 (originally 1695-7).

27. I am most grateful to Robert Evans, Andrew Lintott, and Michael Hurst for their kind invitation to speak and to those who took part in the lively discussion.

6. Comparatively equal: a Spartan approach

1. Carrithers 1993: 18.

2. Miller 1990: 424-7.

3. See, in different contexts, Cartledge 1985b; Golden 1992.

4. Miller 1990: 427.

5. Hanson 1988: 69.
6. Schofield 1999b.
7. Gouldner 1965.
8. Skinner 1988c: 283. Three types of 'use': Skinner 1988a: 9-11.
9. Sen 1980.
10. A 'liberal egalitarian society' is, according to a standard formulation, one 'in which governmental authority is derived from and consistent with the autonomy of every individual' (Gutmann 1980: 287 n. 35). Modern construals of 'State': Skinner 1988b. Liberal democratic freedom and equality defined in relation to the State: Bobbio 1989.
11. Ancient Greek claims to (e.g.) freedom and democracy at most implied or connoted 'rights'; freedom and equality, in any of the modern senses discussed by Dagger 1988, were not construed by the Greeks as rights in themselves: Schofield 1999a: ch. 8 (a critique of Miller 1995); cf. Hansen 1996 and Ostwald 1996. One reason for this key difference is the absence or underdevelopment of the modern notion of State (see previous note): with the partial exception of Sparta, ancient Greek *poleis* were technically 'State-less political communities'. (I acknowledge here especially the help I have received on this basic point from my former graduate pupil, Dr. Moshe Berent, of the Open University of Israel: see Berent 1994, 1998.) However, the ancient *polis* was indeed a form of state, and Gawantka 1985 (cf. Lotze 1990-2) was clearly eccentric in contending that it is (but) a nineteenth-century fabrication.
12. *Galatians* 3.28 and the similar *Colossians* 3.11 have no bearing on *this*-world equality: Ste. Croix 1983: 107-8, 419.
13. For the incommensurable power of the immortal gods, see Bruit-Zaidman & Schmitt-Pantel 1992; Williams 1993.
14. *Concise Oxford Dictionary*, 10th edn (1998), *s.v.* 'Feminism'. Feminist construals of democracy: Mendus 1992; Okin 1979, 1989, 1991: 67-90; Pateman 1983, 1988; Cole 1996. Modern types or instantiations of equality: Lukes 1991: 58, with whom Lee 1990: 105, agrees that liberty and equality can in some respects be mutually reinforcing, and not only rivals.
15. This polarized hierarchy, and especially its manipulation by classical Greek historians, are the informing themes of Cartledge 1997; see also Dougherty 1996.
16. Birth-status in the early *polis*: Morris 1996. Wealth in the developed *polis*: Fuks 1984; and Wood 1996. Ste. Croix 1983 embraces more than the exclusively civic sphere.
17. Sen & Nussbaum eds 1993.
18. As Raaflaub observed (1996: 155), strict economic equality 'was not a serious issue and belonged in the sphere of comic surrealism or abstract theoretical schemes'. Borecky 1963 is a historiographical curiosity.
19. Hansen 1999: 83-4.
20. Aron 1972: 304; cf. Temkin 1994.
21. The standard discussion is Vlastos 1964; cf. Borecky 1971: 5-24; one possible translation – or explication – of the phrase is 'constitutional government with the equal sharing of power by all people' (Graham & Forsythe 1984). Modern slant on justice and equality, from an ancient philosopher: Vlastos 1962.
22. Vapidity: Berlin 1978: 81. 'Imagined communities': Anderson, B. 1991.
23. The choice of *isonomia* by 'Otanes' (Hdt. 3.80.6) to describe an unambiguously democratic form of governance was discursively overdetermined by the imperative necessity of *not* using *dêmokratia*, a term that may actually have been coined by its opponents; cf. Meier 1990, 161ff. By means of partial interpretations

of its very etymology (*dêmos* in the sense of the poor masses or mob, *kratos* in the sense of a forcible grip on the disempowered wealthy few) *dêmokratia* could be construed negatively to mean something approaching mobocracy or the 'dictatorship of the proletariat'.

24. Harvey 1965; cf. Morris 1994: 86.

25. Hansen 1999: 82-3; Dahl 1989. See also Morris 1996.

26. *Isokratia*: Hdt. 5.92a.1, with Ostwald 1972. *Isêgoria* (esp. Hdt. 5.78; Ps.-Xen. *Ath. Pol.* 1.2, 6, 12: Eur. *Supp.* 438-41): Hansen 1999: esp. 83-4.

27. *Isotimia* (the reading at Xen. *Hiero* 8.10 is uncertain): I am indebted to Nathaniel Ober for reminding me of the phrase 'parity of esteem'; *isomoiria*: above, n. 19.

28. Bedau ed. 1971: 12; cf. Berlin 1978: 90, 92, 93.

29. LSJ, 9th ed., s.v. '*isos*' II.2, helpfully collects references, though it is important to distinguish deployment of the phrase within the confines of a *polis* from its uses in relations between *poleis*: e.g., Thuc. 5.79.1 (treaty between Athens and Argos; cf. Ostwald 1972: 52 n. 20) may not bear the same connotations as Dem. 21.112.

30. Aristotle's method: Barnes 1980; Owen 1985. Aristotle on citizen equality: Von Leyden 1985.

31. A textually corrupt clause of the not certainly authentic or authentically early Spartan document known as the 'Great Rhetra' (Plut. *Lyk*. 6) may contain the words *damos* and *kratos*; but, even if that is so, they should not be taken straightforwardly as denoting or even connoting anything like what the Athenians understood by *dêmokratia*: see above, Chapter 3.

32. The old canard that ancient democrats never formulated a theory of democracy should have been laid to rest by Ober 1989 (cf. already Myres 1927) – even if 'theory' is understood as abstract, ivory-towered philosophising by more or less politically disengaged intellectuals. Most but not quite all of the latter were anti-democratic: Roberts 1994; Ober 1998.

33. It is unlikely that at any rate the full-blown democratic ideology of freedom antedated by much if at all the Ephialtic reforms of 462-1.

34. The peculiarly democratic association of sortition is sufficiently demonstrated by Hdt. 3.80.6, Arist. *Pol.* 1294b8, and esp. Arist. *Rhet.* 1365b32; cf. Whibley 1896: 35, 145; and esp. Headlam 1933.

35. Raaflaub 1996; Strauss 1996.

36. Multiplicity of Greek political units: Gehrke 1987; Hansen 1998. Sparta: Cartledge 1987: 99-159; and see above, Chapter 3.

37. Xen. *Hell*. 3.3.5; cf. Hdt. 4.3.4, 7.234.2. 'Spartiatai', denoting full citizens of the *polis* officially called Lakedaimôn, was perhaps the formal counterpart of 'Homoioi'. See on this problem, Hall 2000.

38. One failed revolutionary, Kinadon, allegedly wished 'to be inferior to no one in Sparta' (Xen. *Hell*. 3.3.11). This phrase of Xenophon (not certainly also that of Kinadon) presumably implies that he did wish to be superior to most, inasmuch as the Homoioi (to whose number Kinadon had apparently once belonged) indeed were superior to Lakedaimôn's other classes. Xenophon's rough equivalent of the Spartan Homoioi in the pseudo-Persian context of his fictional *Cyropaedia* was 'Homotimoi' – meaning 'the Same in Honour/ Esteem/ Privilege/ Respect'.

39. Spartan shouting: see Ste. Croix 1972: 348-9; Flaig 1993. Spartan avoidance of sortition: Rhodes 1981. Origin (Athenian?) and significance of the counting (as opposed to other methods of measurement) of votes: Larsen 1949.

40. Compare the demand of the English Royalists in the seventeenth century that, if the House of Commons claimed powers from the people, it would then have to show that *all* the people, every woman and child as well as every adult male, had participated in granting them: Morgan 1988: 289.

41. I cannot, therefore, agree quite with Raaflaub 1996: 153 that Sparta's 'political system was based on strong elements of institutionalized civic equality'.

42. Unlike all other Greeks known to the widely travelled Herodotus (9.11.2, perhaps also 9.55.2), the Spartans alone refused to distinguish between Greek *xenoi* and non-Greek *barbaroi*; instead, they lumped Greeks and non-Greeks together as equally outlandish *xenoi* and practised what they preached in the form of *xenêlasiai*, periodic 'expulsions of *xenoi*'.

43. Plamenatz 1967: 82.

44. Not all that much more space, perhaps: compare and contrast Hanson 1996 and Strauss 1996. Note, however, the apparent negative discrimination against thetes (above, and n. 35); and, with respect at least to its distinction between Spartan militarism and Athenian politics (2.39-40), the Periklean Funeral Speech in Thucydides (2.35-46) seems to represent accurately Athenian democratic ideology as well as practice.

45. Williams 1962: 137. 'Equal say': Beitz 1991.

46. Levi 1987: 390-1. The original version of this chapter was presented on Yom Hashoah (Holocaust Remembrance Day).

47. Terray 1990: 13, concludes his Preface with a series of questions, including 'L'égalité est-elle une condition nécessaire de ces libertés?' To which he adds, 'Sur tous ces points, soyons attentifs à la réflexion grecque: on le voit, les questions qu'elle pose sont aussi les nôtres.' D'accord! For an excellent recent exemplification, see Wood 1995.

48. It was a particular honour for me to participate in a panel on Equality in the capital of the modern country that has the most wholeheartedly embraced 'the democratic gospel of equality' (Aron 1972: 87-8). My sincere thanks to the original organizers and sponsors, especially Josh Ober, and also to the Princeton University Press for most generously waiving its usual reproduction fee.

7. A Spartan education

1. On the Victorians and ancient Greece generally, see Jenkyns 1980; Turner 1981; on the 'Spartan tradition', Rawson 1969: esp. 362-3.

2. Before, that is, it gradually decayed following Sparta's defeat at Leuktra: Cartledge & Spawforth 1989: Index *s.v. agôgê*.

3. From a huge literature on 'orientalism' Saïd 1978 still stands out; cf. Hall 1989; Georges 1994.

4. 'Invention of Athens': Loraux 1986. Sparta as the Athenians' 'other': Millender 1999.

5. On Greek *paideia* generally, and Athenian education in particular, see Garland 1990: esp. 133-6; Golden 1990: esp. ch. 3; and, for the sporty side, Golden 1998.

6. Cartledge 1997: 86-7.

7. Just 1990: esp. 114-18.

8. See recently Powell 1991; but still indispensable is Jeffery 1961; cf. Thomas 1992.

9. Maximal view of Classical male Athenian citizen literacy: Harvey 1966; minimal view: Harris 1989.

10. Pickard-Cambridge 1988: ch. 2, *passim*.

11. Hoplites: Hanson 1989; Hanson ed. 1991; see also Chapter 11, below. Oarsmen: Strauss 1996; 1999: 97-122; Morrison, Coates & Rankov 2000.

12. (Cartledge, anonymously, in) Jones ed. 1984: ch. 6.

13. Kerferd 1981; de Romilly 1992; Cartledge 1999a: ch. 3.

14. Goldhill 1986: ch. 3 ('The city of words'); Hansen 1999.

15. English translation with commentary in both Moore 1983 and Talbert 1988; cf. Higgins 1977: 65-75; Proietti 1987; Rebenich 1998; Lipka (forthcoming).

16. Cartledge 1987: 60-1.

17. Noted in Sallares 1991: 172.

18. See generally below, Chapter 9.

19. For the debate over the precise place of the Karneia, Gymnopaidiai and Hyakinthia festivals within the Spartans' initiatory cycle, contrast Pettersson 1992 with Calame 1977.

20. Garland 1990: ch. 6; Sallares 1991: 178-9; Finley 1981c.

21. Family (life) in Sparta: Pomeroy 1998: 39-66.

22. There is a fascinating footnote in Ehrenberg 1973: 388 n. 52; Ehrenberg had used the 'totalitarian' label in 1946a [originally 1934].

23. Berent 1994, 1998.

24. Momigliano 1985; Cartledge 1996b.

25. See also Ducat 1999b.

26. Arist. *Pol.* 1265b41, 1271a34; cf. MacDowell 1986: 111-14.

27. Above, Chapter 4, p. 49 & n. 52 [Cartledge 1978: 33 & n. 52].

28. Vernant 1991: 241.

29. Cheese-stealing: Xen. *LP* 2.9; cf. Vernant 1991: 236-7. Artemis as patron of *agôgê*: Vernant 1991: 229-30.

30. Parker 1989.

31. For what follows see Chapter 8, below; cf. Vernant 1991: 235-6. For the code of Athenian democratic pederasty, see esp. Halperin 1990: ch. 5 ('The democratic body: prostitution and citizenship in Classical Athens'); and Winkler 1990.

32. Vidal-Naquet 1986a: ch. 5, at 112-14; cf. Jeanmaire 1913; Vidal-Naquet 1986b: 139 n. 8; Cambiano 1995.

33. Cartledge 1987: 32-3.

34. Revisionist trend: e.g. Talbert 1989: 22-40; with my reply: Cartledge 1991: 379-81. See further the Introduction to Chapter 10, below.

35. Again, on the peculiarity of Sparta's 'slave-problem', see Chapter 10, below.

36. Rawson 1969; Ollier 1933-43. Cf. Chapter 12, below.

8. The politics of Spartan pederasty

1. Cf. both the old and the new introductions to Chapter 9, below. Since the subject-matter of that essay overlaps that of the present one, an attempt has been made to avoid unnecessary duplication of references.

2. Jenkyns 1980: 282. One reviewer (the late Peter Levi) of this much-acclaimed book, commenting on two of its themes, remarked that 'Between the sophisticated thuggery of the Spartans and the simpler-minded buggery of English public schools a long sliding scale exists'. This is fundamentally mistaken; rather, as was observed by Paul Veyne (1978: 52), following Michel Foucault, 'La sexualité antique et la nôtre sont deux structures qui n'ont aucun rapport, qui ne sont même pas superposables'; cf. Foucault 1985; Larmour et al. 1997.

3. Dover 1978; Buffière 1980. Patzer 1982 reviews twentieth-century work in the field (but he was wrong to deny the existence in Greek antiquity of any homosexual relationships prolonged into adult life; this is the mirror image of the error of Boswell [n. 7]); cf. Africa 1982; Koch-Harnack 1983.

4. This gulf renders beside the point all pleas, e.g. Eglinton 1971, O'Carroll 1980, for the acceptability of 'Greek love' in our society.

5. 'His' because, apart from Byron's 'burning' Sappho, no females with strong homoerotic proclivities survive to address us. Female homosexuality in Sparta is, however, considered below.

6. Correctness of 'pederasty': Halperin 1986: 64 n. 9, 65 n. 13. 'Homosexuality' first appeared in print, apparently, in its German form 'Homosexualität', in a pamphlet of 1869 (whose author, a Hungarian physician called Kertbeny, wrote under the suitably inverted pseudonym of 'Benkert'). Havelock Ellis, who with J.A. Symonds compiled the first scientific study of what was then generally called 'sexual inversion' (1897-1925), was careful to disclaim responsibility for the word 'homosexual', which he dismissed as 'barbarously hybrid' and 'a bastard term compounded of Greek and Roman elements'. Its earliest attested occurrence in English was in 1890, hence the title of Halperin 1990.

7. See Boswell 1980. But Boswell underplayed Christian hostility to homosexuality before the twelfth century, was quite unjustified in denying that in the Graeco-Roman world most homosexual relationships were between adolescent boys and young men (but see n. 24 below), and has rightly been taken to task (by a gay reviewer, Jeffrey Weeks) for his anachronistic use of 'gay'.

8. Meier's contribution (pp. 3-185) to Meier & Pogey-Castries 1930, was originally published in German in 1837; it is still of some value.

9. See generally Wilkinson 1979: ch. 4. What appears to be an extreme expression of scholarly amoralism may be read in the preface to Dover 1978; less extreme statements appear at Dover 1978, 154 n. 1, 183.

10. Finley 1968.

11. See esp. Brelich 1969: 113-207, esp. 120-1, 198-9, 206, cited by neither Dover nor Buffière. Bremmer 1980 appeared after the essentials of my argument had been worked out and delivered as a paper; though often stimulating, it unfortunately resurrected the 'Dorian' heresy (below) in Indo-European guise and treated the pederasty found among Dorians as a static phenomenon, a form of pederasty 'older' than the more developed pederasty of Classical Athens. See also n. 45, below.

12. There are veiled references to these inclinations in Xen. *Hell.* 4.1.39-40, 5.3.20, *Ages.* 8.2 (perhaps); an explicit one in *Hell. Ox.* 21.4. Maximus of Tyre, a second-century AD sophist, composed a paean to Agesilaos' sexual self-restraint, which he ranked higher on the moral scale than the bravery of Leonidas: *Diss.* 19(25).5. That says more about Maximus than Agesilaos.

13. See generally Marrou 1971: 52. For an undoubted conflation of Agesilaos with Lykourgos by Xenophon (with reference to the alleged purpose of double mess-rations for the two kings), cf. Xen. *Ages.* 5.1 with *LP* 15.4.

14. For Greek moral arguments in favour of sexual self-restraint, which lie at the root of the attack on Spartan sexual mores in general, see Dover 1978: 23, 164; cf. Dover 1973: 61-5; 1974: 178-80, 208-9, 210.

15. 'Probably the most entertaining efforts to conceal homosexuality from the public have been undertaken by the editors of the Loeb Classics': Boswell 1980: 19 n. 7.

16. The polemic is probably directed chiefly at a belief apparently widespread in Athens, or at least frequently ventilated there on the comic stage of his youth, that the Spartans were addicted to buggery. The comic passages are conveniently collected by Henderson 1991: 218, n. 37; cf. Hubbard 1998: 48-59, 73 n. 10. But it should at once be added that the Thessalians and Chalkidians were abused there on precisely the same ground: Jocelyn 1980: 32 and n. 239.

17. On this use of the word *paidika*, see Dover 1978: 16-17 with n. 31, 204.

18. Xenophon, at *Smp.* 4.15, makes Kritoboulos speak of *kaloi* as exerting a certain inspiration (*empnein ti*) upon the amorous, and this use of Spartan technical vocabulary has rightly been taken as evidence of Xenophon's success in turning himself into a Spartiate in all but name: Bourguet 1927: 151-2. Plut. *Kleom.* 3.2 adds that the Spartan word for 'to act as *erastês*' was *empneisthai*; cf. Aelian *VH* 3.12 (*eispnein* at Sparta); Hesych. e 2475 (*empnein*, not tied to any one locality). But Xenophon refrains from using what were almost certainly the Spartan equivalents of *erastês* and *erômenos/paidika*, namely *eispnêlas/os* ('inspirer') and *aïtas* ('hearer'): see Alkman fr. 34 Page; *SEG* XXVIII.404 (inscription of *c.* 550-500 from Perioikic Aigiai naming Hyakinthos as *aïtas*); Theokr. 12.13; Callimach. fr. 68 Pfeiffer, all with the scholia. For Cretan terminology, see below, n. 78.

19. Aelian (*VH* 3.10,12) mentions but does not specify the punishment for an *erastês* found guilty of sexual misconduct and states that pederastic hybris entailed exile or death for both partners. The author of the Plutarchan *Instituta Laconica* 7 (*Mor.* 237bc) states that any *erastês* against whom an accusation of inchastity was levelled was liable to be deprived, for life, of full citizen rights. These sources have no independent value nor, I think, any special claim to our credence.

20. This 'solution' has been cogently resisted by Dover 1978: 81 and n. 37, 190-1.

21. At *Laws* 836a-c Plato goes out of his way to impress his readers with his veracity: 'we're faced with the fact that though in several other respects Crete in general and Sparta give us pretty solid help when we frame laws that flout common custom, in affairs of the heart (*tôn erôtôn*) ... they are totally opposed to us' (Penguin translation by T.J. Saunders). This implies that, had Plato not firmly believed Sparta to be the scene of widespread or universal male homosexual intercourse, he would have been only too happy to take it as a model in sexual as in other matters.

22. Aristotle states (*Pol.* 1272a23-6) that on Crete women are segregated in order to limit population and the legislator (Crete is treated as a single political unit for theoretical purposes) has specifically approved male homosexual intercourse (*homilia*). The ritualized pederastic rape (Ephorus, *FGrHist.* 70 F 149) was presumably followed by physical consummation.

23. I follow the conclusions of Tazelaar 1967. In technical anthropological parlance the *agôgê* is a graded age-set system: Stewart 1977: esp. 8-14, 28-9; cf. Baxter & Almagor eds 1978: 1-35. The pioneering work in this field was Schurtz 1902.

24. An alternative translation is: 'the boys came to be courted by *erastai* from among the reputable (*eudokimoi*) young men'. The relationship between Lysander and Agesilaos is the sole explicitly attested instance: see Section IV, below. 'Agis' at Dover 1978: 202, is clearly a slip; a more serious error is the view of Buffière 1980: 78, that this relationship was one of adolescent homosexuality rather than pederasty. No doubt, though, there was adolescent homosexuality in Sparta: cf. Dover 1978: 193; and generally Steward 1946: 175-80.

25. *Diss.* 20(26).8; cf. n. 12.

26. Above, n. 19.

27. I suspect both Plutarch and Aelian may be generalizing from the relationship of Lysander and Agesilaos – or rather from their understanding of it.

28. Hartley & Hartley 1952: 504; Devereux 1967: 78.

29. On institutionalization, see e.g. Smith 1974: 42.

30. Dover 1978: 171; Buffière 1980: esp. 605-17.

31. For an example see below, n. 79. On the beard as terminating *erômenos* potential, most explicitly stated at Xen. *Anab.* 2.6.28, see Dover 1978: 85-6; Buffière 1980: 146, 318-19, 611-13, 617.

32. The *paidika* who died fighting beside the Spartan harmost Anaxibios (Xen. *Hell.* 4.8.39) was not necessarily a Spartan, if the behaviour of another harmost (Plut. *Mor.* 773ef) is anything to judge by. A certainly non-Spartan *paidika*, a slave from Thracian Argilos, belonged to Regent Pausanias (Thuc. 1.132.5, with Gomme's commentary; Nepos, *Paus.* 4.1).

33. For completeness' sake I add the testimony of Cicero's *de re publica* 4.4 ('in pederasty the Spartans permit everything except *stuprum*', that is, they allow *conplexus* and *concubitus* so long as cloaks are interposed between the lovers); 3.3 (the Greeks generally deem it shameful for *adulescentes* not to have *amatores*). The former passage suggests bundling (I am grateful to Prof. J.A. Barnes for private correspondence on this interesting topic), but should be treated with scepticism; the latter is at best a gross simplification.

34. Thera: Dover 1978: 113, 122-3, 195; Buffière 1980: 57-9. Thasos: Garlan & Masson 1982 (I am most grateful to Prof. Garlan for private correspondence on his find). Athens: Doyer 1978: 111-24. See generally Robinson & Fluck 1937: 15-45 (though I can hardly agree that Thera is 'the most appropriate place to study Spartan pederasty').

35. See Chapter 9, p. 114 & n. 47 [Cartledge 1981: 92 and n. 47]. For the depiction of women (not only in Sparta) as young men *plus* breasts and *minus* external genitalia, see Dover 1978: 70-1; Buffière 1980: 123, 130; Stewart 1997: 108-18. I agree with Dover 1978: 68, that a fragment of the laconophile Kritias (88 B 48 D-K) 'cannot be used, unless it is firmly supported by independent evidence, to show that female characteristics in a youth or boy were a stimulus to homosexual desire'.

36. This expertly painted fragment is CP 16 in Dover's useful 'List of Vases' (1978: 212); the heterosexual interpretation was suggested by Devereux 1970: 21, n. 1; but Powell 1998: 130-3 and Fig. 4 fancies it may be homosexual. For alleged anal penetration of *parthenoi* by Spartan males see below, n. 69; and on heterosexual anal intercourse generally in Sparta, Dover 1964: 37. There is no evidence for intercrural/interfemoral homosexual copulation in Sparta; but see Stibbe 1976: 7ff., no. 1, for a homosexual courting-scene on a Lakonian b.f. cup from Cerveteri.

37. Dickins 1929: 165, 172-5. There is a sudden development in the popularity of dedicating masks in the sixth century, and Dickins notes (167) that Types B ('Youths') and C ('Warriors') stand out from the mass by reason of their 'moderate and human appearance'. See generally Carter 1988.

38. Now in the Ashmolean Museum, Oxford: Vafopoulou-Richardson 1981, pl. 7A; in 1980 it was displayed with the caption 'Irrumator Ipsius' ('Self-fellator'). On fellation generally see Dover 1978: 99, 101, 182-3; Jocelyn 1980: 18 and n. 66, 31-4.

39. Bethe 1907.

40. E.g. Havelock Ellis (n. 6); soon to appear were Karsch-Haack 1911; Hirschfeld 1920. Westermarck 1912-17, vol. II: 752 commented on the 'remarkable activity' in the field between the first (1906-8) and second (1912-17) editions of his *The Origin and Development of the Moral Ideas*.

41. On anthropology's contribution to changing sexual attitudes, see Bullough 1976: 650.

42. Edward Gibbon, who in the *Decline and Fall* counted pederasty 'a more odious vice' even than adultery, elsewhere wrote of 'The virtuous, but almost incredible loves of the Spartans, without sensual desire or jealousy of rivals': Gibbon 1972: 329.

43. Carpenter 1919: 133; he emphasizes (91) that the seventh-century Dorians probably did not draw our sharp distinction between the physical and the spiritual.

44. Hostile (not only on scholarly grounds): Semenov (Semyonov) 1911: 146-50; Ruppersberg 1911: 151-4. Favourable: Jeanmaire 1939: 456-8. Middle-of-the-road: Dover 1964: 37, 42 n. 35; 1978: 189 n. 12, 202 n. 13.

45. Incomprehensibly, Buffière (1980: 49, 52, 89-106) persisted in treating the Boiotians and Thessalians as 'Dorians'.

46. Karsch-Haack 1911 wrote 400 pages on homosexuality and gave a sixty-page bibliography of items stretching back to 1533. More realistically, Ford & Beach 1952: ch. 7, using the Human Relations Area Files in Yale, found evidence on homosexuality, including negative evidence, in only 76 out of the 190 small-scale societies analysed; in 49, homosexuality in some form was considered normal and socially acceptable, but in the remainder it was reportedly totally absent, rare or secret. For rather different results obtained by using a different sample of 186 societies from the same data-base, see Broude & Greene 1976: 409-29 (at 410-11 they give a good summary of the 'problems with ethnographic data'). We can be confident that both sets of figures appreciably understate the incidence of homo-sexuality in these communities. (I am grateful to Dr P. Spencer for a most illuminating letter on the difficulty of research in the field on this subject.)

47. Finley 1986b: 116-17. This has not been appreciated by all who have applied comparative ethnographic evidence to Spartan social institutions (esp. the *agôgê*, *diamastigôsis* or ritual flagellation, and the Krypteia or 'Secret Service'): Nilsson 1908; Jeanmaire 1913; Decker 1913; Ferguson 1918; Knauth 1933; Jeanmaire 1939: 463-591; Den Boer 1954: Pt. III; Brelich 1969.

48. Jeanmaire 1939: 7, 156-71, esp. 163-4.

49. For a stimulating essay on a whole complex of phenomena involving initiation and homosexuality in the area, see Dundes 1976. See further Herdt 1980; Herdt ed. 1985.

50. Strehlow 1913: 98.

51. Williams 1936: ch. 11.

52. Cf. Landtman 1927: 236-7; Layard 1942: 489; and van Baal 1966: 143.

53. van Baal 1966: 669-72, 817-18, 950.

54. Brelich 1969: 113-26.

55. He thus seriously weakened his general position on the *agôgê* by allowing for development from an original rite akin to that of (e.g.) the Marind. On rites of passage generally, secular as well as sacred, see van Gennep 1909, who stressed that 'almost any rite can be interpreted in several ways, depending on whether it occurs within a complete system or in isolation, whether it is performed at one occasion or another' (166). For surveys of the various modern theories of initiation, a highly contentious subject, see Allen 1967: 1-27; Brelich 1969: 14-19; cf. Brown 1991: 12 n. 24; on Sparta specifically, Sergent 1996: 402-23.

56. For the date and possible circumstances see Cartledge 1979: ch. 7.

57. On the *agôgê*, see above, Chapter 7. For a sample of approaches to the study of socialization, see Mayer 1970.

58. Cartledge 1977. For examples of the secularization of initiatory rites among pre-state societies see Webster 1908: 56-7, 80-2.

59. The second-century BC Spartan writer Sosikrates (*FGrHist*. 461 F 7) reports that the Spartans sacrificed to Eros before battle in the belief that victory and safe return depended on *philia* (mutual affection: Konstan 1997) in the ranks; the earliest reference to Eros in a Spartan context is Alkman fr. 58 Page. In Sparta even Aphrodite was represented armed (Paus. 3.14.10); and the Spartans were, according to the Plutarchan *Erôtikos*, among the 'most martial' peoples who are also 'the most devoted to pederasty' (*Mor.* 761d). Pederasty, however, never became the basis of Spartan military organization.

60. References in ch. 9 [Cartledge 1981: 91 and] n. 38; add Calame 1977: I.420, II.12, 86-97, 145; cf. Dover 1978: 195.

61. Calame follows Brelich in interpreting the *agôgê* as a cycle of tribal initiation, but, unlike Brelich, he argues (I.350-7) for a parallel feminine cycle and so takes Plut. *Lyk.* 18.9 to be a reference to the feminine equivalent of the *erastês-erômenos* relationship. But even if we believe Plutarch's assertion that 'fine and upstanding women (*kalas kai agathas*) were lovers of (*eran*) maidens', we cannot definitely attribute this to the time of Alkman.

62. Dover 1978: 195 and n. 20; but he rightly notes their strongly Homeric flavour, and homosexuality does not obtrude in the Homeric poems, if indeed it is there at all. Few perhaps will accept the conclusion of Clarke 1978 that 'homoeroticism, if not homosexuality, does indeed exist in the *Iliad*'. On the other hand, the silence or discretion of Homer does not in my view 'make it reasonable to look for the point of origin of Greek homosexuality neither in the Bronze Age nor in Ionia' (Dover 1978: 194), since Homer was not a historian but a poet (or poets).

63. The Thera graffiti (n. 34) may go back to the seventh century (but see Graf 1979: 3 n. 15), and Thera was reputedly a Spartan 'colony'; but this link can only suggest the possibility of homosexuality in Sparta by this date and tells us nothing about its social location there.

64. Relevant here is Benedict 1939: 570: 'There is no axiom of cultural study which is more clearly established than the fact that a whole array of familial, political, economic and religious institutions mutually condition one another and conversely are unintelligible when considered in isolation'.

65. I leave on one side Freudian theories of psycho-dynamics, mainly on the ground that the historian 'is usually unable to penetrate the bedroom, the bathroom and the nursery': Stone 1987: 53. There is much of interest in Slater 1971: 33-49 (narcissism), 53-63 (homosexuality); but see the comments of Bullough 1976: 96; Arthur 1976: 395-7.

66. Gouldner 1965: ch. 2; cf. Murray 1993: esp. ch. 12. Worth mentioning is the Elakateia, a Spartan *agôn* commemorating an *erômenos* of Herakles (Sosibios, *FGrHist.* 595 F 16). On the agonistic quality of social relations in contemporary Mediterranean societies, see Pitt-Rivers 1977.

67. Fehling 1974: 27.

68. Cf. Eyben 1972: 695-6. Willetts 1955: 11, fails to make the important distinction between social and physiological puberty; cf. van Gennep 1909: 65-6.

69. Dover 1978: 193, rather exaggerates the extent to which 'the young Spartan was not involved, as he grew up, in a simple opposition between sexual love for women and sexual loyalty to the males of his own unit' and (188, 193, 197 n. 2) places too much confidence in Hagnon's report (*ap.* Athen. 13.602d) that 'before marriage it is customary for the Spartans to have intercourse with maidens as with *paidika*'; see Brelich 1969: 158 n. 138.

70. Jenkyns 1980: 283.

71. Buffière 1980: ch. 34; Wilkinson 1979: ch. 3; Starr 1977: 130-3. The earliest Greek gymnasia are of either the seventh or the sixth century.

72. For relationships between a Spartiate and a non-Spartiate see above, n. 32.

73. Buffière 1980: 246.

74. The crown princes of the two royal houses were alone exempted from this requirement; but Agesilaos II, as the son of Archidamos II's second marriage, had not been expected to succeed his older half-brother Agis II. See further on this and all other matters relating to Agesilaos II, Cartledge 1987; Hamilton 1991; Shipley, D.R. 1997.

75. This holds true of Spartan pederasty generally at all periods; it is of course a separate question whether the Spartans of the age of Xenophon viewed pederastic copulation in the way suggested by Bethe. For the apparent increase of sexual inhibition in the fourth century, which may have unduly influenced our sources, see Dover 1978: 151, 183.

76. Gouldner 1965: 61, speaking of Greece generally. There is also reason to believe that pederasty permitted what Gouldner (62) calls 'mutual revelation and validation of the selves involved' to an extent and in ways not possible in heterosexual relationships; cf. Dover 1978: 88, 201.

77. Plutarch (*Lys.* 1) states that Lysander, though a Heraklid by birth, had been brought up in poverty; Aelian (*VH* 12.43) specifies that he was a *mothax*. For a possible explanation, see Cartledge 1979: 315; for a recent discussion of *mothax* status, cf. Hodkinson 1997a: 55-62.

78. The major piece of evidence for the Cretan institution (Ephorus, *FGrHist.* 70 F 149) is well discussed by Jeanmaire 1939: 450-5; see now Link 1999. I would lay particular stress on the fact that the Cretan *philêtôr* (*erastês*) introduced his *kleinos* (*erômenos*) to his common mess: in Sparta, admission to membership of a common mess or (literally) 'common tent' was a condition of full citizenship.

79. Archidamos, as heir-apparent, had not been obligated to go through the *agôgê* (cf. n. 74) and so had perhaps not been involved previously in institutionalized pederasty. Sphodrias' son Kleonymos had just completed the *agôgê* (Xen. *Hell.* 5.4.25), but Xenophon's use of the imperfect tense (*toutou de erôn etugkhanen*) suggests to me that the relationship had begun while Kleonymos was still a *pais*.

80. Cf. Ste. Croix 1972: 134-5.

81. Dover 1978: 54 n. 29, points out that Xenophon's *paidikoi logoi* could possibly mean 'boyish chat' but adds that it would probably have been taken to mean 'talk about *paidika*'. Agesilaos' own homoerotic proclivities were strong (n. 12), but they did not of course prevent him marrying, procreating and indeed taking pleasure in playing with his children.

82. The penultimate draft of the original version of this chapter was astringently criticized by Moses Finley, Simon Price, and Dick Whittaker. The end-product is my sole responsibility.

9. Spartan wives: liberation or licence?

1. The *O.E.D.*, Supp. I (Oxford, 1972) defined 'feminism' as 'advocacy of the rights of women (based on the theory of equality of the sexes)'. It is usually anti-feminists who impute to 'feminism' the aim of achieving female domination.

2. Flacelière 1962, reviewing Vogt 1960; cf. Flacelière 1971.

3. By contrast, the women of Liechtenstein voted for the first time in the history of the principality on 17 April 1977.

4. Ste. Croix 1970b: 273.

5. Notably in the United States: see, e.g., *Arethusa* 6 (1973), which includes a bibliography by S. Pomeroy with D. Schaps, and 11 (1978), two special issues repr. in one volume as Sullivan & Peradotto eds 1984; and Pomeroy ed. 1991.

6. Pomeroy 1976 (reprinted in the nineties); cf. her more recent book on Classical and Hellenistic Greek 'families': Pomeroy 1997.

7. Reade 1934: 57.

8. Rawson 1969.

9. Two contrasting eighteenth-century representatives of this tradition, Helvétius and Rousseau, may raise a smile: Rawson 1969: 241, 243.

10. Rawson 1969: 10.

11. Pomeroy 1976: 42: 'Dorian women, in contrast to Ionian women, enjoyed many freedoms and among Dorians the Spartans were the most liberated of all'; followed in different ways by Kunstler 1983, 1987; and Zweig 1993; see also below, n. 112.

12. Cf. the opening remarks of Just 1975.

13. Greek *gunê*, like *femme*, meant both woman and wife: cf. Humphreys 1973: 258, reviewing Vatin 1970.

14. Redfield 1977/8 in fact says relatively little on its ostensible subject. But see now MacDowell 1986: chs IV-V; Dettenhofer 1993; Dettenhofer ed. 1994; Ducat 1998, 1999a; Thommen 1999.

15. Degler 1974.

16. By 'minority' Degler understands 'any group that is differentiated from the majority by some recognizable characteristics, be they physical or social ... In the case of women ... the group has less power than the majority even though it is numerically larger' (1974: 20 n. 15); cf. de Beauvoir 1972: 608-39.

17. This point has been developed at length by Ste. Croix 1983: 98-111.

18. Ollier 1933-43, vol. I: chs 5-6, esp. 164-88; Tigerstedt 1965-78, vol. I: 155-6; and on Lakonomania, Cartledge 1999b. For Aristotle's treatment of Sparta in general, see Tigerstedt 1965-78, vol. I: 280-304; Laix 1974; David 1982/3; Herrmann-Otto 1998.

19. Besterman 1976: 9. On 'Aristotle's woman' see Clark 1982; Lloyd 1983: 94-105; Cartledge 1997: 66-70.

20. This adverse judgement is restated, with further supporting arguments, at *Pol.* 1333b5-34a10.

21. The MS reading *akolastôs* has been questioned, but it is retained in the Oxford Classical Text (ed. W.D. Ross), to whose numeration all my citations refer.

22. de Beauvoir 1972: 222.

23. Cf. Plato, *Rep.* 8.548b, where this defect is said to be characteristic of a timarchy; clearly (cf. *Rep.* 545a) Plato has Sparta in mind.

24. The translation of Redfield – 'much is managed by women in their regime' – seems untenable. On the political rôle of Spartan women, see generally Bradford 1986; Dettenhofer 1993; Ducat 1998; Powell 1999. On their possible contribution to the fourth-century 'crisis': Hamilton 1987; Hodkinson 1996; French 1997.

25. Some (e.g. Redfield 1977/8) have taken Aristotle to have meant '*un*like women in other states', but the prevailing male Greek view since Homer (*Il.* 6.490-3 = *Od.* 1.356-9) was that war was a man's business; cf. e.g. Thuc. 3.74.2; Aristoph. *Lys.* 520; and generally Plato, *Alc.* 1. 126e-127a. On Plut. *Ages.* 31.5, see Shipley 1997: 340-1; generally, see now Ducat 1999a.

26. The doubt registered by Aristotle's *phasi* (rendered here by 'traditionally') presumably concerns the manner whereby the women evaded the laws of 'Lykourgos'. Translated into modern historical language, this would amount to asking how the Spartan women became an exception to the rule that 'the segregation and legal and administrative subordination of women received their original impetus from the fragmentation of the early Greek world into small, continuously warring states': Dover 1973: 65.

27. For an unconvincingly apologetic account of Aristotle's view, see Fortenbaugh 1977: 135-9; contrast the works cited above, n. 19.

28. Cf. Keaney 1970: 326-36.

29. The unreliable Aelian (*VH* 6.6), writing in the second/third century AD, says *five* or more.

30. On the *Lak. Pol.* see Ollier 1934; Higgins 1977: 65-75 (dating the whole work to the 350s); Rebenich 1998; Lipka (forthcoming); on its authorship, see also Humble 1999: 347-8 n. 9. The essay was written for a non-Spartan audience and is restricted to those points of contrast between Sparta and other states which in the author's view most accounted for Spartan supremacy. On Xenophon's treatment of other women, see Cartledge 1993b.

31. For surviving fragments of the Aristotelian *Lak. Pol.*, one of the 158 *Constitutions* compiled by Aristotle and his pupils, see V. Rose's Teubner edition (frr. 532-45) and Herakleides Lembos, *Excerpta Politiarum*, ed. M.R. Dilts (372. 9-373. 13).

32. For a source-critical examination of the *Life*, see Kessler 1910. On Plutarch as an interpreter of Sparta, see Ollier 1933-43, vol. II: 165-215; Tigerstedt 1965-78, vol. II (1974): 226-64; Shipley, D.R. 1997.

33. We do not know whether newborn girls were subjected to the ritualized and/or hygienic wine-baths endured by their brothers (Plut. *Lyk.* 16. 3). Nor do we know whether the Spartan wet-nurses who acquired something of a cachet outside Sparta (Plut. *Alk.* 1.3, *Lyk.* 16.5) were of citizen status. The nannies praised by Plutarch (*Lyk.* 16.4) were perhaps unfree.

34. Lacey 1968: 197; Pomeroy 1976: 36. The passage in question also contains a reference to the possibility of abortion (cf. *Mor.* 242c; [Hippokr.], *On the Nature of the Child* 13.2); but there is no direct evidence for this (as opposed to infanticide) for our period.

35. However, Germain 1969: 177-97, at pp. 179-80, doubts whether exposure was frequent in our period.

36. Exposure in Sparta (esp. Plut. *Lyk.* 16. 2): Glotz 1906: 187-27, at pp. 188, 192, and esp. pp. 217-19; Roussel 1943: 5-17. Shortage of women in Sparta: the direct evidence is weak (no spinsters attested *versus* attested polyandry, and only one known instance of bigamy, below), but see generally Pomeroy 1976: 227-8. Possibly, too, infant mortality, which was no doubt high in ancient Greece, affected girls more than boys.

37. Such anecdotes may of course legitimately be construed as retrojections of later practice; but it can be rash to generalize from royal practice, and, secondly, Lykourgos' injunction – that his brother's posthumous offspring, if born female, should be handed over to the women – does not entail that she would then be reared, since she might be born deformed or feeble: cf. Garland 1995.

38. Page 1951: 66-7 tentatively attributed this homosexuality to the close association between women and girls in cult and in the gymnasia. Calame 1977: I. 433-6, argues that it had an educative function. Dover 1978: 181 (following Judith Hallett) writes in this connection of 'an overt sub-culture, or rather counterculture in which women and girls received from their own sex what segregation and monogamy denied them from men'. According to Pomeroy 1976: 55, 'the most important factor, both at Sparta and at Lesbos, in fostering female homoerotic attachments was that women in both societies were highly valued'; but note that Parker 1993: 325-31, at 327 nn. 37-8, denies the comparability of Archaic Sparta and Sappho's Lesbos.

39. Nilsson 1908. See also below, nn. 42, 63.

40. Clothesmaking: Herfst 1922: 18-24. Cooking: Herfst 1922: 24-32. Exemption of Spartan women: Herfst 1922: 112-13. But it was Spartan women who each year ritually wove the tunic (*chitôn*) for the cult-statue of Apollo of Amyklai (Paus. 3.16.2).

41. The sixth-century bronze figurines of girl runners from Sparta (Inv. 3305), Delphi (Inv. 3072), Albania (London, B.M. 208) and Dodona (Athens, N.M. Carapanos 24 = Ch. 12, Plate 7) are very possibly all of Spartan 'womanufacture': Stewart 1997: 108-18. The dress of the third, leaving one breast bare, vividly recalls Paus. 5.16.3 (race between virgins at Olympia in honour of Hera, on which see Serwint 1993).

42. Calame 1977: esp. I. 350-7, has ingeniously reconstructed a Spartan cycle of female initiation conforming to the model of Van Gennep. However, although his case for the initiatory function of at least some aspects of the cults discussed seems well grounded, the reconstruction as a whole remains far from demonstrated.

43. We do, however, learn from Athenaios (13.566E) of mixed wrestling between adolescents on the island of Chios.

44. This idea may lie behind the *ben trovato* apophthegm (Plut. *Mor.* 232c) purporting to explain why Spartan virgins did not wear veils in public, whereas Spartan wives did; cf. Cairns 1996: 80 n.18. For the topic in general see North 1966: 68-84 (Euripides), 95-6 (Kritias), 128 and n. 17 (Xenophon), 197-211 (Aristotle); Humble 1999 (Xenophon).

45. The dress of the women seems to have been no more inhibiting than that of the girls: Plut. *Mor.* 241b; Teles *ap.* Stob., *Flor.* 108.83 – *anasyramenê* might be translated colloquially as 'flashing'; for acute discussion of the gesture's gendered moral significance, cf. King 1986: 63-7 and n. 48.

46. Cf. Eur. *Andr.* 597-8, *Hec.* 933-4, Soph. fr. 788N, Pollux 2.187, 7.54-5; Clement, *Paed.* 2.10.114.1. For thighs as an erotogenic feature see Athen. 13.602 e; they certainly functioned as such in male-male homoerotics. For the way that female clothing has often been deliberately designed to hinder activity, see de Beauvoir 1972: 190; cf. 323, 429, 442.

47. The series includes the four items cited above (n. 41), together with Athens, N.M. 15897, 15900; Berlin (Charlottenburg) 10820, 31084; New York, Met. 38.11.3, 06.11.04; Paris, Louvre; Sparta Mus. 594, 3302; Vienna, Kunsthistorisches Mus. VI 2925, 4979. Th. Karageorgha, *AD* 20. 1. 1965: 96-109, publishes Sparta 3302 with further comparanda; all are discussed in Häfner 1965; and more specifically Congdon 1981; cf. Rolley 1977b: 130. They were almost certainly made by men, some of whom could have been Spartan citizens. But the mirrors at any rate could have been commissioned and/or dedicated by women; cf. below, n. 54. We may add a unique sixth-century Spartan clay *kylix* (drinking cup) on the interior of which are depicted three nude and long-haired girls disporting themselves by a river: Stibbe 1972: 133, 280, no. 209.

48. The chief sources are Aristoph. *Lys.* 1105, 1148, 1174, fr. 338, with Ehrenberg 1962: 180 and n. 7; Xen. *LP* 2.12-14; Plato, *Laws* 8.836a-c; Plut. *Lyk.* 18.8-9, *Ages.* 2.1, *Mor.* 761d; Cic. *de rep.* 4.4.4; Hesychius, Suda, Photius s.v. *'Lakônikôn tropôn'.* Dover 1978: 185 ff., seems to me somewhat to understate this feature of Spartan society.

49. Cf. Perlman 1983: 122 n. 34. I suspect, however, that the alleged Spartan practice of stripping virgins in front of foreigners or guest-friends (*xenoi*: Athen. 13.566e) is pure invention.

50. See below, n. 72.

51. On the apophthegms – those attributed to Spartan women are Plut. *Mor.* 240c-242d – see Tigerstedt 1965-78, vol. II (1974): 16-30. Contrast the conventional male Athenian attitude to free public speech for women: Soph. *Ajax* 293; Eur. *Her.* 476-7, fr. 61; Thuc. 2.45.2, 46.

52. Wender 1973.

53. But see MacDowell 1971: *ad loc.*

54. From the late seventh century onwards we have ex-votos from Sparta inscribed with the name of a dedicatrix. Since the recipient deities were also female and a fair proportion of the uninscribed offerings have feminine associations, many of the dedications were probably offered by women. However, the names of only about a dozen Spartan women are attested epigraphically in our period (the corresponding figure for men is about a hundred), as against about fifty in the literary sources: Poralla-Bradford 1985.

55. See above, Chapter 4, where I also discuss brachylogy.

56. The position of Roman women, at least those of the highest social class, seems to me parallel in this respect: cf. Daube 1972: 23 ff.

57. For a succinct exposition of the structure of Spartan society as it had been remodelled by the fifth century, see Finley 1968.

58. Esp. *Od.* 13. 412 (the only use of the epithet *kalligynaika* in the *Odyssey*); and the probably seventh-century oracle discussed in Parke & Wormell 1956: I 82-3, II. no. 1. See also Theopompos, *FGrHist.* 115 F 240, Herakl. Lembos *ap.* Athen. 13.566a. Such internal estimation and praise by outsiders are remarkable, given that the 'cult of beauty' was universally Greek: Bickerman 1976b: 231.

59. We are not told whether Lampito had suckled children; if she had, the Athenian Lysistrata might have been envious that Lampito's breasts had not lost their shape.

60. The best discussion, with full modern bibliography, of Alkman's maidensongs is Calame 1977 (updated vol. I, 1997).

61. For the latter, cf. Aristoph. *Lys.* 1312 and the cup (above, n. 47).

62. E.g. Hesiod, *Op.* 695-8; [Hippokr.], *Peri Parthenôn* I.16; Plato, *Rep.* 5.460e-461a, *Laws* 6.785b; Arist. *Pol.* 1334b29ff.; cf. Aristoph. *Lys.* 595-7; Xen. *Oec.* 7.4-5. For comparative Roman evidence, cf. Hopkins 1965; 1966: esp. 260-4.

63. However, as is correctly observed by Vidal-Naquet 1986a: 150, 'what we know of a [Spartan] girl's infancy and adolescence gives less the impression of being a preparation, punctuated by rituals, for marriage, than an imitation of institutions for males'.

64. Daube 1977: 11, suggests that they were introduced *c.* 500 BC to strengthen the male citizen population in the face of the growing Persian threat. If that dating is correct, this would no doubt have been a part of their motivation; but fear of the size of the native Greek serf population, the Helots, might have been an even weightier factor.

65. Amundsen & Diers 1969; cf. Angel 1972: 97.

66. Seltman 1956: 80.

67. See, e.g., Tazelaar 1967; Kennell 1995; Lupi 2000.

68. Lacey 1968: 318 n. 50. This figure is at least not contradicted by the evidence mustered in White 1964: 140-52, although White herself thinks that the men married at thirty. For a range of overlapping ideas on the proper age for a Greek man to marry, see Solon fr. 27.9-10 West; Plato, *Laws* 6.772de; Arist. *Pol.* 1335a28-30.

69. This seems to me to contradict the view of Bickerman 1976a: 2, that 'the Athenians, and doubtless all the civilized peoples around the Mediterranean, regarded marriage, in the age of Plato, simply as a family affair in which the State was not involved'. But I agree with the main thesis of this article, that the chief purpose of Greek marriage was to establish legitimacy of offspring and so rights of succession to hereditary private property. For the Roman conception of marriage, cf. Williams 1958.

70. Plato, *Laws* 7.804d, 11.923a; Arist., *Pol.* 1334b29 ff., 1335b28-9. For Sparta, see Plut. *Lyk.* 15.14, *Pyrrhus* 28.6, *Mor.* 223a; cf. Napolitano 1985.

71. Statue (Sparta Mus. Inv. 364): Boardman 1978: 62, fig. 80; Pipili 1987: 58-60, Cat. 156. Terracottas: Dawkins ed. 1929: 51 and fig. 29.

72. In the light of epigraphical evidence (*IG* 5.1.713-14, and perhaps 824), Plutarch *Lyk*. 27. 2 ('priestesses in office') was emended by K. Latte to read 'women in childbed'. Though plausible enough – see Pomeroy 1976: 36 and n. 8 ; cf. Garland 1989: 13-14 at 14 n. 54 – this reading lacks MS support.

73. Leigh Fermor 1958: 69. Rawson, 1969: 292, 321, 358, cites sources representing the Maniotes as Spartans *redivivos*.

74. Bickerman 1976b: 237, 244, 247.

75. So strong was the connection at Sparta between beauty and marriage, at least royal marriage, that Plutarch (*Mor.* 1d) misrepresents Archidamos II (reigned *c.* 469-27) as being fined for marrying an ugly woman. In the original version, related by Theophrastos (*ap.* Plut. *Ages.* 2.6), the ground of his guilt was the wife's diminutive stature.

76. For the existence of a true Spartan aristocracy, see Oliva 1971: 118-22, 136; Meier 1998; and on 'privileged families' at Sparta, see Ste. Croix 1972: 137-8, 353-4, following Chrimes 1949: chs 3-6, 10-11.

77. Finley 1977: 103; Gernet 1968: 344-59.

78. Although a 'descendant of Herakles' by birth (Plut. *Lys.* 2.1), Lysander seems to have risen to political prominence from a lowly economic station.

79. We should not be deceived either by Xenophon's rhetorical question (*LP* 7. 3) – 'what need was there to worry about wealth in a society where equal contributions to the mess and a uniform standard of living excluded the search for wealth in order to obtain luxury?' – or by Plutarch's assertion (*Lyk.* 10.4) that under the 'Lykourgan' regime wealth was deprived of its very being and became as it were blind.

80. For a fuller discussion of the Spartan property-regime see Cartledge 1979: ch. 10; Hodkinson 1986 (esp. 394-404), 1989, 2000; and for the catastrophic decline in male citizen numbers between 480 and 371, Cartledge 1979: ch. 14; Hodkinson 1983, 1996. Christien 1974 is stimulating, but to me often unconvincing.

81. Ste. Croix 1970b: 273-4.

82. *SIG*[3] 306. 4-9, 48-57; cf. *IG* 5.2.159 (fifth century BC).

83. Toynbee 1969: 329-37; Huxley 1971: 513-14.

84. The standard edition, with translation, of the Gortyn Code is Willetts 1967; cf. Paoli 1976: 481-507.

85. Wolff, RE XXIII, *s.v. 'proix'* (1957), cols. 133-70, at 166-7. Contrast Schaps 1979: 43-4, 88. However, as Schaps himself observes (1979: 88; cf. 6, 7, 12-13), our other evidence seems to support the conclusion that Spartan women were indeed possessors of wealth in their own right; and he appositely cites Xen. *Ages.* 9. 6 (the wealth in racehorses owned by Kyniska sister of Agesilaos II); cf. Schaps 1979: 117 n. 87. See now Hodkinson 2000.

86. Hermippos fr. 87; Plut. *Mor.* 227f; cf. 242b; Aelian *VH* 6. 6; Justin 3.3.8.

87. Philo's evidence is doubted, though without adequate reason, by Erdmann 1934: 183-5. Jannet 1880: 95, argued that such marriages would have been excluded in practice, but his argument rested on two false assumptions exemplifying the tendency to regard 'Greek law' as a unitary system: first, that the Athenian *anchisteia* rule, whereby an heiress was bound to marry her nearest male kin, 'existed in Sparta in all its rigour' (p. 91); second, that daughters had no share in the paternal inheritance.

88. On incest generally, see, e.g., Fox 1967: 54-76.

89. Cf. Ste. Croix 1970a: 309, reviewing Harrison 1968; also de Beauvoir 1972: 40, 111.

90. Lacey 1968: 201.

91. The topics considered in the foregoing section may usefully be reviewed in the light of comparative evidence from Goody, Thirsk & Thompson eds 1976, esp. Goody (10-36).

92. A fundamental study of *enguê* is Bickerman 1976a: 'it is the institution of *enguê* which gives Athenian marriage its peculiar character' (8). The usage of Herodotus is ambiguous: either he believed (wrongly) that Athenian *enguê* existed at Sparta, or, as Bickerman 1976a: 19-20 suggests, he meant that an 'affianced' heiress could not be married against her wishes to another man; the latter reading seems the more likely. Since *enguê* was specifically Athenian, Bickerman speaks vaguely of *accordailles* at Sparta, to convey the notion that such arrangements did not necessarily imply legitimacy for any future offspring. Such *accordailles*, however, were apparently legally binding (Plut. *Lys*. 30.6).

93. The existence of the *kyrieia* at Sparta is denied by Bickerman, who rightly observed (1976a: 20) that 'the position of the woman at Sparta was quite different from that of the Athenian woman'. A *non liquet* is registered by Beasley 1906: 212-13.

94. The difficulty of interpretation in the passage of Xenophon stems from the ambiguity of *anandria*: see Moore 1983: 85. I do not think my interpretation in the text, which is supported by Plut. *Ages*. 30.3, is contradicted by Xenophon's omission of women from the list of items controlled by a man (*LP* 6. 1). See also below, nn. 112, 117.

95. I put 'engaged' in inverted commas, because *harmosamenos* should technically mean 'having got married but not yet having consummated the marriage'.

96. On 'marriage by capture', see e.g. Mair 1970: 110 ff. (chiefly African examples); cf. Ball 1989.

97. Starcke 1889: 19.

98. Cf. Finley 1986b: esp. pp. 116-17: 'what anthropology illuminates about Sparta, paradoxically, are certain aspects of her lost early history rather than the Sparta from which the fossilized evidence comes'.

99. Erdmann 1934: 199-200, with the review by Rose 1935: 256-7; Ball 1989; Evans-Grubbs 1989: 68. On Spartan marriage customs generally, see now Lupi 2000.

100. Cf. de Beauvoir 1972: 106, 394, 396.

101. Nilsson 1906: 371-2.

102. This prohibition is directly attested only in the Aristotelian *Lak. Pol*. as excerpted by Herakleides Lembos (373.13 Dilts); but it is implied in Lucian, *Fugitivi* 27; and perhaps also Xenophon of Ephesos 5.1.7 (a reference I owe to Ewen Bowie).

103. See Cartledge 1977: 15 and n. 39. It is true, as is pointed out by Vidal-Naquet 1986a: 149, that this does not constitute a *rite de passage* in the same sense as the dedication of severed locks; but adolescent Spartan boys, like the married women, wore their hair close-cropped. On the bride's hair-cropping, see also Vernant 1985: 42-5; Clark 1996: 159 n. 58; and generally on Spartan hair-related social protocols, David 1992.

104. Gernet 1933: 40; Delcourt 1958: 7, 11 (with bibliography at 132); see now Leitao 1995: 137 and n. 38, 162-3.

105. Devereux 1967: 76, 84. For Spartan (mainly pederastic) homosexuality, see above, Chapter 8.

106. As Lacey 1968: 200, remarks, initial secrecy would have been facilitated if marriages in Sparta were generally contracted in the winter months, as they seem to have been in the rest of Greece (Arist. *Pol*. 1335a37-9).

107. For the references, see Griffiths 1972: 10-11; but he has not convinced me that the most famous of Alkman's maiden-songs (fr. 1 Page; cf. Calame 1977) is really an *epithalamion*.

108. Nilsson 1908: 855; Lacey 1968: 318 n. 56. Bickerman 1976a: 232-3, suggests that such marriages are quite usual in agrarian societies.

109. The office of Gynaikonomos (Controller of Women) is not attested in Sparta before the Augustan age: Cartledge & Spawforth 1989: 200-1; but the earliest references to the magistracy as such are in Aristotle's *Politics*: see generally Wehrli 1962. I can make little of the 'Lakonian key', first attested in Aristophanes (*Thesm.* 423), which apparently worked only from the outside: Barton 1972; Whitehead 1990.

110. Hdt. 4. 104; Arist. *Pol.* 1262a20ff.; Caesar, *BG* 5.14-15; Strabo 11.9.1, C515; 16.4. 25, C783. For the modern world, see Starcke 1889: 128-40.

111. See Thiel 1930: 403 (this article is devoted to plural marriage and polykoity).

112. This is of course to imply the existence of the *kyrieia*. Pomeroy 1976: 37, however, finds it 'easier to believe that the women also initiated their own liaisons, whether purely for pleasure or because they accepted the society's valuation of childbearing'.

113. This suggestion is borne out by the context in which the polyandry is introduced by Polybius, that is, the mixed marriages between slave men and free women at the time of the foundation of Lokroi in southern Italy *c.* 700 BC; cf. Moscati Castelnuovo 1991 (Helots and the foundation of Taras).

114. Leach 1971: 154. The Spartan system, incidentally, does not contradict Leach's hypothesis that polyandry 'is consistently associated with systems in which women as well as men are the bearers of property-rights'.

115. In addition to Leach 1971, see Adams 1960.

116. The only attested instance is that of Kleonymos (uncle of Areus I, who reigned *c.* 309-265) with Chilonis (Plut. *Pyrrhus* 27.17-19, 28.5-6): see McQueen 1990; Mossé 1991. The simplest explanation of such marriages is that the man is remarrying on the death (frequently perhaps in childbed: see n. 72) of his first wife.

117. Plutarch (*Mor.* 242b) has the same idea that the husband must be persuaded, but here the emphasis is laid upon the wife's duty of obedience in the first instance to her father and thereafter to her husband – again, the *kyrieia* seems to be implied.

118. We might add that, if a daughter were produced, she and the existing son(s) would be *homomatrioi* and so, following Philo (n. 87), entitled to marry. They would thus unite in the succeeding generation the property of their married parents with that of the extra-marital partner.

119. Den Boer 1954: 216-17.

120. Lacey 1968: 207-8. Lacey's study is misleading, however, to the extent that it equates the Greek *oikos* (household) with our 'family' (cf. Pomeroy 1997) and employs an ideal-typical model of 'the family in the city-state', as if this had everywhere in Greece served the same functions and had the same history.

121. But his strained attempt to prove that Spartan men were more modest even than the women (*LP* 3.4-5) suggests that the accusation of female indiscipline (*anesis*) in Sparta was already current: see generally Humble 1999.

122. Xen. *Ages.* 4.5; Plut. *Alk.* 23.7-9, *Ages.* 3.1ff., *Mor.* 467f; Anon. *ap.* Athen. 13. 574cd (= Kock, *Comicorum Graecorum Fragmenta* iii. 398).

123. Pembroke 1970; Vidal-Naquet 1970: 72-5.

124. Lotze 1962, followed in the main by Toynbee 1969: 343-6; Oliva 1971: 174-7; see now Hodkinson 1997a.

125. Athen. 13. 574cd, 591e; Clement, *Paed*. II. 10.105.2. There is a single representation of flute-girls in sixth-century Lakonian vase painting (Stibbe 1972: 243, 279, no. 191), but this probably owes more to artistic convention than real Spartan life; cf. on Lakonian sixth-century iconography generally, Pipili 1987.

126. Cf. Pembroke 1967. Sparta in our period certainly does not meet Thomas' acceptable definition of a matriarchal society as 'one in which women enjoy recognizable economic, social and religious privileges which, in sum, give them greater authority than men'.

127. This huge vessel (H. 1.64m) is of disputed origin, but a cogent case for manufacture in Sparta can be made out; see Rolley 1977b: 131-2, 139 (though Rolley himself prefers a South Italian manufacture). Around its neck there progresses a stately file of armed men; above them, in the form of a lid-handle, rises the crowning figure of a demure, draped woman.

128. de Beauvoir 1972: 89; cf. 120-1, 143, 157, 174, 189, 446, 598.

10. Rebels and *sambos* in Classical Greece: a comparative view*

*The title of this chapter is adapted from Stampp 1971.

1. Hobsbawm 1971: 42.

2. Unless otherwise qualified, 'slave(s)' and 'slavery' will here mean chattel slave(s) and slavery throughout. This should not be allowed to disguise the fact that the Greeks devised an extraordinarily rich vocabulary to describe these and rarely used it with the sociological precision one could wish: Kretschmer 1930: 71-81; Gschnitzer 1963-76; Mactoux 1980.

3. As Zimmern put it (1928: 106), 'Every decade or half decade sees a new book on the subject: the same authors are ransacked the same evidence is marshalled: the same references are transferred, like stale tea-leaves, from one learned receptacle to another'. That nice – but now obsolete (see n. 5) – observation does not apply to the classic product of nineteenth-century historiography in this field, Wallon 1879 (1st ed., 1847); in scope (vol. I, ch. 9 for our purposes), this is unmatched by any one subsequent work.

4. Exemplified in the unfavourable reactions of Ste. Croix 1957 and Brunt 1958 to the inadequate survey by Westermann 1955, and in the work of Finley, conveniently collected with bibliographical addenda in Finley 1981a: chs 6-10.

5. Apart from the work of Ste. Croix (below, n. 7), one might mention Finley 1980/1998: esp. ch. 3 ('Slavery and Humanity'); and Garlan 1988; further bibliography in Brockmeyer 1979: 16-73, 105-33; and by W. Scheidel in Miller ed. 1993-8, vol. II. The first ancient slavery sourcebook in English translation is Wiedemann 1981.

6. 'Seemingly', for two reasons: first, because there may have been unreported revolts in minor states; second, because 'when it is dangerously threatened, a propertied class will often conceal (if it can), and even deny, the very existence of those who seek to overthrow it' (Thompson 1952: 12).

7. The quotation is from Ste. Croix 1983: 146, in a section entitled 'Slavery and other forms of unfree labour' (133-74); a similar formulation already in Ste. Croix 1972: 90. On ancient justifications of slavery, see Ste. Croix 1975a, 1983: ch. VII; cf. Garnsey 1996.

8. See reviews of Ste. Croix 1983 (originally 1981), by Browning 1983: 147-56, and Anderson 1983: 57-73. Germane to this central theme are also Ste. Croix 1975b, 1984a, 1985.

9. Finley 1979: 248; cf. Stampp 1956. Useful samplings of the literature, together with helpful bibliographies, may be found in Weinstein & Gatell eds 1968; 1973; Weinstein, Gatell & Sarasohn eds 1979. For the full works, see Miller ed. 1993-8. See too nn. 12, 16.

10. Hopkins 1978a: 99-100; cf. Hopkins 1978b: 64. This figure is related to the fact that, in the three modern slave societies for which more or less reliable statistics are available, slaves accounted for about one third of the total population: table in Patterson 1982: 353-64.

11. See Finley 1980/1998: ch. 2; Ste. Croix 1983, *passim*. This qualitative role of slavery is perfectly compatible with (and should not be confused with) the fact that the greater part of the gross domestic product in antiquity before the Later Roman Empire was always and everywhere contributed by 'peasants' of one kind and another: Ste. Croix 1983: 208-26, 261-6; cf. Garnsey ed. 1980. Note too the methodologically important response to an ancient historian's basic misconceptions by a leading Americanist: Degler 1959, refuting Starr 1958 (see further text and n. 47, below).

12. Davis 1974: 11.

13. For discussion of early Christian attitudes to slavery in the Graeco-Roman world, see Ste. Croix 1975a, and 1983: 419-25. For the persistent tendency among classical scholars of 'humanist' outlook to portray Classical Greek slavery, with the exception of mine-slavery, as relatively mild, see the salutary objections of Finley 1980/1998: 56, with special reference to the work of and inspired by Vogt (see also n. 41, below). On marxist study of ancient slavery, I am indebted to the unpublished doctoral thesis of my former pupil, Dr Niall McKeown.

14. Another example is Ike Ward, who died in January 1982 at the age of 119 (I take this further opportunity of correcting an error in Cartledge 1982a: 1028, my review of the French original (1982) of Garlan 1988).

15. Dio's Fifteenth *Discourse* 'On Slavery and Freedom' is translated in Wiedemann 1981: no. 235; as is Athen. VI.262b-273c = 1981: no. 80.

16. Not a few of these have claimed either to use types of sources incomprehensibly neglected by predecessors in the field or to have unearthed fresh deposits of familiar kinds of data that totally invalidate conclusions based on the data hitherto known and used. Paradigmatic in these respects are respectively Blassingame 1972, and Fogel & Engerman 1974: but see respectively Gilmour ed. 1978, and Gutman 1975, or David ed. 1976. For balanced bibliographical surveys of these and other works, see Parish 1979; Smith 1998.

17. Finley 1982: 201-4; the debate concerned Finley 1985a: esp. ch. III (original edn, 1973), and 1980/1998.

18. I am here concerned principally with chattel slaves and slavery (above, n. 2); but on the separate question whether it is justified to speak of 'slavery' as a general category for purposes of description and comparative analysis see Runciman 1983: 78-81; cf. Finley 1986d: 73-4 (in an essay entitled 'Generalisations in ancient history').

19. See briefly Vogt 1974: 39-92 ('The structure of ancient slave wars'), with bibliographical supplement, 215-16; but note the critical review, of the book as a whole and this chapter in particular, by Finley, *TLS* 14 November 1975. Cf. Hoben 1978; Bradley 1989; and see n. 73, below.

20. See, e.g., the classic study of James 1980; or Pluchon 1980.

21. See, e.g., Foner & Genovese eds 1969; Degler 1971: 39-52; and other works cited in Weinstein, Gatell & Sarasohn eds 1979: 314-16. Also Craton 1983.

22. 'Classic' but flawed is Aptheker 1943; cf. Shapiro 1984; for other studies, cf. Weinstein, Gatell & Sarasohn eds 1979: 294-6.

23. Genovese 1979; cf. now Williams Myers 1996.

24. Genovese 1975: 587-97 (the promise at 787 n. 1); but the section on 'resistance' (597-660) is fully developed.

25. The opposition, for instance, between blacks and whites in factors (1), (5) and (6). There were some black slaves in Classical Greece: Snowden 1970; but racial prejudice between blacks and whites was a post-Classical invention (subsequent to both Greek and Roman antiquity): Snowden 1983. This does not of course mean that the Classical Greek stereotypes of slaves were any less derogatory for not being technically racist: text and n. 57, below.

26. Cf. Elkins 1976: 229, cf. 306-7.

27. Rawick 1972 introduces a nineteen-volume edition of slave narrative materials; cf. Blassingame 1977; Blassingame is also editor of the speeches, letters, essays and diaries of the most articulate ex-slave, Frederick Douglass (see Douglass 1845, 1855). For discussion of the difficulties in using such materials see Bailey 1980; or briefly Henige 1982: 116-18.

28. Daube 1979: 69, quoted in Ste. Croix 1983: 643, n. 11.

29. See generally Ste. Croix 1983: ch. VII, which includes a section on 'The ideology of the victims of the class struggle' (441-52); cf. Ste. Croix 1984b.

30. See generally Milani 1972; on the doctrine of 'natural' slavery, see Ste. Croix 1983: 416-18; Garnsey 1996: esp. 107-27; Schofield 1999a: ch. 8.

31. See e.g. Finley 1980/1998: 118.

32. Quoted in Genovese 1975: 65; cf. Blassingame 1972: 160, 195, where he describes the lash as the 'linchpin of [the planters'] regime'.

33. Elkins 1976: 245-6; this was even more true of planters in the English colonies of the Caribbean: Hogg 1979: 45-6.

34. The estimate is that of Curtin 1969, whose figures are somewhat modified in Lovejoy 1982: 473-501.

35. Frederickson's review of Gutman 1976 (repr. in Weinstein, Gatell & Sarasohn eds 1979: 273-86) seems too favourable to Gutman's stability hypothesis.

36. Perhaps the most forceful expression of the slave-outsider equation is in Finley 1977b: 157. On the slave trade in Classical Greece, see Finley 1981a: ch. 10; cf. Wallon 1879: ch. 5.

37. Bömer 1957-63 (4 vols, esp. vol. I); Bömer found that slaves in Greece enjoyed far less religious independence than their counterparts in the Roman world. The Kronia festival (Philochoros, *FGrHist*. 328 F 97; Bömer III.173-95), in which masters and slaves briefly exchanged roles, was intended, like the parallel Roman Saturnalia, to reinforce the norm of inequality and subordination. On the other hand, both masters and (Greek-speaking) slaves might be initiated into the Mysteries at Eleusis.

38. See, e.g., Levine 1979: 143-72; Levine 1977. Levine stresses that such accommodation was far from passive.

39. Elkins 1976; with the responses in Lane ed. 1971.

40. This is the burden of Stampp 1971. For a similar anti-Elkins emphasis, cf. the chapter of Craton 1983 entitled 'Quashee [the Jamaican counterpart of 'Sambo'] as hero'.

41. See e.g. Westermann 1955: 18; Vogt 1974: 4. Contrast, for an individual documented instance of slaves actively resisting self-consciously mild treatment in the Old South, May 1980: 551-70; a good illustration of Douglass' informed view (quoted by Stampp 1956: 89, from Douglass 1855: 263-4) that the well-treated slave would tend to dream unhealthily of freedom.

42. Stampp 1956: 86-140 ('A troublesome property') remains fundamental; see also works cited above, nn. 22, 24.

43. Dockès 1982: 215.

44. Schlaifer 1936: 181.

45. Mintz 1974: 60-1.

46. See Tod 1948: no. 196 (inscription of the early 320s recording 'gifts' of grain from Cyrene to forty-one communities and two individuals) with Tod's commentary; and cf. Garnsey 1985.

47. These are some of the factual points that Degler was able to make against Starr (above, n. 11).

48. Xenophon passages: Gauthier 1976: 142-3. Mine-slaves: Lauffer 1979.

49. Ehrenberg 1962: 162 n. 6 remarks with all due caution that 'There is no evidence, as far as I can see, which could justify the widely held view that the 120 were employed in the shield factory alone'.

50. Contrast Jones 1957: 17, 84; but his interpretation of Dem. 24.197 was refuted by Ste. Croix 1957: 59.

51. Pritchett 1956: 276-81; cf. Jones 1956: 189-90; Finley 1981a: 227; and for prices and the cost of living, see further the appendix to Markle 1985: 265-97.

52. Jameson 1977-8: 137; cf. Guiraud 1893: 452-4; Heitland 1921: 37.

53. See Ste. Croix 1983: 144 and Appendix II ('Some evidence for slavery (especially agricultural) in the Classical and Hellenistic periods').

54. The hypothesis of an average holding of three to twelve slaves for the more prosperous Athenian households may not be a bad guess, in light of what little we know about the size of their landed estates; cf. Ste. Croix 1966: 109-14; Jameson 1977-8.

55. Lintott 1982: chs 3-8; Fuks 1984. *Stasis* at Sparta: Paradiso 1994-5.

56. Galenson 1981: 39-47, with discussion at 48-9.

57. Ste. Croix 1983: 416-18 (and see n. 7, above); cf. Diller 1937: ch. 1; Baldry 1965: e.g. 23-4; Cartledge 1997: ch. 3.

58. Hence such common slave names as Manes (Phrygian) and Thrax/Thratta ('Thracian'): cf. Masson 1973: 9-23; Treu 1983: 39-42; and generally Finley 1981a: ch. 10.

59. David Hume 1963 (originally 1742): 424-7; his ten arguments are cumulatively overwhelming but individually of varying cogency and not always based on accurate reporting of the ancient sources; cf. Westermann 1941.

60. On the character of the Corinthian economy, see Salmon 1984: chs 10-11; the phrase 'could well have been' in my text is imposed by the near-total dearth of positive evidence (Salmon 1984: 159).

61. Sargent 1924: 13-43, is still not entirely superseded; Ste. Croix 1972: 45 was prepared to go above 100,000. A key datum is the 'more than 20,000 slaves, the (a?) greater part of whom were skilled manual workers' reported by Thucydides (7.27.5) as having run away from Attica within the final decade of the Peloponnesian War; despite Ste. Croix 1983: 506, this report could have been based ultimately on a documentary source, namely the records of the Spartan bootysellers (*laphuropôlai*) operating at Dekeleia.

62. The question of the total population of Attica at any time is a well-trodden battleground, but for reasons there is not the space to enter into here I would accept a figure of 200,000-250,000 in 431 and one of perhaps not very much fewer at the time of Demetrios of Phaleron's census in *c.* 310.

63. Theopompos, *FGrHist.* 115 F 122, with Vidal-Naquet 1973. For the inference from Thuc. 8.40.2, see Finley 1981a: 102; and already Hume 1963 [1742]: 426.

64. See text and n. 7, above. For the restricted amount of breeding, see Ste. Croix 1983: 229-30.

65. Starobin 1970: ch. 3 ('Patterns of resistance and repression'); cf. more briefly Starobin 1974: ch. 6 ('Rebellion').

66. Quoted in Starobin 1970: 90.

67. Perotti 1974, 1976; Jacob 1928.

68. For Roman manumission practices, see Hopkins 1978a: 115-31; cf. Ste. Croix 1983: 174-5.

69. Chiefly, the much used and abused Athenian manumission *stelai* of probably the 320s: *IG* 2^2 1553-78, discussed with a couple of additional fragments by Lewis 1959: 208-38; 1968: 368-80; see also Rädle 1969; and the review by Whitehead 1980: 246-9, of four recent works on the subject. Jameson 1977-8: 133-5 rightly concludes that the *stêlai* 'do not give us a cross-section of Athenian slavery as a whole'; cf. Todd 1993: 191.

70. Westermann 1943: 31; cf. the similarly exaggerated view of Bourriot 1974: 35-47. For Brazil, see (in addition to the works cited in n. 21, above) the classic if somewhat outdated Freyre 1946.

71. Flory 1979; further bibliography in Genovese 1979:150-3.

72. Nymphodoros, *FGrHist.* 572 F 4, discussed by Finley 1980/1998: 113-14; cf. Fuks 1968: 102-11; Vogt 1973: 213-19. Archaeological evidence of late Classical and Hellenistic date unearthed by V. Lambrinoudakis on Mt Aipos in northern Chios may be somehow relevant to the Drimakos affair.

73. Patterson 1970: 289-325; Genovese 1979: 65-6. For a suggestive application of the concept of *marronage* to the Sicilian slave revolts of the late second century BC, see Bradley 1983: 435-51; 1989.

74. Moore 1966: ch. 9, at 479-80; cf. Wolf 1971; further bibliography in Shanin ed. 1971: 425-6.

75. Fuller and more extensively documented treatments of the Helots may be found in Cartledge 1979: ch. 10, with a selection of sources in translation in Appendix 4; Cartledge 1987: ch. 10; see also Oliva 1981 and, a general study, Ducat 1990. For recent archaeological and epigraphic evidence for the Messenian Helots, see respectively Davis et al. 1997: 456-7; and perhaps Bauslaugh 1990.

76. Two other partial exceptions are (i) the servile interregnum at Argos, involving slaves and Perioikoi, which followed the Argives' disaster at Sepeia in (probably) 494: Hill 1951, Index IV.3.1; and (ii) the revolt led by Douketios of the non-Greek Sicels of east-central Sicily in the 450s: Hill 1951, Index V.3.8.

77. On the concepts of 'exploitation' and 'surplus' in this context, see above all Ste. Croix 1983, Index *s.vv.*

78. Helots as state-serfs: Ste. Croix 1983: 149-50 (in a general discussion of serfdom in the ancient Greek world, 147-62); it may not be superfluous to add that the definition of 'serfdom' adopted by Ste. Croix (1983: 135-6) is not applicable solely to mediaeval Europe.

79. Stampp 1971.

80. Roobaert 1977 is far too quick to ascribe the Helot danger to the fevered imaginations of the Spartans and, perhaps not surprisingly, omits even to mention the successful revolt of 370/69. Talbert 1989 has also sought to re-position the Helots as less of a real threat than conventionally believed by outsiders since at least Thucydides, but see my rejoinder, Cartledge 1991. Whitby 1994 persists in a Talbertian vein.

81. Genovese 1979: xiv, 82.

82. However, the Perioikoi (on their status see recently Mertens 1999; Hall 2000) of the offshore island of Kythera were included among the recipients: Tod 1948: no. 196, lines 48, 52. See also n. 46, above.

83. Figueira 1984 is an interesting but methodologically unsound attempt to analyse economic relations between the Spartans and the Helots in quantitative terms.

84. The useful expression 'Spartan mirage' is due to Ollier 1933-43.

85. Pausanias is unlikely to have envisaged giving full citizenship to Helots, but a later 'king' of Sparta, Nabis, did just that in the late third century: Mossé 1964; Cartledge & Spawforth 1989: ch. 5. He had been preceded at Syracuse by Dionysios I (to the Kyllyrioi), at Herakleia Pontikê by Klearchos (to the Mariandynoi), and perhaps at Sikyon by Euphron (to the Katônakophoroi): on the latter, see Cartledge 1980a; Whitehead 1981.

86. Another possible case of cause and effect are the political manoeuvring of Kleomenes I in the late 490s and a possible Helot revolt at the time of Marathon, but there is no evidence linking Kleomenes and Helots, and the evidence for a revolt in 490 is less than conclusive: Cartledge 1979: 153-4.

87. During the Peloponnesian War Athens had made some effort to take advantage of Helot disaffection: e.g., Thuc. 4.41.2-3, 55.1; 7.26.2. But this stopped short of fullscale incitement to revolt *en masse*, and in 421 one of the clauses which the Athenians swore to uphold in their defensive alliance with the Spartans committed them to helping the Spartans in the event of a revolt by 'the slave class' (*hê douleia*), that is, the Helots: Thuc. 5.23.3.

88. Moses Finley, David Harvey, Michael Jameson and Paul Millett generously read and searchingly criticized the penultimate draft of this essay in its original published version. More recently, I have benefited from the enormous learning and sage advice of Stan Engerman and Walter Scheidel.

11. The birth of the hoplite: Sparta's contribution to early Greek military organization

1. Havelock 1972; Sagan 1991: 228-47 ('Warfare and Genocide').

2. Ancient historians: Garlan 1989, with my review in *Gnomon* 62, 1990, 464-6; Rich & Shipley eds 1993. Historical sociologists: Runciman 1989, esp. 258-9; Bryant 1990, 1996: esp. 46-57. See also Cartledge 1993a: 323-8; and n. 12, below.

3. Momigliano 1966a; Villard 1981; Manicas 1982; Finley 1985b: 67-87 ('War and Empire'); Garlan 1989: esp. 21-40 ('Les causes de la guerre chez Platon et Aristote').

4. Cartledge 1996b. See further Chapter 6, above.

5. Honourable exceptions include Lorimer 1947; and Kirk 1968. Stubborn problems of interpretation remain. Was the so-called 'Dipylon shield' a genuine item of an early hoplite's equipment, or merely a heroic artistic convention? See J. Boardman's discussion of the Karditsa Late Geometric bronze warrior figurine (Athens, N.M. 12831): *Cambridge Ancient History (CAH), Plates to Volume III* (Cambridge, 1984) 255-6, no. 333. Did early hoplites use chariots on the battlefield as a 'taxi-service' in the Homeric manner? are early visual depictions of chariots in battle examples of contemporary realism? See Boardman, *CAH Plates* III, 256, no. 334; cf. Greenhalgh 1973. Did early hoplite helmets have stilted crests, as represented on an Attic *krater* of *c.* 570 (Athens, N.M. Acr. 606), or are these as conventional a depiction as the absence of a tunic beneath the hoplites' (really bronze) bell corslet? See Boardman, *CAH Plates* III, 260-1, no. 340.

6. Models: Finley 1985b. Marx: Ste. Croix 1975b. Weber: Nippel 1994.

7. Hoplite equipment: Cartledge 1977: 12-15; Hanson 1989; Lazenby 1989; Anderson 1991; Mitchell 1996.

8. As noted by, e.g., Holladay 1982: 101.

9. Contrast Krentz 1985, Cawkwell 1989, and Goldsworthy 1997, on the one hand, with (e.g.) Adcock 1957; Cartledge 1977: esp. 15-16; Holladay 1982; Anderson, J.K. 1984; Hanson 1989; and Hanson 1991: esp. 80-1 and nn. 11-12, on the other.

10. This problem is not of course peculiar to the reconstruction of a *hoplite* battle: see Whatley 1964. See also Sekunda 1986 for some brilliant full-colour imaginative reconstructions (by Angus McBride) of hoplites at rest and in action.

11. Lissarrague 1989 contains a usefully compendious repertory of original hoplite imagery; one of the most evocative of all representations is on an Attic red-figure vase in the Louvre showing a near-complete panoply *minus* its hoplite user: Lissarrague 1989: 51, fig. 72. The earliest successful representation of the phalanx in action is on the so-called Chigi olpe from Italy: Hurwit 1985: 158-63, with fig. 67. Remarkably, a near copy by the same Corinthian painter has been found at Erythrai: Akurgal 1992.

12. Nilsson 1929; Lorimer 1947; Andrewes 1956: 31-6; Snodgrass 1965; Cartledge 1977; Salmon 1977; Bryant 1990 (an avowedly Weberian restatement of the case for 'a revolution in military technology and tactics', 494); Snodgrass 1993a; Goldsworthy 1997. Add now Runciman 1998, another sociological view of Greek hoplite culture generally.

13. Latacz 1977; Pritchett 1985: 7-44; Morris 1987: 196-201; Pritchett 1991c: 181-90; Bowden 1993; Raaflaub 1991: esp. 225-30; Raaflaub 1997.

14. Van Wees 1986, 1988, 1992, 1994, 1995.

15. Since the Greeks' religion was not one of dogma and orthodoxy, the epics could not be regarded as a source of infallible religious doctrine: see (e.g.) Bruit-Zaidman & Schmitt-Pantel 1992.

16. Oral tradition: Anderson 1987; Powell 1991; Thomas 1993: 45-51. Homeric inconsistency: Leimbach 1980 (a review of Latacz 1977); Snodgrass 1993a: 54-5.

17. Homeric 'period': Greenhalgh 1973. Homeric 'world': Finley 1978; cf. Fritz Lang (playing himself) in Jean-Luc Godard's film 'Le Mépris' (1963). Critique of alleged 'Homeric society': Snodgrass 1974; see also the works cited in n. 67, below.

18. Raaflaub 1993.

19. Morris 1986.

20. This is one of the main points of Latacz's revisionist case, followed and developed by Van Wees (above, n. 14) and (unlike most of his other points) accepted by Snodgrass 1986a.

21. Esp. Van Wees 1994.

22. The extrapolation is made by Pritchett 1991c: 186.

23. Quotations from Van Wees 1994: 15 n. 12; cf. Bryant 1990, 512-13 n. 9.

24. Greenhalgh 1973; Van Wees 1994: 18 n. 45.

25. Quotation from Bryant 1990: 501.

26. Role-models: Morris 1986; Van Wees 1995.

27. Snodgrass 1964; Ahlberg 1971.

28. Long ago pointed out by Cartledge 1977: 20 and n. 72.

29. 'Conquest-state' terminology: Finley 1983.

30. Cartledge 1979: 123ff.

31. Origins of the Greek 'state' and/or *polis*: Runciman 1982; Snodgrass 1986b; Starr 1986; Morris 1991; Raaflaub 1993.

32. Aristotle, *Politics* 1297b16-28; cf. 1279b3.

33. Bordes 1982. See further Cartledge 1996a.

34. Bryant 1990 rightly stresses the political significance of the self-supply system; cf. Ste. Croix 1983: 282-3.

35. Greek 'Renaissance': Starr 1961: Pt. III; Hägg & Marinatos eds 1983.

36. Snodgrass 1971; Sallares 1991: 64; Thomas 1993: 69-82.

37. Demography: Snodgrass 1977; modified by Morris 1987: esp. 156-9; and by Sallares 1991: 84-8.

38. Pastoralism-agriculture shift (alleged): Snodgrass 1987: 193-209.

39. Greeks' political debt to the Orient: Morris 1992: e.g., 123-4.

40. Standard account: Ehrenberg 1969. Acute discussion of Weber's contribution: Nippel 1994.

41. Quotation: Bryant 1990: 495; cf. de Polignac 1995.

42. Among its many merits, Hanson 1983 properly emphasizes the distinction between ravaging and plundering. For a catalogue of literary references to military booty, see Pritchett 1991a: 505-41.

43. See, e.g., Holladay 1982.

44. Ducat 1990: 74 and n. 15.

45. Osborne 1987: ch. 7.

46. Andrewes 1956: ch. 2; Salmon 1977; Bryant 1990: 499.

47. Snodgrass 1986a: 47-58.

48. *Ethnos*-type polities: Snodgrass 1980: 45, fig. 9. Absence of early tyrants therein: Bryant 1990: 500.

49. Weber, *Economy and Society*, as quoted by Bryant 1990: 485.

50. Connor 1988; de Polignac 1995.

51. Sallares 1991: 164ff., esp. p. 172; Vidal-Naquet 1968, 1986c in Vidal-Naquet 1986a; Dover 1978: 201.

52. Ober 1991: 188.

53. Detienne 1968: 123-4.

54. Brelich 1961; Lonis 1979; Jameson 1991: esp. 220.

55. Andrewes 1938; Lorimer 1947; Latacz 1977; Bryant 1990.

56. Van Wees 1995.

57. Lissarrague 1990b; cf. Cartledge 1977: 23-4.

58. Kurtz & Boardman 1971: 201.

59. Sanctuaries: Snodgrass 1980: 52-65; miniature Spartan hoplite figurines: Cartledge 1977: 27 and n. 108.

60. Schnapp 1979; Schnapp 1989; Vidal-Naquet 1986a, 1986b.

61. Snodgrass 1967: 57; Lissarrague 1989: 39-52; Lissarrague 1990b: ch. II; Hoffmann 1994.

62. Contrast the anomic behaviour of the Spartan Aristodamos at Plataia in 479: Hdt. 9.71 (with 7.229).

63. Triremes: Morrison, Coates & Rankov 2000. Peltasts: Cartledge 1987: ch. 15. Hoplite ideology: Loraux 1986; Vidal-Naquet 1986c.

64. Raaflaub 1993.

65. Monarchy: Carlier 1984. Aristocracy: Stein-Hölkeskamp 1989.

66. Compare and contrast Alföldi 1967 with Raaflaub 1990.

67. Former 'orthodoxy': Finley 1978. For a variety of more or less 'revisionist' views on household, kinship, friendship, socio-economic stratification and consequent military organization in early Greece, see Geddes 1984; Donlan 1985, 1989; Andreev 1988; Ulf 1990: esp. 139-49; Welwei 1992; Van Wees 1992: esp. 338 n. 81; Raaflaub 1997. On sympotic groups in particular, see Murray 1983; Stein-Hölkeskamp 1992.

68. Bryant 1990: 492.

69. See further Raaflaub 1999.

70. Lazenby 1985: 63-80; Bryant 1996: 57-66; Ducat 1999c.

71. Parker 1989; Murray 1991: 93-7.

72. Cartledge 1977: 27 and n. 110; cf. generally Groeschel 1989.

73. Vidal-Naquet 1986b.

74. Roussel 1976: esp. chs 5-6. The Lakedaimonian Perioikoi, some of whom fought as hoplites and eventually in the same units as Spartans, are a separate and special classificatory problem: see recently Hall 2000 (though I myself prefer not to see them as second-class citizens, or indeed as citizens of Lakedaimon in any strong sense at all). See also Chapter 12, n. 18 below.

75. Less narrow, however, than that of Delbrück 1920.

76. 'Military Participation Ratio': Andreski 1954. Community reassertion: Lissarrague 1990a: 116.

77. Ste. Croix 1972: ch. IV; Gschnitzer 1978; Cartledge 1987: ch. 13; Baltrusch 1994.

78. This chapter has benefited in particular from the kindness of Kurt Raaflaub, who shared with me in advance of publication his paper Raaflaub 1997, and of Hans Van Wees, who performed the same service in regard to Van Wees 1995.

12. The mirage of Lykourgan Sparta: some brazen reflections

1. Rawson 1969; Tigerstedt 1965-78; Powell & Hodkinson eds. 1994; Cartledge 1999b; Hodkinson 2000: chs 1-2.

2. Hodkinson 1999a: 151 questions whether Eur. *Andromache* 595-601 can be interpreted in this way, but that seems to me the passage's clear implication.

3. See Chapter 3.

4. Nafissi 1991; Link 1994.

5. Finley 1986; Morris 1998.

6. Coulson 1985; Eder 1998.

7. For a full review of bronze and all other classes of Archaic Lakonian artefacts, readers are referred to Förtsch 1994 (an exhaustive Köln Habilitationsschrift), and, once more, to Hodkinson 2000 (forthcoming at the time of writing). Meanwhile see also Hodkinson 1997b (though I cannot agree that there is little or no connection between the history of Lakonian art and Spartan socio-political developments), and 1999a.

8. Cartledge 1979: App. 5.

9. A. Spawforth in Cartledge & Spawforth 1989: 221, no. 38.

10. For certain purposes some Perioikoi were sometimes counted as Lakedaimonioi: Shipley, G. 1997; Hall 2000.

11. Snodgrass 1977. The hypothesis of de Polignac 1995 regarding the role of Amyklai is dubitable; see Chapter 2, above.

12. Desborough 1952: 283-90, 293; 1972: 84, 240-3, 283; Coulson 1985; Coldstream 1968: ch. 9 and 340-1, 364-5; 1977: 157-60; Margreiter 1988.

13. See Dawkins ed. 1929, pl. 77a.

14. Zimmermann 1989: ch. 5.

15. Ste. Croix 1972, App. XXVIII; cf. Hodkinson 1999a: 148 and n. 1; modifications in Hodkinson 2000: ch. 10.

16. Some seals remain unpublished, e.g., Cartledge 1977: 26, fig. 1.

17. Parker 1989; Pettersson 1992.

18. On the Perioikoi generally see Shipley, G. 1992, 1997; Mertens 1999; Hall 2000; on their economic functions, Ridley 1974.

19. I am most grateful to Steve Hodkinson for comments on this chapter in its penultimate state.

13. The importance of being Dorian: an onomastic gloss on the Hellenism of Oscar Wilde

1. Stanford 1976: 236 (in a chapter entitled 'Faith and Morals').

2. For a précis of his university career, see Stanford 1976: 232-9; Mason 1914: 99-101. See also below, n.19. After going down from Oxford, Wilde submitted 'The Rise of Historical Criticism' [sc. in ancient Greece] for the Chancellor's Essay Prize in 1879; the Prize was not awarded, but Wilde's essay, still worth reading, was published posthumously in his *Essays and Lectures*, 1909: 1-108.

3. I owe this reference to Ewen Bowie, a former Editor of *JHS*.

4. See especially Turner 1981: ch. 2 ('Varieties of Victorian Humanistic Hellenism', with an attempted definition at 15-17); cf. Jenkyns 1980; Clarke ed. 1989; Wallace 1997; and esp. Dowling 1994.

5. Rawson 1969. It is one of this splendid book's few flaws that it overlooks Wilde; but see below, n. 14 (Rawson on Walter Pater). See also Africa 1993.

6. For the publishing history in detail, see Mason 1914: 105-10 (1890); 341-5 (1891); there is a modern critical edition: Murray 1974; cf. Lawler ed. 1988. Of the several currently available impressions, all giving the text presented by Ross (cf. below, n. 20), I would single out Ellmann's Bantam Classic edition, 1982. For discussion of the artistic improvements registered by the book-novel, see Murray 1972: 220-31, esp. 224 (Dorian's relationship with Lord Henry) and 227-8 (transformation of Basil Hallward).

7. Meyers 1977; see in detail below. For a conspectus of English-language scholarship, see Maier 1984, with bibl. (329-39).

8. Rajec 1978. To which one might add Passage 1982.

9. On his own Christian names, see especially the anecdotes quoted by Ellmann 1987: 16 and n. 49; for his last-minute anxiety to replace 'Ashton' ('a gentleman's name') with 'Hubbard' as the name for the picture-framer in the book version of *Dorian Gray*, see Ellmann ed. 1977: 304. The importance of being 'Ernest' in a certain play by Wilde needs no further comment.

10. Nassaar 1974: 42 (from the chapter on *Dorian Gray* entitled 'The Darkening Lens', 37-72); cf. Pfister 1986: 138-51 ('Zum literaturhistorischen Kontext: Ästhetizismus, Symbolismus, Dekadenz').

11. Meyers 1977: 14, who devotes a chapter to 'Wilde: *The Picture of Dorian Gray*' (20-31); cf. Pfister 1986: 127-38 ('Die anderen Viktorianer: zur sexuelle Frage'). Millett 1969: 155, more accurately but less sympathetically comments that *Dorian Gray* 'just misses being the first important homosexual novel because it is too timid to tell us what Dorian's crime really was ...'. See also Dale 1995.

12. Ellmann 1987: 301; cf. his 1982 introduction (above, n. 6). For an informative appreciation of the Ellmann biography by a Classically educated novelist and critic, see Brophy 1989: 175-82.

13. Meyers 1977: 24, quoting Symonds 1896: 118.

14. On Walter Pater's aestheticism and Hellenism generally, see Turner 1981: esp. 68-74; and the no fewer than five books on Pater reviewed by Ian Fletcher, *TLS* August 5-11, 1988: 858. On Pater's relation to the Spartan tradition, esp. through his 'Lacedaemon' (Pater 1893), see Rawson 1969: 361, 362-3; and, more severely, Jenkyns 1980: 223, 225; see also n. 28, below. For Pater's influence on Wilde (esp. through his *Studies in the Renaissance*, 1873), see Ellmann 1987: 238, 252, 272, 284; and Murray 1974: ix-x, xii, xx. Nassaar 1974: 39 acutely noticed that, if Dorian died in 1890, the action of the novel (such as it is: see below, text and n. 29) began in 1873, the date of Pater's *Studies*.

15. Holmes 1980: 99. See now Wallace 1997: esp. 105-6.

16. The *Discourse* is easily accessible in Holmes ed. 1980: 101-12; cf. Holmes 1974: 414-38, at 429-38 ('The Platonist: Bagno di Lucca 1818'). On Byron and 'Greek love', see now Dover 1988: 299-302 (emphasizing that male homosexual copulation was a capital offence under English law in the early nineteenth century).

17. Müller 1839: 306-13 (note the fervent abjuring of 'so black a stain', 'so horrible a crime', 310-11).

18. Relevant literature is cited above, Chapter 8.

19. Stanford & McDowell 1971: esp. 38-42; 79-88 (Mahaffy and Wilde); 155-8 (Mahaffy on Greek male homosexuality, most of which was expunged from the 1875 edition).

20. Ellmann 1987: 260 (Wilde was allegedly initiated into the practice of homosexuality in 1886 by the Cambridge Kingsman – and his future editor and literary executor – Robbie Ross).

21. 'Hellenism' was privately printed in 1979 by the Tragara Press, Edinburgh; it is not innocent of factual error.

22. Wilde's Oxford commonplace book, with its laudatory references to Aristophanes, may now be read conveniently in Smith II & Helfland eds 1989.

23. Mahaffy 1874: 309.

24. Müller 1830: II.306-7, cf. 313.

25. The deletions are usefully itemised in Mason 1912: 231-57. One sufficiently telling example is Basil Hallward's musing 'Somehow I have never loved a woman'.

26. Ollier 1933-43.

27. On Symonds, see Weeks 1977: ch. 4. I have not seen Edward Carpenter's 1894 pamphlet *Homogenic Love* (Manchester), which is listed in *A Bibliography of Edward Carpenter* ... (Sheffield, 1949); but for a relevant quotation from Carpenter 1919: 133, see Chapter 8, n. 43 above.

28. For the conventional, but inaccurate, contrast between the 'highland' Dorians and the 'littoral, fluid' Ionians, see, e.g., Pater 1893: 201; with Dowling 1989: 3. Wilde himself spoke of 'the noble Dorian music' (though music, it has to be said, was not Wilde's *forte*): Ellmann ed. 1970: 368.

29. Murray 1974: viii, cf. xix.

30. For bibliographical and other guidance I am indebted to Professor Richard Jenkyns and to my one-time English teacher Dr Peter Raby (see also Raby 1988, Raby ed. 1997). Neither of these, of course, should be implicated criminally in my foray into Victoriana and Wildeiana.

Bibliography

** = Reprinted in this volume; see p. 235.

Aalders, G.J.D. (1968) *Die Theorie der gemischsten Verfassung im Altertum*, Amsterdam

Adams, R.N. (1960) 'An inquiry into the nature of the family' in *Essays in the Science of Culture in Honor of Leslie A. White*, New York: 30-49

Adcock, F.E. (1924) 'Some aspects of ancient Greek diplomacy', *PCA* 21: 92-116

Adcock, F.E. (1948) 'The development of ancient Greek diplomacy', *AC* 17: 1-12

Adcock, F.E. (1953) 'Greek and Macedonian Kingship', *PBA* 39: 163-80

Adcock, F.E. (1957) *The Greek and Macedonian Art of War*, California & London

Adcock, F.E. & D.J. Mosley (1975) *Diplomacy in Ancient Greece*, London

Africa, T.W. (1982) 'Homosexuals in Greek history', *Journal of Psychohistory* 9: 401-20

Africa, T.W. (1993) 'The owl at dusk: two centuries of classical scholarship', *JHI* 54: 143-63

Ahlberg, G. (1971) *Fighting on Land and Sea in Greek Geometric Art*, Stockholm

Akurgal, M. (1992) 'Eine protokorinthische Oinochoe aus Erythrai', *Istanbuler Mitteilungen* 42: 83-96

Alcock, S.E. & R.G. Osborne (1994) eds *Placing the Gods: Sanctuaries and Sacred Space in Ancient Greece*, Oxford

Alföldi, A. (1967) 'Die Herrschaft der Reiterei in Griechenland und Rom nach dem Sturz der Könige', *AK* Supp. 4: 13-47

Allen, M.R. (1967) *Male Cults and Secret Initiation in Melanesia*, Melbourne, London & New York

Amundsen, D.W. & C.J. Diers (1969) 'The age of menarche in classical Greece', *Human Biology* 41: 125-32

Andersen, Ø. (1987) 'Mündlichkeit und Schriftlichkeit im frühen Griechenland', *A&A* 33: 29-44

Anderson, B. (1991) *Imagined Communities: Reflections on the Origins and Spread of Nationalism*, 2nd edn, London

Anderson, J.K. (1970) *Military Theory and Practice in the Age of Xenophon*, California & London

Anderson, J.K. (1984) 'Hoplites and heresies: a note', *JHS* 104: 152

Anderson, J.K. (1991) 'Hoplite weapons and offensive arms' in Hanson ed. 1991: 15-37

Anderson, P. (1983) Review of Ste. Croix 1983, *History Workshop Journal* 16: 57-73

Andreev, J.V. (1975) 'Sparta als Typ einer Polis', *Klio* 57: 73-82

Andreev, J.V. (1988) 'Die homerische Gesellschaft', *Klio* 70: 5-85

Andreski, S. (1954) *Military Organisation and Society*, London

Andrewes, A. (1938) 'Eunomia', *CQ* n.s. 32: 89-102

231

Bibliography

Andrewes, A. (1954) *Probouleusis: Sparta's Contribution to the Technique of Government*, Oxford (Inaugural Lecture)

Andrewes, A. (1956) *The Greek Tyrants*, London

Andrewes, A. (1966) 'The government of classical Sparta' in Badian ed. 1966: 1-20

Andrewes, A. (1978) 'Spartan imperialism?' in C.R. Whittaker & P. Garnsey eds *Imperialism in the Ancient World*, Cambridge: 91-102

Angel, J.L. (1972) 'Ecology and population in the eastern Mediterranean', *World Archaeology* 4: 88-105

Aptheker, H. (1943) *American Negro Slave Revolts*, New York [new edn 1969]

Aron, R. (1972) *Progress and Disillusion: The Dialectics of Modern Society*, Harmondsworth

Arthur, M.B. (1976) 'Review essay: Classics', *Signs* 2: 382-403

Austin, M. & P. Vidal-Naquet (1972) *Economies et Sociétés en Grèce ancienne*, 2nd edn, Paris

Baal, J. van (1966) *Dema: Description and Analysis of Marind-Anim Culture (South New Guinea)*, The Hague

Badian, E. (1966) ed. *Ancient Society and Institutions: Studies Presented to Victor Ehrenberg on his 75th Birthday*, Oxford

Bailey, D.T. (1980) 'A divided prism: two sources of black testimony on slavery', *Journal of Southern History* 46: 381-404

Baker, J. (1987) *Arguing for Equality*, London

Baldry, H.C. (1965) *The Unity of Mankind in Greek Thought*, Cambridge

Ball, A.J. (1989) 'Capturing a bride: marriage practices in classical Sparta', *AH* 19: 75-81

Baltrusch, E. (1994) *Symmachie und Spondai: Untersuchungen zum griechischen Völkerrecht*, Berlin & New York

Baltrusch, E. (1998) *Sparta: Geschichte, Gesellschaft, Kultur*, Munich

Barnes, J. (1980) 'Aristotle and the methods of ethics', *RIPh* 34: 490-511

Barton, I.M. (1972) 'Tranio's Laconian key', *G&R* n.s. 19: 25-31

Bauslaugh, R.A. (1990) 'Messenian dialect and dedications of the "Methanioi" ', *Hesperia* 39: 661-8

Baxter, W. & U. Almagor (1978) eds *Age, Generation and Time: Some Features of East African Age Organizations*, London

Bayle, P. (1992) *Sparta nel 'Dizionario'*, ed. A. Paradiso, Palermo [with 'Note' by L. Canfora (9-18)]

Beasley, T.W. (1906) 'The *kyrios* in Greek states other than Athens', *CR* 20: 210-13

Beauvoir, S. de (1972) *The Second Sex*, Harmondsworth [French original, Paris, 1949; trans. 1953]

Beck, F.A. (1993) 'Spartan education revised', *History of Education Review* 22: 16-31

Bedau, H.A. (1971) ed. *Justice and Equality*, Englewood Cliffs, N.J.

Beitz, C.R. (1991) *Political Equality: An Essay in Democratic Theory*, Princeton

Benedict, R. (1939) 'Sex in a primitive society', *American Journal of Orthopsychiatry* 9: 570-5

Bengtson, H. (1975) ed. *Die Staatsverträge des Altertums* II. *Die Verträge der griechisch-römischen Welt von 700-338 v. Chr.*, 2nd edn, Munich

Bérard, C. et al. (1989) *A City of Images*, Princeton [French original 1984]

Berent, M. (1994) 'The Stateless Polis. Towards A Re-evaluation of the Classical Greek Political Community', unpublished diss. Cambridge

Berent, M. (1998) 'Stasis, or the Greek invention of politics', *HPTh* 19: 331-62

Berlin, Ira (1998) *Many Thousands Gone: The First Two Centuries of Slavery in America*, Cambridge, MA

Berlin, Isaiah (1978) 'Equality' (1956) repr. in *Concepts and Categories*, ed. H. Hardy, Oxford: 81-102

Berve, H. (1967) *Die Tyrannis bei den Griechen*, 2 vols, Munich

Besterman, T. (1976) *Voltaire*, 2nd edn, Oxford

Bethe, E. (1907) 'Die dorische Knabenliebe. Ihre Ethik und ihre Idee', *RhM* n.F. 62: 438-75

Bickerman, E.J. (1950) 'Remarques sur le droit des gens dans la Grèce classique', *RIDA* 4: 99-127

Bickerman, E.J. (1952) *'Origines gentium'*, *CPh* 47: 65-88

Bickerman, E.J. (1958) *'Autonomia*. Sur un passage de Thucydide (1.144.2)', *RIDA* 3rd ser. 5: 313-44

Bickerman, E.J. (1976a) 'La conception du mariage à Athènes', *BIDR* 3rd ser. 17: 1-28

Bickerman, E.J. (1976b) 'Love story in the Homeric Hymn to Aphrodite', *Athenaeum* n.s. 54: 229-54

Birgalias, N. (1999) *L'Odyssée de l'éducation spartiate*, Athens

Birt, T. (1913) *Das Antike Buchwesen*, Munich

Blassingame, J.W. (1972) *The Slave Community: Plantation Life in the Antebellum South*, New York, London & Toronto

Blassingame, J.W. (1977) ed. *Slave Testimony: two centuries of letters, speeches, interviews, and autobiographies*, Baton Rouge

Boardman, J. (1963) 'Artemis Orthia and chronology', *ABSA* 58: 1-7

Boardman, J. (1978) *Greek Sculpture: The Archaic Period*, London

Boardman, J. (1999) *The Greeks Overseas: Their Early Colonies and Trade*, 4th edn, London

Bobbio, N. (1989) *Democracy and Dictatorship: The Nature and Limits of State Power*, Oxford

Boegehold, A.L. (1972) 'The establishment of a central archive at Athens', *AJA* 76: 23-30

Bölte, F. (1929) 'Sparta', *RE* IIIA: 1265-1373

Boffo, L. (1995) 'Ancora una volta sugli "Archivi" nel mondo Greco: conservazione e "pubblicazione" epigrafica', *Athenaeum* n.s. 83: 91-130

Bogdanor, V. (1995) *The Monarchy and the Constitution*, Oxford

Bolgar, R.R. (1969) 'The training of élites in Greek education', in R. Wilkinson ed. *Governing Elites: Studies in Training and Selection*, New York: 23-49

Bömer, F. (1957-63) *Untersuchungen über die Religion der Sklaven in Griechenland und Rom*, 4 vols, Wiesbaden

Bommelaer, J.-F. (1977) *Lysandre de Sparte: Histoire et traditions*, Paris

Bonnard, G.A. (1966) ed. *Edward Gibbon: Memoirs of My Life*, London

Bonner, R.J. & G. Smith (1942) 'Administration of Justice in Sparta', *CPh* 37: 113-29

Bordes, J. (1982) *Politeia dans la pensée grecque jusqu' à Aristote*, Paris

Borecky, B. (1963) 'The primitive origin of the Greek conception of equality' in V. Varcl & R.F. Willetts eds *GERAS: Studies Presented to George Thomson on the Occasion of his 60th Birthday*, Prague: 41-60

Borecky, B. (1971) 'Die politische Isonomie', *Eirene* 9: 5-24

Boswell, J. (1980) *Christianity, Social Tolerance and Homosexuality: Gay People in Western Europe from the Beginning of the Christian era to the Fourteenth Century*, Chicago & London

Bourguet, E. (1927) *Le dialecte laconien*, Paris

Bourriot, F. (1974) 'L'évolution de l'esclave dans les comédies d'Aristophane et

Bibliography

l'essor de l'affranchissement au IVe siècle' in *Mélanges d'histoire ancienne offerts à W. Seston*, Paris: 35-47

Bowden, H. (1993) 'Hoplites and Homer: warfare, cult and the ideology of the Polis' in Rich & Shipley eds 1993: 45-63

Bradford, A.S. (1986) 'Gynaikokratoumenoi: did Spartan women rule Spartan men?', *AncW* 14: 13-18

Bradley, K.R. (1983) 'Slave kingdoms in ancient Sicily', *Historical Reflections/Réflexions historiques* 10: 435-51

Bradley, K.R. (1989) *Slavery and Rebellion in the Roman World, 140 BC-70 BC*, Bloomington, Indianapolis & London

Brelich, A. (1961) *Guerre, agoni e culti nella Grecia arcaica*, Bonn

Brelich, A. (1969) *Paides e parthenoi* I, Rome

Bremmer, J. (1980) 'An enigmatic Indo-European rite: paederasty', *Arethusa* 13: 279-98

Bringmann, K. (1980) 'Die soziale und politische Verfassung Spartas: ein Sonderfall der griechischen Verfassungsgeschichte?', *Gymnasium* 87: 465-84

Brockmeyer, N. (1979) *Antike Sklaverei*, Darmstadt

Brophy, B. (1989) 'The Great Celtic/Hibernian School' in her *Reads: A Collection of Essays*, London: 173-82

Broude, G.J. & S.J. Greene (1976) 'Cross-cultural codes in twenty sexual attitudes and practices', *Ethnology* 15: 409-29

Brown, C. (1985) 'The "correct" understanding of *eu diabas*', *AJPh* 106: 356-9

Brown, C.G. (1991) 'The prayers of the Corinthian women (Simonides Ep. 15 Page)', *GRBS* 32: 5-14

Browning, R. (1983) Review of Ste. Croix 1983, *P&P* 100: 147-56

Bruit-Zaidman, L. & P. Schmitt-Pantel (1992) *Religion in the Ancient Greek City*, ed. and trans. P.A. Cartledge, Cambridge

Brunt, P.A. (1958) Review of Westermann 1955, *JRS* 48: 164-70

Bryant, J.M. (1990) 'Military technology and socio-cultural change in the ancient Greek city', *Sociological Review* 38: 484-516

Bryant, J.M. (1996) *Moral Codes and Social Structure in Ancient Greece: A Sociology of Greek Ethics from Homer to the Epicureans and Stoics*, Albany, N.Y.

Buckler, J. (1985) 'Epameinondas and the *embolon*', *Phoenix* 39: 134-43

Buffière, F. (1980) *Eros adolescent: La pédérastie dans la Grèce antique*, Paris

Bullough, V.L. (1976) *Sexual Variance in Society and History*, New York [repr. Chicago, 1980]

Burn, A.R. (1960) *The Lyric Age of Greece*, London [repr. 1978]

Busolt, G. (1893) *Griechische Geschichte* I, 2nd edn, Gotha

Cairns, D.L. (1996) 'Off with her *aidos* – Herodotus 1.8.3-4', *CQ* n.s. 46: 78-83

Calame, C. (1977) *Les choeurs de jeunes filles en Grèce archaïque*, 2 vols, Rome [vol. 1 trans. in a 2nd edn as *Choruses of Young Women in Ancient Greece: Their Morphology, Religious Role, and Social Functions* (Lanham, MD & London 1997)]

Cambiano, G. (1995) 'Becoming an Adult' in J.-P. Vernant ed. *The Greeks*, Chicago: 86-119 [Italian original 1991]

Carlier, P. (1977) 'La vie politique à Sparte sous le règne de Cléomène Ier: essai d'interprétation', *Ktema* 2: 65-84

Carlier, P. (1984) *La Royauté en Grèce avant Alexandre*, Strasbourg

Carpenter, E. (1894) *Homogenic Love*, Manchester

Carpenter, E. (1919) *Intermediate Types among Primitive Folk: A Study in Social Evolution*, 2nd edn, London

Carrithers, M. (1993) *Why Humans Have Cultures*, Oxford

Bibliography

Carter, J.B. (1984) *Greek Ivory-Carving in the Orientalizing and Archaic Periods*, Ann Arbor

Carter, J.B. (1988) 'Masks and poetry in early Sparta' in R. Hägg & G.C. Nordquist eds *Early Greek Cult Practice*, Stockholm: 89-98

Cartledge, P.A. (1975) 'Toward the Spartan revolution', *Arethusa* 8: 59-84

Cartledge, P.A. (1976a) 'Did Spartan citizens ever practise a manual *tekhne*?', *LCM* 1: 115-19

Cartledge, P.A. (1976b) 'The new Spartan treaty', *LCM* 1: 87-92

Cartledge, P.A. (1977) 'Hoplites and Heroes: Sparta's contribution to the technique of ancient warfare', *JHS* 97: 11-27 [repr. in German trans., with add., in Christ ed. 1986: 387-425, 470]

**Cartledge, P.A. (1978), 'Literacy in the Spartan oligarchy', *JHS* 98: 25-37

Cartledge, P.A. (1979) *Sparta and Lakonia: A Regional History 1300-362 BC*, London, Henley & Boston

Cartledge, P.A. (1980a) 'Euphron and the *douloi* again', *LCM* 5: 209-11

**Cartledge, P.A. (1980b) 'The peculiar position of Sparta in the development of the Greek city-state', *PRIA* 80C: 91-108

**Cartledge, P.A. (1981a) 'The politics of Spartan pederasty', *PCPhS* n.s. 27: 17-36 [repr. with add. in Siems ed. 1988: 385-415]

**Cartledge, P.A. (1981b) 'Spartan wives: liberation or licence?', *CQ* n.s. 31: 84-105

Cartledge, P.A. (1982a) Review of Garlan 1982, *Annales (ESC)* 37: 1028-32

Cartledge, P.A. (1982b) 'Sparta and Samos in the Archaic period: a "special relationship"?', *CQ* n.s. 32: 243-65

Cartledge, P.A. (1983) ' "Trade and Politics" revisited: Archaic Greece' in P. Garnsey et al. eds *Trade in the Ancient Economy*, London: 1-15

Cartledge, P.A. (1985a) 'The Greek religious festivals' in P. Easterling & J. Muir eds *Greek Religion and Society*, Cambridge: 98-127

**Cartledge, P.A. (1985b) 'Rebels and *Sambos* in Classical Greece: a comparative view' in Cartledge & Harvey eds 1985: 16-46

Cartledge, P.A. (1987) *Agesilaos and the Crisis of Sparta*, London & Baltimore

Cartledge, P.A. (1990) Review of Garlan 1989, *Gnomon* 62: 464-6

Cartledge, P.A. (1991) 'Richard Talbert's revision of the Spartan-Helot struggle: a reply', *Historia* 38: 379-81

**Cartledge, P.A. (1992a) 'A Spartan education' in *Apodosis: Essays Presented to Dr W.W. Cruickshank to Mark his Eightieth Birthday*, London: 10-19 [St Paul's School, privately printed]

Cartledge, P.A. (1992b) 'Early Lakedaimon: the making of a conquest-state' in Sanders ed. 1992: 49-55

Cartledge, P.A. (1993a) 'Review Article: Ancient Warfare', *International History Review* 15: 323-8 [review-article of Hanson ed. 1991 et al.]

Cartledge, P.A. (1993b) 'Xenophon's women: a touch of the other' in H.D. Jocelyn ed. *Tria Lustra: Essays and Notes Presented to John Pinsent*, Liverpool: 5-14

Cartledge, P.A. (1995a) 'Vindicating Gibbon's good faith', *Hermathena* 148: 133-47

Cartledge, P.A. (1995b) ' "We are all Greeks"? Ancient (especially Herodotean) and modern contestations of Hellenism', *BICS* n.s. 2: 75-82

Cartledge, P.A. (1996a) 'La nascita degli opliti e l'organizzazione militare' in S. Settis ed. *I Greci II. Una Storia Greca 1. Formazione*, Turin, 681-714

Cartledge, P.A. (1996b) 'La politica' in S. Settis ed. *I Greci I: Noi e I Greci*, Turin: 39-72

Cartledge, P.A. (1996c) 'Putting the Greek gods in their places', review-article of Alcock & Osborne eds 1994 et al., *IHR* 18: 104-12

Cartledge, P.A. (1997) *The Greeks: A Portrait of Self and Others*, rev. edn, Oxford [German trans., with Nachwort, Stuttgart 1998]

Cartledge, P.A. (1998a) *Democritus and Atomistic Politics*, London

Cartledge, P.A. (1998b) 'Writing the history of Archaic Greek political thought' in N. Fisher & H. Van Wees eds *Archaic Greece: New Approaches and New Evidence*, London: 379-99

Cartledge, P.A. (1999a) *Aristophanes and his Theatre of the Absurd*, rev. edn, Bristol

Cartledge, P.A. (1999b) 'The Socratics' Sparta and Rousseau's' in Hodkinson & Powell eds 1999: 311-37

Cartledge, P.A. (2000) ' "To Poseidon the Driver": an Arkado-Lakonian ram dedication' in Tsetskhladze et al. eds 2000: 60-7

Cartledge, P.A. & A.J.S. Spawforth (1989) *Hellenistic and Roman Sparta: A Tale of Two Cities*, London & New York [corr. pb. repr. 1991]

Cartledge, P.A. & F.D. Harvey (1985) eds *CRUX: Essays in Greek History Presented to G.E.M. de Ste. Croix on his 75th Birthday*, Exeter & London

Casson, S. (1935) 'Early Greek inscriptions on metal', *AJA* 39: 510-17

Catling, H.W. (1976-77) 'Excavations at Sparta, 1973-76', *AR* 23: 27-35

Catling, H.W. (1990a) 'Lakonia, Aphyssou, Tsakona', *AR* 36: 22-4

Catling, H.W. (1990b), 'A sanctuary of Zeus Messapeus: excavations at Aphyssou, Tsakona, 1989', *ABSA* 85: 15-35

Catling, H.W. & H. Cavanagh (1976) 'Two inscribed bronzes from the Menelaion, Sparta', *Kadmos* 15: 145-57

Cavanagh, W.G. (1991) 'Surveys, cities and synoecism' in Rich & Wallace-Hadrill eds 1991: 97-118

Cavanagh, W.G. & J.H. Crouwel (1988) 'Lakonia Survey, 1988', *Lakonikai Spoudai* 9: 77-88

Cavanagh, W.G., J.H. Crouwel, R.W.V. Catling & D.J.G. Shipley (1996) *Continuity and Change in a Greek Rural Landscape: The Lakonia Survey* II: *Archaeological Data*, British School at Athens, Supplementary Volume 27, London

Cavanagh, W.G., J.H. Crouwel, R.W.V. Catling & D.J.G. Shipley (1997) *Continuity and Change in a Greek Rural Landscape: The Lakonia Survey* I: *Methodology and Interpretation*, British School at Athens, Supplementary Volume 26, London

Cavanagh, W.G. & S.E.C. Walker (1998) eds *Sparta in Laconia* (Proceedings of the 19th British Museum Classical Colloquium: B.S.A. Studies 4), London

Cawkwell, G.L. (1989) 'Orthodoxy and hoplites', *CQ* n.s. 39: 375-89

Cawkwell, G.L. (1993) 'Cleomenes', *Mnemosyne* 4th ser. 46: 506-27

Chrimes, K.M.T. (1949) *Ancient Sparta: A Re-examination of the Evidence*, Manchester [repr. Oxford 1999]

Christ, K. (1986) ed. *Sparta* (Wege der Forschung 622), Darmstadt

Christien, J. (1974) 'La loi d'Épitadeus: un aspect de l'histoire économique et sociale à Sparte', *RD* 4th ser. 52: 197-221

Christien, J. (1998) 'Sparte et le Péloponnèse après 369 BC', *Praktika tou E' Diethnous Synedriou Peloponnesiakôn Spoudôn* (Argos-Nafplion 6-10 September 1995), Athens: 433-67

Christou, Ch. (1964) '*Spartiatikoi arkhaïkoi taphoi kai epitaphios met' anagluphôn amphoreus tou lakônikou ergastêriou*', *AD* 19A: 123-63

Clark, C.A. (1996) 'The gendering of the body in Alcman's *Partheneion* 1: narrative, sex, and social order in archaic Sparta', *Helios* 23: 143-72

Clark, S.R.L. (1982) 'Aristotle's woman', *HPTh* 3: 177-91

Bibliography

Clarke, G.W. (1989) ed. *Rediscovering Hellenism: The Hellenic Inheritance and the English Imagination*, Cambridge

Clarke, W.M. (1978) 'Achilles and Patroclus in love', *Hermes* 106: 381-96

Clauss, M. (1983) *Sparta: Eine Einführung in seine Geschichte und Zivilisation*, Berlin

Cloché, P. (1949) 'Sur le rôle des rois de Sparte', *LEC* 17: 113-38, 343-81

Coldstream, J.N. (1968) *Greek Geometric Pottery*, London

Coldstream, J.N. (1977) *Geometric Greece*, London

Coldstream, J.N. & G.L. Huxley (1972) eds *Kythera*, London

Cole, S.G. (1981) 'Could Greek women read and write?', *Women's Studies* 8: 129-55 [repr. in H. Foley ed. *Reflections of Women in Antiquity*, New York, 1981: 219-46]

Cole, S.G. (1996) 'Oath ritual and the male community at Athens' in Ober & Hedrick eds 1996: 227-48

Congdon, L.O.K. (1981) *Caryatid Mirrors of Ancient Greece*, Mainz

Connor, W.R. (1988) 'Early Greek land warfare as symbolic expression', *P&P* 119: 3-29

Coulson, W.D.E (1985) 'The dark age pottery of Sparta', *ABSA* 80: 29-84

Cook, R.M. (1962) 'Spartan history and archaeology', *CQ* n.s. 12: 156-8

Craton, M. (1983) *Testing the Chains: Resistance to Slavery in the British West Indies*, Ithaca

Curtin, P.D. (1969) *The Atlantic Slave Trade: A Census*, Madison

Dagger, R. (1988) 'Rights' in T. Ball, J. Farr & R.L. Hanson eds *Political Innovation and Conceptual Change*, Cambridge: 292-308

Dahl, R.A. (1989) *Democracy and Its Critics*, New Haven

Dale, P.A. (1995) 'Oscar Wilde, crime and the glorious shapes of art', *Victorian Newsletter* 88: 1-5

Daube, D. (1972) *Civil Disobedience in Antiquity*, Edinburgh

Daube, D. (1977) *The Duty of Procreation*, Edinburgh

Daube, D. (1979) 'Three footnotes on civil disobedience in antiquity', *Humanities in Society* 2: 69-82

David, E. (1979) 'The pamphlet of Pausanias', *PP* 34: 94-116

David, E. (1982/3) 'Aristotle on Sparta', *AncSoc* 13/14: 67-103

David, E. (1985) 'The trial of Spartan kings', *RIDA* 32: 131-40

David, E. (1989a) 'Dress in Spartan society', *AncW* 19: 3-13

David, E. (1989b) 'Laughter in Spartan society' in Powell & Hodkinson eds 1989: 1-25

David, E. (1992) 'Sparta's social hair', *Eranos* 90: 11-21

David, E. (1993) 'Hunting in Spartan society and consciousness', *EMC/CV* 37: 393-417

David, P.A. (1976) ed. *Reckoning with Slavery: A Critical Study in the Quantitative History of American Negro Slavery*, New York

Davidson, J. (1997) *Courtesans and Fishcakes: The Consuming Passions of Classical Athens*, New York & London

Daviero-Rocchi, G. (1988) *Frontiera e confini nella Grecia antica*, Rome

Davis, D.B. (1974) 'Slavery and the post-World War II historians', *Daedalus* 103: 1-16

Davis, J. et al. (1997) 'The Pylos Regional Archaeological Project 1. Overview and the archaeological survey', *Hesperia* 66: 391-494

Davison, J.A. (1968) 'Literature and literacy in Ancient Greece' in *From Archilochus to Pindar: Papers on Greek Literature of the Archaic Period*, London & New York: 86-128

Dawkins, R.M. (1929) ed. *The Sanctuary of Artemis Orthia at Sparta. Excavated* and described by Members of the British School at Athens, 1906-1910 (*JHS* Supp. V), London

Decker, J. (1913) 'La genèse de l'organisation civique des Spartiates' in *25th Bulletin Instituts Solvay = Archives sociologiques* 4, Brussels: 306-13

Degler, C.N. (1959) 'Starr on Slavery', *Journal of Economic History* 19: 271-7

Degler, C.N. (1971) *Neither Black Nor White: Slavery and Race Relations in Brazil and the United States*, New York & London

Degler, C.N. (1974) *Is There a History of Women?*, Oxford (Inaugural Harmsworth Lecture)

Delbrück, H. (1920) *Geschichte der Kriegskunst im Rahmen der politischen Geschichte*, vol. I, 3rd edn [new edn ed. K. Christ 1964; Eng. trans. 1975]

Delcourt, M. (1958) *Hermaphrodite: Mythes et rites de la bisexualité dans l'antiquité classique*, Paris

Den Boer, W. (1954) *Laconian Studies*, Amsterdam

Desborough, V.R.D'A. (1952) *Protogeometric Pottery*, Oxford

Desborough, V.R.D'A. (1972) *The Greek Dark Ages*, London

Detienne, M (1968), 'La phalange: problèmes et controverses' in Vernant ed. 1968: 119-42

Detienne, M. (1988) 'L'espace de la publicité: ses opérateurs intellectuels dans la cité' in Detienne ed. 1988: 29-81

Detienne M. (1988) ed. *Les savoirs de l'écriture. En Grèce ancienne*, Lille

Dettenhofer, M. (1993) 'Die Frauen von Sparta: gesellschaftliche Position und politische Relevanz', *Klio* 75: 61-75 [= Dettenhofer ed. 1994: 15-40]

Dettenhofer, M. (1994) ed. *Reine Männersache? Frauen in Männerdomänen der antiken Welt*, Cologne

Devereux, G. (1967) 'Greek pseudo-homosexuality and the "Greek miracle" ', *SO* 42: 69-92

Dickins, G. (1908) 'The art of Sparta', *Burlington Magazine* 14: 66-84

Dickins, G. (1929) 'The terracotta masks' in Dawkins ed. 1929: 163-86

Diller, A. (1937) *Race Mixture among the Greeks before Alexander*, Urbana

Dockès, P. (1982) *Medieval Slavery and Liberation*, Chicago & London

Donlan, W. (1985) 'The social groups of Dark Age Greece', *CPh* 80: 293-308

Donlan, W. (1989) 'The pre-State community in Greece', *SO* 64: 5-29

Dougherty, C. (1996) 'Democratic contradictions and the synoptic illusion of Euripides' *Ion*' in Ober & Hedrick eds 1996: 249-70

Douglass, F. (1845) *Narrative of the Life of Frederick Douglass, an American Slave*, Boston [repr. Harmondsworth 1982]

Douglass, F. (1855) *My Bondage and My Freedom*, New York

Dover, K.J. (1973) 'Classical Greek attitudes to sexual behaviour', *Arethusa* 6: 59-73 [repr. in Sullivan & Peradotto eds 1984: 143-57]

Dover, K.J. (1974) *Greek Popular Morality in the Time of Plato and Aristotle*, Oxford

Dover, K.J. (1978) *Greek Homosexuality*, London [repr. with add. Cambridge, MA 1989]

Dover, K.J. (1988) 'Byron on the Ancient Greeks' in his *The Greeks and their Legacy. Collected Papers* II, Oxford: 292-303

Dow, S. (1942) 'Corinthiaca', *HSPh* 43: 89-119

Dowling, L. (1989) 'Ruskin's pied beauty and the constitution of a "homosexual" code', *The Victorian Newsletter* 75: 1-8

Dowling, L. (1994) *Hellenism and Homosexuality in Victorian Oxford*, Ithaca

Drews, R. (1983) *BASILEUS: The Evidence for Kingship in Geometric Greece*, New Haven & London

Bibliography

Ducat, J. (1983) 'Sparte archaïque et classique. Structures économiques, sociales, politiques (1965-1982)' *REG* 96: 194-225

Ducat, J. (1990) *Les Hilotes* (*BCH* Supp. XX), Paris

Ducat, J. (1998) 'La femme de Sparte et la cité', *Ktema* 23: 385-406

Ducat, J. (1999a) 'La femme de Sparte et la guerre', *Pallas* 51: 159-71

Ducat, J. (1999b) 'Perspectives on Spartan education in the classical period' in Hodkinson & Powell eds 1999: 43-66

Ducat, J. (1999c) 'La société spartiate et la guerre' in F. Prost ed. *Armées et sociétés de la Grèce classique: Aspects sociaux et politiques de la guerre aux Ve et IVe s. av. J.-C.*, Paris: 35-50

Dundes, A. (1976) 'A psychoanalytic study of the bullroarer', *Man* n.s. 11: 220-38

Eder, B. (1990) ed. *Staat, Herrschaft, Gesellschaft in frühgriechische Zeit: Eine Bibliographie 1978-1991/2*, Vienna

Eder, B. (1998) *Argolis, Lakonien, Messenien: Vom Ende der mykenischen Palastzeit bis zur Einwanderung der Dorier*, Vienna

Eder, W. (1990) ed. *Staat und Staatlichkeit in der frühen römischen Republik*, Stuttgart

Eglinton, J.Z. (1971) *Greek Love*, London

Ehrenberg, V. (1924) 'Spartiaten und Lakedaimonier', *Hermes* 59: 22-76 [repr. in Christ ed. 1986: 144-94]

Ehrenberg, V. (1946a) 'A totalitarian State' in *Aspects of the Ancient World*, Oxford: 94-104 [repr. in German in Christ ed. 1986: 217-28]

Ehrenberg, V. (1946b) 'Eunomia' in *Aspects of the Ancient World*, Oxford: 70-93

Ehrenberg, V. (1962) *The People of Aristophanes: A Sociology of Old Attic Comedy*, 3rd edn, New York

Ehrenberg, V. (1969) *The Greek State*, 2nd edn, London

Ehrenberg, V. (1973) *From Solon to Socrates*, 2nd edn, London

Elkins, S.M. (1976) *Slavery: A Problem in American Institutional and Intellectual Life*, 3rd edn, Chicago & London

Ellis, H. (1897) *Sexual Inversion*, London (= *Studies in the Psychology of Sex* I)

Ellis, H. (1925) *Studies in the Psychology of Sex* II, London

Ellmann, R. (1970) ed. *The Artist as Critic: Critical Writings of Oscar Wilde*, 2nd edn, London

Ellmann, R. (1977) ed. *Oscar Wilde. The Picture of Dorian Gray and Other Writings*, Toronto

Ellmann, R. (1987) *Oscar Wilde*, London [repr. Harmondsworth 1988]

Erdmann, W. (1934) *Die Ehe im alten Griechenland*, Munich

Euben, J.P., J.R. Wallach & J. Ober (1994) eds *Athenian Political Thought and the Reconstruction of American Democracy*, Ithaca & London

Evans, R. (1998) *In Defence of History*, London

Evans-Grubbs, J. (1989) 'Abduction marriage in antiquity: a law of Constantine (*CT* IX.24.1) and its social context', *JRS* 79: 59-83

Eyben, E. (1972) 'Antiquity's view of puberty', *Latomus* 31: 677-87

Farrar, C. (1988) *The Origins of Democratic Thinking: The Invention of Politics in Classical Athens*, Cambridge

Fehling, D. (1974) *Ethologische Überlegungen auf dem Gebiet der Altertumskunde*, Munich

Ferguson, J. (1975) *Utopias of the Classical World*, London

Ferguson, W.S. (1918) 'The Zulus and the Spartans: a comparison of their military systems', *Harvard African Studies* 2: 197-234

Figueira, T.J. (1984) 'Mess contributions and subsistence at Sparta', *TAPhA* 114: 87-109

Figueira, T.J. (1999) 'The evolution of the Messenian identity' in Hodkinson & Powell eds 1999: 211-44

Finley, M.I. (1959) 'Was Greek civilization based on slave labour?', *Historia* 8: 145-64 [repr. in Finley ed. 1968: 53-72; Finley 1981a: 97-115]

Finley, M.I. (1962a) 'The myth of Sparta', *The Listener*, August 2: 171-3

Finley, M.I. (1962b) 'The slave trade in antiquity: the Black Sea and Danubian regions', *Klio* 40: 51-9 [repr. in Finley 1981a: 167-75]

Finley, M.I. (1963-4) 'Between slavery and freedom', *CSSH* 6: 233-49 [repr. in Finley 1981a: 116-32]

Finley, M.I. (1968) 'Sparta' in J.-P. Vernant ed. *Problèmes de la guerre en Grèce ancienne*, Paris: 141-60 [repr. in Finley 1981a: 24-40; 1986a: 161-77]

Finley, M.I. (1975) *The Ancient Greeks*, rev. edn, Harmondsworth

Finley, M.I. (1976) 'The freedom of the citizen in the Greek world', *Talanta* 7: 1-23 [repr. in Finley 1981a: 77-96]

Finley, M.I. (1977a) 'The ancient city: from Fustel de Coulanges to Max Weber and beyond', *CSSH* 19: 305-27 [repr. in Finley 1981a: 3-23]

Finley, M.I. (1977b) 'Aulos Kapreilios Timotheos, slave trader' in his *Aspects of Antiquity*, rev. edn, Harmondsworth: 154-66

Finley, M.I. (1978) *The World of Odysseus*, 2nd edn, London

Finley, M.I. (1979) 'Slavery and the historians', *Histoire sociale – Social History* 12: 247-61 [repr. in Finley 1980/1998: 285-309, and in French trans. in Finley 1981b: 41-62]

Finley, M.I. (1980/1998) *Ancient Slavery and Modern Ideology*, original edn London, repr. in expanded edn, ed. B.D. Shaw, Princeton

Finley, M.I. (1981a) *Economy and Society in Ancient Greece*, ed. B.D. Shaw & R.P. Saller, London [repr. Harmondsworth 1983]

Finley, M.I. (1981b) *Mythe, mémoire, histoire*, ed. F. Hartog, Paris

Finley, M.I. (1981c) 'The elderly in classical antiquity', *G&R* n.s. 28: 156-71

Finley, M.I. (1982) 'Problems of slave society: some reflections on the debate', *Opus* 1: 201-11 [repr. in Finley 1980/1998: 265-84]

Finley, M.I. (1983) *Politics in the Ancient World*, Cambridge

Finley, M.I. (1985a) *The Ancient Economy*, 2nd edn, California & London [repr. with new intro. by I. Morris, California 1999]

Finley, M.I. (1985b) *Ancient History: Evidence and Models*, London

Finley, M.I. (1985c) 'Censorship in Classical Antiquity' (1977), repr. in *Democracy Ancient and Modern*, 2nd edn, London, 142-72

Finley, M.I. (1985d) 'Town and country' in Finley 1985a: 123-49

Finley, M.I. (1986a) *The Use and Abuse of History*, 2nd edn, London

Finley, M.I. (1986b) 'Anthropology and the Classics' (1972) in Finley 1986a: 102-19

Finley, M.I. (1986c) 'Archaeology and History' (1971) in Finley 1986a: 87-101

Finley, M.I. (1986d) 'Generalizations in ancient history' (1963), rev. repr. in Finley 1986a: 60-74

Finley, M.I. (1968) ed. *Slavery in Classical Antiquity*, Cambridge

Finley, M.I. (1974) ed. *Studies in Ancient Society*, London

Fisher, N. & H. Van Wees (1998) eds *Archaic Greece: New Approaches and New Evidence*, London

Fitzhardinge, L.F. (1980) *The Spartans*, London

Flacelière, R. (1948) 'Sur quelques passages des *Vies* de Plutarque', *REG* 41: 67-103, 391-429

Flacelière, R. (1962) 'D'un certain féminisme grec', *REA* 64: 109-16

Flacelière, R. (1971) 'Le féminisme dans l'ancienne Athènes', *CRAI*: 698-706

Bibliography

Flaig, E. (1993) 'Die spartanische Abstimmung nach der Lautstärke. Überlegungen zu Thukydides 1.87', *Historia* 42: 139-60

Flory, T. (1979) 'Fugitive slaves and free society: the case of Brazil', *Journal of Negro History* 44: 116-30

Flower, M. (1988) 'Agesilaus of Sparta and the origins of the ruler cult', *CQ* n.s. 38: 123-34

Förtsch, R. (1994) 'Kunstverwendung und Kunstlegitimation im archaischen und frühklassischen Sparta', Habilitationsschrift Köln

Fogel, R.W. & S.L. Engerman (1974) *Time on the Cross: The Economics of American Negro Slavery*, 2 vols, Boston

Foner, L. & E.D. Genovese (1969) eds *Slavery in the New World: A Reader in Comparative History*, Englewood Cliffs, N.J.

Ford, C.S. & F.A. Beach (1952) *Patterns of Sexual Behaviour*, London

Fornara, C.W. (1983) *Archaic Times to the End of the Peloponnesian War*, 2nd edn, Cambridge

Forrest, W.G. (1963) 'The date of the Lykourgan reforms in Sparta', *Phoenix* 17: 157-79

Forrest, W.G. (1968) *A History of Sparta 950-192 BC*, London [repr. 1980]

Forsdyke, E.J. (1957) *Greece before Homer*, London

Fortenbaugh, W.W. (1977) 'Aristotle on slaves and women' in J. Barnes, M. Schofield & R. Sorabji eds *Articles on Aristotle*, 4 vols, London, vol. 2: 135-9

Foucault, M. (1985) *The History of Sexuality* vol. 2, London [French original, Paris 1984]

Fox, R. (1967) *Kinship and Marriage*, Harmondsworth

Foxhall, L. & J. Salmon (1998) eds *Thinking Men: Masculinity and its Self-representation in the Classical Tradition*, London & New York

Foxhall, L. & J. Salmon (1999) eds *When Men Were Men. Masculinity, Power and Identity in Classical Antiquity*, London & New York

Francis, E.D. (1991-3) 'Brachylogia laconica: Spartan speeches in Thucydides', *BICS* 38: 198-212

French, V. (1997) 'The Spartan family and the Spartan decline: changes in child-rearing practices and failure to reform' in Hamilton & Krentz eds 1997: 241-74

Freyre, G. (1946) *Masters and Slaves*, New York

Frost, F.J. (1984) 'The Athenian military before Cleisthenes', *Historia* 33: 283-94

Fuks, A. (1968) 'Slave war and slave troubles in Chios in the third century BC', *Athenaeum* n.s. 46: 102-11 [repr. in Fuks 1984]

Fuks, A. (1984) *Social Conflict in Ancient Greece*, Leiden & Jerusalem

Galenson, D.W. (1981) 'White servitude and the growth of black slavery in Colonial America', *Journal of Economic History* 46: 39-47

Gallo, L. (1984) 'La donna greca e marginalità', *QUCC* 47: 7-51

Gareau, E. (1972) ed. *Classical Values and the Modern World*, Ottawa

Garlan, Y. (1972) *La Guerre dans l'antiquité*, Paris [abridged Eng. trans. 1975]

Garlan, Y. (1988) *Slavery in Ancient Greece*, Ithaca & London [French original 1982]

Garlan, Y. (1989) *Guerre et économie en Grèce ancienne*, Paris

Garlan, Y. & O. Masson (1982) 'Les acclamations pédérastiques de Kalami (Thasos)', *BCH* 106: 3-22

Garland, R. (1989) 'The well-ordered corpse. An investigation into the motives behind Greek funerary legislation', *BICS* 36: 1-15

Garland, R. (1990) *The Greek Way of Life: From Conception to Old Age*, London

Garland, R. (1995) *In the Eye of the Beholder: Deformity and Disability in the Graeco-Roman World*, London.

Bibliography

Garnsey, P.D.A. (1985) 'Grain for Athens' in Cartledge & Harvey eds 1985: 62-75 [repr. with add. in Garnsey 1998: 183-200]

Garnsey, P.D.A. (1998) *Cities, Peasants and Food in Classical Antiquity: Essays in Social and Economic History*, ed. W. Scheidel, Cambridge

Garnsey, P.D.A. (1980) ed. *Non-slave Labour in the Greco-Roman World*, Cambridge

Gauthier, P. (1976) *Un commentaire historique des Poroi de Xénophon*, Paris

Gawantka, W. (1985) *Die sogenannte Polis: Entstehung, Geschichte und Kritik der modernen althistorischen Grundbegriffe der griechische Staat, die griechische Staatsidee, die Polis*, Stuttgart

Geddes, A.G. (1984) 'Who's who in Homeric society', *CQ* n.s. 34: 17-36

Geertz, C. (1983) 'Centers, kings, and charisma: reflections on the dynamics of power' (1977), repr. in *Local Knowledge: Further Essays in Interpretive Anthropology*, New York & London: 121-46

Gehrke, H.J. (1987) *Jenseits von Athen und Sparta: Das Dritte Griechenland und seine Staatenwelt*, Munich

Gennep, A. van (1909) *Les rites de passage*, Paris [Eng. trans. *The Rites of Passage*, trans. G.L. Kaffee & M.B. Vizedom, London, 1960]

Genovese, E.D. (1975) *Roll, Jordan, Roll: The World the Slaves Made*, London [U.S. edn 1974]

Genovese, E.D. (1979) *From Rebellion to Revolution: Afro-American Slave Revolts in the Making of the Modern World*, Baton Rouge & London

Georges, P. (1994) *Barbarian Asia and the Greek Experience: From the Archaic Period to the Age of Xenophon*, Baltimore & London

Germain, L.R.F. (1969), 'Aspects du droit d'exposition en Grèce', *RD* 4th ser. 47: 177-97

Gernet, L. (1933) *Le génie grec dans la religion*, Paris [repr. with bibl. add. 1970]

Gernet, L. (1968) 'Mariages de tyrans' (1954), repr. in *Anthropologie de la Grèce antique*, ed. J.-P. Vernant, Paris: 344-59

Gibbon, E. (1972) *English Essays*, ed. P.B. Craddock, Oxford

Gilbert, G. (1895) *Greek Constitutional Antiquities* I, 2nd edn, London

Gilmour, A.-T. (1978) ed. *Revisiting Blassingame's 'The Slave Community': The Scholars Respond*, Westport

Glotz, G. (1906) 'L'exposition des enfants' in *Etudes sociales et juridiques sur l'antiquité grecque*, Paris: 187-227

Golden, M. (1990) *Children and Childhood in Classical Athens*, Baltimore & London

Golden, M. (1992) 'The uses of cross-cultural comparison in ancient social history', *EMC/CV* 11: 309-31

Golden, M. (1998) *Sport and Society in Ancient Greece*, Cambridge

Goldhill, S.D. (1986) *Reading Greek Tragedy*, Cambridge [corr. impr. 1988]

Goldhill, S. and Osborne, R. (1994) eds *Art and Text in Ancient Greek Culture*, Cambridge

Goldsworthy, A.K. (1997) 'The *othismos*, myths and heresies: the nature of hoplite battle', *War in History* 4: 1-26

Gomme, A.W. (1945) *A Historical Commentary on Thucydides* I, Oxford

Goody, J. (1976) 'Inheritance, property and women: some comparative considerations' in Goody, Thirsk & Thompson eds 1976: 10-36

Goody, J. & I. Watt (1968) 'The consequences of literacy' (1962/3), repr. in Goody ed. 1968: 28-68

Goody, J. (1968) ed. *Literacy in Traditional Societies*, Cambridge

Bibliography

Goody, J., J. Thirsk & E.P. Thompson (1976) eds *Family and Inheritance: Rural Society in Western Europe 1200-1800*, Cambridge

Gordon, R.L. (1981) ed. *Myth, Religion and Society. Structuralist essays by M. Detienne, L. Gernet, J.-P. Vernant and P. Vidal-Naquet*, Cambridge

Gouldner, A.W. (1965) *Enter Plato: Classical Greece and the Origins of Social Theory*, New York [2nd edn 1967]

Graf, F. (1979) 'Apollon Delphinios', *MH* 36: 381-96

Graham, A.J. & G. Forsyth (1984) 'A new slogan for oligarchy in Thucydides III.82.6', *HSPh* 88: 24-45

Gray, V.J. (1994) 'Images of Sparta: writer and audience in Isocrates' *Panathenaicus'* in Powell & Hodkinson eds 1994: 223-71

Green, P. (1985) *Retrieving Democracy: In Search of Civic Equality*, London

Greenhalgh, P.A.L. (1973) *Early Greek Warfare: Horsemen and Chariots in the Homeric and Archaic Ages*, Cambridge

Greenhalgh, P.A.L. (1978) 'How are the mighty fallen?', *AClass* 21: 1-38

Greenidge, A.H.J. (1896) *A Handbook of Greek Constitutional History*, London

Griffiths, A.H. (1972) 'Alcman's *Partheneion*: the morning after the night before', *QUCC* 14: 1-30

Griffiths, A. H. (1989) 'Was Kleomenes mad?' in Powell ed. 1989: 51-78

Groeschel, S.-G. (1989) *Waffenbesitz und Waffeneinsatz bei den Griechen*, Frankfurt/Main

Grote, G. (1888) *History of Greece*, 10-vol. edn, London

Gschnitzer, F. (1963-76) *Studien zur griechischen Terminologie der Sklaverei* I-II, Wiesbaden

Gschnitzer, F. (1978) *Ein neuer spartanischer Staatsvertrag und die Verfassung des Peloponnesischen Bundes*, Meisenheim am Glan

Gschnitzer, F. (1991) 'Zum Verhältnis von Siedlung, Gemeinde und Staat in der griechischen Welt' in E. Olshausen & H. Sonnabend eds *Stuttgarter Kolloquium zur historischen Geographie des Altertums* 3, Bonn: 429-42

Guiraud, P. (1893) *La propriété foncière en Grèce jusqu'à la conquête romaine*, Paris

Gutman, H.G. (1975) *Slavery and the Numbers Game: A Critique of 'Time on the Cross'*, Urbana

Gutman, H.G. (1976) *The Black Family in Slavery and Freedom*, New York

Gutmann, A. (1980) *Liberal Equality*, Cambridge

Hackett, J. (1989) ed. *Warfare in the Ancient World*, London

Häfner, U. (1965) 'Das Kunstschaffen Lakoniens in archaischer Zeit', diss. Münster

Hägg, R. & N. Marinatos (1983) eds *The Greek Renaissance of the Eighth Century BC: Tradition and Innovation*, Stockholm

Hall, E. (1989) *Inventing the Barbarian: Greek Self-definition through Tragedy*, Oxford

Hall, J.M. (2000) 'Sparta, Lakedaimon and the nature of Perioikic dependency' in P. Flensted-Jensen ed. *Further Studies in the Ancient Greek Polis* (*Historia Einzelschrift 139*), Stuttgart: 73-89

Halperin, D.M. (1986) 'Plato and erotic reciprocity', *CA* 5: 60-80

Halperin, D.M. (1990) *One Hundred Years of Homosexuality and Other Essays on Greek Love*, New York & London

Hamilton, C.D. (1987) 'Social tensions in Classical Sparta', *Ktema* 12: 31-41

Hamilton, C.D. (1991) *Agesilaus and the Failure of Spartan Hegemony*, Ithaca & London

Hamilton, C.D. & P. Krentz (1997) eds *Polis and Polemos: Essays on Politics, War and History in Ancient Greece in honor of Donald Kagan*, Claremont, CA

243

Bibliography

Hammond, M. (1972) *The City in the Ancient World*, Cambridge, MA

Hammond, N.G.L. (1973) *Studies in Greek History*, Oxford

Hansen, M.H. (1987) *The Athenian Assembly in the Age of Demosthenes*, Oxford

Hansen, M.H. (1995) 'Kome. A study in how the Greeks designated and classified settlements which were not poleis' in Hansen & Raaflaub eds 1995: 45-81

Hansen, M.H. (1996) 'The ancient Athenian and the modern liberal view of liberty as a democratic ideal' in Ober & Hedrick eds 1996: 91-104

Hansen, M.H. (1998) *Polis and City State: An Ancient Concept and its Modern Equivalent*, Copenhagen

Hansen, M.H. (1999) *The Athenian Democracy in the Age of Demosthenes*, rev. edn, Bristol & London

Hansen, M.H. (1993) ed. *The Ancient Greek City-State*, Copenhagen

Hansen, M.H. & K.A. Raaflaub (1995) eds *Studies in the Ancient Greek Polis*, *Historia* Einzelschrift 95, Stuttgart

Hanson, R.L. (1988) 'Democracy' in T. Ball, J. Farr & R.L. Hanson eds *Political Innovation and Conceptual Change*, Cambridge: 68-89

Hanson, V.D. (1983) *Warfare and Agriculture in Classical Greece*, Pisa [rev. edn, California 1998]

Hanson, V.D. (1989) *The Western Way of War: Infantry Battle in Classical Greece*, New York [rev. edn, California 2000]

Hanson, V.D. (1991) 'Hoplite technology in phalanx battle' in Hanson ed. 1991: 63-84

Hanson, V.D. (1996) 'Hoplites into democrats: the changing ideology of Athenian infantry' in Ober & Hedrick eds 1996: 289-312

Hanson, V.D. (1991) ed. *Hoplites: The Classical Greek Battle Experience*, London & New York

Harris, W.V. (1989) *Ancient Literacy*, Cambridge, MA

Harrison, A.R.W. (1968) *The Law of Athens: The Family and Property*, Oxford

Hartley, E.L. & R.E. Hartley (1952) *Fundamentals of Social Psychology*, New York

Hartog, F. (1988) *The Mirror of Herodotus*, California & London [French original 1980; new French edn 1991]

Harvey, F.D. (1965) 'Two kinds of equality', *C&M* 26: 101-46 [corrigenda, *C&M* 27 (1966): 99-100]

Harvey, F.D. (1966) 'Literacy in the Athenian democracy', *REG* 79: 585-635

Havelock, E.A (1972) 'War as a way of life in Classical culture' in Gareau ed. 1972: 19-78

Havelock, E.A. (1982) *The Literate Revolution in Ancient Greece and its Cultural Consequences*, Princeton

Headlam, J.W. (1933) *Election by Lot at Athens*, 2nd edn, Cambridge

Heilmeyer, W.D. (1979) *Olympische Forschungen* XII, Munich

Heilmeyer, W.D. (1992) ed. *Euphronios und seine Zeit*, Berlin

Heitland, W.E. (1921) *Agricola: A Study of Agriculture and Rustic Life in the Greco-Roman World from the Point of View of Labour*, Cambridge

Henderson, J. (1991) *The Maculate Muse: Obscene Language in Attic Comedy*, 2nd edn, New York

Henige, D.P. (1982) *Oral Historiography*, London, New York & Lagos

Herdt, G.H. (1980) *Guardians of the Flutes: Idioms of Masculinity*, New York & London

Herdt, G.H. (1985) ed. *Ritualized Homosexuality in Melanesia*, Berkeley

Herfort-Koch, M. (1986) *Archaische Bronzeplastik Lakoniens*, Münster

Herfst, P. (1922) *Le travail de la femme dans le Grèce ancienne*, Paris

Herman, G. (1987) *Ritualised Friendship and the Greek City*, Cambridge

Bibliography

Herrmann, H.-V. (1964) 'Werkstätten geometrischer Bronzeplastik', *JDAI* 79: 17-71

Herrmann-Otto, E. (1998) 'Verfassung und Gesellschaft Spartas in der Kritik des Aristoteles', *Historia* 47: 18-40

Hiersche, R. (1970) *Grundzüge der griechischen Sprachgeschichte bis zur klassischen Zeit*, Wiesbaden

Higgins, W.E. (1977) *Xenophon the Athenian: The Problem of the Individual and the Society of the Polis*, Albany

Hill, G.F. (1951) *Sources for Greek History Between the Persian and Peloponnesian Wars*, ed. R. Meiggs & A. Andrewes, Oxford

Hirsch, E. & M. O'Hanlon (1995) eds *The Anthropology of Landscape: Perspectives on Place and Space*, Oxford

Hirschfeld, M. (1920) *Die Homosexualität des Mannes und des Weibes*, 2nd edn, Berlin

Hoben, W. (1978) *Terminologische Studien zu den Sklavenerhebungen der römischen Republik*, Wiesbaden

Hobsbawm, E.J. (1971) 'Social history to the history of society', *Daedalus* 100: 20-45

Hodkinson, S. (1983) 'Social order and the conflict of values in Classical Sparta', *Chiron* 13: 239-81

Hodkinson, S. (1986) 'Land tenure and inheritance in Classical Sparta', *CQ* n.s. 36: 378-406

Hodkinson, S. (1989) 'Inheritance, marriage and demography: perspectives upon the decline and success of Classical Sparta' in Powell ed. 1989: 79-121

Hodkinson, S. (1996) 'Spartan society in the fourth century: crisis and continuity' in P. Carlier ed. *Le IVe siècle av. J.-C. Approches historiographiques*, Paris, 85-101

Hodkinson, S. (1997a) 'Servile and free dependants of the classical Spartan "oikos" ' in M. Moggi & G. Cordiano eds *Schiavi e Dipendenti nell' ambito dell' 'oikos' e della 'familia'*, Pisa: 45-71

Hodkinson, S. (1997b) 'The development of Spartan society and institutions in the archaic period' in Mitchell & Rhodes eds 1997: 83-102

Hodkinson, S. (1998) 'Patterns of bronze dedications at Spartan sanctuaries, c. 650-350 BC: towards a quantified database of material and religious investment' in Cavanagh & Walker eds 1998: 55-63

Hodkinson, S. (1999a) 'An agonistic culture? Athletic competition in archaic and classical Spartan society' in Hodkinson & Powell eds 1999: 147-87

Hodkinson, S. (1999b) 'Introduction' in Hodkinson & Powell eds 1999: ix-xxvi

Hodkinson, S. (2000) *Property and Wealth in Classical Sparta*, London

Hodkinson, S. & C.A. Powell (1999) eds *Sparta: New Perspectives*, London

Hoffmann, H. (1994) *'Dulce et decorum est pro patria mori*: Heroic immortality imagery on Greek painted vases' in Goldhill & Osborne eds 1994: 28-51

Hogg, P. (1979) *Slavery: The Afro-American Experience*, London

Hölkeskamp, K.-J. (1992) 'Written law in Archaic Greece', *PCPhS* n.s. 38: 87-117

Holladay, A.J. (1977) 'Spartan austerity', *CQ* n.s. 27: 111-26

Holladay, A.J. (1982) 'Hoplites and heresies', *JHS* 102: 94-103

Holmes, R. (1974) *Shelley: The Pursuit*, London

Holmes, R. (1980) ed. *Shelley on Love*, London

Hönle, A. (1968) 'Olympia in der Politik der griechischen Staatenwelt, von 776 bis zum Ende des 5. Jahrhunderts', diss. Tübingen

Hooker, J.T. (1980) *The Ancient Spartans*, London

Bibliography

Hopkins, M.K. (1965) 'The age of Roman girls at marriage', *Population Studies* 18: 309-27

Hopkins, M.K. (1966) 'On the probable age structure of the Roman population', *Population Studies* 20: 245-64

Hopkins, M.K. (1978a) *Conquerors and Slaves (Sociological Studies in Roman History* I), Cambridge

Hopkins, M.K. (1978b) 'Economic growth and towns in classical antiquity' in P. Abrams & E.A. Wrigley eds *Towns in Societies: Essays in Economic History and Historical Sociology*, Cambridge: 35-77

Hubbard, T.K. (1998) 'Popular perceptions of elite homosexuality in classical Athens', *Arion* 6: 48-78

Hume, D. (1963) 'Of the populousness of ancient nations' in *Essays Moral, Political and Literary*, Oxford: 381-451 [orig. publ. 1742]

Humble, N. (1999) '*Sophrosynê* and the Spartans in Xenophon' in Hodkinson & Powell eds 1999, 339-54

Humphreys, S.C. (1973) Review of Vatin 1970, *JHS* 93: 258-9

Humphreys, S.C. (1978) *Anthropology and the Greeks*, London, Henley & Boston

Hunt, P. (1998) *Slaves, Warfare, and Ideology in the Greek Historians*, Cambridge

Hurwit, J. (1985). *Art and Culture of Early Greece, 1100-480 BC*, Ithaca

Huxley, G.L. (1962) *Early Sparta*, London

Huxley, G.L. (1971) 'Crete in Aristotle's *Politics*', *GRBS* 12: 505-15

Huxley, G.L. (1973) 'Aristotle as antiquary', *GRBS* 14: 271-86

Huxley, G.L. (1979) *On Aristotle and Greek Society*, Belfast

Jacob, O. (1928) *Les esclaves publics à Athènes*, Liège

James, C.L.R. (1980) *The Black Jacobins: Toussaint L'Ouverture and the San Domingo Revolution*, rev. edn, London

Jameson, M.H. (1977-8) 'Agriculture and slavery in classical Athens', *CJ* 73: 122-45

Jameson, M.H. (1991) 'Sacrifice before battle' in Hanson ed. 1991: 197-227

Jameson, M.H., C.N. Runnels & T.H. van Andel (1994, 1995) *A Greek Countryside: The Southern Argolid from Prehistory to the Present Day*, Stanford & Cambridge

Jannet, C. (1880) *Les institutions sociales et le droit civile à Sparte*, 2nd edn, Paris

Jeanmaire, H. (1913) 'La cryptie lacédémonienne', *REG* 26: 121-50

Jeanmaire, H. (1939) *Couroi et Courètes: Essai sur l'éducation spartiate et sur les rites d'adolescence dans l'antiquité grecque*, Lille

Jeffery, L.H. (1961) *The Local Scripts of Archaic Greece*, Oxford [rev. edn by A.W. Johnston 1990]

Jeffery, L.H. (1967) '*Archaia grammata*: some ancient Greek views' in W.C. Brice ed. *Europa: Studien zur Geschichte und Epigraphik der frühen Ägäis. Festschrift für Ernst Grumach*, Berlin: 152-66

Jeffery, L.H. (1976) *Archaic Greece: The City-States c. 700-500 BC*, London

Jenkyns, R. (1980) *The Victorians and Ancient Greece*, Oxford

Jocelyn, H.D. (1980) 'A Greek indecency and its students: *laikazein*', *PCPhS* n.s. 26: 12-66

Jones, A.H.M. (1956) 'Slavery in the ancient world', *Economic History Review* 2nd ser. 9: 185-99 [repr. in Finley ed. 1968: 1-15]

Jones, A.H.M. (1957) *Athenian Democracy*, Oxford

Jones, A.H.M. (1967) *Sparta*, Oxford

Jones, P.V. (1984) ed. *The World of Athens*, Cambridge

Jordan, B. (1990), 'The ceremony of the Helots in Thucydides IV.80.4', *AC* 59: 37-69

Bibliography

Jost, M. (1975) 'Statuettes de bronze archaïques provenant de Lykosoura', *BCH* 99: 339-64

Just, R. (1975) 'Conceptions of women in Classical Athens', *Journal of the Anthropological Society of Oxford* 6: 153-70

Just, R. (1985) 'Freedom, slavery and the female psyche in the ancient Athenian world' in Cartledge & Harvey eds 1985: 169-88

Just, R. (1990) *Women in Athenian Law and Life*, London & New York

Karageorgha, T. (1965) '*Lakôniko katoptro sto mouseio tîs Spartîs*', *AD* 20: 96-109

Karsch-Haack, F. (1911) *Forschungen über gleichgeschlechtliche Liebe* I. *Das gleichgeschlechtliche Liebe der Naturvölker*, Berlin

Kautsky, J.H. (1983) *The Politics of Aristocratic Empires*, Chapel Hill, N.C.

Keaney, J.J. (1970) 'The date of Aristotle's *Athenaiôn Politeia*', *Historia* 19: 326-36

Kelly, T. (1985) 'The Spartan skutale' in J.W. Eadie & J. Ober eds *The Craft of the Ancient Historian: Essays in Honor of C.G. Starr*, Lanham, MD: 141-69

Kennell, N.M. (1995) *The Gymnasium of Virtue: Education and Culture in Ancient Sparta*, Chapel Hill & London

Kerferd, G.B. (1981) *The Sophistic Movement*, Cambridge

Kessler, E. (1910) *Plutarchs Leben des Lykurgos*, Berlin

Kiechle, F. (1966) 'Die Ausprägung der Sage von der Rückkehr der Herakliden', *Helikon* 6: 493-517

Kienast, D. (1973) 'Presbeia', *RE* Supp. XIII: 499-628

King, H. (1986) 'Agnodike and the profession of medicine', *PCPhS* n.s. 32: 53-77

Kirk, G.S. (1968) 'War and the warrior in the Homeric poems' in Vernant ed. 1968: 93-119

Kirsten, E. (1956) *Die griechische Polis als geographisch-historisches Problem des Mittelmeerraumes*, Bonn

Kirsten, E. (1984) *Landschaft und Geschichte in der antiken Welt*, Bonn

Knauth, W. (1933) 'Die spartanische Knabenerziehung im Licht der Völkerkunde', *Zeitschrift für Geschichte der Erziehung und des Unterrichts* 23: 151-85

Koch-Harnack, G. (1983) *Knabenliebe und Tiergeschenke*, Berlin

Konstan, D. (1997) *Friendship in Classical Antiquity*, Cambridge

Krentz, P. (1985) 'The nature of hoplite battle', *CA* 4: 50-61

Kretschmer, E. (1930) 'Beiträge zur Wortgeographie der altgriechischen Dialekte', *Glotta* 18: 67-100

Kufofka, D. (1993) 'Die Paidiskoi im System der spartanischen Altenklasse', *Philologus* 137: 197-205

Kunstler, B.L. (1983) 'Women and the Development of the Spartan Polis: A Study of Sex Roles in Classical Antiquity', diss. Boston University

Kunstler, B.L. (1987) 'Family dynamics and female power in ancient Sparta' in M. Skinner ed. *Rescuing Creusa: New Methodological Approaches to Women in Antiquity* (*Helios* Supp. 13.2), Austin, TX: 32-48

Kurtz, D.C. & J. Boardman (1971) *Greek Burial Customs*, London & New York

Lacey, W.K. (1968) *The Family in Classical Greece*, London [repr. Auckland 1980]

Laix, R.A. de (1974) 'Aristotle's conception of the Spartan constitution', *JHPh* 12: 21-30

Landtman, G. (1927) *The Kiwai Papuans of British New Guinea: A Nature-born Instance of Rousseau's Ideal Community*, London

Lane, A. (1971) ed. *The Debate over Slavery: Stanley Elkins and his Critics*, Urbana, Chicago & London

Lamb, W.M. (1929) *Greek and Roman Bronzes*, London [repr. with add. Chicago 1969]

Lang, M. (1974) *Graffiti in the Athenian Agora*, Agora Picture Book, Princeton

Bibliography

Larmour, D., P.A. Miller & C. Platter (1997) eds *Rethinking Sexuality: Foucault and Classical Antiquity*, Princeton

Larsen, J.A.O. (1949) 'The origin and significance of the counting of votes', *CPh* 44: 164-81

Larsen, J.A.O. (1968) *Greek Federal States*, Oxford

Lasserre, F. (1976) 'Hérodote et Protagoras: le débat sur les constitutions', *MH* 33: 65-84

Latacz, J. (1977) *Kampfparänese, Kampfdarstellung und Kampfwirklichkeit in der Ilias, bei Kallinos und Tyrtaios*, Munich

Latacz, J. (1991) ed. *Zweihundert Jahre Homer-Forschung: Rückblick und Ausblick*, Stuttgart

Lauffer, S. (1979) *Die Bergwerkssklaven von Laureion*, 2nd edn, 2 vols, Wiesbaden

Lawler, D.L. (1988) ed. *The 'Picture of Dorian Gray': Authoritative Texts, Background, Reviews, Reactions, Criticism*, New York & London

Layard, J. (1942) *The Stone Men of Malekula*, London

Lazenby, J.F. (1985) *The Spartan Army*, Warminster

Lazenby, J.F. (1989), 'Hoplite warfare' in Hackett ed. 1989: 54-81

Lazenby, J. & D. Whitehead (1996), 'The myth of the hoplite's *hoplon*', *CQ* n.s. 46: 27-33

Leach, E.R. (1971) 'Polyandry, inheritance and the definition of marriage' in J. Goody ed. *Kinship*, Harmondsworth: 151-62

Lee, S. (1990) *The Cost of Free Speech*, London

Leigh Fermor, P. (1958) *Mani*, London

Leimbach, R. (1980), Review of Latacz 1977, *Gnomon* 52: 418-25

Leitao, D. (1995), 'The perils of Leukippos: *initiatory transvestism* and male gender ideology in the Ekdusia at Phaistos', *CA* 14: 130-63

Leontis, A. (1995) *Topographies of Hellenism*, Ithaca & London

Lendon, J.E. (1997) 'Spartan honor', in Hamilton & Krentz eds 1997: 105-25

Lepore, E. (1978) 'Città-stato e movimenti coloniali: struttura economica e dinamica sociale' in R. Bianchi Bandinelli ed. *Storia e Civiltà dei Greci* I, Milan: 183-253

Levi, P. (1987) *If This Is a Man* and *The Truce*, London [Italian originals 1947 & 1963]

Levine, L.W. (1977) *Black Culture and Black Consciousness: Afro-American Folk Thought from Slavery to Freedom*, New York

Levine, L.W. (1979) 'Slave songs and slave consciousness: an exploration in neglected sources' in Weinstein, Gatell & Sarasohn eds 1979: 143-72

Lévy, E. (1977) 'La grande rhètra', *Ktema* 2: 85-103

Lewis, D.M. (1959) 'Attic manumissions', *Hesperia* 28: 208-38

Lewis, D.M. (1968) 'Dedications of *phialai* at Athens', *Hesperia* 37: 368-80

Lewis, D.M. (1977) *Sparta and Persia*, Leiden

Lewis, N. (1974) *Papyrus in Classical Antiquity*, Oxford

Leyden, W. von (1985) *Aristotle on Equality and Justice*, London

Link, S. (1994) *Der Kosmos Sparta*, Darmstadt

Link, S. (1999) 'Der geliebte Burger: paideia und paidika in Sparta und Kreta', *Philologus* 143: 3-25

Lintott, A.W. (1982) *Violence, Civil Strife and Revolution in the Classical City 750-330 BC*, London & Canberra

Lipka, M. (forthcoming) *Xenophon's Lakedaimonion Politeia. Introduction. Text. Commentary*

Lissarrague, F. (1989) 'The world of the warrior' in Bérard ed. 1989: 39-52

248

Bibliography

Lissarrague, F. (1990a) *The Aesthetics of the Greek Banquet*, Princeton [French original 1987]

Lissarrague, F. (1990b) *L'Autre Guerrier: Archers, peltastes, cavaliers dans l'imagerie attique*, Paris & Rome

Lloyd, G.E.R. (1983) *Science, Folklore and Ideology: Studies in the Life Sciences in Ancient Greece*, Cambridge

Lloyd, G.E.R. (1991) *Methods and Problems in Ancient Science*, Cambridge

Lonis, R. (1979) *Guerre et religion en Grèce à l'époque classique*, Paris

Loraux, N. (1986) *The Invention of Athens: The History of the Funeral Oration in the Classical City*, trans. A. Sheridan, Cambridge, MA [French original 1981]

Loraux, N. (1993) *The Children of Athena*, trans. C. Levine, Princeton [French original 1984]

Lorimer, H.L. (1947) 'The hoplite phalanx, with special reference to the poems of Archilochus and Tyrtaeus', *ABSA* 42: 76-138

Losemann, V. (1977) *Nationalsozialismus und Antike*, Hamburg

Lotze, D. (1959) *Metaxy Eleutheron kai Doulon: Studien zur Rechtsstellung unfreier Landbevölkerungen in Griechenland bis zum 4. Jahrhundert v. Chr.*, Berlin

Lotze, D. (1962) '*Mothakes*', *Historia* 11: 427-35

Lotze, D. (1990-2) 'Die sogenannte Polis', *AAntHung* 33: 237-42

Lotze, D. (1994) 'Bürger zweiter Klasse: Spartas Periöken. Ihre Stellung und Funktion im Staat der Lakedaimonier' in *Sitzungsberichte der Akademie der Wissenschaften zu Erfurt, Geistwissenschaftliche Klasse 1994*: 37-51

Lovejoy, P.E. (1982) 'The volume of the Atlantic slave trade', *Journal of African History* 23: 473-501

Lukes, S. (1991) 'Equality and liberty: must they conflict?' in D. Held ed. *Political Theory Today*, Oxford: 48-66

Lupi, M. (2000) *L'ordine delle generazioni. Classi di età e costumi matrimoniali nell'antica Sparta*, Bari

McCarter, P.K. jr. (1975) *The Antiquity of the Greek Alphabet and the Early Phoenician Scripts*, Missoula

MacDowell, D.M. (1971) ed. *Aristophanes Wasps*, Oxford

MacDowell, D.M. (1986) *Spartan Law*, Edinburgh

McQueen, E.I. (1990) 'The Eurypontid house in Hellenistic Sparta', *Historia* 39: 163-81

Mactoux, M. (1980) *Douleia: esclavage et pratiques discursives dans l'Athènes classique*, Paris

Mahaffy, J.P. (1874) *Social Life in Greece from Homer to Menander*, London

Maier, W. (1984) *Oscar Wilde. 'The Picture of Dorian Gray': eine kritische Analyse der anglistischen Forschung von 1962 bis 1982*, Frankfurt

Mair, L. (1970) *Marriage*, Harmondsworth

Malkin, I. (1994) *Myth and Territory in the Spartan Mediterranean*, Cambridge

Mallwitz, A. (1972) 'Zu den Arbeiten im Heiligtum von Olympia während der Jahre 1967 bis 1971', *AD* 27: 272-80

Manicas, P.T. (1982) 'War, *stasis* and Greek political thought', *CSSH* 24: 673-88

Manso, J.F.C. (1800) *Sparta*, 3 vols, Berlin

Marangou, E.-L.I. (1969) *Lakonische Elfenbein- und Beinschnitzereien*, Tübingen

Markle III, M.M. (1985) 'Jury pay and Assembly pay at Athens' in Cartledge & Harvey eds 1985: 264-97

Margreiter, I. (1988) *Frühe lakonische Keramik der geometrischen bis archaischen Zeit (10. bis 6. Jahrhundert v. Chr.)*, Bayern

Marrou, H.-I. (1971) *Histoire de l'éducation dans l'antiquité*, 7th edn, Paris

Bibliography

Martin, R. (1974) *L'urbanisme dans l'antiquité grecque*, 2nd edn, Paris

Mason, S. (1912) *Oscar Wilde: Art and Morality*, 2nd edn, London

Mason, S. (1914) *Bibliography of Oscar Wilde*, London

Masson, O. (1973) 'Les noms des esclaves dans la Grèce antique' in *Actes du Colloque 1971 sur l'esclavage*, Ann. litt. Univ. Besançon 140, Paris: 9-23

May, R.E. (1980) 'John A. Quitman and his slaves: reconciling slave resistance with the proslavery defense', *Journal of Southern History* 46: 551-70

Mayer, P. (1970) ed. *Socialization: The Approach from Social Anthropology*, London & New York

Meier, C. (1990) *The Greek Discovery of Politics*, trans. D. McLintock, Cambridge, MA [abridgement of 1980 German original]

Meier, C. (1994) ed. *Die Okzidentale Stadt nach Max Weber: Zum Problem der Zugehörigkeit in Antike und Mittelalter*, Munich

Meier, M. (1998) *Aristokraten und Damoden: Untersuchungen zur inneren Entwicklung Spartas im 7. Jahrhundert v. Chr. und zur politischen Funktion der Dichtung des Tyrtaios*, Stuttgart

Meier M.-H.-E. & L.R. de Pogey-Castries (1930) *Histoire de l'amour grec*, Paris [orig. pub. in J.S. Ersch & J.G. Gruber eds *Allgemeine Encylopädie der Wissenschaften und Künsten*, Leipzig, 1837, 3rd ser, vol. 9: 149-88]

Meiggs, R. & D.M. Lewis (1989) eds *A Selection of Greek Historical Inscriptions to the End of the Fifth Century BC*, rev. edn, Oxford

Mendus, S. (1992) 'Losing the faith: feminism and democracy' in J. Dunn ed. *Democracy: The Unfinished Journey 508 BC to AD 1993*, Oxford: 7-20

Mertens, N. (1999) 'Die Periöken Spartas', MA diss. Freie Universität Berlin

Meyer, E. (1892) *Forschungen zur alten Geschichte I*, Halle

Meyers, J. (1977) *Homosexuality and Literature 1870-1930*, London

Milani, P. (1972) *La schiavitù nel pensiero politico: dai Greci al Basso Medio Evo*, Milan

Millender, E.G. (1999) 'Athenian ideology and the empowered Spartan woman' in Hodkinson & Powell eds 1999: 355-91

Miller, D. (1990) 'The resurgence of political theory', *Political Studies* 38: 421-37

Miller, D.A. (1998) 'The Spartan kingship: some extended notes on complex duality', *Arethusa* 31: 1-17

Miller, F.D. jr (1995) *Nature, Justice and Rights in Aristotle's Politics*, Oxford

Miller, J.C. (1993-8) ed. *Slavery and Slaving in World History: A Bibliography* vol. I. *1900-1991*, Charlottesville, VA. II. *1992-1996*, Armonk, NY, & London

Millett, K. (1969) *Sexual Politics*, New York

Mintz, S.W. (1974) 'The Caribbean region', *Daedalus* 103: 45-71

Mitchell, L.G. & P.J. Rhodes (1997) eds *The Development of the Polis in Archaic Greece*, London & New York

Mitchell, S. (1996) 'Hoplite warfare in ancient Greece' in A.B. Lloyd ed. *Battle in Antiquity*, London: 87-105

Moggi, M. (1976) ed. *I sinecismi interstatali greci I. Dalle origini al 338 a.C.*, Pisa

Momigliano, A.D. (1966a) 'Some observations on causes of war in ancient historiography' (1958), repr. in his *Studies in Historiography*, London: 112-26

Momigliano, A.D. (1966b) 'The place of Herodotus in the history of historiography' (1958), repr. in his *Studies in Historiography*, London: 127-42

Momigliano, A.D. (1985) 'Marcel Mauss and the quest for the person in Greek biography and autobiography' in M. Carrithers, S. Collins & S. Lukes eds *The Category of the Person: Anthropology, Philosophy, History*, Cambridge: 83-92

Moore, B. jr. (1966) *Social Origins of Dictatorship and Democracy: Lord and*

Bibliography

Peasant in the Making of the Modern World, Boston [latest repr. Harmondsworth 1984]

Moore, J.M. (1983) *Aristotle and Xenophon on Democracy and Oligarchy*, 2nd edn, Cambridge

Morgan, C.A. (1990) *Athletes and Oracles: The Transformation of Olympia and Delphi in the Eighth Century BC*, Cambridge

Morgan, E.S. (1988) *Inventing the People: The Rise of Popular Sovereignty in England and America*, New York & London

Morley, N. (1999) *Writing Ancient History*, London

Morpurgo, A. (1963) *Mycenaeae Graecitatis Lexicon*, Rome

Morris, I.M. (1986) 'The use and abuse of Homer', *CA* 5: 81-138

Morris, I.M. (1987) *Burial and Ancient Society: The Rise of the Greek City-state*, Cambridge

Morris, I.M. (1991) 'The early *polis* as city and state' in Rich & Wallace-Hadrill eds 1991: 24-57

Morris, I.M. (1994) 'Everyman's grave' in A.L. Boegehold & A.C. Scafuro eds *Athenian Identity and Civic Ideology*, Baltimore & London: 67-101

Morris, I.M. (1996) 'The strong principle of equality and the archaic origins of Greek democracy' in Ober & Hedrick eds 1996: 19-48

Morris, I.M. (1998) 'Archaeology and Archaic Greek society' in Fisher & Van Wees eds 1998: 1-91

Morris, I.M. (2000) 'Equality for men' in *Archaeology as Cultural History*, Oxford, 109-54

Morris, S.P. (1992) *Daidalos and the Origins of Greek Art*, Princeton

Morrison, J.S., J.F. Coates & N.B. Rankov (2000) *The Athenian Trireme: The History and Reconstruction of an Ancient Warship*, 2nd edn, Cambridge

Moscati Castelnuovo, L. (1991) 'Iloti e fondazione di Taranto', *Latomus* 50: 64-79

Mosley, D.J. (1979) 'Spartanische Diplomatie' in E. Olshausen ed. *Antike Diplomatie* (Wege der Forschung 462), Darmstadt: 183-203

Mossé, C. (1964) 'Un tyran grec à l'époque hellénistique: Nabis, "roi" de Sparte', *CH* 9: 313-23

Mossé, C. (1991) 'Women in the Spartan revolutions of the third century BC' in S. Pomeroy ed. *Women's History and Ancient History*, Chapel Hill & London: 138-53

Müller, K.O. (1839) *The History and Antiquities of the Doric Race* II, 2nd edn, London

Müller, R. (1991) 'Literarische Kommunikation in Griechenland in 5. und 4. Jahrhundert v. u. Z.', *Philologus* 135: 4-23

Munson, R.V. (1993) 'Three aspects of Spartan kingship in Herodotus' in R.M. Rosen & J. Farrell eds *NOMODEIKTES: Greek studies in Honor of Martin Ostwald*, Ann Arbor: 39-54

Murray, I. (1972) 'Some elements in the composition of *The Picture of Dorian Gray*', *DUJ* 64: 220-31

Murray, I. (1974) ed. *Oscar Wilde. The Picture of Dorian Gray*, Oxford

Murray, O. (1983) 'The symposium as social organization' in Hägg & Marinatos eds 1983: 195-9

Murray, O. (1991) 'War and the Symposium' in Slater ed. 1991: 83-104

Murray, O. (1993) *Early Greece*, 2nd edn, Glasgow

Murray, O. & S. Price (1990) eds *The Greek City from Homer to Alexander*, Oxford

Myres, J.L. (1927) *The Political Ideas of the Greeks*, Berkeley, Los Angeles & London

Nagel, T. (1991) *Equality and Partiality*, Oxford

Bibliography

Nafissi, M. (1989) 'Distribution and trade' in Stibbe 1989: 68-77, 136-46

Nafissi, M. (1991) *La nascita del kosmos: Studi sulla storia e la società di Sparta*, Perugia

Napolitano, M.L. (1985) 'Donne spartane e *teknopoiia*', AION 7: 19-50

Nassaar, C.S. (1974) *Into the Demon Universe: A Literary Exploration of Oscar Wilde*, New Haven & London

Neils, J. et al. (1992) *Goddess and Polis: The Panathenaic Festivals in Ancient Athens*, Dartmouth & Princeton

Nenci, G. (1998) 'Sul grafito di una coppa laconica di Alpea dell' Archäologische Sammlung dell' Università di Zurigo', *SFIC* 16: 3-7

Newman, W.L. (1887) *The Politics of Aristotle* I, Oxford

Nicholls, R.V. (1950) 'Laconia', *ABSA* 45: 282-98

Nilsson, M.P. (1906) *Griechische Feste von religiöser Bedeutung mit Ausschluss der Athenischen*, Leipzig [repr. 1957]

Nilsson, M.P. (1908) 'Die Grundlagen des spartanischen Lebens', *Klio* 12: 308-40 [repr. in *Opera Selecta*, 3 vols, Lund, 1951-60: II.826-69]

Nilsson, M.P. (1929) 'Die Hoplitentaktik und das Staatswesen', *Klio* 22: 240-9 [repr. in *Opera Selecta*, 3 vols, Lund, 1951-60: II.897-907]

Nippel, W. (1980) *Mischverfassungs-Theorie und Verfassungs-Realität in der Antike und Frühe Neuzeit*, Stuttgart

Nippel, W. (1994) 'Max Weber zwischen Althistorie und Universalgeschichte: Synoikismos und Verbrüderung' in Meier ed. 1994: 35-57

Noethlichs, K. (1987) 'Bestechung, Bestechlichkeit und die Rolle des Geldes in der spartanischen Aussen- und Innenpolitik von 7. bis 2. Jh. v. Chr.', *Historia* 36: 129-70

Nordern, E. (1913) *Agnostos Theos: Untersuchungen zur Formengeschichte religiöser Rede*, Leipzig

Norman, R. (1987) *Free and Equal: A Philosophical Examination of Political Values*, Oxford

North, H. (1966) *Sophrosyne: Self-knowledge and Self-restraint in Greek Literature*, Ithaca

Nylander, C. (1968) '*Assyria grammata*. Remarks on the 21st letter of Themistocles', *OAth* 8: 119-36

Ober, J. (1989) *Mass and Elite in Democratic Athens: Rhetoric, Ideology, and the Power of the People*, Princeton

Ober, J. (1991) 'Hoplites and obstacles' in Hanson ed. 1991: 173-96

Ober, J. (1998) *Political Dissent in Democratic Athens: Intellectual Critics of Popular Rule*, Princeton

Ober, J. & C.W. Hedrick (1996) eds *Demokratia: A Conversation on Democracies, Ancient and Modern*, Princeton

O'Carroll, T. (1980) *Paedophilia: The Radical Case*, London

Ogden, D. (1994) 'Crooked speech: The genesis of the Spartan rhetra', *JHS* 114: 85-102

Okin, S.M. (1979) *Women in Western Political Thought*, Princeton [7th printing, 1992, has a new Afterword]

Okin, S.M. (1989) *Justice, Gender and the Family*, New York

Okin, S.M. (1991) 'Gender, the public, and the private' in D. Held ed. *Political Theory Today*, Oxford: 67-90

Oliva, P. (1971) *Sparta and its Social Problems*, Amsterdam & Prague

Oliva, P. (1981) 'Heloten und Spartaner', *Index* 10: 43-54

Oliva, P. (1998) 'Politische Praxis und Theorie in Sparta' in W. Schuller ed. *Politische Praxis und Theorie im Altertum*, Darmstadt: 30-42

Ollier, F. (1933-43) *Le mirage spartiate*, 2 vols, Paris [repr. in 1 vol., New York, 1973]

Ollier, F. (1934) ed. *Xénophon, la République des Lacédémoniens*, Lyon

Osborne, R.G. (1987) *Classical Landscape with Figures: The Ancient Greek City and Its Countryside*, London

Osborne, R.G. (1991) 'Pride and prejudice, sense and subsistence: exchange and society in the Greek city' in Rich & Wallace-Hadrill eds 1991: 119-45

Osborne, R.G. (1996) *'Classical Landscape revisited'*, *Topoi* 6: 49-64

Ostwald, M. (1969) *Nomos and the Beginnings of the Athenian Democracy*, Oxford

Ostwald, M. (1972) 'Isokratia as a political concept (Herodotus 5.92a.1)' in V. Brown, A.H. Hourani & S.M. Stern eds *Islamic Philosophy and the Classical Tradition: Essays Presented by his Friends and Pupils to Richard Walzer*, Oxford: 277-91

Ostwald, M. (1996) 'Shares and rights: "citizenship" Greek style and American style' in Ober & Hedrick eds 1996: 49-61

Owen, G.E.L. (1985) *'Tithenai ta phainomena'* in his *Logic, Science and Dialectic: Collected Papers in Greek Philosophy*, ed. M.C. Nussbaum, London: 239-51

Pack, R.A. (1965) *The Greek and Latin Literary Texts from Greco-Roman Egypt*, 2nd edn, Ann Arbor

Page, D. (1951) *Alcman. The Partheneion*, Oxford

Paoli, U. (1976) 'L'antico diritto di Gortina' in *Altri Studi di diritto greco e romano*, Milan: 481-507

Paradiso A. (1991) *Forme di Dipendenza nel mondo greco: Ricerche sul VI libro di Ateneo*, Bari

Paradiso, A. (1994/5) 'Tucidide, Aristotele, la *Stasis* a Sparta: due modelli interpretativi', *Métis* 9-10: 151-70

Parish, P.J. (1979) *Slavery*, Durham

Parke, H.W. (1930) 'The development of the Second Spartan Empire', *JHS* 50: 37-79

Parke, H.W. (1945) 'The deposing of Spartan kings', *CQ* 39: 106-12

Parke, H.W. & D.E.W. Wormell (1956) *The Delphic Oracle*, 2nd edn, 2 vols, Oxford

Parker, H.N. (1993) 'Sappho schoolmistress', *TAPhA* 123: 309-51

Parker, R. (1989) 'Spartan Religion' in Powell ed. 1989: 142-72

Passage, C.E. (1982) *Character Names in Dostoevsky's Fiction*, Ann Arbor

Pateman, C. (1983) 'Feminism and democracy' in G. Duncan ed. *Democratic Theory and Practice*, Cambridge: 204-17

Pateman, C. (1988) *The Sexual Contract*, Cambridge

Pater, W. (1893) 'Lacedaemon' in his *Plato and Platonism*, London: 197-234

Patterson, O. (1970) 'Slavery and slave revolts: a sociohistorical analysis of the First Maroon War, 1665-1740', *Social and Economic Studies* 19: 289-325

Patterson, O. (1982) *Slavery and Social Death: A Comparative Study*, Cambridge, MA & London

Patzer, H. (1982) *Die griechische Knabenliebe*, Wiesbaden

Peek, W. (1974) 'Ein neuer Spartanische Staatsvertrag', *ASAW* 65: 3-15

Pembroke, S.G. (1967) 'Women in charge: the function of alternatives in early Greek tradition and the ancient idea of matriarchy', *JWI* 30: 1-35

Pembroke, S.G. (1970) 'Locres et Tarente: le rôle des femmes dans la fondation de deux colonies grecques', *Annales (ESC)* 25: 1240-70

Perlman, P. (1983) 'Plato *Laws* 833c-834d and the bears of Brauron', *GRBS* 24: 115-30

Perotti, E. (1974) 'Esclaves *chôris oikountes*' in *Actes du colloque 1972 sur l'esclavage*, Ann. litt. Univ. Besançon 163, Paris: 47-56

Bibliography

Perotti, E. (1976) 'Contribution à l'étude d'une autre catégorie d'esclave attique: les *andrapoda misthophorounta'* in *Actes du colloque 1973 sur l'esclavage*, Ann. litt. Univ. Besançon 182, Paris: 179-91

Pettersson, M. (1992) *Cults of Apollo at Sparta: The Hyakinthia, the Gymnopaidiai and the Karneia*, Stockholm

Pfister, M. (1986) *Oskar Wilde 'The Picture of Dorian Gray'*, Munich

Phelps Brown, H. (1988) *Egalitarianism and the Generation of Inequality*, Oxford

Piccirilli, L. (1984) 'Il santuario, la funzione guerriera della dea, la regalità: il caso di Atena Chalkioikos' in M. Sordi ed. *Santuari e la guerra nel mondo antico*, Milan: 3-19

Pickard-Cambridge, A.W. (1988) *The Dramatic Festivals of Athens*, 2nd edn, ed. D. Lewis and J. Gould, repr. with add., Oxford

Pipili, M. (1987) *Laconian Iconography of the Sixth Century BC*, Oxford

Pitt-Rivers, J. (1977), *The Fate of Shechem, or the Politics of Sex: Essays in the Anthropology of the Mediterranean*, Cambridge

Plamenatz, J. (1967), 'Diversity of rights and kinds of equality' in J.R. Pennock & J.W. Chapman eds *Equality (NOMOS IX)*, New York: 79-98

Pluchon, P. (1980) *Toussaint L'Ouverture: de l'esclavage au pouvoir*, Paris

Podlecki, A.J. (1968) 'Simonides: 480', *Historia* 17: 257-75

Polignac, F. de (1994) 'Mediation, competition and sovereignty: the evolution of rural sanctuaries in Geometric Greece' in Alcock & Osborne eds 1994: 3-18

Polignac, F. de (1995) *Cults, Territory, and the Origins of the Greek City-State*, 2nd edn, Chicago [French original 1984]

Pollitt, J.J. (1972) *Art and Experience in Classical Greece*, Cambridge

Pomeroy, S.B. (1976) *Goddesses, Whores, Wives and Slaves: Women in Classical Antiquity*, London

Pomeroy, S.B. (1997) *Families in Classical and Hellenistic Greece: Representations and Realities*, Oxford

Pomeroy, S.B. (1991) ed. *Women's History and Ancient History*, Chapel Hill, NC & London

Poralla, P. & A.S. Bradford (1985) *A Prosopography of Lacedaemonians from the Earliest Times to the Death of Alexander the Great (X-323 BC) / Prosopographie der Lakedaimonier bis auf die Zeit Alexanders des Grossen*, 2nd edn, Chicago [original German edition, 1913]

Powell, B.B. (1989) 'Why was the Greek alphabet invented: the epigraphical evidence', *CA* 8: 321-50

Powell, B.B. (1991) *Homer and the Origins of the Greek Alphabet*, Cambridge

Powell, C.A. (1989) 'Mendacity and Sparta's use of the visual' in Powell ed. 1989: 173-92

Powell, C.A. (1998) 'Sixth-century Lakonian vase-painting: continuities and discontinuities with the "Lykourgan" ethos' in Fisher & Van Wees eds 1998: 119-46

Powell, C.A. (1999) 'Spartan women assertive in politics? Plutarch's Lives of Agis and Kleomenes' in Hodkinson & Powell eds 1999: 393-419

Powell, C.A. (1989) ed. *Classical Sparta: Techniques Behind Her Success*, London & New York

Powell, C.A. (1995) ed. *The Greek World*, London & New York

Powell, C.A. & S. Hodkinson (1994) eds *The Shadow of Sparta*, London & New York

Pritchett, W.K. (1956) 'The Attic Stelai II', *Hesperia* 25: 178-317

Pritchett, W.K. (1985a) *The Greek State at War* vol. IV, California & London

Pritchett, W.K. (1985b) 'The pitched battle' in Pritchett 1985a: 1-93

Pritchett, W.K. (1991a) *The Greek State at War* vol. V, California & London

Pritchett, W.K. (1991b) *Studies in Ancient Greek Topography* vol. VII, Amsterdam

Pritchett, W.K. (1991c) 'A recent theory of Homeric warfare' in Pritchett 1991b: 181-90

Proietti, G. (1987) *Xenophon's Sparta: An Introduction*, Leiden

Quass, F. (1971) *Nomos und Psephisma: Untersuchung zum griechischen Staatsrecht*, Munich

Raaflaub, K.A. (1990) 'Expansion und Machtbildung in frühen Polis-Systemen' in Eder ed. 1990: 511-45

Raaflaub, K.A. (1991) 'Homer und die Geschichte des 8.Jh.s v. Chr.' in Latacz ed. 1991: 205-56

Raaflaub, K.A. (1993) 'Homer to Solon: the rise of the Polis (the written evidence)' in Hansen ed. 1993: 41-105

Raaflaub, K.A. (1996) 'Equalities and inequalities in Athenian democracy' in Ober & Hedrick eds 1996: 139-74

Raaflaub, K.A. (1997) 'Citizens, soldiers, and the evolution of the early Greek Polis' in Mitchell & Rhodes eds 1997: 49-59

Raaflaub, K.A. (1999) 'Archaic and Classical Greece' in K. Raaflaub & N. Rosenstein eds *War and Society in the Ancient and Medieval Worlds: Asia, the Mediterranean, Europe and Mesoamerica*, Cambridge, MA & London: 129-61

Raby, P.H. (1988) *Oscar Wilde*, Cambridge

Raby, P.H. (1997) ed. *The Cambridge Companion to Oscar Wilde*, Cambridge

Rädle, H. (1969) *Untersuchungen zur griechischen Freilassungswesen*, Munich

Rahe, P.A. (1980) 'The selection of Ephors at Sparta', *Historia* 29: 385-401

Rajec, E.M. (1978) *The Study of Names in Literature: A Bibliography*, New York

Raschke, W.J. (1988) ed. *The Archaeology of the Olympics*, Madison

Rawick, G.P. (1972) *From Sundown to Sunup: The Making of the Black Community*, Westport

Rawson, E. (1969) *The Spartan Tradition in European Thought*, Oxford [repr. 1991]

Reade, W. (1934) *The Martyrdom of Man*, repr. edn, London

Rebenich, S. (1998) *Xenophon: Die Verfassung der Spartaner*, Darmstadt

Reden, S.V.I.A. von (1998) 'The well-ordered polis: topographies of civic space' in P.A. Cartledge, P.C. Millett & S.V.I.A. von Reden eds *KOSMOS: Order, Conflict and Community in Classical Athens*, Cambridge: 170-90

Redfield, J. (1977/8) 'The women of Sparta', *CJ* 73: 146-61

Reinsberg, C. (1989) *Ehe, Hetärentum und Knabenliebe im antiken Griechenland*, Munich

Renfrew, A.C. and Cherry, J. (1986) eds *Peer Polity Interaction and the Development of Sociocultural Complexity*, Cambridge

Rhodes, P.J. (1981) 'The selection of ephors at Sparta', *Historia* 30: 498-502

Rich, J.W. & G. Shipley (1993) eds *War and Society in the Greek World*, London & New York

Rich, J. & A. Wallace-Hadrill (1991) eds *City and Country in the Ancient World*, London

Richer, N. (1999) *Les Éphores: Études sur l'histoire et l'image de Sparte (VIIIe – IIIe siècle avant Jésus-Christ)*, Paris

Ridley, R.T. (1974) 'The economic activities of the Perioikoi', *Mnemosyne* 4th ser. 27: 281-92

Risch, E. (1954) 'Die Sprache Alkmans', *MH* 11: 20-37

Ritook, Z. (1991) 'Alkidamas über die Sophisten', *Philologus* 135: 157-63

Robb, K. (1994) *Literacy and Paideia in Ancient Greece*, Oxford

Roberts, J.T. (1994) *Athens on Trial: The Antidemocratic Tradition in Western Thought*, Princeton

Bibliography

Robertson, N. (1992) *Festivals and Legends: The Formation of Greek Cities in the Light of Public Ritual*, Toronto

Robinson, D.M. & E.J. Fluck (1937) *A Study of the Greek Love-names, Including a Discussion of Paederasty and a Prosopography*, Baltimore

Roemer, J.E. (1994) *Egalitarian Perspectives: Essays in Philosophical Economics*, Cambridge

Rolley, C. (1963) 'Hydries de bronze dans le Péloponèse du Nord', *BCH* 87: 459-84

Rolley, C. (1969) *Fouilles de Delphes* V.2. *Monuments figurés: les statuettes de bronze*, Paris

Rolley, C. (1977a) *Fouilles de Delphes* V.3. *Les trépieds à cuve clouée*, Paris

Rolley, C. (1977b) 'Le problème de l'art laconien', *Ktema* 2: 125-40

Rolley, C. (1986) *Les Bronzes Grecs*, Fribourg

Romilly, J. de (1959) 'Le classement des constitutions d'Hérodote à Aristote', *REG* 72: 81-99

Romilly, J. de (1992) *The Great Sophists in Periclean Athens*, trans. J. Lloyd, Oxford

Roobaert, A. (1977) 'Le danger hilote?', *Ktema* 2: 141-55

Rose, H.J. (1935) Review of Erdmann 1934, *JHS* 55: 256-7

Rose, P.W. (1997) 'Ideology in the *Iliad*: Polis, *Basileus, Theoi*', *Arethusa* 30: 151-99

Roussel, D. (1976) *Tribu et Cité*, Paris

Roussel, P. (1943) 'L'exposition des enfants à Sparte', *REA* 45: 5-17

Runciman, W.G. (1982) 'Origins of States: the case of Archaic Greece', *CSSH* 24: 351-77

Runciman, W.G. (1983) *A Treatise on Social Theory* I. *The Methodology of Social Theory*, Cambridge

Runciman, W.G. (1989) *A Treatise on Social Theory* II. *Substantive Social Theory*, Cambridge

Runciman, W.G. (1990) 'Doomed to extinction: the polis as an evolutionary dead-end' in Murray & Price eds 1990: 347-67

Runciman, W.G. (1998) 'Greek hoplites, warrior culture and indirect bias', *JRAI* 4: 731-51

Ruppersberg, A. (1911) '*Eispnêlas*', *Philologus* 70: 151-4

Ruzé, F. (1997) *Délibération et pouvoir dans la cité grecque de Nestor à Socrate*, Paris

Sagan, E. (1991) *The Honey and the Hemlock: Democracy and Paranoia in Ancient Athens and Modern America*, Princeton

Saïd, E. (1978) *Orientalism*, New York [repr. with new Afterword, Harmondsworth 1995]

Ste. Croix, G.E.M. de (1957) Review of Westermann 1955, *CR* n.s. 7: 54-9

Ste. Croix, G.E.M. de (1966) 'The estate of Phaenippus (Ps.-Dem. xlii)' in Badian ed. 1966: 109-14

Ste. Croix, G.E.M. de (1970a), 'Athenian family law', *CR* n.s. 20: 307-10

Ste. Croix, G.E.M. de (1970b), 'Some observations on the property rights of Athenian women', *CR* n.s. 20: 273-8

Ste. Croix, G.E.M. de (1972), *The Origins of the Peloponnesian War*, London & Ithaca

Ste. Croix, G.E.M. de (1974) 'Ancient Greek and Roman Maritime Loans' in H. Edey & B.S. Yamey eds *Debits, Credits, Finance and Profits: Studies in Honour of W.T. Baxter*, London: 41-59

Ste. Croix, G.E.M. de (1975a) 'Early Christian attitudes to property and slavery', *Studies in Church History* 12: 1-38

Bibliography

Ste. Croix, G.E.M. de (1975b) 'Karl Marx and the history of classical antiquity', *Arethusa* 8: 7-41

Ste. Croix, G.E.M. de (1983) *The Class Struggle in the Ancient Greek World: From the Archaic Age to the Arab Conquests*, corrected impr., London & Ithaca [original 1981]

Ste. Croix, G.E.M. de (1984a) 'Class in Marx's conception of history, ancient and modern', *New Left Review* 146: 94-111

Ste. Croix, G.E.M. de (1984b) 'A worm's-eye view of the Greeks and Romans and how they spoke: martyr-acts, fables, parables and other texts', *Latin Teaching* 37: 16-30

Ste. Croix, G.E.M. de (1985) 'Karl Marx and the interpretation of ancient and modern history' in B. Chavance ed. *Marx en Perspective* (Actes du Colloque E.H.E.S.S., Paris, December 1983), Paris: 159-87

Sakellariou, M.B. (1975) ed. *History of the Hellenic World* II. *The Archaic Period*, Athens & London

Sakellariou, M.B. (1989) *The Polis-State: Definition and Origin*, Athens

Salapata, G. (1997) 'Hero warriors from Corinth and Lakonia', *Hesperia* 66: 245-60

Sallares, J.R. (1991) *The Ecology of the Ancient Greek World*, London

Salmon, J.B. (1977) 'Political hoplites?' *JHS* 97: 84-101

Salmon, J.B. (1984) *Wealthy Corinth: A History of the City to 338 BC*, Oxford

Sanders, J.M. (1992) ed. *Philolakôn: Lakonian Studes in honour of Hector Catling*, London & Athens

Sargent, R.L. (1924) *The Size of the Slave Population at Athens during the Fifth and Fourth Century BC*, Chicago

Sartre, M. (1979) 'Aspects économiques et aspects politiques de la frontière dans les cités grecques', *Ktema* 4: 213-24

Scanlon, T.F. (1988) '*Virgineum gymnasium*: Spartan females and early Greek athletics' in Raschke ed. 1988: 185-216

Schaps, D.M. (1979) *Economic Rights of Women in Ancient Greece*, Edinburgh

Schlaifer, R.L. (1936) 'Greek theories of slavery from Homer to Aristotle', *HSPh* 47: 165-204 [repr. in Finley ed. 1968: 93-132]

Schnapp, A. (1979) 'Pratiche e immagini di caccia nella Grecia antica', *DArch* n.s. 1: 36-59

Schnapp, A. (1989) 'Eros the Hunter' in Bérard ed. 1989: 71-88

Schofield, M. (1999a) *Saving the City: Philosopher-kings and Other Classical Paradigms*, London & New York

Schofield, M. (1999b) 'Ideology and philosophy in Aristotle's theory of slavery' (1990), repr. with Additional Note in Schofield 1999a: 115-40

Schurtz, H. (1902) *Altersklassen und Männerbünde: Eine Darstellung der Grundformen der Gesellschaft*, Berlin

Scott, J.W. (1986) 'Gender: a useful category of historical analysis', *AHR* 95: 1053-76 [repr. in her *Gender in History*, New York, 1988]

Sealey, R. (1976) *A History of the Greek City States ca. 700-338 BC*, Berkeley

Sekunda, N. (1986) *The Ancient Greeks: Armies of Classical Greece, 5th and 4th centuries BC*, London

Seltman, C.T. (1956) *Women in Antiquity*, London

Semenov, A. (1911) 'Zur dorische Knabenliebe', *Philologus* 70: 146-50

Sen, A. (1980) 'Equality of what?' in S.L. McMurrin ed. *The Tanner Lectures on Human Values*, vol. I, Salt Lake City & Cambridge: 195-220

Sen, A. (1992) *Inequality Re-Examined*, Oxford

Sen, A. & M.C. Nussbaum (1993) eds *The Quality of Life*, Oxford

Bibliography

Sergent, B. (1996) *Homosexualité et initiation chez les peuples indo-européens*, Paris

Serwint, N. (1993) 'The female athletic competition at the Heraia and prenuptial initiation rites', *AJA* 97: 403-22

Shanin, T. (1971) ed. *Peasants and Peasant Societies*, Harmondsworth

Shapiro, H. (1984) 'The impact of the Aptheker thesis: a retrospective view of American-Negro slave revolts', *Science & Society* 48: 52-73

Shey, H.J. (1976) 'Tyrtaeus and the art of propaganda', *Arethusa* 9: 5-28

Shipley, D.R. (1997) *Plutarch's Life of Agesilaos*, Oxford

Shipley, G. (1992) *'Perioikos*: the discovery of classical Laconia' in Sanders ed. 1992: 211-26

Shipley, G. (1996) 'Ancient history and landscape histories' in Shipley & Salmon eds 1996: 1-15

Shipley, G. (1997) ' "The Other Lakedaimonians": the dependent Perioikic *poleis* of Laconia and Messenia' in M.H. Hansen ed. *The Polis as an Urban Centre and as a Political Community*, Copenhagen: 189-281

Shipley, G. (2000) *The Greek World After Alexander 323-30 BC*, London

Shipley, G. & J. Salmon (1996) eds *Human Landscapes in Classical Antiquity: Environment and Culture*, London & New York

Sickinger, J.P. (1999) ed. *Public Records and Archives in Classical Athens*, Chapel Hill

Siems, A.K. (1988) ed. *Sexualität und Erotik in der Antike* (Wege der Forschung 605), Darmstadt

Singor, H.W. (1999) 'Admission to the *syssitia* in fifth-century Sparta' in Hodkinson & Powell eds 1999: 67-89

Skinner, Q.R.D. (1988a) 'Language and political change' in T. Ball, J. Farr & R.L. Hanson eds *Political Innovation and Conceptual Change*, Cambridge: 6-23

Skinner, Q.R.D. (1988b) 'The State' in T. Ball, J. Farr & R.L. Hanson eds *Political Innovation and Conceptual Change*, Cambridge: 90-131

Skinner, Q.R.D. (1988c) 'A reply to my critics' in J. Tully ed. *Meaning and Contexts: Quentin Skinner and his Critics*, Cambridge: 231-88

Slater, P. (1971) *The Glory of Hera*, Princeton [repr. 1992]

Slater, W.J. (1991) ed. *Dining in a Classical Context*, Ann Arbor

Smith II, P.E. & M.S. Helfland (1989) eds *Oscar Wilde's Oxford Notebooks: A Portrait of a Mind in the Making*, Oxford

Smith, M.G. (1974) *Corporations and Society*, London

Smith, M.M. (1998) *Debating Slavery: Economy and Society in the Antebellum American South*, Cambridge

Smith, T.J. (2000) 'Dancing spaces and dining places: Archaic komasts' in Tsetskhladze et al. eds 2000: 309-19

Snell, B. (1969) *Tyrtaios und die Sprache des Epos*, Göttingen

Snodgrass, A.M. (1964) *Early Greek Armour and Weapons from the End of the Bronze Age to 600 BC*, Edinburgh

Snodgrass, A.M. (1965) 'The hoplite reform and history', *JHS* 85: 110-22

Snodgrass, A.M. (1967) *Arms and Armour of the Greeks*, London & New York

Snodgrass, A.M. (1971) *The Dark Age of Greece*, Edinburgh

Snodgrass, A.M. (1974) 'An historical Homeric society?', *JHS* 94: 114-25

Snodgrass, A.M. (1977) *Archaeology and the Rise of the Greek State*, Cambridge

Snodgrass, A.M. (1980) *Archaic Greece: The Age of Experiment*, California & London

Snodgrass, A.M. (1986a) 'Interaction by design: the Greek city-state' in Renfrew & Cherry eds 1986: 47-58

Bibliography

Snodgrass, A.M. (1986b) 'La formazione dello stato greco', *Opus* 5: 7-21

Snodgrass, A.M. (1987) *An Archaeology of Greece: The Present State and Future Scope of a Discipline*, California & London

Snodgrass, A.M. (1991) 'Structural history and classical archaeology' in J. Bintliff ed. *The Annales School and Archaeology*, Leicester: 57-72

Snodgrass, A.M. (1993a) 'The "hoplite reform" revisited', *DHA* 19: 47-61

Snodgrass, A.M. (1993b) 'The rise of the polis: the archaeological evidence' in Hansen ed. 1993: 30-40

Snowden, F.M. (1970) *Blacks in Antiquity*, Cambridge, MA

Snowden, F.M. (1983) *Before Color Prejudice: The Ancient View of Blacks*, Cambridge, MA

Sokolowski, F. (1962) ed. *Lois sacrées des cités grecques (Supp.)*, Paris

Stampp, K.M. (1956) *The Peculiar Institution: Slavery in the Ante-Bellum South*, New York

Stampp, K.M. (1971) 'Rebels and Sambos: the search for the Negro's personality in slavery', *Journal of Southern History* 37: 367-92 [repr. in *The Imperiled Union. Essays on the background of the Civil War*, New York 1980]

Stanford, W.B. (1976) *Ireland and the Classical Tradition*, Dublin

Stanford, W.B. & R.B. McDowell (1971) *Mahaffy: A Biography of an Anglo-Irishman*, London

Starcke, C.N. (1889) *The Primitive Family in its Origins and Development*, London

Starobin, R.S. (1970) *Industrial Slavery in the Old South*, New York

Starobin, R.S. (1974) ed. *Blacks in Bondage: Letters of American Slaves*, New York

Starr, C.G. (1958) 'An overdose of slavery', *Journal of Economic History* 18: 17-32 [repr. in Starr 1979: 43-58]

Starr, C.G. (1961a) 'The decline of the early Greek kings', *Historia* 10: 129-38 [repr. in Starr 1979: 134-43]

Starr, C.G. (1961b) *The Origins of Greek Civilization 1100-650 BC*, New York

Starr, C.G. (1965) 'The credibility of early Spartan history', *Historia* 14: 257-72 [repr. in Starr 1979: 144-59]

Starr, C.G. (1977) *The Economic and Social Growth of Early Greece 800-500 BC*, New York

Starr, C.G. (1979) *Essays on Ancient History: A Selection of Articles and Reviews*, ed. A. Ferrill & T. Kelly, Leiden

Starr, C.G. (1986) *Individual and Community: The Rise of the Polis 800-500 BC*, New York

Staveley, E.S. (1972) *Greek and Roman Voting and Elections*, London & New York

Steinhauer, G. (1972) 'Archaiotîtes kai mnîmeia Lakônias', *AD* 27: 242-50

Steinhauer, G. (1978) *The Museum of Sparta*, Athens

Stein-Hölkeskamp, E. (1989) *Adelskultur und Polis-Gesellschaft: Studien zum griechischen Adel in archaischer und klassischer Zeit*, Stuttgart

Stein-Hölkeskamp, E. (1992) 'Lebensstil als Selbstdarstellung: Aristokraten beim symposion' in Heilmeyer ed. 1992: 39-49

Steward, G.H. (1946) *Sex and the Social Order*, New York & London

Stewart, A. (1997) *Art, Desire and the Body in Ancient Greece*, Cambridge

Stewart, F.H. (1977) *Fundamentals of Age-group Systems*, New York & London

Stibbe, C.M. (1972) *Lakonische Vasenmaler des sechsten Jahrhunderts v. Chr.*, Amsterdam

Stibbe, C.M. (1976) 'Neue Fragmente lakonischer Schalen aus Cerveteri', *MNIR* 38: 7-16

Stibbe, C.M. (1989) *Mixing Bowls: A History of the Krater Lakonikos from the Seventh to the Fifth Century BC*, Amsterdam

259

Bibliography

Stibbe, C.M. (2000) 'Lakonische Bronzegefässe aus Capua', *AK* 43: 4-16

Stone, L. (1987) 'Prosopography' (1971), repr. in his *The Past and the Present Revisited*, London: 45-73

Strauss, B.S. (1996) 'The Athenian trireme, school of democracy' in Ober & Hedrick eds 1996: 313-25

Strauss, B.S. (1999) *Rowing Against the Current: On Learning to Scull at Forty*, New York

Strehlow, C. (1913) *Die Aranda- und Loritja-Stämme in Zentral-Australien* IV.1, Frankfurt am Main

Stroud, R.S. (1968) *Drakon's Law on Homicide*, Berkeley

Sullivan, J.P. & J. Peradotto (1984) eds *Women in Classical Antiquity: The Arethusa Papers*, Buffalo

Symonds, J.A. (1896) *A Problem in Modern Ethics: Being an Enquiry into the Phenomenon of Sexual Inversion Addressed Especially to Medical Psychologists and Jurists*, 2nd edn, London [1st edn, 1891]

Talbert, R. (1988) ed. *Plutarch on Sparta*, Harmondsworth

Talbert, R. (1989) 'The role of the Helots in the class struggle at Sparta', *Historia* 40: 22-40

Taplin, O. (1989) *Greek Fire*, London

Tausend, K. (1992) *Amphiktyonie und Symmachie: Formen zwischenstaatlicher Beziehungen im archaischen Griechenland*, *Historia* Einzelschrift 73, Stuttgart

Tazelaar, C.M. (1967) '*Paides kai ephêboi*: some notes on the Spartan stages of youth', *Mnemosyne* 4th ser. 20: 127-53

Temkin, L.S. (1994) *Inequality*, Oxford

Terray, E. (1990) *La Politique dans la Caverne*, Paris

Thiel, J.H. (1930) 'De feminarum apud Dores condicione ii', *Mnemosyne* 2nd ser. 58: 402-9

Thomas, C.G. (1973) 'Matriarchy in early Greece: the Bronze and Dark Ages', *Arethusa* 6: 173-95

Thomas, C.G. (1974) 'On the role of the Spartan kings', *Historia* 23: 257-70

Thomas, C.G. (1983) 'Spartan diarchy in comparative perspective', *PP* 38: 81-104

Thomas, C.G. (1993) *Myth Becomes History: Pre-Classical Greece*, Claremont, CA

Thomas, R. (1992) *Literacy and Orality in Ancient Greece*, Cambridge

Thommen, L. (1996) *Lakedaimonion Politeia: Die Entstehung der spartanischen Verfassung*, *Historia* Einzelschrift 103, Stuttgart

Thommen, L. (1999) 'Spartanische Frauen', *MH* 56: 129-49

Thommen, L. (2000) 'Spartas Umgang mit der Vergangenheit', *Historia* 49: 40-53

Thompson, E.A. (1952) 'Peasant revolts in Late Roman Gaul and Spain', *P&P* 2: 11-23 [repr. in Finley ed. 1974: 304-20]

Tigerstedt, E.N. (1965-78) *The Legend of Sparta in Classical Antiquity*, 3 vols, Stockholm, Uppsala & Göteborg

Tod, M.N. (1933) 'A Spartan grave on Attic soil', *G&R* 2: 108-11

Tod, M.N. (1948) *A Selection of Greek Historical Inscriptions* II. *From 403 to 323 BC*, Oxford

Todd, S.C. (1993) *The Shape of Athenian Law*, Oxford

Toher, M. (1991) 'Greek funerary legislation and the two Spartan funerals' in M. Toher & M. Flower eds *Georgica: Greek Studies in Honour of George Cawkwell (BICS* Supp. 58), London: 159-75

Toher, M. (1999) 'On the *eidôlon* of a Spartan king', *RhMus* n.F. 142: 113-27

Toynbee, A.J. (1969) *Some Problems of Greek History*, Oxford

Travlos, J. (1971) *Pictorial Dictionary of Ancient Athens*, London

Treu, K. (1983) 'Zu den Sklavennamen bei Menander', *Eirene* 20: 39-42

Bibliography

Tsetskhladze, G.R., A.J.N.W. Prag & A.M. Snodgrass (2000) eds *Periplous: Papers on Classical Art and Archaeology Presented to Sir John Boardman*, London

Turner, E.G. (1971) *Greek Manuscripts of the Ancient World*, Oxford

Turner, F.M. (1981) *The Greek Heritage in Victorian Britain*, New Haven & London

Ulf, C. (1990) *Die homerische Gesellschaft: Materialien zur analytischen Beschreiben und historischen Lokalisierung*, Munich

Vafopoulou-Richardson, C.E. (1981) *Greek Terracottas*, Oxford

Van Effenterre, H. & F. Ruzé (1994-5) eds *Nomima: Recueil d'inscriptions politiques et juridiques de l'archaïsme grecque*, 2 vols, Rome

Van Wees, H. (1986) 'Leaders of Men? Military organization in the *Iliad*', *CQ* n.s. 36: 285-303

Van Wees, H. (1988) 'Kings in combat: battles and heroes in the *Iliad*', *CQ* n.s. 38: 1-24

Van Wees, H. (1992) *Status Warriors: War, Violence, and Society in Homer and History*, Amsterdam

Van Wees, H. (1994) 'The Homeric way of war: the *Iliad* and the hoplite phalanx (I-II)', *G&R* n.s. 41: 1-18, 131-55

Van Wees, H. (1995) 'Politics on the battlefield: Ideology in Greek warfare' in Powell ed. 1995: 153-78

Van Wees, H. (1999) 'Tyrtaeus' *Eunomia*: Nothing to do with the Great Rhetra' in Hodkinson & Powell eds 1999: 1-41

Vatin, C. (1970) *Recherches sur le mariage et la condition de la femme mariée à l'époque hellénistique*, Paris

Vayiakakos, D.V. & I.G. Taïphakos (1975) '*Lakônikê Bibliographia*', *Lakônikai Spoudai* 2: 417-87

Vernant, J.-P. (1968) ed. *Problèmes de la guerre en Grèce ancienne*, Paris & The Hague

Vernant, J.-P. (1985) *La mort dans les yeux: Figures de l'Autre en Grèce ancienne*, Paris

Vernant, J.-P. (1991) 'Between shame and glory: the identity of the young Spartan warrior' in *Mortals and Immortals: Collected Essays*, ed. F. Zeitlin, Princeton: 220-43

Veyne, P. (1978) 'La famille et l'amour sous le Haut-Empire romain', *Annales (ESC)* 33: 35-63

Vidal-Naquet, P. (1968) 'The Black Hunter and the origin of the Athenian *ephebia*', *PCPhS* n.s. 14: 49-64 [repr. in Vidal-Naquet 1986a: 106-28]

Vidal-Naquet, P. (1970) 'Esclavage et gynécocratie dans la tradition, le mythe, l'utopie' in C. Nicolet ed. *Recherches sur les structures sociales dans l'Antiquité classique*, Paris: 63-80 [Eng. trans. in Vidal-Naquet 1986a: 205-23]

Vidal-Naquet, P. (1973) 'Réflexions sur l'historiographie grecque de l'esclavage' in in *Actes du Colloque 1971 sur l'esclavage*, Ann. litt. Univ. Besançon 140, Paris: 25-44 [Eng. trans. in Vidal-Naquet 1986a: 168-88]

Vidal-Naquet, P. (1974) 'Les jeunes. Le cru, l'enfant grec, et le cuit' in J. le Goff & P. Nora eds *Faire de l'histoire* III, Paris: 137-68 [Eng. trans. in Vidal-Naquet 1986a: 129-56]

Vidal-Naquet, P. (1986a) *The Black Hunter: Forms of Thought and Forms of Society in the Greek World*, trans. A. Szegedy-Maszak, Baltimore & London

Vidal-Naquet, P. (1986b) 'The Black Hunter revisited', *PCPhS* n.s. 32: 126-44

Vidal-Naquet, P. (1986c) 'The tradition of the Athenian hoplite' (1968) in Vidal-Naquet 1986a: 85-105

Villard, P. (1981) 'Sociétés et armées civiques en Grèce: de l'union à la subversion', *RH* 105: 297-310

Bibliography

Vlastos, G. (1962) 'Justice and equality' in R.B. Brandt ed. *Social Justice*, Englewood Cliffs, N.J.: 31-62

Vlastos, G. (1964) *'Isonomia politike'* in J. Mau & E.G. Schmidt eds *Isonomia: Studien zur Gleichheitsvorstellung im griechischen Denken*, Berlin: 1-35

Vogt, J. (1960) *Von der Gleichwertigkeit der Geschlechter in der bürgerlichen Gesellschaft der Griechen*, Mainz

Vogt, J. (1973) 'Zum Experiment des Drimakos: Sklavenhaltung und Raüberstand', *Saeculum* 24: 213-19

Vogt, J. (1974) 'The structure of ancient slave wars' in his *Ancient Slavery and the Ideal of Man*, Oxford: 39-92, 215-16

Wace, A.J.B. (1906-7) 'Excavations at Sparta 1907: the city walls', *ABSA* 13: 5-16

Wade-Gery, H.T. (1958) *Essays in Greek History*, Oxford

Walbank, F.W. (1970) 'An experiment in Greek union', *PCA* 67: 13-37

Walbank, F.W. (1985) 'The problem of Greek nationality' (1951), repr. in his *Selected Papers: Essays in Greek and Roman History and Historiography*, Cambridge: 1-19

Wallace, J. (1997) *Shelley and Greece: Rethinking Romantic Hellenism*, London & New York

Wallon, H. (1879) *Histoire de l'esclavage dans l'antiquité*, 3 vols, 2nd edn, Paris

Waterhouse, H.E. & R. Hope Simpson (1960-1) 'Prehistoric Laconia, Part I', 'Prehistoric Laconia, Part II', *ABSA* 55: 67-107; 56: 114-75

Webster, H. (1908) *Primitive Secret Societies: A Study in Early Politics and Religion*, New York

Weeks, J. (1977) *Coming Out! Homosexual Politics in Britain, from the Nineteenth Century to the Present*, London

Wehrli, C. (1962) 'Les gynéconomes', *MH* 19: 33-8

Weinstein, A.M. & F.O. Gatell (1979) eds *American Negro Slavery: A Modern Reader*, 2nd edn, New York [1st edn 1968]

Weinstein, A.M., F.O. Gatell & D. Sarasohn (1979) eds *American Negro Slavery: A Modern Reader*, 3rd edn, New York

Welles, C.B. (1966) 'Isocrates' view of history' in L. Wallach ed. *The Literary Tradition: Literary and Historical Essays in Honor of Harry Caplan*, Ithaca: 3-25

Welwei, K.-W. (1992) 'Polisbildung, Hetairos-Gruppen und Hetairien', *Gymnasium* 99: 481-500

Wender, D. (1973) 'Plato: misogynist, paedophile and feminist', *Arethusa* 6: 75-90

West, M.L. (1974) *Studies in Greek Elegy and Iambus*, Berlin & New York

West, S. (1988) 'Archilochus' message-stick', *CQ* n.s. 38: 42-8

Westen, P. (1990) *Speaking of Equality: An Analysis of the Rhetorical Force of 'Equality' in Moral and Legal Discourse*, Princeton

Westermann, W.L. (1941) 'Athenaeus and the slaves of Athens' in *Athenian Studies Presented to William Scott Ferguson (HSPh Supp. 1)*: 451-70 [repr. in Finley ed. 1968: 73-92]

Westermann, W.L. (1943) 'Slavery and the elements of freedom in Ancient Greece', *Quarterly Bulletin of the Polish Institute of Arts and Sciences* 2: 1-14 [repr. in Finley ed. 1968: 17-32]

Westermann, W.L. (1955) *The Slave Systems of Greek and Roman Antiquity*, Philadelphia

Westermarck, E. (1912-17) *The Origin and Development of the Moral Ideas*, 2 vols, 2nd edn, London

Whatley, N. (1964) 'On the possibility of reconstructing Marathon and other ancient battles', *JHS* 84: 119-39

Bibliography

Whibley, L. (1896) *Greek Oligarchies: Their Character and Organization*, London [repr. Chicago 1975]

Whitby, M. (1994) 'Two shadows: images of Spartans and helots' in Powell & Hodkinson eds 1994: 87-126

White, M.E. (1964) 'Some Agiad dates: Pausanias and his sons', *JHS* 84: 140-52

Whitehead, D. (1980) Review of L.C. Reilly *Slaves in Ancient Greece*; H. Raffeiner *Sklaven und Freigelassene*; K.-D. Albrecht *Rechtsprobleme in den Freilassungen der Böoter, Phoker, Ost- und Westlokrer*; K.-W. Welwei *Unfreie im antiken Kriegsdienst*, *JHS* 100: 246-9

Whitehead, D. (1981) 'The serfs of Sicyon', *LCM* 6: 37-41

Whitehead, D. (1986) *The Demes of Attica 508/7 to ca. 250 BC*, Princeton

Whitehead, D. (1990) 'The Laconian key', *CQ* n.s. 40: 267-8

Whitley, J. (1997) 'Cretan laws and Cretan literacy', *AJA* 101: 635-61

Wide, S. (1893) *Lakonische Kulte*, Leipzig

Wiedemann, T. (1981) *Greek and Roman Slavery: A Sourcebook*, Beckenham

Wilde, O. (1909) *Essays and Lectures*, 2nd edn, London

Wilkinson, L.P. (1979) *Classical Attitudes to Modern Issues*, London

Will, E. (1979-82) *Histoire politique du monde hellénistique*, 2 vols, 2nd edn, Nancy

Willetts, R.F. (1955) *Aristocratic Society in Ancient Crete*, London

Willetts, R.F. (1967) *The Law Code of Gortyn*, Berlin

Williams, B.A.O. (1962) 'The Idea of Equality' in P. Laslett & W.G. Runciman eds *Politics, Philosophy and Society*, 2nd edn, Oxford: 110-37 [repr. in Bedau ed. 1971: 116-37]

Williams, B.A.O. (1993) *Shame and Necessity*, Berkeley, Los Angeles & London

Williams, F.E. (1936) *Papuans of the Trans-Fly*, Oxford [repr. 1969]

Williams, G. (1958) 'Some aspects of Roman marriage ceremonies and ideals', *JRS* 48: 16-30

Williams Myers, A.J. (1996) 'Slavery, rebellion and revolution in the Americas: a historiographical scenario on the theses of Genovese and others', *Journal of Black Studies* 26: 381-400

Winkler, J.J. (1990) *The Constraints of Desire: The Anthropology of Sex and Gender in Ancient Greece*, New York & London

Wolf, E.R. (1971) *Peasant Wars of the Twentieth Century*, London

Wood, E.M. (1995) *Democracy Against Capitalism: Renewing Historical Materialism*, Cambridge

Wood, E.M. (1996) 'Demos versus "We, the People": freedom and democracy ancient and modern' in Ober & Hedrick eds 1996: 121-37

Woodward, A.M. (1928/9) 'Excavations at Sparta, 1924-27', *ABSA* 30: 241-52

Wycherley, R.E. (1962) *How the Greeks Built Cities*, 2nd edn, London

Wycherley, R.E. (1978) *The Stones of Athens*, Princeton

Youtie, H.C. (1971) '*Bradeôs graphôn*: between literacy and illiteracy', *GRBS* 12: 239-61

Youtie, H.C. (1973) *Scriptiunculae* II, Amsterdam

Zimmermann, J.-L. (1989) *Les Chevaux de bronze dans l'art géométrique grec*, Mainz & Geneva

Zimmern, A.E. (1928) *Solon and Croesus*, London

Zweig, B. (1993) 'The only women to give birth to men: a gynocentric, cross-cultural view of women in ancient Sparta' in M. de Forest ed. *Women's Power, Men's Game: Essays in Classical Antiquity in Honor of Joy King*, Wasconda, IL: 32-53

Index Locorum

References in bold type are to the pages and notes of this book.

Inscriptions, Papyri

General Index